Learning to Teach Reading

Setting the Research Agenda

Cathy M. Roller, Editor

INTERNATIONAL
Reading
Association

800 Barksdale Road, PO Box 8139
Newark, Delaware 19714-8139, USA
www.reading.org

The International Reading Association attempts, through its publications, to provide a forum for a wide spectrum of opinions on reading. This policy permits divergent viewpoints without implying the endorsement of the Association.

Director of Publications   Joan M. Irwin
Editorial Director, Books and Special Projects   Matthew W. Baker
Special Projects Editor   Tori Mello Bachman
Permissions Editor   Janet S. Parrack
Associate Editor   Jeanine K. McGann
Production Editor   Shannon Benner
Editorial Assistant   Tyanna L. Collins
Publications Manager   Beth Doughty
Production Department Manager   Iona Sauscermen
Art Director   Boni Nash
Supervisor, Electronic Publishing   Anette Schütz-Ruff
Senior Electronic Publishing Specialist   Cheryl J. Strum
Electronic Publishing Specialist   Lynn Harrison
Proofreader   Charlene M. Nichols

Project Editor   Tori Mello Bachman

Cover Design   Cindy Doerzbach

Library of Congress Cataloging-in-Publication Data

Learning to teach reading : setting the research agenda / Cathy M. Roller, editor.
    p.   cm.
   Includes bibliographical references and index.
ISBN 0-87207-295-9
   1. Reading teachers–Training of. 2. Reading. I. Roller, Cathy M.
LB2844.1.R4 L43   2001
424.4'071–dc21
2001000288
Second Printing August 2001

CONTENTS

SECTION THREE
INSERVICE TEACHER EDUCATION

SECTION FOUR
CONCLUSION

Introduction

Learning to Teach Reading: Setting the Research Agenda contains a set of chapters developed from presentations at the International Reading Association's Reading Research 2000 conference of the same title. Learning to teach reading is an important and timely topic in the reading-focused reform environment of education at the start of the millennium. Teacher education in general and reading teacher education, specifically, are under attack. Teacher educators are accused of not preparing teachers who are capable of teaching reading to all children.

This is not the first time reading instruction has been the subject of national debate. However, this most recent wave of criticism is the first to focus so directly on teacher education and reading teacher preparation. As noted in Chapter 3 of this volume, if we are not guilty of the direct charges—which is a matter for extended discussion—we are definitely guilty of not having direct data to either support or refute these charges. As teacher educators we are guilty of not systematically studying our practice for continuous evaluation and improvement.

However, as P. David Pearson demonstrates in the opening chapter, "Learning to Teach Reading: The Status of the Knowledge Base," our knowledge of preparation for reading instruction is not a void. We do have correlational evidence. And while some claims are not supported by experimental and/or quasiexperimental studies, the preponderance of evidence supports the following claims:

Totally prepared and certified teachers are better rated and more successful with students in terms of promoting achievement than are teachers who lack either subject matter or teaching knowledge.

Teachers admitted to the profession with less than full preparation are less satisfied with their training, and have greater difficulties planning curriculum, managing the classroom, diagnosing student learning needs, and adapting their instruction to specific situations and students.

More fully prepared teachers are more effective in each of those performance areas.

The research agenda we hope to propel has considerable empirical evidence at its foundation. Pearson's chapter provides an excellent overview of what we know about teacher education in the area of reading. In the second chapter, Dorothy Strickland provides us with a masterful overview of the reform environment in which we are operating. She gives a history of the reform effort and helps us see reading teacher preparation issues in the current educational and political context. The discussion situates teacher quality as the last frontier of systemic reform.

The second section of the book focuses on preservice teacher preparation. Chapter 3 presents the results of a survey of International Reading Association members who are teacher educators. It provides demographic information about reading educators and a description of current practices in reading teacher education. It also compares reading educators' values of certain practices (such as course requirements, field placements, and assessments) with the educators' ratings of the programs in which they work. In Chapter 4, Pamela Grossman and her colleagues present case studies of five beginning elementary teachers' writing instruction practices. The chapter follows the beginning teachers through their first 4 years of teaching and describes the various influences on their teaching practices. The authors discuss the impact of the teacher education program in relation to the heavy influences of school context.

Chapter 5 reports preliminary findings from the International Reading Association's study of beginning reading teachers from two sites of the National Commission on Excellence in Elementary Teacher Preparation for Reading Instruction. Amy Seely Flint and her coauthors report similarities and differences among Commission Program Beginning Teachers and Comparison Beginning Teachers. Although the beginning teachers from both groups shared many characteristics, there were differences in the ways that program-prepared teachers approached reading instruction in the school context. Chapter 6, by Rosary Lalik and Ann Potts, is a study of a teacher education program based on a social reconstruction framework. This qualitative analysis was based on interviews with nine program graduates and two program faculty. The interviews reveal ways the program influenced teachers and led to strong practice and leadership in the field. Teacher survival in the midst of standards reform is a major theme of the chapter. In the final chapter of this section, Chapter 7, Kathryn Au and Margaret Maaka describe a teacher education program that was designed to produce teachers who would be successful and stay in teaching on the Wai'anae Coast of Oahu, Hawaii. Schools on the Wai'anae Coast serve a predominately native Hawaiian population, and recruiting and attracting competent teachers is a difficult issue for these schools.

The final section of this volume focuses on inservice teacher education. In Chapter 8, Richard Allington and Peter Johnston showcase effective fourth-grade reading teachers. They focus on what we can learn from successful practitioners to improve our professional development efforts with teachers. Chapter 9 focuses on one aspect of a joint professional development effort by researchers and their local school district. Authors Robert Calfee, Kimberly Norman, Guy Trainin, and Kathleen Wilson have focused the chapter primarily on research methodology for studying professional development in real school contexts. Labeled the "design experiment," this research breaks important ground in suggesting a powerful approach to research design that can give us good information about real children and real teachers in real schools.

In Chapter 10, Barbara Taylor and P. David Pearson of the Center for the Improvement of Early Reading Achievement (CIERA) report findings from a Web-based school change program instituted in seven school districts across the United States. Teachers at each site analyze their own situations and choose from a menu of Web-based resources. These include readings, video clips, chat rooms, and others. Teachers on site form weekly study groups and observe each other's practice to support positive change. Jennifer Berne in Chapter 11 reports outcomes of a study focused on the way teachers interact with standards documents. The central tenet of the chapter is that standards should be viewed as hypotheses rather than as authoritative statements. In this way, teachers can actually interact with standards in a way that encourages reflective practice and professional growth.

The conclusion section of this volume synthesizes and draws from the previous chapters some important questions that must be answered if teacher education is to become research based.

Finally, the appendixes contain executive summaries of three important documents related to the preparation of reading teachers: National Board Certification and the Reform Agenda; Report of the NEA Task Force on Reading 2000; and Teaching Reading IS Rocket Science: What Expert Teachers of Reading Should Know and Be Able to Do.

The chapters presented in this volume will provide readers with a foundation for future research about reading teacher education, and will help propel the needed investment in research on teacher preparation for reading instruction.

THE CONTEXT

CHAPTER 1

Learning to teach reading:
The status of the knowledge base

P. David Pearson

CENTER FOR THE IMPROVEMENT OF EARLY READING ACHIEVEMENT (CIERA), MICHIGAN STATE UNIVERSITY

It is highly appropriate at this juncture in the history of reading research and pedagogy that we turn to matters of teacher learning, teacher education, and professional development. These terms appear in book titles, are featured in articles about school reform, and are even mentioned by politicians eager to let voters know that they intend to be either supportive of or tough on education. Reformers of every stripe—their political ideology does not seem to matter—try to capture teacher education as *their* agenda, as *their* tool of reform. In fact, citing teacher education as a core problem, and then recommending changes in teacher education and staff development is the policy strategy of choice among politicians and reformers. It is the common element in all reform movements.

After a decade of laying the blame for the ills of U.S. education at the feet of teachers, reformers have shifted the blame to teacher educators, who get blamed for just about every problem in U.S. education and many in U.S. society. Teacher education is now the answer to two of the most important questions in the reform rhetoric: (1) What's wrong? and (2) How do we fix it?

I originally set out to write a paper with the challenging title "The Science and Art of Reading Teacher Education." I say challenging because it was challenging to find either the science or the art. Some pundits (such as Finn & Petrilli, 2000) argue that we have had all too much art and not enough science. Others (such as Coles, 2000; O'Hanion, 1999) argue that science (and/or the emphasis on standards and/or standards that usually accompa-

ny scientific rhetoric) will never take us where we want to go in teacher education. My personal experience suggests that conducting research on teacher education, particularly the improvement of teacher education, is especially challenging to anyone who aspires to apply traditional experimental perspectives to the problem. Why? Because it defies every attempt we make to apply controls and measure outcomes. First, it is not altogether clear what counts as evidence of its effectiveness. Is it the knowledge, skills, and dispositions that our prospective teachers gather in teacher education programs? Is it successful entry into the profession, or perhaps staying power within the profession? Or is it the capacity to help students learn? Second, if we think student achievement counts most, we must face the fact that it is nearly impossible to measure a given teacher's contribution to the achievement of a given group of students, much less the contribution of his or her teacher education program to that achievement. How does one sort out the contribution of teacher education from personal qualities, postgraduate professional development as a practicing teacher, community norms, and family factors, all of which surely impact student learning?

The Urgency of the Problem

In a perfect and yet-to-be-discovered world, we could spend 3 years determining the right questions to ask about teacher education, another 3 years determining the right variables to study, and another 10 years designing and implementing studies to fine tune the variables and answer the questions. The problem is that we do not have 16 years to answer these questions—not if we want policy, education, licensure, and certification to be as informed by our research efforts as it will inevitably be informed by political ideologies and economic interests. Simply put, there is incredible impatience in the policy world. The public and the policy makers want the problems identified, and they want them fixed now.

Policy makers who administer federal projects like the Reading Excellence Act or the Improving America's Schools Act, as well as the Foundation personnel (Carnegie Corporation, 2000), express alarm at the pace that we in higher education, teacher education, and professional development adopt in moving toward solving the problems in teacher education. They believe that the window for action is quite narrow, that we cannot wait for the definitive research to inch its way toward a solution to these vexing problems.

The Central Role of Standards

Like it or not, standards are playing—and will continue to play—a major role in shaping reforms in teacher education and professional development. As part of the larger standards-based reform movement, most states are now in the process of changing their standards for initial and permanent certification. The demand for new research-based standards for teacher education, while strong everywhere, is nowhere stronger than it is in the K–6 and the pre-K–3 arena.

The current model of standards-based reform, so prevalent in the discourse of national and state efforts, positions content standards as the primary driving force behind just about every other educational phenomenon. As depicted in Figure 1, content standards are driving performance standards and assessments, teacher education standards, and curriculum frameworks. Reform, in this model, is the consequence of implementing policy tools that are all aligned with content standards. Teacher

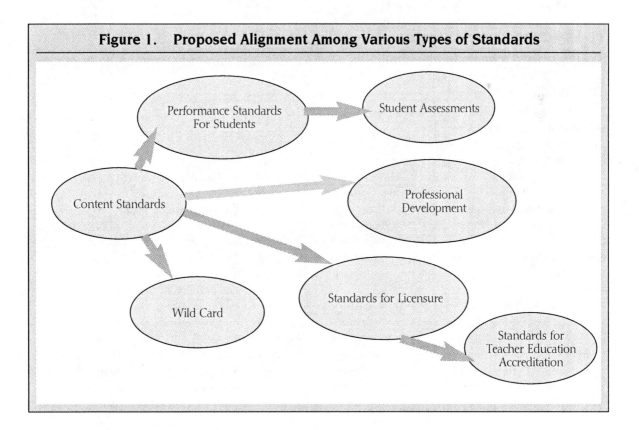

Figure 1. Proposed Alignment Among Various Types of Standards

standards are a part of the model, and the primary criterion for judging the new standards in teacher education and teacher licensure is the degree to which they align with standards for students.

The sense of urgency about attending to standards in general and standards for teacher education in particular prompted me to change the title of this chapter to its current instantiation—the status of the knowledge base for teaching reading. I believe that the knowledge base, whether it comes from science, art, or values, is something that we must address right now, in the next year or two. In this chapter, I hope to extend the conversation about what this knowledge base might look like. The question before us is how me might develop this knowledge base, and what standards and assessments will we create or choose in order to give it life.

The Policy Context in Which We Work

First we should deal with a few contextual issues so that we fully understand the manner in which teacher education is being portrayed in policy debates and what that portrayal does to our professional energies.

The Manufactured Crisis

We need to make sure that we deal with real, not manufactured, problems of teacher education. The primary manufactured problem regarding teacher education is that *our current approaches to teacher education and professional development are ineffective, and do not result in higher student achievement.* That is simply not true! Two recent reviews, both completed by Linda Darling-Hammond (1999, 2000), portray a completely different picture about the efficacy of teacher education. The data cited in these reviews dispel the myth of teacher education ineffectiveness.

Research reviews since 1970 conclude that totally prepared and certified teachers are better rated and more successful with students in terms of promoting achievement than are teachers who lack either subject matter or teaching knowledge. Teachers admitted to the profession with less than full preparation are less satisfied with their train-

ing, and have greater difficulties planning curriculum, managing the classroom, diagnosing student learning needs, and adapting their instruction to specific situations and students. More fully prepared teachers are more effective in each of these performance areas.

DATA FROM STATE AND LOCAL STUDIES. Several studies indicate that certification is correlated with significant effects, such as

> higher pass rates on state exams for students in North Carolina whose teachers scored higher on the NTE (Strauss & Sawyer, 1986);
>
> higher achievement in language arts for Dallas, Texas, students whose teachers were traditionally versus alternatively certified (Gomez & Grobe, 1990);
>
> higher performance in reading and math for students whose teachers scored higher on the Texas Teacher Licensing Exam (Ferguson, 1991);
>
> higher pass rates on Texas student exams in schools with more fully certified teachers (Fuller, 1999);
>
> higher test scores for math students whose teachers were fully certified (Goldhaber & Brewer, 1999); and
>
> higher scores in Los Angeles, California, for students, at all income levels, whose teachers were more fully certified (LA County Office of Education, 1999).

The data from Los Angeles are interesting because they show reading achievement by relative poverty level *and* the percentage of untrained teachers at those schools. They compare schools serving students from low, moderate, and higher income families. The study suggested that regardless of income, the higher the percentage of certified teachers, the higher the achievement of the schools across each of those levels (see Figure 2 on facing page). These data on certification certainly suggest that our profession does make a difference.

When we consider average retention rates for teachers who pursue differing pathways into teaching, the data show that one of the outcomes of more rigorous teacher education programs is that

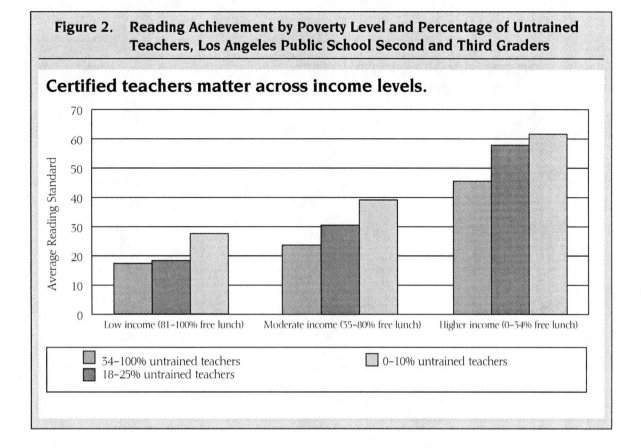

Figure 2. Reading Achievement by Poverty Level and Percentage of Untrained Teachers, Los Angeles Public School Second and Third Graders

Certified teachers matter across income levels.

Average Reading Standard

Low income (81–100% free lunch)   Moderate income (35–80% free lunch)   Higher income (0–34% free lunch)

☐ 34–100% untrained teachers   ☐ 0–10% untrained teachers
☐ 18–25% untrained teachers

people remain in the profession longer. As suggested by the data in Figure 3 (see page 8), 4-year programs provide the smallest yield of teachers entering the field, even smaller than alternative certification pathways; however both 4- and 5-year programs promote greater longevity in the profession, with 5-year programs showing a substantial edge even over 4-year programs. Overall, these data suggest that the investment individuals make in 5-year preparation programs promotes greater initial and long-term commitment to teaching.

DATA FROM THE NATIONAL ASSESSMENT OF EDUCATIONAL PROGRESS (NAEP). In analyses of the relationship between contextual factors and student achievement on the NAEP (see Darling-Hammond, 2000), the largest share of the total variance in state student achievement is explained by teacher quality variables, including certification, training, and professional development. These findings hold both

before *and* after controlling for student poverty and language background. Teacher quality indexes explain somewhere between 67% and 87% of the variance in state scores. The best predictor is the percentage of well-qualified teachers in the state—those who are fully certified in the major of the field in which they teach. This explains between 40% and 60% of the variance on NAEP achievement.

FINDINGS FROM THE NATIONAL READING PANEL. Recent findings from the National Reading Panel report (NRP, 2000), particularly the teacher education portion, are interesting mainly because the teacher education section is one that provides unequivocally good news. They could not determine, from the studies they researched, which elements of teacher preparation were most effective or most desired, primarily because there is not a good database on how teachers are prepared. However, they did find that specific interventions at the preservice level al-

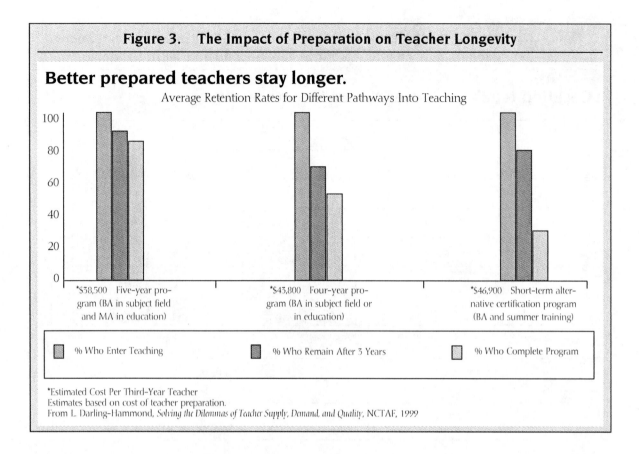

Figure 3. The Impact of Preparation on Teacher Longevity

Better prepared teachers stay longer.

Average Retention Rates for Different Pathways Into Teaching

*\$38,500   Five-year pro-
gram (BA in subject field
and MA in education)

*\$43,800   Four-year pro-
gram (BA in subject field or
in education)

*\$46,900   Short-term alter-
native certification program
(BA and summer training)

■ % Who Enter Teaching   ■ % Who Remain After 3 Years   ■ % Who Complete Program

*Estimated Cost Per Third-Year Teacher
Estimates based on cost of teacher preparation.
From L. Darling-Hammond, *Solving the Dilemmas of Teacher Supply, Demand, and Quality*, NCTAF, 1999

most always resulted in aspiring teachers learning the skills they were taught. In addition, the Panel found that student performance improved on skills associated with inservice training teachers had received. The students whose teachers benefited from inservice instruction increased their performance on assessments of skills related to that instruction. Interestingly, many more of these studies addressed the acquisition of pedagogical skills for teaching comprehension than other areas of the reading curriculum. That finding demonstrates that professional teachers actively engage and make effective use of opportunities to refine their knowledge and skills, and they are able to transform that knowledge in ways that benefit their students. The findings from the National Reading Panel Report do show that teacher learning benefits student learning, particularly at the inservice level, and especially on comprehension measures.

The Consequences of Manufactured Crises

THE MALDISTRIBUTION OF TEACHER EXPERTISE. Manufactured crises are not just idle misinformation; they are destructive because they may divert our attention from more substantive issues that really should concern us—for example, the fact that the distribution of teacher knowledge *is* correlated with the distribution of student achievement. We do not know whether it is the environment or the teachers that cause the learning differences, but we have data suggesting that our very best teachers, in terms of the knowledge and skills they possess, are teaching in the schools that probably need them least. Our higher performance schools are populated by our more knowledgeable teachers. Poorer school districts and minority children get the least qualified, least knowledgeable teachers (see Figure 4).

There is an alarming difference between the two types of environments.

There is at least some anecdotal evidence that the widespread legislative initiatives to reduce class size, mostly in the primary grades, may actually exacerbate the inverse relationship between school needs and teacher expertise. With increased positions available (the open slots in primary grades), wealthy suburban schools, which usually offer higher salaries and better working conditions, are in a position to bid for the services of the best urban teachers, thus contributing to this problem. The natural result of this migration—and nowhere is this more evident than in California's largest urban districts—is an increase in reliance on partially certified teachers. This falls under the rubric of a conspiracy of good intentions.

HIRING PRACTICES. Many districts do not hire the best-qualified applicants for teaching positions even when qualified applicants are available. The shortages are preventable, but not prevented. In 1999, in the city of New York, there were about 37,000 qualified applicants for approximately 5,000 teaching positions. The city ended up hiring about 2,000 people on emergency credentials (Darling-Hammond, 2000). The most probable explanation is that the districts failed to make most of hiring decisions until after Labor Day, when the better qualified applicants had taken positions elsewhere.

OTHER PRACTICES. There are the issues of pay and working conditions to consider. Some districts prefer having low-paid personnel, especially if they are restricted by a tight budget. Selection procedures remain a problem. There are still many districts in the United States where patronage of one sort or another—special advantage given to particular groups such as city residents, veterans, or the like— is still the norm. Inefficient and ineffectual screening

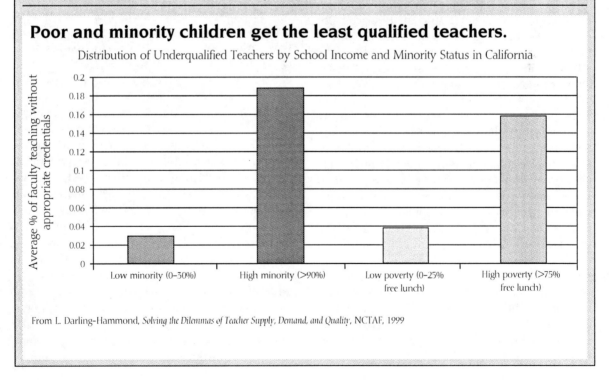

Figure 4. The Relationship Among School Racial Distribution, School Poverty, and Teacher Qualification

Poor and minority children get the least qualified teachers.

Distribution of Underqualified Teachers by School Income and Minority Status in California

From L. Darling-Hammond, *Solving the Dilemmas of Teacher Supply, Demand, and Quality*, NCTAF, 1999

processes, unprofessional treatment of applicants, late hiring decisions and, the lack of licensing reciprocity among the states continue to hinder recruitment efforts. The United States is divided into the producers and consumers of teachers. Many states are over-producers while other states are over-consumers of new teachers. Aligning supply and demand would be a lot easier to accomplish if reciprocity were more common among states.

Alternatives to Standards-Based Professional Models

There are competitive alternatives to standards-based professional models, and they are supported widely by those who are suspicious of the teacher education establishment. Finn and Petrilli (2000) have a very different vision of how to improve the quality of teaching. They have a strictly marketplace vision. The idea is to invite all comers and then weed out the chaff. You admit anyone into the teaching profession, and if they do not produce results—if the gain scores of their students are not up to standard—they are invited to leave the profession. Furthermore, schools not producing results would become history, too. Student performance becomes the sole criterion for retaining teachers and schools. It is a strict marketplace economy, and output results, in the form of student performance measures, are the single criterion by which quality and therefore longevity, either for an individual teacher or a program, is judged.

Finn and Petrilli argue that we have used the wrong metaphor for teaching, at least in terms of teacher preparation. We have used the medical metaphor, arguing that teachers, like doctors, need to meet professional standards, serve in internships, pass professional examinations prior to being licensed, and once a practitioner, continue to participate in professional development activities to update their knowledge and practices and keep their licensure current. Finn and Petrilli argue that we should be using a metaphor more like journalism. In journalism you can become a journalist with a degree in journalism, and indeed you may have an advantage with such a degree. But, in most instances a journalism degree is not actually required. Journalists are a varied lot, with backgrounds or degrees in English, law, history, and other areas. Finn and Petrilli propose to allow people to come into the profession from all routes, and then let quality, as indexed by student performance, carry the day.

Linda Darling-Hammond has tried to characterize the difference between the National Commission on Teaching and America's Future (NCTAF) view and the Fordham Foundation (led by Chester Finn) view. It is a difference between professional accountability and marketing accountability: Using professional accountability as a guide, the system and the teachers are held accountable for possessing the best possible knowledge they can about what works. This is the promise any profession makes to its constituents—that its members will know as much as they can about their work. In the market economy model, on the other hand, anyone is allowed to enter, and you eliminate those who do not perform adequately. The goal of the professional accountability model is to ensure access to subject matter and teaching knowledge. The goal of the market economy is simply gain: "What matters are the results." The goal of the professional model is to ensure the standards are there before and after hiring, through licensing, induction, evaluation, and professional development. It is truly a developmental model, one that allows you to begin with minimal level of skills and evolve from that starting point. By contrast, in the market model, a veteran teacher who suddenly has a bad year would be as vulnerable as a newcomer—truly a Willy Loman model of teacher quality.

Most salient among the many problems with the marketplace model is the question of what happens to the children and parents who must wait for this system to work. Also problematic is the question of compensation: What would be the consequences of salaries based on achievement gain from one year to the next? Although market devotees would argue that such a model would force teachers to work harder to help students learn more, it is equally as plausible to argue that teachers will work harder at selecting the students with whom they would be willing to work.

In an early 2000 posting on the National Reading Conference listserv (Johnson, 2000), the marketplace approach was caricatured by likening it to dentists being held accountable for the number of cavities developed by their patients. Would that motivate dentists to work harder at cleaning, prevention, and care? Or would it motivate them to choose their patients more carefully? Measuring the value added of a single teacher's work by the gain made by either an individual student or even a group of students is rife with problems and potentially corrupt practices. Students are diverse in terms of background, dispositions, and performance. They come with histories. It is hard to imagine how such a system could be made equitable.

Scaling Up

There is much pressure in the current policy context to extend promising findings to any and all situations in which they might prove helpful. The pressure to "scale up" findings from teacher education is as strong as in research on school curriculum reform. The great irony in teacher learning is that in the face of enormous pressure to scale up, we have a rich body of evidence suggesting that "scaling down" is what really works (see Richardson, in press; Wilson & Berne, 1999). Our best research shows that learning in communities, especially local, school-based communities, is most effective. But the political pressures are in favor of rapid, wide-scale change immediately. If we look at staff development studies in literacy (for example, Richardson & Anders, 1994) we find that community-based staff development facilitates teachers in

> becoming confident in their decision making,
>
> taking responsibility for what occurs in their classrooms,
>
> developing a sense of individual autonomy,
>
> becoming empowered to make changes, and
>
> over time nurturing growth in student performance.

In this regard, it is important to emphasize that in the work completed by Richardson and Anders (1994), it took 3 years just to get the community going. It is hard to imagine how scaling up would work in the face of strong evidence that developing communities of learners takes so much time and patience.

Wilson and Berne (1999) completed an extensive review on the development of professional knowledge; in the process they examined several large-scale community knowledge development projects. Looking across all of those hefty community-based model developments, they found several consistent patterns and trends. First, teachers who are learning are in the process of redefining their teaching practice. Second, teacher learning is better thought of as activated, rather than packaged and delivered. That idea encompasses the notion of "I can't give it to you, but I can start you on the pathway to figuring out for yourself what really matters." Third, teacher learning flourishes in a context of privileged interactions among teachers. Cooperation, conversation, and dialogue are absolutely essential to the process. Fourth, teacher learning is more substantial when there is a personal, not just professional, learning goal involved. This means that for many teachers, it is important to become a more interesting person—not just a more knowledgeable professional.

The community/collegial view is also supported by the work of the late Susan Rosenholtz, who provided enormously rich work in the late 1980s on schools that do and do not work (Rosenholtz, 1989). She looked inside what she called "learning enriched" and "learning impoverished" schools, as defined by student learning indexes, and then examined teacher beliefs about their own professional efficacy. She found two very different sets of beliefs about teacher learning. In the "learning enriched" schools, people had a *sustained* view of teacher learning. That is, pedagogical skills were not considered something that one developed in a weekend, or a day, or even a week. The assumption was that teaching skill requires hard work and collegial support. It is a dynamic process. It is ever changing, and the focus is on academics and motivation. By contrast, in the "learning impoverished" schools, teachers possessed a *terminal* view of teacher learning. The terminal view suggests that teaching skill is something bestowed on you without any work or effort—a natural, God-given talent of sorts. It is also viewed as an individual gift—teaching prowess is an individualized, isolated, solitary phenomenon. Those who do not consider themselves as blessed with this "gift" approach teaching as routine, with the focus placed on managing behavior and curriculum demands. These divergent views of teacher learning and skill development are associated with two very different learning environments. Apparently a school-wide learning ethos does matter, for both students and teachers.

These data, however compelling they may be, leave us on the horns of a dilemma. In terms of improving the quality of teaching, it seems reasonable to recommend some level of external intervention. Because we know that not all teachers know—nor can easily learn what they need to know—on their own, a little external nudge to spur an increase in efforts to improve teacher knowledge seems in order. However, we can also be confident that if and when the allegedly needed knowledge is handed to teachers on a silver platter or force-fed through some ill-conceived mandate, they may reject it, or more likely, engage in mock compliance. Assuring officials that they are implementing the reform when, in fact, they are just waiting for it to run its course.

The Knowledge Base Question

Potential Knowledge Sources for Setting Teacher Standards

The fundamental question regarding teacher knowledge is, Who determines what teachers need to know and be able to do? In other words, from where or whom should the standards for teachers come? Four sources seem plausible.

First, and most ideal, especially to an anxious public, is research demonstrating that teachers who possess a certain body of knowledge promote better student learning. This is the rarest kind of information at our disposal. It is rare because it requires that we do research on the relationship between teacher learning and student learning—an endeavor that is difficult and expensive and, ultimately, may not be possible, at least to the degree that would allow us to pinpoint the precise relationship between the knowledge and efforts of a given teacher in a given year and the learning of students who were in his or her class during that period.

Second, we can determine what approaches work best with students, and then make sure that teachers possess the knowledge and skills required

to use those approaches. This is what much of the current rhetoric in the reform movement is about. Chapter 9 of *Preventing Reading Difficulties in Young Children* (Snow, Burns, & Griffin, 1998) contains many recommendations for teacher education policy and practice. These recommendations are not a listing of understandings that have been empirically validated as causing student learning. Instead, they are things that teachers would have to know if they were going to implement the sorts of practices validated in their review of research on classroom reading instruction. (See Strickland, Chapter 2 of this volume, for further discussion of these recommendations.) *Teaching Reading IS Rocket Science: What Expert Teachers of Reading Should Know and Be Able to Do*, the influential document published by the Learning First Alliance (full text available at http://www.aft.org/edissues/rocketscience.htm), is driven by exactly the same logic. (See Appendix C of this volume for a summary of *Teaching Reading IS Rocket Science*.)

The third model is really a variant of the second. Instead of examining research about student performance, we look instead to existing standards for students and from them draw inferences about standards for teachers. I want to illustrate the reality of this third approach, which assumes that there should be a close relationship between content standards for students and standards for teacher education, by quoting from a document that I received in the mail a few weeks ago. The document came from the state of Ohio, where the Board of Regents sought ideas on how to align curriculum throughout K–12 and higher education. The message on the letter, which was endorsed by the American Association of Colleges for Teacher Education (AACTE), read, "not only is it important for you to share your perspective on the standards for English and language arts, it is also important for you to indicate to the Board of Regents how the standards will impact the role of teacher education at colleges and universities around the country". (State of Ohio, personal communication, April 2000). There is a widespread presumption that there should be a close relationship between student standards and teacher standards, as depicted earlier in Figure 1 (see page 5).

So where do we look to find a solid set of student standards? In 1999, every state in the United States was required submit standards to the U.S. Department of Education in order to receive Title I funds; thus, groups from almost any state could look to their own student standards. We could look to the *Standards for the English Language Arts* (IRA/NCTE, 1996), although it is not clear that these standards have widespread recognition and acceptance. And some nonprofit organizations, New Standards (NCEE, 1999) for example, have developed their own standards for the primary grades.

The fourth model, "professional consensus" about what teachers should know and be able to do, is the model used most often in setting national and state standards for teaching. Typically, in implementing this model, we do the following:

1. Convene a group of professionals and have them use their professional judgment to negotiate a set of proposed standards.

2. Send the document to many different groups to solicit feedback.

3. Repeat that process until we have a set of standards objected to by few if any constituencies.

Presumably, the experts we select will use many different kinds of research—research about basic processes in literacy, research about instructional practices, and research about teacher development and learning—to inform their discussions and the resulting standards. But the research is always filtered through individual judgment and group negotiation.

The Knowledge Source Matters

My search for an answer to the question, What should teachers know and be able to do?, leads me to the conclusion that the answer you get depends on where you look. If one looks to the National Board for Professional Teaching Standards (NBPTS), or the International Reading Association/National Council of Teachers of English (IRA/NCTE) standards, or many state standards documents, one gets a highly situated, organic, decidedly constructive view of teaching and learning from those documents. Teachers and students are both empowered

beings. Teachers facilitate. Students accept responsibility. Consider the standard for language study in the NBPTS early adolescent English/language arts standards. It begins, "...accomplished early adolescent language arts teachers know that language is an artifact of human ingenuity and a constantly evolving media.... They recognize that each individual speaks what is, in effect, a personal dialect reflecting his or her own particular regional upbringing, occupation, age, and socioeconomic status. Whereas teachers celebrate the diversity of language forms in the United States, they understand the sociopolitical reality that some forms carry with them both greater prestige and the potential for greater access..." (NBPTS, 1998, p. 37). This document is very situated and constructivist in tone and feel.

By contrast, if one appeals to the teacher learning standards implicit in *Preventing Reading Difficulties* (Snow, Burns, & Griffin, 1998), one gets a rich, thorough description of the linguistic, psychological, and pedagogical knowledge base. However, there is little acknowledgment of the teacher as a learner. Snow and her colleagues provide a list of the pieces of knowledge that teachers would need to be able to teach in research-proven ways. There is no sense of how people acquire that knowledge. And there is no notion of when in the course of a career particular kinds of knowledge ought to become a part of a teacher's repertoire. (See Strickland, Chapter 2 of this volume, for a summary of this list.)

Examining an Influential Knowledge Source—*Teaching Reading IS Rocket Science: What Expert Teachers of Reading Should Know and Be Able To Do*

I want to single out one particular document—one account of what teachers should know and be able to do—because it has attracted so much attention in 1999 and 2000, and it appears to be taken seriously by states as they revise standards for teachers. It is the American Federation of Teachers (AFT)-sponsored document, *Teaching Reading IS Rocket Science: What Expert Teachers of Reading Should Know and Be Able To Do*. The document asserts that because of a surge in the research base, we now know how to teach reading effectively. In representing effective classroom programs, the document pays attention to most of the elements of a balanced program—phonemic awareness, phonics, comprehension, composition, and oral language. The underlying logic is that if we can specify the knowledge that teachers need in order to teach that curriculum, then we will know what to teach in teacher education programs.

The document proposes a set of action steps to improve teacher education. It is an important document to read, both for its potential influence and for its solid content. Indeed, if I were building a knowledge base or a set of standards, I would include most of the content AFT has included in the document. However, I would order and situate the components differently.

As I suggested, their action steps for changing reading instruction are, according to the authors, based on research. There is a presumption in the document that for the last decade and a half, we generally have been using opinion to guide the profession. The document suggests that we need to establish core standards, curriculum, and entry-level assessments for new teachers, and we need to align teacher education, curriculum standards for students, and licensing requirements.

The document also recommends professional development institutes for professors and classroom teachers, which some states, such as California, have done. Others are doing it as part of the Reading Excellence Act (REA) grants that were awarded in 1999 or 2000. According to *Rocket Science*, we also need to press the developers of textbooks and instructional materials to align those products as well. Twenty years ago reformers called for improvements and changes in basal programs; today they are calling for improvements and changes in the textbooks that are used in professional courses. Finally the document suggests that in order to promote a high quality of professional development for teachers, we need to further invest in higher salaries and improved working environments.

The core curriculum as posed by the *Rocket Science* document is divided into five areas of emphasis:

1. psychology of reading and reading development

2. knowledge of language structure and its application

3. practical skills for instruction in the comprehensive program

4. assessment of classroom reading

5. assessment of writing skills

Each area is sensibly subdivided into important topics. The psychology area, for example, includes the cognitive characteristics of proficient reading, cognitive characteristics of poor reading, environmental and physiological factors that influence reading ability, and the development of reading, writing, and spelling as intellectual phenomenon. The language area focuses on phonetics, phonology, morphology, semantics, syntax, and text structure. Again, these are topics that would be on my list, not necessarily because I believe teachers need to teach any of these elements directly, but because teachers need to know what these elements are and how each of them affects their students' learning. Regarding assessment, it would be hard for anyone to argue against teacher knowledge of the conceptual and psychometric characteristics of assessments and the consequences of their use.

All these aspects seem eminently reasonable to me, but my major concern about the document focuses more on what it fails to address than what it does address. The most notable omission is any discussion of language in use. Language, as it is listed and discussed in the *Rocket Science* document, has a static feel to it—as if it were a set of objects out there that one could accumulate. What is missing is the dynamic, dialogic quality that we know language has when we see it in use (see, for example, Gee, 1999; Gee & Green, 1998). I wonder, as I read this section, what happened to the last 20 years of literacy research in the areas of pragmatics, discourse analysis, and sociolinguistics?

My second concern can be expressed as a series of questions: What is figure, and what is ground? What gets privileged? What gets marginalized in the presentation? One test of privilege can be carried out by examining the kinds of questions put forward by the authors to illustrate the kind of knowledge that expert teachers ought to possess. For example, the questions the teachers can answer if they have knowledge about the psychology of reading are questions such as

> Why is it useful to know if a student can read nonsense words such as *flep*, *tridding*, and *pertollic*?

> What does it mean if a 5-year-old writes, "Please take me with you" as *pez tak me yet u*?

> Which words do good readers skip as they read along?

A teacher who has knowledge of language can answer questions such as

> What sounds will children confuse with /p/ and what can a teacher do to help children avoid confusion?

> Why do children spell *dress* with a "J" or a "G" at the beginning?

> Are *love*, *dove*, and *give* exception words in English?

> How many meaningful parts are in the word *contracted*?

A teacher who has knowledge of teaching skills can answer questions such as

> Can the words *shoe*, *do*, *flew*, and *you* be used to teach rhyming?

> How fast should a second or third grader be able to read?

> When in the instructional sequence should a teacher ask a child to think about the meaning of a passage to decipher a word?

In reference to assessment, an expert teacher should be able to answer

> What specific skills should be present at the end of first grade that might predict later reading achievement?

> Are running records or oral reading tests reliable or valid indicators of reading ability?

> When are children typically expected to spell the words *trapped*, *offered*, *plate*, *illustrate*, and *preparing*?

> Why is it important to test comprehension with material that the child has not read before?

These questions reveal an additional concern about this influential document. Where are the questions about the comprehension process? Why are there no questions about composition? Why are there no questions about the relationship between knowledge and comprehension? These questions reveal the privilege accorded to phonemic awareness, phonics, and spelling and the corresponding marginalization of comprehension, context, and composition. These higher order processes are barely alluded to and then only with items that suggest highly circumscribed roles for them.

Finally, the *Rocket Science* publication gives no sense of the professional teacher as a learner. There is no acknowledgment that pedagogical knowledge develops over time, or how such knowledge is acquired in the first place. This is unfortunate, because there is a mass of solid information to be found in this document about the technical aspects of reading and writing. I would not want to see any of that information ignored because some key perspectives are omitted.

Unwarranted Isomorphism

This next point is not a criticism of the AFT document, but of virtually all documents that attempt to extrapolate standards for teachers on the basis of standards for students. All the approaches that begin by specifying what students need to know and should be able to do, whether they start with research or professional consensus, assume a direct link that may or may not be justified. The idea that the teacher learning is isomorphic to student learning is an assumption that needs to be tested. When this idea is tested, I predict that we will find many things that teachers should know in order to shape curriculum or instructional activities that students need never have to learn in order to read well. These things make up a segment of the knowledge that teachers need in order to make good decisions about what to do with students.

So is there an alternative to *Rocket Science*? There are several, but none is well-enough developed to provide a definitive and useful alternative at the time this chapter went to press. Let me introduce them, however, in order to encourage others to get involved in this important task.

First, the Carnegie Corporation has just funded an effort that involves a host of literacy educators, policy makers, teachers, and teacher educators. The purpose of the Carnegie effort is to specify the knowledge base of teachers of our youngest children (pre-K through Grade 3); Catherine Snow and Dorothy Strickland are heading up the project.

Second, a group of us are working on the reading and language arts portion of the Interstate New Teachers Assessment and Support Consortium (INTASC) standards for initial elementary certification.[1] INTASC is a unit within the Council of Chief State School Officers (CCSSO). Its mission is to develop standards and assessments for initial teacher licensure. It is attempting to do for beginning certification what the National Board for Professional Teaching Standards has done for advanced certification. It has now expanded to more than 20 states. At this time, our group has identified several fundamental principles to guide the development of INTASC's standards, but as yet, none of their ideas are official. Nonetheless, a few of the more general principles are worth sharing because of their provocative nature.

LITERACY AS FOUNDATIONAL KNOWLEDGE. It is time to stop conceptualizing literacy education as a distinct subject matter that is on a par with math, social studies, science, art, or physical education. Instead, we should regard literacy as *foundational knowledge*, just like learning theory or social foundations, that is required for learning in the subject areas of the elementary school. It is not hard to make such a case for language and literacy. The constructs of language and discourse are central to building knowledge in any subject area—not only language and discourse in general, but also language and discourse in those particular disciplines. And literacy, in the sense of mastery, is central to most disciplines, and it is captured in our use of terms like mathematical literacy, scientific literacy, and civic literacy.

LITERACY IS NOT SOMETHING THAT CAN BE DELIVERED TO CHILDREN. It requires active participation, ongoing, interesting and relevant interchange between student and teacher. It has to be active, alive, and lively for the student to gain access to it. It comes with and through engaging in the everyday practices of literacy.

THE FRAMEWORK ONE SELECTS TO ORGANIZE IDEAS ABOUT LANGUAGE AND LITERACY IS AS IMPORTANT AS THE PARTICULAR IDEAS INCLUDED IN THE FRAMEWORK. The infrastructure of language is fully represented, as are all of the components that comprise the *Rocket Science* list (semantics, syntax, morphology, phonology, and pragmatics). However, the INTASC document will also consider the nature of living language, and the fact that we learn it in interaction with others. This perspective emphasizes how language develops both in and out of school settings. It considers the language system, the learners' development, and the ways in which formal education can support each. Also important are the functional aspects of language and literacy. We put these tools to work to achieve other ends—to inform, persuade, direct, entertain, control, subvert. The document accepts the Halliday and Hassan (1976) triad: We learn language, we learn through language, and we learn about language.

TEXT PLAYS A MAJOR ROLE IN BOTH WRITTEN AND ORAL COMMUNICATION. Teachers need to know a great deal about text—how to define it, how it relates to language, its major genres, and the structures within those genres. Like the *Rocket Science* document, the INTASC document will also address the full range of written language topics, including the oral-written language relationship, orthography and its methods of representation (including the alphabetic principle), and the specifics of the cipher in English orthography (for instance, the mapping of sound to symbol and symbol to sound).

---

1. The committee for the INTASC effort includes Barbara Diamond, Susan Florio-Ruane, Sandra Gibbs (NCTE), Miriam Martinez, Kathleen Paliokas (INTASC staff), Michelle Parker, P. David Pearson, Taffy Raphael, Cathy Roller (IRA), Jean Smith (INTASC staff), Karen Smith, and Dorothy Strickland.

The final document is likely to include most, if not all, of the elements that are currently seen in the *Rocket Science* publication. But the new document will differ in some fundamental ways. First and most important will be the inclusion of the "language in use" perspective. Second is how the knowledge base is organized and contextualized. Third, and this is sheer speculation, I predict that the two documents will be translated into very different kinds of teacher assessment. The *Rocket Science* framework lends itself to multiple-choice tests of teacher knowledge. I would be surprised to learn of anything short of a multiple measures approach, with a teacher-created portfolio leading the way but flanked by some multiple-choice testing and some essay-like assessment center tasks.

The question of level of expertise keeps haunting us, as it haunts all attempts to develop standards and assessments for professionals operating at different levels of experience. I believe that we desperately need developmental models of teacher learning, with a trajectory that plots the increasing sophistication of teacher knowledge over time. We need a model that identifies and includes the stages encountered by teachers as they refine their craft. How might standards for initial licensure differ from standards for permanent certification? The National Board for Professional Teaching Standards presents a rich model of what expert teaching looks like. However, knowing how much novice teachers know prior to placing them in classrooms is much more difficult for us to gauge. I do not believe we have a strong enough notion of how far along the path toward expertise one needs to be prior to entering the field. We may need a developmental rubric that recognizes that the sophistication of knowledge increases over time. My rubric would begin with (a) initial awareness of an idea or a body of knowledge, to (b) use of the knowledge to plan and implement instruction, to (c) use of the knowledge to adapt instruction and assessment, and to (d) use of the knowledge to reinvent oneself through critical reflection on practice.

A Coda

I would like to conclude with a success story about teacher education policy. The story has un-folded over the last 14 years in the state of Connecticut, where they have devoted a great deal of work to the enhancement of teacher education, both preservice and inservice. They have increased and equalized salaries for teachers around the state, raised licensing standards, subsidized and intensified teacher preparation, and created a beginning teacher mentoring and assessment program that has affected most teachers. The state has implemented middle school and high school English/language arts permanent certification by peer review of professional portfolios. They have stimulated and improved teacher evaluation, initiated the portfolio review, and invested in widespread professional development using sound principles of elementary literacy instruction.

At the same time as all this investment in teacher development was taking place, Connecticut dramatically improved its NAEP scores. From 1994 to 1998, Connecticut gained 10 scale score points—an unprecedented jump for any state of any size. Typically and with arduous effort, a state might change 2 or 3 points in an NAEP cycle. But a jump of such magnitude demands attention. Connecticut hired an external firm to conduct a policy analysis to determine the reasons behind this dramatic change. First, they found that the positive shift in gain scores occurred in the face of declining wealth, and an increase in minority and low-income populations within the state. Neither class size nor instructional time changed during the period measured. What did change, however, was the approach to reform adopted by the Connecticut State Department of Education. The Department linked higher teacher salaries to licensing and teacher preparation reforms. New teacher induction procedures were instituted. A low-stakes, high-information, performance-based assessment system was put into place. The alignment of student and teaching standards was thus achieved. Low-achieving districts were provided categorical aid. The bottom line is that Connecticut succeeded at what so many of us aspire to achieve: They took a set of policy tools and made them work in a positive way for schools, parents, teachers, and learners. There may be a lesson to learn from Connecticut.

The Long-Term Strategy—Research

Most of all, we need research—research that we can use to replace all the informed professional judgment we have had to rely on for all too long. First, as difficult as it will be, we definitely need more work on the relationship between teacher learning and student learning. It is a very difficult issue to investigate empirically; design issues and political issues will be difficult to negotiate. We need to develop better tools to measure teacher learning. Second, we need longitudinal studies of teacher learning if we are to develop theories of teacher development that are conceptually based, empirically driven, and not simply a compendium of opinions regarding what develops. Third, and at a much more basic level, we desperately need a basic database that will allow us to answer the question, What does reading teacher education look like?

In a perfect world, we could wait for the definitive studies to be done before we enter the policy phase. We do not live in that perfect world. So, we must implement imperfect models while we continue to learn more about perfection. What we need to do is develop and implement—and continue to improve—a set of standards to guide our profession and our teacher education programs. We also need to make tentative assessment decisions. My vote goes for the model that is currently being implemented in Connecticut and by the National Board for Professional Teaching Standards. I know what seems to be in the plans for INTASC, and those are portfolio reviews monitored by the profession. It is much more costly than sit-down multiple choice exams that so many of the states use. My question is whether we can "afford" those cheaper assessments.

Finally, given the choice between Finn and Petrilli's marketplace model and Darling-Hammond's professional model for improving the quality of teaching in the United States, I know where I am going to focus my energy. To promote the standards-based model is to hold on to the ideal that we can and must be a true profession. To promote the marketplace model is to mock our profession and to neglect our obligations to children and their parents. That is a trust we must not break.

REFERENCES

Coles, G. (2000). *Misreading reading: The bad science that hurts children*. Portsmouth, NH: Heinemann.

Darling-Hammond, L. (1999). *Teacher quality and student achievement: A review of state policy evidence*. Seattle, WA: Center for Teaching Policy, University of Washington.

Darling-Hammond, L. (2000). *Solving the dilemmas of teacher supply, demand, and standards: How we can ensure a competent, caring, and qualified teacher for every child. National Commission on Teaching and America's Future*. New York: Teachers College Press.

Ferguson, R. (1991). Paying for public education: New evidence on how and why money matters. *Harvard Journal of Legislation, 28*, 465–498.

Finn, C.E. Jr., & Petrilli, M.J. (Eds.). (2000). *The state of state standards, 2000: English, history, geography, mathematics, science* [Online]. Available: www.edexcellence.net/library/soss2000/2000soss.html

Fuller, E.J. (1999). *Does teacher certification matter? A comparison of TAAS performance in 1997 between schools with low and high percentages of certified teachers*. Austin, TX: University of Texas at Austin, Charles A. Dana Center.

Gee, J.P. (1999). *An introduction to discourse analysis: Theory and method*. London: Routledge.

Gee, J.P., & Green, J.L. (1998). Discourse analysis, learning and social practice. A methodological study. *Review of Research in Education, 23*, 119–171.

Goldhaber, D.D., & Brewer, D.J. (1999). *Does teacher certification matter? High school certification states and student achievement*. Unpublished manuscript.

Gomez, D.L., & Grobe, R.P. (1990, April). *Three years of alternative certification in Dallas: Where are we?* Paper presented at the annual meeting of the American Educational Research Association, Boston, MA.

Halliday, M.A.K., & Hassan, R. (1976). *Cohesion in English*. London: Longman.

Hirsh, E., Koppich, J., & Knapp, M. (1988). *What states are doing to improve the quality of teaching: A brief review of current patterns and trends*. Seattle, WA: Center for Teaching Policy, University of Washington.

International Reading Association & National Council of Teachers of English. (1996). *Standards for the English language arts*. Newark, DE, & Urbana, IL: Authors.

Johnson, F. (2000, March 29). High stakes dentistry. Electronic mail from the National Reading Conference Listserv.

Learning First Alliance/American Federation of Teachers (AFT). (1999). *Teaching Reading IS Rocket Science: What expert teachers of reading should know and be able to do* . Washington, DC: Learning First Alliance.

National Board for Professional Teaching Standards (NBPTS). (1998). *Early adolescence/English language arts standards*. Washington, DC: Author.

National Reading Panel (NRP). (2000). *Report of the National Reading Panel: Teaching children to read*. Washington, DC: National Institute of Child Health & Human Development.

National Center on Education and the Economy (NCEE). (1999). *New standards* [Online]. Available: www.ncee.org/Our Programs/nsPage.html

Ohanian, S. (1999). *One size fits few: The folly of educational standards.* Portsmouth, NH: Heinemann.

Richardson, V., & Anders, P. (1994). A theory of change. In V. Richardson (Ed.), *Teacher change and the staff development process: A case of reading instruction* (pp. 199–216). New York: Teachers College Press.

Rosenholtz, S.J. (1989). *Teachers' workplace: The social organization of schools* (Research on Teaching Monograph Series). New York: Teachers College Press.

Strauss, R.P., & Sawyer, E.A. (1986). Some new evidence on teacher and student competencies. *Economics of Education Review, 5*(1), 41–48.

Snow, C.E., Burns, M.S., & Griffin, P. (1998). *Preventing reading difficulties in young children.* Washington, DC: National Academy Press.

Wilson, S.M., & Berne, J. (1999). Teacher learning and the acquisition of professional knowledge: An examination of research on contemporary professional development. In A. Iran-Nejad & P.D. Pearson (Eds.), *Review of Research in Education, 24,* 173–209.

CHAPTER 2

The interface of standards, teacher preparation, and research: Improving the quality of teachers

Dorothy S. Strickland
RUTGERS UNIVERSITY

Improving the quality of teachers has come to the forefront as a crucial element in educational reform. In his 1997 State of the Union Address, President Clinton issued a "Call to Action" that included as a priority improving the quality of teachers in every U.S. classroom (National Center for Education Statistics, 1999). An increasing number of educational leaders are also calling for greater emphasis on teacher quality. When the president of the National Education Association (NEA) and the superintendent of the District of Columbia public schools were asked at a forum to name their prescriptions for fixing education, they suggested the same remedy: high-quality teachers (Bradley, 2000).

This chapter explores topics related to improving the quality of teachers of reading. Specifically, it addresses issues concerning teacher preparation and professional development, the development of standards for teachers, and related research implications.

Teacher Quality: The Last Frontier of Systemic Reform

For the past several decades, the improvement of U.S. schools has been a major area of concern. A recent survey (National Public Radio, Kaiser, Kennedy School survey, 1999) revealed that Americans believe education is so important that they are willing to pay higher taxes if it means improving public schools. Suggested improvements include increasing pay for teachers, reconstructing old and dilapidated schools, and enforcing academic standards. The primary goal is to improve academic achievement and to bring "standards-based reform" to the forefront of the debate. The standards-based reform movement is predicated on the belief that student achievement will be advanced by establishing clear and challenging goals in specific subject areas for each grade, focusing teaching on helping students achieve these goals, and developing accurate measures to determine student progress. On the surface, this appears to be a very straightforward set of goals and principles. Operationalized, it involves a very complex set of components and has inevitably led to the promulgation of standards for virtually every aspect of education, including standards for teachers and for their preparation and ongoing professional development. A brief history of the standards movement helps to explain the evolution.

The Origins of Systemic Reform

The publication of *A Nation at Risk* (National Commission on Excellence in Education, 1983) focused widespread attention on the inadequacies of our public schools and inspired policy makers and legislatures at the state level, in particular, to scrutinize public education in unprecedented ways. Several waves of school reform emerged. The first wave involved state efforts to raise coursework standards for high school graduation and standards for prospective teachers (Goertz, Floden, & O'Day, 1995). The second wave focused on school restructuring. It included a call for higher and common expectations for *all* students, an emphasis on new and more challenging teaching practices, and dramatic changes in the organization and management of public schools (Elmore, 1990).

In their review of policy-oriented research on literacy standards and assessment, Valencia and Wixson (1999) point out that "these waves of reform did little to change the content of instruction, especially with their focus on basic skills" (p. 3). Nor did these reform efforts result in the desired changes in teaching, learning, and student achievement (Cuban, 1990; Firestone, Fuhrman, & Kirst, 1989). Fragmented and contradictory policies diverted teachers' attention, provided little or no support for the type of professional learning they needed, and made it difficult to sustain the very promising reforms taking shape in individual schools or clusters of schools (Cohen & Spillane, 1992; Goertz, Floden, & O'Day, 1995).

In 1989, increased concern about the educational preparation of the U.S. youth prompted President Bush and the nation's governors to hold an educational summit in Charlottesville, Virginia. The summit established six broad educational goals to be reached by the year 2000 (National Education Goals Panel, 1991). This was followed by the work of a bipartisan group, the National Council on Education Standards and Testing (NCEST), which issued a report recommending national content standards and a national system of assessments based on the new standards. Once broad agreement had been achieved on what is to be taught and learned, then everything else in the system (such as tests, professional development, textbooks, software) could be redirected toward reaching those standards. This has come to be known as "systemic reform" (Valencia & Wixson, 1999).

Studies of systemic reform efforts suggest the need to understand thoroughly the context of policy implementation from both the system perspective and the day-to-day lives of teachers and students. Research also suggests that without some form of professional development, the effects of such policies are highly variable. Jennings (1995), Spillane (1994, 1998), and Spillane and Jennings (1997) examined the impact of the reading policy in Michigan on a racially and economically diverse urban district, a relatively affluent suburban district, and a small group of teachers within the suburban district. Spillane's (1994) study revealed that even when they operate from the same state-generated document, local policies may differ widely.

The suburban district used the revision of the state reading test as a lever to move in a different direction from the central administration, which advocated a basic skills curriculum. The urban district used the state's reading policy to support its efforts to move in a different direction. It adopted a new basal program and curriculum guide that supported traditional ideas about teaching reading by encouraging teachers to teach isolated bits of vocabulary, decoding skills, and comprehension skills. These examples make it clear that contextual factors such as local needs, beliefs, and priorities play a major role in how reform efforts are addressed.

The complexity of effecting change has led many advocates of systemic reform to place a high priority on changing teachers as the most efficient and direct way to affect students' learning. Standards for students and teachers are linked. They focus on creating new policy instruments such as content standards and curricular frameworks, assessments that are aligned with content standards, and changes in both preservice and inservice teacher education (Cohen, 1995). As a result, in recent years policy makers and educators have turned their attention to strengthening and improving the quality of teachers. Fortunately, there is a growing body of information to support emphasis in this area. Unfortunately, the need for large numbers of highly qualified teachers has never been greater, making the challenge to prepare and upgrade the skills of large numbers of teachers a daunting task.

The Teacher Shortage

Compounding the issues related to improving teacher quality are problems associated with an impending shortage of qualified teachers; a high turnover of teachers, particularly in areas where there is chronic low achievement; and the upgrading of paraprofessionals. According to the National Center for Education Statistics (2000), in 1999 there were 53.2 million students in public and private elementary and secondary schools—almost half a million more than in 1998. Increases in the student population are expected to continue, resulting in 54.3 million public and private school students in 2008. Among public schools, the student enrollment will rise from 47 million in 1999 to 48 million in 2008. A significant amount of that increase will be comprised of minority and limited English proficient students. By 2010, 40% of Americans ages 5 to 19 will be Latino, African American, Asian American, or Native American. These students frequently pose unique challenges for teachers because of their social and economic backgrounds. They are frequently over represented among those who are not achieving well in reading. Thus, it is critical that they have highly knowledgeable and competent literacy teachers.

State and local class-size reduction programs have also created an increased demand for teachers. In some cases, class-size reduction has caused pressure to get teachers into classrooms without strict attention to qualifications. Although most class-size reduction programs focus on the early grades, efforts to expand these initiatives through Grade 6 could conceivably create an additional strain on the ability to improve teacher quality.

Another factor contributing to the teacher shortage is the massive number of experienced teachers hired in the late 1960s and 1970s who are beginning to retire. In 1996, almost 26% of teachers were over the age of 50. This was up from 15.5% in 1976 and 21.2% in 1986 (American Federation of Teachers, 1998).

To some extent, the shortage of teachers is due to an uneven distribution of individuals entering teacher preparation programs (Feistritzer, 1998). Many school districts are concerned about the lack of qualified teachers in the areas of math, science, special education, and English as a second language. The area of reading has a unique role to play because it transcends all aspects of the curriculum. Ideally, every teacher should have a strong background in the areas of reading and writing instruction, regardless of the subjects or student population in which they specialize.

Complicating the need for more and better prepared teachers of reading is the fact that paraprofessionals, funded under Title I or other special programs, often have responsibility for teaching reading to children without the direct supervision of teachers. The qualifications of paraprofessionals in Title I programs has caused a contentious debate in Washington, D.C., where many policy makers would make the provisions for paraprofessionals more stringent.

Lawmakers are proposing that requirements for Title I paraprofessionals be upgraded from a minimum high school diploma or GED within 2 years of being employed as an aide, to at least 2 years of college with an associate's degree, or the ability to meet a rigorous standard of quality that demonstrates the knowledge and ability to assist in instruction in reading, writing, and math. New standards would also require that Title I teachers be "fully qualified" and that teacher qualifications be reported to parents on annual report cards (Jennings & Rentner, 1999).

Improving teacher quality in the face of a teacher shortage has caused educators and policy makers to seek a variety of ways to confront the challenge. One of the most significant initiatives is an attempt to strengthen teacher preparation and professional development through the development of teacher standards.

The Development of Teacher Standards

Research indicates that teachers who enter the profession better prepared to teach are more likely to remain in the profession for the long term. "States that want to develop a stable, high-quality teaching force can invest their training resources more wisely by emphasizing program models that prepare effective, career teachers" (Darling-Hammond, 1999a, p. 6). Studies indicate that policy makers can support new teachers and reduce attrition through the establishment of induction programs that provide direct support from a mentor or master teacher (Gold, 1996). Professional development programs that link directly to state initiatives have also led to better teaching.

A study of a Vermont initiative designed to align relevant professional development opportunities for teachers involved in a state-instituted portfolio assessment concluded that the initiative resulted in improved teaching (Hirsch, Koppich, & Knapp, 1998). Other examples include professional development schools, such as the Mayerson Academy in Cincinnati, Ohio, which focus on effective professional development for new and veteran teachers, and the California Subject Matter Projects, which provide training in content and teaching methods through Saturday workshops, teacher-led leadership academies, newsletters, and a summer institute. Efforts such as these are prompted by systemic reform. Specifically, they reflect the desire to raise standards for teachers and to link them to the standards already established for students. A number of states and national, nongovernmental organizations have developed explicit standards for teachers. Some examples follow.

The state of Illinois produced a policy document (2000) that clearly supports an approach to teaching and learning that links standards for students and teachers. The document grew out of concern that while the Illinois Learning Standards defined what students were expected to know and be able to do, "no similar expectations existed for teachers or administrators" (p. i). It was also noted that many certification requirements had not changed for more than 20 years, and although certification of educators continues to be based on the successful completion of specific courses and the accumulation of credit hours, the reviews of teacher training programs confirm dramatic differences among institutions in the content and quality of these courses.

The Illinois Content-Area Standards for Educators (ISBE, 2000) combines standards-based certification requirements for teachers and administrators with a requirement that all approved preparation programs must meet the Illinois Professional Teaching Standards or the Illinois School Leader Standards, as well as the appropriate content area standards. The new system requires teacher education candidates to demonstrate knowledge and performance competencies in technology, language arts, and special education as well as in their field of teaching specialization.

Rhode Island has moved quite far along the path of linking preservice teacher education programs to statewide standards for students. In presentations at the National Reading Conference, Susan Pasquarelli, Rachel McCormack, and Marie DiBiasio (1999) described elaborate portfolio assessment procedures that link student performance directly to the preservice curriculum at Roger Williams College. The procedures assess student knowledge as well as their ability to demonstrate specific competencies. One important outcome of this process is the sense of clarity and purpose that results for both students and professors.

A compelling influence on all states to add teacher education standards to their reform efforts is the 1998 Higher Education Act. Title II of that law (Sec. 207) contains new, mandatory requirements for states and for institutions of higher education that prepare teachers. Specifically, institutions must provide the state with

> the institution's graduates' pass rate on the state's teacher licensure assessments, to be compared with the average pass rate for other institutions in the state;
>
> the number of students in the teacher education program, the average number of hours of supervised practice teaching required, and the student-faculty ratio in supervised practice teaching;
>
> a statement of whether the institution is approved or accredited by the state to prepare teachers; and
>
> whether the teacher education program has been designated by the state as low-performing.

It is felt that when states publish the passing rates of graduates of teacher education programs, for example, the public will have yet another piece of data to add to its perception of the quality of teaching. Low-performing schools of education would be labeled as such—so that students could choose successful schools instead—and could eventually lose federal aid. The legislation includes amendments that encourage the states to improve their schools of education and rely less on unqualified teachers. April 2000 was set as the deadline for the first institutional reports, which were to be sent to the state where the data would be compiled and sent to the U.S. Department of Education, where it would become the framework of a national report card on teacher education to be submitted to Congress by the Secretary of Education (American Association of Colleges for Teacher Education, 1999).

According to published reports (*The New York Times*, 2000), Massachusetts, New York, Florida, and Texas are all complying with the law. Several states and universities have failed to reveal the information needed for the report card, fearing that exposure will cost them prestige and federal aid. Several states that fought the legislation in Congress continued to do so even after it was passed. The U.S. Department of Education announced just prior to the writing of this chapter that the report cards, originally due out in April of 2000, would be a year late.

In addition to state initiatives, several national, nongovernmental agencies have either set standards for teachers or produced documents that have influenced those who do. Virtually all have been involved in setting standards for teachers responsible for reading instruction. Among these organizations are the International Reading Association (IRA), the American Federation of Teachers (AFT), National Council for the Accreditation of Teacher Education (NCATE), the National Board for Professional Teaching Standards (NBPTS), the Interstate New Teachers Assessment and Support Consortium (IN-TASC), and the Educational Testing Service (ETS), through its widely used PRAXIS exam, designed to assess beginning teachers.

It is no surprise that the International Reading Association has a long history of providing direction for setting standards and priorities in the teaching of reading. More recently, organizations such as the American Federation of Teachers have produced position papers and other documents designed to establish or influence standards in reading (see, for example, *Teaching Reading IS Rocket Science: What Expert Teachers of Reading Should Know and Be Able to Do*, 2000, available http://www.aft.org/edissues/rocketscience.htm; see also Appendix C of this volume).

The Interstate New Teachers Assessment and Support Consortium (INTASC), under the auspices of the Council of Chief State School Officers, is a consortium of 30 states and professional associations that has developed a set of standards that are based on knowledge of effective learning and teaching and on the student learning standards developed by professional associations such as the International Reading Association and the National Council of Teachers of English (1998).

An increasing number of states now require teacher education institutions to be accredited by the National Council for the Accreditation of Teacher Education (NCATE) or some other nationally recognized accrediting agency. Many states now give special incentives to teachers who seek national board certification from the National Board of Professional Teaching Standards. These standards are designed for accomplished teachers.

States are not only setting higher standards for preservice teacher education and linking them to student standards, but some are attempting to work in similar ways with ongoing professional development. In order to foster high quality professional development, New Jersey established a Professional Teaching Standards Board, which had the responsibility to produce standards for effective professional development. These standards are meant to support the content standards already developed for students and to provide guidance the state's newly established requirements for ongoing professional development of teachers (New Jersey Department of Education, 1999). Not only do these standards address issues related to the content and implementation of professional development, they give guidelines for its assessment as well. For example, the first standard relates to content: *Enhances knowledge of subject content.* This standard includes the following subheads:

> assists educators in acquiring content knowledge within their own discipline(s) and in application(s) to other disciplines
>
> enables classroom professionals to help students achieve the New Jersey Core Curriculum Content Standards (CCCS)
>
> routinely reviews the alignment of professional development content with CCCS and with the Frameworks in all disciplines.

Standard number eight relates to the implementation process: *Results from clear coherent strategic planning that is embraced and supported by the district's governing body and by all levels of the school system.* Subheads for this standard include:

> supports a clearly delineated vision and is aligned with the district and school goals
>
> fosters the use of reflection and self-assessment in professional and intellectual growth
>
> allows educators to pursue personal educational opportunities.

Standard number seven provides for evaluation: *Is periodically assessed to show its impact on teaching practice and/or student learning.* This standard includes the following subheads:

> results from a careful analysis of student data
>
> uses educators' self-assessment to evaluate the impact of professional development
>
> uses classroom, school, and other data to guide future professional development efforts. (p. 1–3)

New Jersey is also among several states that have recently changed their certification requirements to include a specific certification for teachers of young children. Rather than obtaining a more general, kindergarten-through-elementary certification, teachers may choose to opt for a more targeted certificate for prekindergarten through primary grades. In some states they may not have an option. The theory is that districts will want to hire teachers who have the more specific degree to work with young children. This, of course, has implications for the kind of knowledge and experiences relevant to reading instruction that these teachers bring to the early childhood classroom.

In an effort to upgrade the quality of early literacy instruction, some states are also raising the standards for prekindergarten teachers as well (based on data reported at a meeting of the National Advisory Board, Center for the Improvement of Early Reading Achievement, University of Michigan, October 20, 2000). Once again, federal legislation has added impetus to this trend. In an effort to upgrade the quality of literacy instruction in Head Start programs, the U.S. federal government included the following educational performance standards and performance measures in the 1998 Head Start Reauthorization Act:

- develop phonemic, print, and numeracy awareness;
- understand and use oral language to communicate for different purpose;
- understand and use increasingly complex and varied vocabulary;
- develop and demonstrate an appreciation of books; and
- in the case of non-English background children, progress toward acquisition of the English language.
- know that letters of the alphabet are a special category of visual graphics that can be individually named;
- recognize a word as a unit of print;
- identify at least 10 letters of the alphabet;
- associate sounds with written words.

In addition to setting literacy standards for children, the 1998 Head Start Reauthorization also established professional requirements for classroom teachers. Each classroom must be assigned one teacher who has demonstrated competency, including the ability to plan and implement learning experiences that advance the intellectual development of children. Moreover, by 2003, at least 50% of classroom teachers nationwide in center-based programs must have an associate's degree in early childhood education. Although these standards for children and teachers may seem modest to some, they represent a significant attempt to upgrade the quality of education experienced by the nation's youngest learners. Because Head Start is a national effort, these standards have the potential to affect large numbers of children and to have implications for the qualifications of early childhood staff in other settings as well. An increasing number of public school districts in low-income areas now offer prekindergarten programs. These teachers of 3- and 4-year-old children are expected to have full certification and to provide high-quality literacy programs that are both challenging and developmentally appropriate. Many in the field anticipate that an increasing number of teacher education programs for early childhood educators will include strong literacy components.

States such as Connecticut, Kentucky, North Carolina, and Texas have attempted to bring a variety of these elements together to form a unified whole. For example, during the past decade Connecticut initiated several initiatives that link together to improve teacher quality. Over $300 million was spent to boost minimum beginning teacher salaries in an equaling fashion that made it possible for low-wealth districts to compete in the market for qualified teachers. At the same time the state raised licensing standards by requiring a major in the discipline to be taught plus extensive knowledge of teaching and learning as part of preparation. It also instituted performance-based examinations in subject matter and knowledge of teaching as a basis for receiving a license; created a state-funded mentoring program that supported trained mentors for beginning teachers in their first year on the job; and created a sophisticated assessment program using state-trained assessors to determine which first-year teachers could continue in teaching (Connecticut State Department of Education, 1991).

Connecticut also required teachers to earn a master's degree in education for a continuing license and supported new, content-based professional development strategies in universities and school districts. It further extended its performance-based teacher licensing system to incorporate the INTASC standards and to develop portfolio assessments modeled on those of the National Board for Professional Teaching Standards (NBPTS) (Darling-Hammond, 1999b).

Although there is considerable variability among the approaches to systemic reform described here, virtually all have attempted to upgrade student and teacher standards and to link them in some way. This is due to a sense of urgency and concern about student achievement, rather than a clear sense of direction provided by the research. While the research base for what young literacy learners should know and be able to do is fairly robust, research on teacher preparation and professional development has been largely neglected or ignored. Fortunately, systemic reform and the standards movement has caused renewed interest in this area.

Research Issues and the Quality of Teachers of Reading

In his review of the new scholarship in teacher education, Zeichner (1999) states, "There is also widespread agreement that teacher education research has had very little influence on policy making about teacher education both in the U.S. and elsewhere" (p. 12). Zeichner makes a case for remaining somewhat circumspect about many of the policy initiatives described in this chapter. His synthesis of teacher education research suggests that policy makers, operating on the basis of common sense reasoning and hearsay and in response to political pressures, pay very little attention to teacher education research and to the historically politically weak constituency of teacher educators. In doing so, they often oversimplify and distort complex issues by mandating quantitative requirements that do not correspond to the complexity of the issues involved. Thus, simply requiring a specific number of courses in a particular area or a certain number of hours for continuing professional development may not advance teacher quality. The issues surrounding teacher education are complicated and challenging. Yet they can and must be addressed. There are positive signs that researchers are turning their attention to this area in an effort to improve policy and practice.

Clearly, there is a need to bring the policy and the teacher education communities together to set a research agenda to better inform the formulation of regulations and rules affecting teachers' standards. That research agenda would be based on what is already known about how children learn to read and write, how they are best taught, and how we can best prepare their teachers. Several recent documents have called attention to what is known about teacher education and the implications for reading instruction. One of the best publicized is *Preventing Reading Difficulties in Young Children* (Snow, Burns, & Griffin, 1998), which concludes that "...teacher preparation for the teaching of reading has not been adequate to bring about the research-based changes in classroom practices that result in success" (p. 289). The report outlines several conclusions from the research about the knowledge base of qualified teachers of reading, which were summarized by Bickart (1998):

> They must have knowledge about how children develop and learn, what they know, and what they are capable of doing.
>
> They must have a range of teaching methods that they can use to meet the individual needs of children.
>
> They must be able to identify children's individual strengths and weaknesses and to prepare instructional strategies that will enable each child to make progress.
>
> They must understand, master, and integrate the knowledge and concepts in the different content areas that young children study.

The report also outlines several obstacles thought to restrict the quality of teacher education programs:

> They lack a solid apprenticeship component.
>
> They offer a course-by-course approach that hinders the integration of information.
>
> The find it difficult to convey effectively complex current knowledge about best classroom practices.
>
> They have not been successful in helping new teachers master the skills needed to understand the knowledge base and then use the knowledge to teach those children most in need of instruction.

These observations are confirmed and extended by findings from research on common features found in successful teacher preparation programs (Darling-Hammond, 1999):

1. a common clear vision of good teaching that is apparent in all coursework and clinical experiences;

2. well-defined standards of practice and performance that are used to guide and evaluate courses and clinical work;

3. a rigorous core curriculum;

4. extensive use of problem-based methods, including case studies, research on teaching issues, performance assessments, and portfolio evaluation;

5. intensively supervised, extended clinical experiences; and

6. strong relationships with reform-minded local schools. (pp. 31-32)

These features provide a roadmap for the direction of future research in teacher preparation. However, teacher education is filled with complexities that can confound the variables that researchers attempt to study. Following are some specific challenges that researchers will need to address as they pursue the larger issues:

- Issues regarding recruitment include the recruitment of minority teachers and the need to publicize teacher education in ways that enable prospective students and the public to view entering the field of education as challenging and desirable.

- Curriculum issues center around striking a proper balance between the content to be taught and developing student competency in a variety of instructional strategies; linking teacher education with liberal arts courses; and utilizing adjunct instructors to teach methods courses.

- Field experience issues include the challenges involved in providing a series of well-planned, coordinated, and monitored practical field experiences that link to coursework and the quality of field sites and supervision.

- Other related issues include the quality of the preparation of special education teachers in the area of reading; the preparation of paraprofessionals in such programs as Title I and Basic Skills; and the quality of prekindergarten teachers, administrators, and those seeking certification through nontraditional routes. Teacher preparation programs have a responsibility to be actively involved with the design and implementation of programs providing alternate routes to certification (Turley & Nakai, 2000).

- Finally, there is a need for well-designed research to inform the ongoing support of new and accomplished teachers. Research has found that the attrition rates of new teachers are five times higher than those of their more experienced counter parts (Asian-Pacific Economic Cooperation, 1997). Support structures for new teachers helps to ease the transition into full-time teaching and improve the quality of instruction.

Although the considerations outlined here are complex and challenging, renewed interest in research on improving the quality of teachers holds promise for improving the education of educators and their students. In their report on teacher education and reading instruction, the National Reading Panel (2000) concluded that appropriate teacher education does produce higher achievement in students. Much more must be known about the conditions under which this conclusion holds (p. 5.2).

Summary

Both recent and past reform efforts indicate that teacher quality is a crucial factor in children's reading and literacy achievement. Various governmental and nongovernmental national and state initiatives have been implemented to improve teacher quality. Most link to established standards for student achievement. Though many of the initiatives are highly promising and commendable, the research base to support them is frequently lacking or uneven. There is a need for a national and international agenda in the areas of improving teacher preparation and ongoing professional development for teachers of reading/language arts. The agenda would include,

1. Clear and focused guidelines for the content and clinical experiences of preservice and inservice teachers that are linked to content and performance standards established for students. Teacher standards would emphasize three levels of professional development—initial preservice, the induction period, and ongoing professional development.

2. Teacher preparation institutions and ongoing professional development efforts would align programs to meet established standards for what teachers should know and be able to do at various career levels, and would initiate various formative and summative means for assessment.

3. A research agenda to select and support promising lines of inquiry to improve existing programs and develop exemplary models would be put in place.

REFERENCES

American Association of Colleges for Teacher Education. (1999). *Negotiations on report card guidelines continue.* Briefs, 20. Unpaged.

American Federation of Teachers. (1998). *Teacher salary trends* [Online]. Available: http://www.att.org/research

American Federation of Teachers. (2000). *Teaching reading is rocket science: What teachers of reading should know and be able to do.* Washington, DC: Author.

Asian-Pacific Economic Cooperation. (1997). *Overview of teacher induction policy and practice: Results of the exploratory survey* (Issue brief No. 97-HR-01.1). Washington, DC: Asian-Pacific Economic Cooperation.

Bickart, T. (1998). *Summary report of* Preventing Reading Difficulties in Young Children. Washington, DC: Paper prepared for the U.S. Department of Education Reading Summit, September 18-19.

Bradley, A. (2000, March 29). RX for education: High-quality teachers. *Education Week*, p. 10.

Cohen, D.K. (1995). What is the system in systemic reform? *Educational Researcher, 24,* 11-17.

Cohen, D.K., & Spillane, J. (1992). Policy and practice: The relations between governance and instruction. In G. Grant (Ed.), *The review of research in education* (pp. 3-49). Washington, DC: American Educational Research Association.

Connecticut State Department of Education Division of Research, Evaluation, and Assessment. (1991). *Research bulletin, school year 1990-91.* Hartford, CT: Bureau of Research and Teacher Assessment.

Cuban, L. (1990). Reforming again, again, and again. *Educational Researcher, 19,* 3-13.

Darling-Hammond, L. (1999a). *Solving the dilemmas of teacher supply, demand, and standards: How we can ensure a competent, caring, and qualified teacher for every child.* New York: National Commission on Teaching & America's Future.

Darling-Hammond, L. (1999b). Educating teachers: The academy's greatest failure or its most important future? *Academe, 85*(1), 29.

Elmore, R.F. (1990). Introduction: On changing the structure of public schools. In R.F. Elmore (Ed.), *Restructuring schools: The next generation of educational reform* (pp. 1-28). San Francisco: Jossey-Bass.

Feistritzer, C.E. (1999). *The making of a teacher* [Online]. Available: http://www.ncei.com/makingteacher-blts.htm

Firestone, W.A., Fuhrman, S.H., & Kirst, M.W. (1989). *The progress of reform: An appraisal of state education initiatives.* New Brunswick, NJ: Consortium for Policy Research in Education, Rutgers University.

Goertz, M.E., Floden, R.E., & O'Day, J. (1995). *Studies of education reform: systemic reform: Findings and conclusions* (Vol. 1). New

Brunswick, NJ: Consortium for Policy Research in Education, Rutgers University.

Gold, Y. (1996). Beginning teacher support: Attrition, mentoring and induction. In J.P. Sikula, T.J. Buttery, & E. Guyton. (Eds.), *Handbook of research on teacher education.* New York: Simon & Schuster/Macmillan.

Hirsch, E., Koppich, J.E., & Knapp, M.S. (1998). *What states are doing to improve the quality of teaching: A brief review of current patterns and trends.* Seattle, WA: Center for the Study of Teaching and Policy.

Illinois State Board of Education (ISBE). (2000). *Content-area standards for educators.* Springfield, IL: Illinois State Department of Education.

Interstate New Teacher Assessment and Support Consortium (1995). *INTASC Core Standards* [Online]. Available: http://develop.ccsso.cybercentral.com/intascst.htm

Jennings, J.F., & Rentner, D.S. (1999, Winter). Policymaking in mid-stream. *Phi Delta Kappa Washington Newsletter, 9,* 11.

Lewis, A.C. (2000). High-quality teachers for all Americans. *Phi Delta Kappan, 81,* 339–340.

National Center for Education Statistics. (1998). *Projections of education statistics to 2008* [Online]. Available: http://nces.ed.gov/pubs98/pj2008/p98t01.html

National Center for Education Statistics. (1999). *Teacher quality: A report on the preparation and qualifications of public school teachers.* Washington, DC: U.S. Office of Education.

National Center for Education Statistics. (2000). *Teacher quality: A report on the preparation and qualifications of public school teachers.* Washington, DC: U.S. Department of Education, Office of Educational Research and Improvement.

National Commission on Excellence in Education. (1983). *A nation at risk: The imperative for educational reform.* Washington, DC: U.S. Government Printing Office.

National Council on Education Standards and Testing. (1992). *Raising standards for American education.* Washington, DC: U.S. Government Printing Office.

National Educational Goals Panel. (1991). *National educational goals report: Building a nation of learners.* Washington, DC: U.S. Government Printing Office.

National Projections of the United States by Age, Sex, Race, and Hispanic Origin: 1995 to 2050, Current Population Reports. (1996). Washington, DC: U.S. Department of Commerce, Bureau of the Census, Economics and Statistics Administration.

National Public Radio, The Henry Kaiser Family, Harvard University's John F. Kennedy School of Government. (Producer). (1999, September 7). *Americans willing to pay for improving school* [Press release].

National Reading Panel. (2000). *Teaching children to read: An evidence-based assessment of the scientific research literature on reading and its implications for reading instruction.* Washington, DC: National Institute of Child Health and Human Development.

New Jersey Department of Education. (1999). *Survey of draft professional development standards for teachers.* Trenton, NJ: Author.

New York Times. (2000, January 23). Editorial. New York: Author.

Pasquarelli, S., McCormack, R.L., & DiBiasio, M. (1999). *Are we teaching what we say we are? Matching Rhode Island beginning teacher standards to preservice elementary teachers' portfolios.* Individual presentations at the National Reading Conference, Orlando, FL.

Snow, C., Burns, S., & Griffin, P. (Eds.). (1998). *Preventing reading difficulties in young children.* Washington, DC: National Academy Press.

Spillane, J.P. (1994). How districts mediate between state policy and teachers' practice. In R. Elmore & S.H. Fuhrman (Eds.), *The governance of curriculum* (pp. 167–185). Alexandria, VA: Association for Supervision and Curriculum Development.

Spillane, J.P. (1998). State policy and the non-monolithic nature of the local school district: Organizational and professional considerations. *American Educational Research Journal, 35,* 33–63.

Spillane, J.P., & Jennings, N.E. (1997). Aligned instructional policy and ambitious pedagogy: Exploring instructional reform from the classroom perspective. *Teachers College Record, 98,* 449–481.

Strickland, D.S. (1995). Pre-elementary programs: A model for professional development. In S. Wepner, J. Feeley, & D. Strickland (Eds.). *The administration and supervision of reading programs.* New York: Teachers College Press.

Turley, S., & Nakai, K. (2000). Two routes to certification: What do student teachers think? *Journal of Teacher Education, 51.* 122–134.

Valencia, S.W., & Wixson, K.K. (1999). *Policy-oriented research on literacy standards and assessment.* Ann Arbor, MI: Center for the Improvement of Early Reading Achievement.

Wise, A.E., & Leibbrad, J.A. (2000). Standards and teacher quality: Entering the new millennium. *Phi Delta Kappan, 621,* 612–616.

Zeichner, K. (1999, December). The new scholarship in teacher education. *Educational Researcher,* 4–15.

PRESERVICE TEACHER PREPARATION

The IRA Excellence in Reading Teacher Preparation Commission's report: Current practices in reading teacher education at the undergraduate level in the United States

James V. Hoffman
UNIVERSITY OF TEXAS—AUSTIN

Cathy M. Roller
INTERNATIONAL READING ASSOCIATION

The National Commission on Excellence in Elementary Teacher Preparation for Reading Instruction

The professionalization of teaching was a primary concern to the leaders in the field of reading in the late 1950s and early 1960s. One of the major goals of the International Reading Association (IRA), as it took shape and formed its identity during this period, was a commitment to the improvement of reading teacher education. Mary Austin, one of the Association's early presidents, used the attacks on schools and reading methodology raging at that time as an opportunity to focus attention on the preparation of teachers. Specifically, she was interested in the quantity and quality of preparation offered to prospective elementary teachers in the area of reading.

Working with her then-student and later-colleague, Coleman Morrison, Austin conducted a study of the requirements, content, and processes used in the undergraduate programs that were preparing teachers. Relying primarily on survey methodology, Austin and Morrison collected data on a large sample of programs across the United States. In their final report, titled *The Torch Lighters* (1962), Austin and Morrison decried the lack of attention to reading in the undergraduate preparation programs and criticized the quality of much of what was offered. They presented a set of specific recommendations for changes in programs that they believed, if implemented, would have a profound impact on the quality of teaching and learning in schools.

By today's standards, the recommendations seem obvious and even minimalist. They include,

> The class time devoted to reading instruction, whether taught as a separate course or integrated with the language arts, be equivalent to at least three semester hours of credit.

The staff responsible for teaching reading and/or language arts courses be sufficiently augmented to allow each instructor time in which to observe and confer with students during the practice teaching experience and to consult with the cooperating teacher and administrative panel.

None of the recommendations for change were grounded explicitly in any research or theory of teacher education. They just seemed to make sense to the authors of the report.

The report served as a rallying point for the profession. The findings were used as a leverage point within colleges and universities, as well as at the state level, to raise standards and requirements for reading teacher education. The International Reading Association, under the leadership of Ted Clymore, launched its first commission into reading teacher preparation. This initiative was linked to the competency-based teacher education movement that was taking shape in the broader context of teacher education at this same time. The reading profession set out to identify the specific set of competencies necessary for the effective teaching of reading. Further, the profession set out to identify the specific ways in which aspiring teachers could be trained in these competencies to a "mastery" level.

Barely 10 years later, a follow-up study was conducted by Morrison and Austin (1974), using similar survey methodology, to check on the progress that had been made regarding their recommendations. A majority of the recommendations were judged to have been realized. We applauded ourselves on a job well done. We were so pleased, it seemed, that we decided that the challenge of how to deliver quality reading teacher education had been resolved. There was no attempt at the time to collect any data that might be useful in understanding the effects of this investment in reading teacher education. The profession seemed content with the fact that the changes made good sense and that "more" must be "better." That was 25 years ago, and from that point the profession stopped thinking seriously about reading teacher education.

Today, again as in the 1960s, we find ourselves under attack for our shortcomings in teaching reading—only this time the attack is not on teachers or schools, but it is leveled directly at the teacher education community. We are charged with failure in preparing teachers with the knowledge and skills they need to be effective. We are charged with failure to infuse our programs of preparation with understandings from research on teaching and learning to read.

Whether we are guilty of these charges or not is a matter for extended discussion. What is true and what we are clearly guilty of is having no data to respond to these attacks. We know little more today than we did 25 years ago about what is going on in reading teacher education. In this regard, and without question, we have been professionally irresponsible and negligent—not just because we have not collected the data that would allow us to confront the absurd attacks being made, but because we have not been continuously collecting data from which we can learn how to make ongoing improvements in reading teacher education. We are a community of reading researchers active in teacher education who have not been systematic about studying our own practices.

Hoffman (first author of this chapter) has participated in the writing of two different reviews of the research literature on reading teacher education, one for *Reading Research Quarterly* (Hoffman & Pearson, 2000), and one for the *Handbook of Reading Research (Vol. 3)* (Anders, Hoffman, & Duffy, 2000). We have read other reviews including that of the National Reading Panel (2000) and *Preventing Reading Difficulties in Young Children* (Snow, Burns, & Griffin, 1998). There is just not much there to defend the present or guide us toward the future.

IRA's Recent Research About Reading Teacher Preparation

Recently IRA has launched a research initiative into the preparation of elementary teachers in the area of reading. The Association has invested substantial resources in this effort. In fact, this program of research marks the first time that IRA has invested on this scale in a major research initiative. The initial work of this commission is focused on the preparation of teachers in 4-year undergraduate programs. This was a focusing decision that allowed us to concentrate on one set of issues and contexts. In the long run, we must broaden our investigation to include 5-year, fifth-year, induction, and inservice programs. The notion of teacher education as a lifelong learning process must be reflected in our own research agenda.

Our overarching goal is to generate findings regarding excellence in reading teacher preparation that will (1) guide and inform program improvement efforts in institutions around the United States; (2) provide leverage for resources to effect the changes that are needed; and (3) provide a rich database that can be used to institutionalize the processes of program development.

The scope of work within the IRA research agenda involves several different programs of research:

- The Features of Excellence Study of effective programs of teacher preparation,
- The Beginning Teacher Follow-up study, and
- The Survey of Current Practices.

In this chapter, we report on the findings from the Survey of Current Practices in Reading Teacher Preparation Programs.

Purpose

The goal of completing this survey was to gather data useful in (1) characterizing current practices in reading teacher preparation in the United States; and (2) assessing the "valuing" of the status quo by reading teacher educators.

Survey Instrument

In designing the questionnaire used in this survey, we considered several data sources: recent reviews of research in reading teacher preparation that identified potential factors of importance in reading teacher preparation (Anders, Hoffman, & Pearson, 2000; Hoffman & Pearson, 2000; National Reading Panel, 2000); findings and concerns raised through prior surveys of reading teacher education programs and practices (see, for example, Austin & Morrison, 1962; Morrison & Austin, 1974); standards for the preparation of reading teachers as proposed by professional organizations (International Reading Association, 1998); and concerns raised by those critical of reading teacher

preparation (see, for example, Brady & Moats, 1997; Moats & Reid, 1996).

There are two parts within the questionnaire. (See Chapter Appendix A on page 51 for a complete version of this questionnaire.) Part I is focused on general demographic data from the respondents, their current activity in reading teacher preparation, and their general perceptions regarding program quality. Part II of the questionnaire consists of 35 items that explore specific features of reading teacher preparation programs. Each of these items is structured the same way: The item begins with a statement regarding reading teacher preparation programs (such as, "It is important to screen applicants who wish to enter teacher education programs in order to maintain high standards for the program.") The respondent is first asked to rate the feature in terms of its importance to program quality using a scale of

1. not at all
2. somewhat
3. substantially
4. very important
5. essential to program success.

Next, the respondent is asked to rate the feature in relation to the program he or she is currently involved with using a scale of

1. not compliant with the standard
2. somewhat compliant with the standard
3. substantially compliant with the standard
4. beyond the standard
5. far exceeding the standard.

All respondents were asked to rate each of the items in Part II on the first scale in terms of its importance. Only those who were actively involved in a 4-year undergraduate teacher preparation program were asked to rate each of the items on the second scale. This structure was devised to compare directly the perceived importance of the features included and the level of compliance with the feature for the existing programs. The items in the survey generally reflect the underlying structure presented in Table 1.

Sampling

The target population for the survey was reading teacher educators who are active in higher education. The survey questionnaire was sent to all members of the International Reading Association who indicated "teacher education" as a primary role and elementary reading as a primary interest. In the fall of 1999, 1,598 questionnaires were mailed from IRA Headquarters. A follow-up reminder letter was sent 4 weeks later. A total of 949 completed surveys were returned to Headquarters, representing a 60% return rate. A preliminary analysis of the returned questionnaires suggested no bias from the sampled population by geographic distribution.

Data Analysis

All the responses from the returned questionnaires were entered into a data file and analyzed using SPSS. There was a minimal amount of "cleaning up" or "pitching out" of the surveys that were returned. If questions or items were left blank, they were simply entered as missing data. If a respondent marked more than one item when only one response was required, it was entered as missing data or "no response" to the item. Our goal was to use as much of the data returned as possible. In many cases, this led to instances where the n size fluctuates substantially from one question to the next. Fortunately, with the high return rate and sample size, these fluctuations did not affect the power of the analyses.

Several a priori decisions were made regarding the procedures to be used in the data analysis.

First, patterns of responses across all items were inspected for differences across three major program context variables: (1) Institutional Mission (Research I institutions, Research II institutions, and Teaching institutions); (2) diversity of students enrolled in the program (dominant minority [more than 50%]; substantial minority representation [30–50%]; some minority representation [10–30%]; and small minority representation [less than 10%]); and (3) number of graduates each year (less than 25; between 25 and 100; between 100 and 300; and more than 300). For analyses involving only categorical variables, chi-square was used. The results for number of graduates each year were very similar to the results for Institutional Mission, and we decided not to report these effects in the interest of efficiency and readability. For the items included in Part II, the differences across the three program context variables were inspected using analysis of variance procedures (with continuous variable assumptions regarding responses); again because of redundancy, we reported on only two.

In addition, for each item we calculated a discrepancy score by converting the item importance and program rating means to Z-scores, and subtracting the importance score from the program rating score. This score allowed us to look at the program ratings of each feature relative to perceived importance of that feature. Z-scores were used rather than raw scores because there were substantial differences in the ways the respondents used the two 5-point scales. The Z-scores transformed the means to standard deviation units that can be com-

Table 1. Survey Structure

Area of focus	Part I items	Part II items
1. Program Context	7, 8, 9, 10, 11, 12	
2. Capacity/Resources	1, 2, 3, 4, 5, 6,	12, 15, 29, 30, 31, 34, 35
3. Control/Structure	14a	11, 14, 16, 17, 18, 19, 23, 32, 33
4. Process	13, 14b	13, 20, 21, 22, 24, 25, 28
5. Commitment/Philosophy		8, 9, 10
6. Content of Programs	15b	1, 2, 3, 4, 5, 6, 7, 26, 27

pared across scales. We arbitrarily set .5 SD as the cut-off point for discrepancies in the importance and program rating scores, judging that a difference of this amount was interesting.

The reader should keep in mind that these data represent the reports of individual reading teacher educators who have expressed themselves, their experiences, and their values. We did not target individual programs or institutions as our sampling strategy. It is possible that some of the individual teacher educators may have responded to the survey in reference to the same teacher preparation program. Any generalizations regarding the features of programs must be considered with this caution in mind.

Results

The respondents indicated their current roles in the following distribution: 78% full-time college or university faculty (tenure track); 10% full-time college or university faculty (nontenure track); 6% part-time college or university faculty; 3% retired; and 3% other. There were effects for Student Diversity on this item $[X^2(24)(n = 895) = 98.956, p = .010]$. The most diverse institutions reported fewer full-time tenure track faculty and more full-time nontenure track faculty. (See Chapter Appendix B, Table 1 on page 56.)

The results and findings will be reported beginning with a description of the background of the respondents and the institutional contexts in which they work. This will be followed by a report of results that reflect the underlying structure for the survey offered in Table 1 on page 35. Each section will report data analyses in detail, including reports of Institutional Mission and Student Diversity effects. The sections conclude with an overall summary. Some readers may wish to go directly to the section summaries.

Area 1: Program Context

In describing their institutional affiliations, the respondents reflected the following contexts for Institutional Mission (Table 2), Support (Table 3), Number of Graduates per Year (Table 4), and Student Population Served (Table 5 on page 38).

For Institutional Mission, there was an effect for Diversity $[X^2(6)(n = 863) = 38.853, p = .000]$. Teaching Institutions were least diverse, and Research I institutions were more Diverse, with Research II institutions falling in the middle (see Chapter Appendix B, Table 2 on page 57).

There was an effect for Institutional Mission on Support $[X^2(8)(n = 864) = 303.623, p = .000]$. Research I institutions tended to be large and public and Teaching institutions tended to smaller and private. There was also an effect for Student Diversity on this item $[X^2(12)(n = 885) = 62.070, p = .000]$. Larger public institutions tended to be more diverse, with small private institutions being less diverse (see Chapter Appendix B, Tables 3 and 4).

There was an effect for Institutional Mission on number of graduates per year $[X^2(6)(n = 854) = 71.928, p = .000]$. As we might expect, Research I institutions tended to graduate larger numbers of

Table 2. Institutional Mission

Research I Institutions. "Research is a very high priority. Research publications and research grants count heavily toward merit and promotion considerations."	18% ($n = 144$)
Research II Institutions. "Research is valued and productivity expected, but there is not an extreme emphasis on productivity."	30% ($n = 239$)
Teaching Institutions "The primary emphasis is on the quality of teaching."	50% ($n = 403$)
Other	2% ($n = 23$)

Table 3. Institutional Support

Major state-supported university (student enrollment at 10,000 or more)	36% ($n = 323$)
Moderate-sized state-supported institution (Student enrollment at 3,000–10,000)	24% ($n = 218$)
Small-sized state-supported institution (Student enrollment at less than 3000)	5% ($n = 74$)
Moderate-to-large private university (Student enrollment over 5,000)	8% ($n = 74$)
Small-sized private college/university (Student enrollment less than 5,000)	26% ($n = 238$)
Other	1% ($n = 12$)

students, and Teaching institutions tended to graduate smaller numbers of students (see Appendix B, Table 5). There was also an effect for Student Diversity $[X^2(9)(n = 877) = 29.951, p = .000]$. Programs graduating fewer than 25 teachers were underrepresented in the predominately diverse category, and larger institutions were underrepresented in the primarily white category. This is consistent with the previous finding that larger public institutions are more diverse and smaller private universities are less diverse (see Appendix B, Table 6).

For age of students served, there was no effect for Institutional Mission, but there was an effect for Student Diversity $[X^2(6)(n = 852) = 90.431, p = .000]$. More diverse institutions reported student populations that were less traditional, while homogeneous institutions reported more traditional-aged students (see Chapter Appendix B, Table 7).

Table 4. Number of Graduates per Year (Estimated)

Less than 25	8% ($n = 67$)
Between 25 and 100	36% ($n = 321$)
Between 100 and 300	38% ($n = 340$)
Over 300	18% ($n = 158$)

Summary of Program Context

A full range of program contexts was reported by respondents across Tables 2 through 5. For all category breakdowns (with the exception of "other"), the minimum percentage of respondents was 5% ($n = 74$) and the maximum was 78% ($n = 661$). Although it is impossible to say if the data are representative given the sampling procedures, it is clear that all the anticipated categories of institutions were represented in significant numbers in the survey.

With respect to Institutional Mission and contexts, there were two predictable effects. Research I institutions tended to be large and public, and Teaching institutions tended to be smaller and private. Research I institutions also graduated larger numbers of students, while Teaching institutions graduated smaller numbers.

The findings with respect to Student Diversity were more interesting and suggest that student diversity varies greatly among institutions and that smaller, private, and Teaching institutions have less-diverse student populations than larger, public, and Research institutions. Perhaps the most troubling finding is that institutions serving the most diverse student populations have a smaller percentage of full-time tenured professors and a larger percentage of full-time nontenured professors. It is difficult to know the reasons behind this finding. One possibility is that faculties at larger, public, and research institutions include more full-time clinical faculty who are not in tenure track lines.

Table 5. Student Population Served

Age of Students

Serves primarily traditional college students (ages 18–25)	78% ($n = 661$)
Serves primarily nontraditional college students (ages over 25)	22% ($n = 188$)

Ethnic Diversity

Serves a predominantly diverse student population (greater than 50% minority)	9% ($n = 85$)
Serves a substantially diverse student population (30–50% minority)	13% ($n = 115$)
Serves a somewhat diverse student population (10–30% minority)	38% ($n = 339$)
Serves a primarily white (Euro-American) student population	40% ($n = 357$)

Area 2: Capacity and Resources

Items and responses included in this section relate to the characteristics and qualities of individuals responding as well as to the commitment of human resources and capacity to program operations.

The responses in this section suggest that those involved in the reading teacher education programs surveyed tend to be highly qualified in terms of academic preparation and credentials. Eighty-nine percent ($n = 777$) of those who responded hold doctorate degrees in education, with the remainder having completed a masters degree program ($n = 91$). There were effects for Institutional Mission on this item [$X^2(4)(n = 874) = 20.080, p = .000$]. Research I and II institutions reported higher percentages of Ph.Ds (93.8% and 93.2% for Research I and II; 85% for Teaching institutions; see Chapter Appendix B, Table 8).

The areas of specialization for these degree programs include Reading (50%), Language Arts (7%), Teacher Education (4%), Elementary Education (7%), General Studies (15%), and Other (17%). There was no effect for Institutional Mission on this item, but there was an effect for Student Diversity [$X^2(18)(n = 897)$ 32.236, $p = .021$]. The institutions serving the most diverse student populations reported a lower percentage of degrees focusing in Reading, Language Arts, General, or Elementary Education and a higher percentage of degrees focusing on other areas. The differences in

Reading-focused degrees are substantial—35.5% as opposed to the overall average of 48.4% (see Chapter Appendix B, Table 9). Although no direct questions were asked regarding age, respondents did indicate the date when they completed their highest degree, which included 1960s (5%), 1970s (21%); 1980s (33%); and 1990s (41%).

The respondents were experienced as classroom teachers. Sixty-four percent of the respondents reported more than 5 years of elementary classroom teaching experience (16% with 3–5 years; 12% with 1–3 years), and less than 8% reported no classroom teaching experience. There was a statistically significant main effect for Institutional Mission on this variable [$X^2(6)(n = 868) = 15.812, p = .0150$], with respondents from Research I institutions having the least teaching experience and those from Teaching institutions with the most. But even here, 73% of the respondents from the Research I institutions reported 3 or more years of teaching experience and only 11% reported none (see Chapter Appendix B, Table 10). There was no effect for diversity.

Respondents were active professionally, with 50% reporting 1–3 state or national presentations per year and 36% reporting over 3 per year. There were no statistically significant differences for presentation activity. In terms of publications, 55% reported 1–3 publications per year, and 13% reported more than 3. There was a statistically significant effect for Institutional Mission [$X^2(6)(n = 808) =$

81.726, $p = .000$]. Respondents from Research I institutions reported a higher level of publication activity (see Chapter Appendix B, Table 11). There was also effect for Student Diversity [$X^2(9)(n = 833) = 38.853$, $p = .000$]. Respondents from the most diverse institutions reported the highest level of publication activity (see Chapter Appendix B, Table 12).

The patterns described earlier and taken from Part I of the survey are reflected again in Part II. The three related items are presented in Table 6. This table includes data on the Importance Rating (from 1 "not at all" to 5 "essential to program success") and on the respondent's evaluation of the program in which he or she is working (from 1 "not compliant with the standard" to 5 "far exceeding the standard"). Table 6 and the tables that follow report item means, standard deviations, Z-scores, and the discrepancy score. Recall that the program rating of compliance and the discrepancy score reflect the difference between the level of rated importance. A positive discrepancy score suggests that an item's level of compliance is higher that one would expect given its rated importance. A negative discrepancy score suggests that the level of compliance is lower than one would expect given its rated importance. We arbitrarily set + or - .5 SD as the discrepancy level of practical significance.

The means for the first two items were rated in the "very important" range, and the third item fell in the "substantially important" range of the scale. With the exception of the importance ratings for teaching experience (#30), there were significant effects for Institutional Mission across all three questions. F-values for $p<.05$ ranged from 5.64 to 59.470. The findings with respect to Institutional Mission are somewhat predictable for both Ph.D./Ed.D degrees (#29) and research activity (#31). Ratings for both importance and program compliance decline from Research I to Research II and Teaching institutions. Research institutions both value and have higher compliance with the standard in these two areas (for relevant means and standards deviations see Chapter Appendix B, Table 13).

With respect to faculty elementary teaching experience, the results are also somewhat predictable. There were no differences in the rated importance of elementary teaching experience by Institutional Mission; however, there was a difference in the program rating [$F_{2,789} = 10.816$, $p = .000$]. Teaching institutions rated themselves higher. (For relevant means and standard deviations, see Chapter Appendix B, Table 14 on page 69.)

There were two effects for Student Diversity on these items. The program compliance with teaching experience [$F_{3,809} = 5.548$, $p = .001$] was lowest for the diverse institutions and highest for the predominantly white institutions. This is a puzzling finding. We offer a hypothesis: It may be that minority teacher educators are in such demand that they move through the early career trajectory quickly, thus spending less or no time teaching in public schools. We know of particular cases in which this is true, although our evidence is anec-

Table 6. Standards and Program Evaluation of Teaching Faculty

Question/Area	Importance Rating	Program Rating	Discrepancy Score
29. The faculty teaching in the reading program area have an earned Ph.D./Ed.D degree in Reading or Language Arts Education.	4.1 (SD = 1.0) Z = .24	3.7 (SD = 1.2) Z = .65	.4
30. The faculty teaching in the reading program area have a minimum of 3 years elementary teaching experience.	4.5 (SD = .8) Z = .92	4.0 (SD = 1.1) Z = 1.14	.2
31. The faculty teaching in the reading program area are engaged in reading research and active in writing and presenting the findings from their work.	3.6 (SD = 1.1) Z = -.78	3.1 (SD = 1.1) Z = -.34	.4

dotal. Program compliance on research activity [$F_{3,833} = 2.867$, $p = .036$] was difficult to interpret. It was lowest for the most diverse institutions, followed by the most homogeneous, and the middle categories were highest.

Two questions explored the resources that can accrue to a reading teacher education program through networking with local schools and with the broader teacher education community. The data for these two questions are presented in Table 7. (See Chapter Appendix B, Table 15, on page 69 for means and standard deviations.)

Among the questions posed in Part II for both the importance and program ratings, networking with public schools is rated among the highest. Teacher educators clearly value their partnerships with public schools and view themselves as very successful in enacting those partnerships. Networking with other programs of teacher education is also valued, but not as highly, nor is the program rating as high. There were no effects for Institutional Mission or Student Diversity on these items.

Availability of Resources

Three other items are related to availability of resources: discretionary budget (#14), class size (item #12), and availability of teaching assistants (#15). As Table 7A on the facing page indicates, program ratings are low for these items. While the importance ratings fall in the "very important" range for class size and discretionary budget and fall in the "substantially important" range for availability of teaching assistants, the program ratings fall in the "compliant" or "somewhat compliant" range of the scale. For the discretionary budget and

teaching assistants items, the institutions rate themselves below standard. In addition the discrepancy score for discretionary budget is the second largest in Part II of the survey, and the discrepancy score for class size is -.50. The negative discrepancy values suggest that given the rated importance of class-size limitations and a discretionary budget, the program ratings are unexpectedly low.

For Class Size (#12) there was an effect for Institutional Mission on program ratings [$F_{2,820} = 12.363$, $p = .000$]. The means indicate that Research I institutions rate their compliance lowest, while Teaching institutions rate their compliance highest. For the discretionary budget there were no effects for either Institutional Mission or Student Diversity. For Teaching Assistants (#15) there are effects of Institutional Mission and Student Diversity for both importance ratings and program ratings, and there were effects for diversity on program ratings. The F-values ranged from 2.945 ($p = .032$) to 32.892 ($p = .000$). For Institutional Mission, Research I institutions rated both the importance and the program compliance for Teaching Assistants higher than Teaching institutions. The Student Diversity effect was not as consistent, but the most diverse institutions rated their programs lower for availability of TAs. (See Chapter Appendix B, Tables 16 and 17, for specific means.)

Summary of Capacity and Resources

The findings in this area suggest that the human resources devoted to reading teacher education are quite strong. Reading teacher educator background, both in terms of content preparation and teaching experience, as well as the valuing and

Table 7. Networking

Question/Area	Importance Rating	Program Rating	Discrepancy Score
1. Active relationships between the teacher education program and the public schools are maintained.	4.5 (SD = .6) Z = 1.16	4.1 (SD = 1.0) Z = 1.26	.1
2. Active relationships with other programs of teacher preparation are maintained.	3.8 (SD = 1.0) Z = -.41	3.1 (SD = 1.2) Z = -.28	.1

Table 7A. Standards and Program Compliance for Resources

Question/Area	Importance Rating	Program Rating	Discrepancy Score
12. Maximum enrollment in organized courses that relate directly to teacher certification is no greater than 25 students.	4.16 (.97) $Z = .30$	3.21 (1.34) $Z = -.19$	-.50
14. The program has a discretionary budget for use in program planning and operations.	3.85 (1.02) $Z = -32$	2.39 (1.16) $Z = -1.5$	-1.21
15. Teaching Assistants are available for supporting course instruction and supervision.	2.95 (1.36) $Z = -2.14$	1.86 (1.23) $Z = -2.37$	.23

expertise in research, are consistent with professional standards. The picture projected by these data is of a highly qualified faculty who have extensive elementary teaching experience. The common stereotype of teacher educators who have never taught is not reflected in these data. The contrasts related to institutional mission reflect the underlying differences among these institutions, yet the consistency (such as the ratings for teaching experience) across the institutional contexts is impressive and reveals a core level of expertise and experience that is valued.

One potentially surprising finding in this area relates to the low program ratings for the teaching background of faculty in programs that serve minority students. This may be the result of high demand for minority teacher educators that results in potential minority teacher educators passing through the early career trajectory very rapidly and hence acquiring little or no actual elementary school teaching experience.

One other important finding in this area is that the respondents rated their programs below standard in the area of discretionary budget. It appears that many teacher educators do not have access to discretionary funds to support their programs. Indeed this is one of the highest areas of discrepancy between rated importance and compliance with standards. Similarly, program ratings are low in the area of access to teaching assistants. The overall picture is one of highly qualified personnel who have little discretionary resources available for support of their programs.

Area 3: Program Structure and Control

The traditional 4-year plan for teacher preparation has been challenged in recent years by alternative structures. Our sample, however, suggests that the 4-year plan is still alive if not dominant. Four-year certification plans were available in 81% of the programs described, and 4-year certification plans were the only plans available in 54% of the programs. Fifth-year and 5-year plans were the only options offered in 9% of the programs. Many of the institutions offered a combination of plans for students to complete that included 4-year, 5-year, fifth-year, and alternative (or nontraditional) programs (27%).

The option to complete a reading specialization, a recommendation included in the original *Torch Lighters* report, as part of the initial preparation program is quite viable. Forty percent of the respondents described programs that offered this option. This option was distributed across institutional contexts: Research I institutions (42%), Research II institutions (48%), and Teaching institutions (35%). While the ratings on the related item of the importance of this option to program quality [Part II, Question 11: $X = 3.3$, SD 1.4, $Z = -1.4$] put it in the "substantially important" range, the Z-score indicates that relative to the other items rated, respondents saw this as less important. They also rated their programs relatively lower [Part II, Question 11: $X = 2.2$, SD $= 1.5$, $Z = -1.85$] on this option. No statistically significant effects were detected for the program ratings on this item by Institutional Mission or by Student Diversity.

Five of the questions in Part II of the survey were focused on program features that deal with students as they move into, through, and beyond the teacher education program, as shown in Table 8.

The responses to these items suggest that the respondents feel it is important to apply high standards for program admission and completion. Generally, importance and program rating means in these areas were in the "substantially important" to "very important" ranges, and the program ratings were in the "substantially compliant" or "exceeds the standards" ranges. However, the Z-scores suggest differences in the relative importance and program ratings. Items 17, 18, and 19 had negative Z-scores for importance, while items 16 and 33 had positive Z-scores for importance. The Z-scores suggest that respondents felt that monitoring admissions and follow-up was more important than interviews or testing. The Z-scores for the program ratings show a similar pattern, except programs rate themselves relatively higher on state assessments even though they view these as less important.

There were statistically significant effects for Institutional Mission with respect to perceived importance for comprehensive examinations [$F_{2,807}$ = 3.218, p = .041] and state assessments [$F_{2,813}$ = 4.76, p = .009]. In both cases, Teaching institutions thought these were relatively more important and Research I institutions rated them relatively less important.

With respect to program ratings, there were significant effects for Institutional Mission on four of the five items. (There was no program rating effect for state assessments.) F-values ranged from $F_{2,813}$ = 10.449, p = .000 to $F_{2,775}$ = 4.003, p = .019. In each case, Teaching institutions rated their programs higher while Research I and Research II institutions rated their programs lower. For admissions and interviews, Research II institutions rated their programs lowest. For comprehensive and state assessments, Research I institutions ranked their programs lowest. There were effects for Student Diversity on program ratings, state assessments [$F_{3,799}$ = 5.070, p = .002], and follow-up [$F_{3,865}$ = 3.395, p = .018]. For state assessments, institutions with 30% or more minority populations rated themselves higher than the less diverse institutions. The pattern for follow-up was less clear. The most diverse institutions rated their programs lowest, while those in the next category rated themselves

Table 8. Program Features Related to Structure and Control

Question/Area	Importance Rating	Program Rating	Discrepancy Score
16. Teacher education students must meet minimum requirements for program admission (e.g., grade point average) that exceed the minimum requirements for matriculation or graduation.	4.1 (SD = .9) Z = .18	3.7 (SD = 1.2) Z = .54	-.4
17. Students are personally interviewed before admission into the program.	3.6 (SD = 1.2) Z = -.89	2.7 (SD = 1.5) Z = -.99	-.2
18. Students are required to successfully complete a comprehensive examination (written or oral, standardized or local) that goes beyond specific course experiences to complete the program of preparation.	3.2 (SD = 1.3) Z = -1.56	3.0 (SD = 1.5) Z = -.99	1.0
19. Students are required to complete state assessments for certification.	3.6 (SD = 1.3) Z = -.86	3.8 (SD = 1.3) Z = .69	1.5
33. Contact is maintained with students and follow-up evaluations of program effectiveness are conducted.	4.1 (SD = .9) Z = .14	3.2 (SD = 1.2) Z = -.24	-.4

highest (see Chapter Appendix B, Tables 18 and 19, for means and SD).

Interestingly, item 18 (related to program-administered comprehensive exams) and item 19 (related to state testing for certification) had the highest positive discrepancy scores (1.0 and 1.5, respectively), suggesting that respondents rated their programs relatively higher in meeting the standard, while they rated the importance of comprehensive test and state assessments relatively lower.

Summary of Program Structure and Control

The findings in this area suggest that the options for those seeking certification are expanding from the relatively limited range available at the time of *The Torch Lighters* and *Torch Lighters Revisited*. Program choices range from the broad structure of the program to the opportunities for specialization. Overall importance rating means for items discussed in this section ranged from 3.2 to 3.8, which puts them in the "substantially important" to "very important" range. The range for program ratings on these items was broader, 2.7 to 3.8, with items related to personal admission interviews and comprehensive exit exams in the "somewhat compliant" to "substantially compliant" range and the others in the "substantially compliant" to "beyond the standard" range. The survey data also suggest that although their programs use tests as a part of accountability and monitoring, these tests are ranked relatively less important. The data suggest that reading educators value accountability and monitoring at each stage of the program.

There were many effects for Institutional Mission on these items. In general, those in Teaching institutions thought items 18 and 19 were more important and ranked their programs higher in relation to admissions standards, admission interviews, comprehensive examinations, and follow-up evaluations. These findings are consistent with stereotypes related to missions, suggesting that monitoring the teacher education program is more important and better at Teaching institutions.

Area 4: Program Processes

The questions posed in this area tended to focus on the quantity of organized courses required in reading in the program and the character of the practicum experiences offered. With respect to the total number of hours in reading required for all students, there appears to be a continuing increase in requirements over the early *Torch Lighters* period. The mean for number of required semester hours of courses for reading only has increased to 6.36 (4.26) and an average of 2.23 (3.02) courses. For the reading specialization the mean is 16.63 (7.30) semester hours. There were no effects for Institutional Mission on these variables. There was, however, an effect for Student Diversity on number of reading courses: The most diverse institutions required more courses.

In response to a question regarding concurrent placement in field experiences, 61% of the respondents indicated "yes." There was an effect for diversity that was somewhat difficult to interpret. The percentage answering yes was lowest for the most diverse institutions (41% [$N = 14$]) and highest for those in the substantially diverse category (71% [$N = 34$]). The moderately diverse group had 57% ($N = 75$) answering yes, and the most homogeneous group had 68% ($N = 79$) answering yes. There was no effect for Institutional Mission on this item.

Several of the items in Part II of the questionnaire related to the process of preparation. These items are included in Table 9 (see page 44).

Noteworthy here is the fact that in each of these areas, with the exception of work with adults, the average program ratings are at a substantially compliant level with the standard expressed in the question. Also clear is the overwhelming recognition of the importance of supervised field experiences in the preparation process. There were two high discrepancy items in this section: #21 related to tutoring adults and #24 related to a minimum 10-week student teaching experience. In the first there was a large discrepancy because the respondents ranked the item lowest among the 35 items for both importance and program ratings, but in general they used a narrower range of the scale for program ratings. In the case of the minimum of 10 weeks for student teaching, the discrepancy results from relatively high program ratings. Many pro-

Table 9. Preparation Processes for All Students

Question/Area	Importance Rating	Program Rating	Discrepancy Score
13. Opportunities for supervised field experiences in reading with local elementary children.	4.7 (.7) $Z = 1.32$	4.0 (1.12) $Z = 1.06$	-.3
20. Tutorials of elementary students directly supervised by the teacher education faculty.	4.0 (1.3) $Z = -.02$	3.1 (1.4) $Z = -.35$	-.3
21. Supervised tutorials of adults.	2.5 (1.3) $Z = -3.13$	1.8 (1.3) $Z = -2.46$	.7
22. Students in university supervised field experience prior to student teaching (10–20 hours per week).	4.1 (1.2) $Z = .20$	3.5 (1.5) $Z = .23$	.0
24. Student teaching for a minimum of 10 weeks full-time.	4.7 (.7) $Z = 1.26$	4.4 (.9) $Z = 1.74$	.5
25. Students working in classrooms with a diverse student background.	4.3 (.8) $Z = .52$	3.6 (1.2) $Z = .37$	-.2
28. Students work with technology in a significant way in their studies.	4.0 (.9) $Z = .08$	3.4 (1.1) $Z = .12$	.2

grams either substantially meet or exceed the standard of 10 weeks.

There were two effects of Institutional Mission on the importance ratings of program processes. For item 20 (tutoring children) [$F_{2,797} = 6.413$, $p = .002$]. Research II institutions rated it most important while Research I institutions rated it least important. For technology use [$F_{2,818} = 3.005$, $p = .05$], Teaching institutions rated it most important followed by Research II institutions and Research I institutions rated technology use lowest.

There was also an effect of Institutional Mission on program ratings of processes for fieldwork [$F_{2,778} = 9.209$, $p = .000$]. For fieldwork, ratings were highest for Research I institutions and lowest for Teaching institutions. (See Chapter Appendix B, Table 20, on page 73.)

There were five effects for Diversity. Two were on the item about working in diverse classrooms [$F_{3,843} = 11.179$, $p = .000$] for importance and [$F_{3,810} = 37.160$, $p = .000$] for program ratings. In both cases ratings decreased as diversity increased. There were differences in program ratings for tutoring adults [$F_{3,746} = 2.713$, $p = .004$] and length of student teach-

ing [$F_{3,795} = 3.885$, $p = .009$]. For tutoring adults, respondents from institutions with substantially diverse student populations ranked their programs highest while those from predominately white institutions ranked their programs lowest. However, tutoring adults was among the lowest rated items in the survey. For length of student teaching, the opposite is true. Program ratings are relatively high. They are highest for predominantly white institutions and lowest for predominantly diverse institutions.

The fifth effect for diversity was on the importance of students being in fieldwork 10–20 hours per week before student teaching [$F_{3,832} = 2.871$, $p = .36$]. Respondents who reported from institutions with predominately diverse student populations rated this most important while those from predominately white student populations rated it least important. (See Chapter Appendix B, Table 21 on page 74.)

Summary for Program Processes

The data reported in this section suggest that the number of reading-only courses and semester hours has increased since *Torch Lighters Revisited*. The respondents described their programs as requiring more than two courses and an average of 6.36 semester hours. The respondents rated items related to fieldwork very high in importance, and they also ranked their programs relatively high in this area.

The effects for Institutional Mission were difficult to interpret on some items (such as tutoring children and using technology). For instance, Research I institutions rated tutoring children and using technology as least important, while Research II institutions rated them most important for fieldwork. The findings in relation to Student Diversity are also somewhat mixed. For the item related to the opportunity to work in diverse classrooms, the trend for both importance and program ratings was clear. As the diversity of the student population increased, the importance and program ratings also increased. The other effects are less consistent.

Area 5: Content

Textbooks Used

Of the 598 respondents who taught introductory reading methods, 76% reported using a basic methods textbook for the course. We asked those responding positively to this question to indicate the first author of that textbook. The most frequently mentioned (over 4%) first authors are presented in Table 10.

The textbooks used most often tend to be fairly eclectic and comprehensive in their attention to the broad goals of a reading program. A second impression is that these tend to be introductory texts that include considerable attention to integrated language arts curriculum with substantial attention to writing and the other language arts.

Program Content

Nine of the questions in the second part of this section of the survey focused on the content of the programs. These data are presented in Table 11 on page 46.

These responses suggest again that in all areas of the content recommended for elementary teachers' programs (except structure of the English language), programs are substantially meeting basic standards or exceeding them. Interestingly, the three areas ranked lowest in terms of the program ratings are in the areas of structure of language, testing and measurement, and technology. All three are areas in which the field has been criticized soundly. Furthermore, these three content areas also rank lowest in the importance ratings, which suggests that a reason for relatively lower program ratings may be that respondents perceive these areas to be relatively less important than other areas.

This interpretation of the data is strongly supported by the discrepancy scores. Of the 35 items in Part II of the survey 13 had discrepancy scores greater than +/-.5 standard deviations, or approximately 40% of the overall items were discrepant. Within the 9 content items, 5 (56%) were discrepant.

Table 10. Methods Textbooks Used in Introductory Classes

First Author	Number of Respondents	Percent of Total (464 respondents)
Tompkins	38	8%
Cooper	36	8%
Reutzel	35	8%
Burns	35	8%
Vacca	31	7%
Gunning	28	6%
May	19	4%

Table 11. Program Content

Question/Area	Importance Rating	Program Rating	Discrepancy Score
1. Students seeking elementary teaching certification should take similar general education courses and meet the same requirements as students seeking a liberal arts degree.	3.9 (.8) Z = -.16	3.8 (.8) Z = .72	.9
2. Students...should take a course or courses that focus on the structure of English language, including attention to phonetics, morphology, syntax, semantics, and sociolinguistic principles.	3.6 (1.2) Z = -.76	2.6 (1.3) Z = (-1.25)	-.5
3. Students...should take a course or courses that focus on the relationship between culture, diversity, and language learning.	4.1 (.9) Z = .22	3.1 (1.3) Z = -.34	-.6
4. Students...should take a course or courses that address principles of testing and measurement.	3.9 (1.0) Z = -.31	3.0 (1.2) Z = -.50	-.2
5. Students...should take a course or courses that address reading foundations and pedagogy.	4.6 (.8) Z = 1.10	3.6 (1.3) Z = .40	-.7
6. Students...should take at least one course that addresses the foundations of language arts and teaching methods.	4.5 (.8) Z = .98	3.7 (1.1) Z = .56	-.4
7. Students should take a least one course that focuses on children's literature.	4.4 (.8) Z = .82	3.4 (1.3) Z = .02	-.8
26. Courses and course content in the teacher education program should deal with issues of diversity in schools and teaching strategies.	4.4 (.8) Z = .78	3.7 (1.0) Z = .60	-.2
27. Students are instructed in the use of electronic media in the teaching of reading.	3.8 (1.0) Z = -.48	3.1 (1.1) Z = -.40	.1

One of those discrepancy scores was positive, item #1, which related to general education requirements. While respondents rated this item relatively unimportant, they rated their programs as exceeding the standard. This pattern probably reflects the fact that reading educators have little control over general education requirements and simply must comply with the standards set by their universities regardless of their perceived importance.

The other four items with discrepancy scores over +/-.5 are items #2 (language structure), #3 (courses related to culture diversity and language learning), #5 (reading foundations and pedagogy), and #7 (children's literature). With the exception of language structure, all of these items were rated very important, and the programs were rated as

substantially meeting or exceeding the standard. The negative discrepancy suggests that although the programs are meeting the standard in these areas, we would expect ratings to be higher, given the importance assigned to them.

In the area of language structure, the rating is between somewhat compliant and substantially compliant, suggesting that the view from within the field reflects the broader criticisms of preparation programs that are coming from outside the field. These are very important areas in which the programs do not rate themselves as high as we might expect.

There were effects of Institutional Mission on importance ratings for #3 (diversity and language [$F_{2,841}$ = 3.438, p = .033]), #5 (reading foundations course [$F_{2,840}$ = 3.094, p = .046]), and #26 (diversity strategies course [$F_{2,825} = 3.180$, $p = .042$]). Two of those items are related to cultural diversity (#3, #26), and Research I respondents rate both items highest while Teaching Institutions rate them lowest. The ratings for the importance of the reading foundation course are lowest for Research I institutions. (See Chapter Appendix B, Table 22, for means and standard deviations.)

There were two effects of Institutional Mission on program ratings—#7 (children's literature [$F_{2,806}$ = 3.343, $p = .036$]) and #27 (technology instruction [$F_{2,786} = 4.329$, $p = .013$]). The pattern of means is difficult to interpret (see Chapter Appendix B, Table 22).

There were also effects for Student Diversity on both importance and program ratings. Four items had effects on both ratings—item #5, foundations ($F_{3,850} = 4.607$, $p = .003$), ($F_{3,814} = 3.215$, $p = .022$); #3, language and diversity ($F_{3,863} = 4.395$, $p = .004$), ($F_{3,828}$ = 4.538, $p = .004$); #7, children's literature ($F_{3,857}$ = 3.462, $p = .016$), ($F_{3,825} = 5.175$, $p = .002$); and #26, diversity strategies ($F_{3,845} = 2.851$, $p = .036$), ($F_{3,812}$ = 11.620, $p = .000$).

The patterns of means are distinctly different for the items related to diversity issues (#3, #26) and the items related to specific coursework (#1, #7), and they are identical for the importance and program ratings. For the diversity items, the trend is the predominantly diverse institutions' ratings are highest and the predominantly white institutions' ratings are lowest. The opposite is true for the coursework items, where both importance ratings and program ratings are highest for the predominantly white institutions and lowest for the predominantly diverse institutions. There is one item (#2) with an effect only for the importance ratings [$F_{3,856} = 2.912$, $p = .034$]. There is no clear pattern in the means. Also for the language arts item (#6), there is a student diversity effect for the program ratings [$F_{3,824} = 3.050$, $p = .28$]. Again, the pattern does not afford a clear interpretation (see Chapter Appendix B, Table 23).

Summary for Content

Perhaps the most significant finding is that with the exception of Structure of Language, the respondents rate the content items in the "very important" to "essential" ranges and in the "substantially compliant" to "beyond the standard" ranges. However, the items ranked lowest by respondents (structure of language, testing and measurement, and technology) are areas in which teacher education has been subject to criticism. The data are consistent with the criticisms and suggest that teacher educators recognize these areas of weakness.

Another interesting finding of this section is that there are strong and consistent effects for diversity across items that focus on diversity and on some items that focus on course content. Respondents from predominantly diverse institutions rank the diversity items highest across both importance and program ratings, and these ratings decline as they move across categories toward predominantly white institutions whose ratings are lowest. The opposite trend consistently holds for two content course items—foundations (#12) and children's literature (#7).

Area 6: Program Commitment and Philosophy

Given the limitations of a survey instrument like this, we did not explore the specifics of the programs and their philosophies. Rather, we queried the importance of having a philosophical stance within the program and the importance of being explicit with students regarding this stance. Three questions were posed in Part Two of the questionnaire that related to this area (see Table 12 on page 48).

There appears to be a general consensus on the need for a program to have a philosophical stance that is shared among faculty and students. Programs appear to be doing a better job of sharing the "procedural" (item #10) side of the program than the philosophical (item #9).

There were effects of Institutional Mission on the importance ratings for philosophical stance. Research I institutions' importance ratings were lower than those of Research II and Teaching institutions. There were effects for Institutional Mission on the program ratings for all three items: philosophical stance (item 8) [$F_{2,809} = 4.614$, $p = .010$]; sharing philosophy (item 9) [$F_{2,810} = 9.059$, $p = .000$]; and program description (item 10) [$F_{2,804} = 6.492$, $p = .002$]. For the two philosophy items (#8, #9), Research I institutions' ratings are lower than those of Research II and Teaching institutions. For the program description item (#10), Research II institutions' ratings are lowest and teaching institutions ratings are highest (see Chapter Appendix B, Table 24).

There was only one effect for diversity on these items. The program ratings for sharing philosophy [$F_{3,829}$ = 3.028, p = .029] were lowest for the predominately diverse institutions and highest for the substantially diverse institutions. The other two categories fell in between (see Chapter Appendix B, Table 25).

Summary for Program Philosophy

All three items related to philosophy and program were rated in the "very important" to "essential" ranges of the scale, and program ratings were in the "beyond the standard" range. In relation to philosophy, Research I institutions rated these items lower than Research II and Teaching institutions.

Area 7: Program Rating

What is the quality of the preparation offered to preservice teachers? We asked this question directly of our respondents with respect to the preparation of general elementary education students as well as those who follow a reading specialization plan (see Tables 13 and 14 on the facing page).

The data for the program ratings related to the quality of the reading specialization did not vary significantly with respect to Institutional Mission or Student Diversity. However, there were statistically significant effects with respect to the *general program* ratings related to Institutional Mission [$X^2(6)(n$ =

845), p = .021] and Student Diversity [$X^2(9)(n$ = 865) = 29.631, p = .001]. (See Chapter Appendix B, Tables 26 and 27.)

Research I and II institutions rated their programs lower than Teaching institutions. The effect for diversity was largely due to lower ratings for the predominately diverse institutions.

Summary for Program Effectiveness

The findings suggest that among reading educators, there is a clear and positive regard for the programs that prepare elementary teachers. This is contrary to the intense criticism of teacher educators from outside the field. The findings in relation to the content of programs may help explain the difference. Teacher educators are very aware of the time constraints under which they work and may feel that under those constraints they are doing an excellent job preparing future teachers.

The program ratings seem to follow predictable patterns: Teaching institutions rate their programs higher than Research institutions, and small programs rate their programs higher than large ones. The fact that the lowest program rating levels are in the programs that serve the most diverse population of future teachers is a matter of concern given the shortage of minority teachers in schools today.

Limitations

Although the sample size is large and the return rate extremely high, this is a survey report about questionnaire data, and it suffers from all of the limitations of this kind of research. Most of the items

Question	Importance Rating	Program Rating	Discrepancy Score
8. The general elementary program has a clearly defined philosophy and goals.	4.5 (.8) Z = .92	3.8 (1.1) Z = .77	-.16
9. The program philosophy and goals are shared explicitly among faculty and with the students.	4.4 (.8) Z = .74	3.5 (1.2) Z = .34	-.4
10. The full description of the program features, components, and requirements are available for inspection by the students.	4.5 (.8) Z = .86	4.0 (1.0) Z = 1.04	-.2

Table 12. Program Philosophy and Commitment

Table 13. Ratings of Quality for the General Elementary Program

Rating	Number	Percent
Outstanding	294	35%
Very Good	431	51%
Satisfactory	104	12%
Poor	16	2%

Table 14. Ratings of Quality for the Reading Specialization Program

Rating	Number	Percent
Outstanding	119	28%
Very Good	205	50%
Satisfactory	65	16%
Poor	18	4%
Missing Data	7	2%

were offered in a closed response format. We are also aware that the sample is biased toward those reading teacher educators who are at least members of the International Reading Association. Whether their views are representative of the broader population of reading teacher educators can be questioned. Any interpretation of these data must be considered within the context of these limitations.

That said, we feel the data presented here are valuable in establishing a measure of current practices and standards for reading teacher preparation at the preservice level. The following conclusions and interpretations are warranted by these data.

Interpretations and Discussion

Preparation programs for teachers continue to expand in the area of reading as compared to previous decades. In Austin and Morrison's original *Torch Lighters* study, less than 3 semester hours of preparation programs were devoted to reading instruction. By the time of *Torch Lighters Revisited* in the 1970s, that had increased to the recommended 3 hours. Our survey respondents report that an average of over 6 semester hours of preparation programs are devoted to reading instruction.

In addition, the variety of program structures has increased. While the traditional 4-year undergraduate program was available in 84% of the programs respondents described, 5-year, fifth-year, masters degree, and alternative format programs were also described. Undergraduate reading specializations were offered in 40% of the programs the respondents described, and the number of hours of additional reading course semester hours required in these specializations was 16.63 semesters hours. There is a substantial percentage of preservice teachers who enter the profession with a great deal of knowledge and practice in reading instruction.

In terms of program content, the respondents reported finding the traditional course components of a reading preparation program both important and up to standard. However, the relative importance ratings of courses in language structure, testing and measurement, and technology were lower than other courses, and respondents rated their programs below standard in language structure. This pattern is consistent with the external criticisms and suggests that teacher educators are aware of some specific program weaknesses.

In the area of capacity, the faculty teaching in preparation programs reported by our respondents appear well qualified. Faculty members hold terminal degrees and have areas of specialization appropriate for reading instruction. These faculty are also active in the areas of publications and presentations and have substantial elementary classroom teaching experience. The frequent stereotypes of ill-prepared teacher educators who are professionally inactive and have never taught in elementary classrooms are simply not reflected in these data. In the area of physical and financial capacities, however, stereotypes of under-resourced programs are supported. Respondents rated their programs below standard in the areas of class size and discretionary budget.

The emphasis on field-based experiences and the coordination of field experiences appears to be growing in the amount of time, supervision, and articulation with coursework. Our respondents' ratings of clinical experiences and opportunities were consistently among the highest of those items in the second section of the survey. Respondents rated the importance of field experience and their programs' provision of those experiences very high.

Our respondents, unlike many of the most vocal critics, rate their program quality high. Only 2% of the respondents ranked their programs "poor," and nearly 86% rated their programs "good" or "outstanding." Ratings of reading specialization programs were similarly high. Our data suggest to us that even though there is disparity in the perceptions of external critics and the respondents to the survey, the respondents are aware of weaknesses. One reason for the discrepancy may be that respondents value the areas of weakness (language structure, tests and measurement, and technology) relatively less than other areas of their programs, although they rate them as very important. In conjunction with serious constraints on class size and discretionary budget, teacher educators believe they are doing an excellent job. Outsiders who focus on specific areas of weakness usually do not consider the relative importance and the amount of resources available for those areas when they level their criticisms.

We have real concerns about the preparation of teachers of diverse backgrounds. It appears that most diverse students are prepared in large research institutions where respondents rate program quality lower than teaching institutions. In addition, on items addressing the opportunities to work in diverse settings and on items addressing the knowledge of diversity issues, the most diverse institutions' importance and program ratings are highest and those ratings at predominantly white institutions are lowest. Given the changing demographics of student populations, this discovery is alarming. We would hope that educators working at predominantly white institutions would recognize the need to teach their predominantly white preservice teachers the information, sensitivities, and practices that these teachers will need to teach well in more diverse classrooms.

In summary, the programs described by our respondents have much to recommend, and there are notable increases in the number of reading courses and the amount of clinical fieldwork in these preparation programs. Although we cannot say from these data that the field as a whole is making progress, we can say that there are many teacher preparation programs around the United States where preservice teachers are receiving excellent preparation for reading instruction. We must acknowledge this excellence and look to these respondents and their programs as we attempt to improve the level of teacher preparation for reading instruction.

We have come a long way toward a vision of placing a well-prepared professional teacher in every classroom. There is room for improvement, however, and we must continue to examine and improve our programs.

REFERENCES

Anders, P.L., Hoffman, J.V., & Duffy, G.G. (2000). Teaching teachers to teach reading: Paradigm shifts, persistent problems, and challenges. In M.L. Kamil, P.B. Mosenthal, P.D. Pearson, & R. Barr (Eds.), *Handbook of reading research: Volume III* (pp. 719–742). Mahwah, NJ: Erlbaum.

Austin, M.C., & Morrison, C. (1962). *The torch lighters: Tomorrow's teachers of reading.* Cambridge, MA: Harvard University.

Brady, S., & Moats, L. (1997). *Informed instruction for reading success: Foundations for teacher preparation.* Baltimore: International Dyslexia Association.

Hoffman, J.V., & Pearson, P.D. (2000). Reading teacher education in the next millennium: What your grandmother's teacher didn't know that your granddaughter's teacher should. *Reading Research Quarterly, 35,* 28–44

Morrison, C., & Austin, M.C. (1977). *The torch lighters revisited.* Newark, DE: International Reading Association.

Report of National Reading Panel. (2000). Washington, DC: National Institute of Health.

Snow, C.E., Burns, M.S., & Griffin, P. (1998). *Preventing reading difficulties in young children.* Washington, DC: National Academy Press.

International Reading Association. (1998). *Standards for reading professionals* (Rev. ed.). Newark, DE: Author.

Moats, L.C., & Reid, G.L. (1996). Wanted: Teachers with knowledge of language. *Topics in Language Disorders, 16,* 73–86.

Reading Teacher Educator Survey

Part I: Respondent Background Information

1. Your <u>highest</u> earned academic degree (check one):

   ___ BA/BS ___ Masters/MED ___ PhD/EdD   **Year Earned:** ___

2. Your <u>highest</u> degree focus (check one)

   ___ General Curriculum and Instruction
   ___ Reading
   ___ Language Arts
   ___ Teacher Education
   ___ Elementary Education
   ___ Other: ___

3. Your current position (check as many as apply):

   ___ full time college/university faculty — tenure track   **Your Rank:** ___
   ___ full time college/university faculty — non-tenure track
   ___ part time college/university faculty.
   ___ public school teacher
   ___ public school administrator
   ___ graduate student (full time)
   ___ graduate student (part time)
   ___ retired
   ___ other: ___

4. Your elementary classroom teaching experience:

   ___ none
   ___ 1-3 years
   ___ 3-5 years
   ___ more than 5 years

5. Your experience teaching as a reading specialist:

   ___ none
   ___ 1-3 years
   ___ 3-5 years
   ___ more than 5 years

6. Your current level of activity in conference presentations and publications (state & national):

not active in **presentations**	not active in **publications**
1-3 per year	1-3 per year
3-5 per year	3-5 per year
more than 5 per year	more than 5 per year

If you are affiliated with a college or university and work in the area of teacher education, answer questions 7 through 16. If you are not affiliated with a college or university, please skip these questions and go directly to Part II of the questionnaire.

7. Which of the following best describes your institution:

   ___ A "**Research I**" Institution. Research is a very high priority. Research publications and research grants count heavily toward merit and promotion considerations.
   ___ A "**Research II**" Institution. Research is valued and productivity expected but there is not an extreme emphasis on productivity
   ___ A **Teaching Institution**. The primary emphasis is on quality of teaching.
   ___ Other: ___

8. Which of the following best describes your institution:

   ___ A major state supported university (student enrollment at 10,000+).
   ___ A moderate-sized state supported institution (student enrollment at 3,000-10,000).
   ___ A small-sized state supported institution (student enrollment at less than 3,000).
   ___ A moderate to large private university (more than 5,000 students enrolled).
   ___ A small-sized private college/university (less than 5,000 students enrolled).
   ___ Other: ___

9. Which of the following best describes your institution:

   ___ Serves primarily traditional college students (ages 18-25).
   ___ Serves primarily non-traditional students (ages 25 and older).

10. Which of the following best describes your institution:

   ___ Serves a predominantly diverse student population (50% or more minority students).
   ___ Serves a substantially diverse student population (30-50% minority students).
   ___ Serves a somewhat diverse student population (10-30% minority enrollment).
   ___ Serves primarily a white (Euro-American) student population (less than 10% minority student enrollment).

11. Which of the following best describes the structure of your institution in relation to its teacher education program? If you have more than one program you may check one for each program.

   ___ 2 year general education + 2 year professional studies (e.g., associates degree + BA).
   ___ 4 year undergraduate preparation program.
   ___ a fifth year certification/degree program leading to an MA/MED/MAT degree.
   ___ a five year certification/degree program leading to a BA/BS degree.
   ___ an alternative (non traditional) teacher education program.
   ___ other: ___

12. How many students (approximate) does your teacher education program(s) graduate each year with an elementary focus?

   ___ less than 25
   ___ between 25 and 100
   ___ between 100 and 300
   ___ more than 300

(continued)

3

13. How many semester hours/courses are **all** students required to take in the area of reading methods (Do not include in your calculation courses that are not directly focused on methods of teaching reading — such as children's literature survey courses, or general language arts methods, or courses that are required for specialization students only).

___ semester hours total
___ courses

14. Does your program offer students an option to major in or specialize in the area of reading?

___ yes
___ no

If your program offers students the option of completing a specialization in the area of reading, how many semester hours/courses are students required to take in the area of reading methods (Do not include in your calculation courses that are not directly focused on methods of teaching reading)

___ semester hours total
___ courses

If your program offers students the option of completing a specialization in the area of reading, respond to the following items:

Students enrolled in the reading specialization program do spend more time in field work than the students general program. ___ yes ___ no

Students enrolled in the reading specialization program do spend more time working with students in supervised tutorials than the students in the general program. ___ yes ___ no

15. Do you teach an introductory reading methods course as part of your responsibility.

___ yes
___ no

If yes, what textbook(s) do you use for this course (author/title/edition):

Are the students enrolled in your reading methods course concurrently placed in a field-experience working with classroom teachers?

___ yes
___ no

16. How would you rate the quality of your:

General Elementary Preparation Program	The Reading Specialization Program (if offered)
___ clearly outstanding	___ clearly outstanding
___ very good	___ very good
___ satisfactory	___ satisfactory
___ poor	___ poor

4

totally substandard ___   ___ totally substandard

Part II: IRA Program Features Analysis

Our goal in this portion of the survey is to understand the features of teacher preparation programs that foster excellence in beginning teachers. Our focus is on the general undergraduate teacher preparation programs at the elementary level. We ask that you rate, in your estimation, the potential for the features to contribute to a quality program. **First,** we ask that you rate, if you are currently teaching in a program and responded to questions 7-16 in Part I, that you rate the program you are working with in terms of these features. If you are working in more than one program, answer for the program you feel is most effective. In most cases, the features are described in terms of an activity or experience as well as an acceptable standard. The features have been derived from an analysis of the professional literature in reading teacher preparation. These are the two scales you will be using:

Importance Rating of this Feature
1. not at all
2. somewhat
3. substantially
4. very important
5. essential to program success

Your Program Rating in Relation to this feature:
1. not compliant with the standard
2. somewhat compliant with the standard
3. substantially compliant with the standard
4. beyond the standard
5. far exceeding the standard in this area

Here is an **example** to illustrate the process:

It is important to screen applicants who wish to enter teacher education programs in order to maintain high standards for the program.

You are to rate your agreement or disagreement with this statement on the first scale. You may, for example, not agree that screening applicants is important to maintaining standards. You might advocate an open door policy with ongoing assessments as a better approach to maintaining high standards. In this case you might circle #1 not at all.

Importance Rating of this Feature
1. not at all
2. somewhat
3. substantially
4. very important
5. essential to program success

If you are not teaching in a program you would go on then to the next area and statement leaving the Program Rating scale blank. If you are currently teaching in a program, however, you would go to the second scale to rate your current program against this feature. Your rating here might be quite different than your personal estimate of importance. Following the same example, your current program might use a minimum GPA requirement for admission to the program. In this case you might circle #3 "substantially compliant with the standard" to indicate that the program you are involved with is attending to the feature identified.

Your Program Rating in Relation to this feature:
1. not compliant with the standard
2. somewhat compliant with the standard
3. substantially compliant with the standard
4. beyond the standard
5. far exceeding the standard in this area

There are no right or wrong answers in these response areas. Your ratings on the two areas might be the same in some instances and different in others. Our goal is to capture the valuing of teacher educators and the degree to which this valuing is consistent with current teacher education practices.

(continued)

5

Respond to all statements in reference to the general elementary program that all students must take (i.e., the minimum) to complete elementary certification not in terms of a Specialization program in Reading or some other area.

Importance Rating of this Feature
1. not at all
2. somewhat
3. substantially
4. very important
5. essential to program success

Your Program Rating in Relation to this feature:
1. not compliant with the standard
2. somewhat compliant with the standard
3. substantially compliant with the standard
4. beyond the standard
5. far exceeding the standard in this area

COLLEGE/UNIVERSITY COURSES

General Foundations

1. Students seeking elementary teaching certification take similar general education courses and meet the same requirements as students seeking a liberal arts degree.

Importance Rating 1 2 3 4 5   Program Rating 1 2 3 4 5

Linguistics

2. Students seeking elementary teaching certification take a course or courses that focus on the structure of the English language including attention to phonetics, morphology, syntax, semantics, and socio-linguistic principles.

Importance Rating 1 2 3 4 5   Program Rating 1 2 3 4 5

Culture

3. Students seeking elementary teaching certification take a course or courses that focus on the relationship between culture, diversity, and language learning.

Importance Rating 1 2 3 4 5   Program Rating 1 2 3 4 5

Testing and Measurement

4. Students seeking elementary teaching certification take a course or courses that address principles of testing and measurement.

Importance Rating 1 2 3 4 5   Program Rating 1 2 3 4 5

Reading

5. Students seeking elementary teaching certificate take at least two courses (six semester hours minimum) that address reading foundations and pedagogy.

Importance Rating 1 2 3 4 5   Program Rating 1 2 3 4 5

6

Importance Rating of this Feature
1. not at all
2. somewhat
3. substantially
4. very important
5. essential to program success

Your Program Rating in Relation to this feature:
1. not compliant with the standard
2. somewhat compliant with the standard
3. substantially compliant with the standard
4. beyond the standard
5. far exceeding the standard in this area

Language Arts

6. Students seeking elementary teaching certification take at least one course (three semester hours minimum) that address the foundations of language arts and teaching methods.

Importance Rating 1 2 3 4 5   Program Rating 1 2 3 4 5

Children's Literature

7. Students seeking elementary teaching certification take at least one course (three semester hours minimum) that focuses on children's literature.

Importance Rating 1 2 3 4 5   Program Rating 1 2 3 4 5

PROGRAM SPECIFICATIONS

Philosophy and Goals Statements

8. The general elementary program has a clearly defined philosophy and goals.

Importance Rating 1 2 3 4 5   Program Rating 1 2 3 4 5

9. The program philosophy and goals are shared explicitly among faculty and with the students who are enrolled.

Importance Rating 1 2 3 4 5   Program Rating 1 2 3 4 5

Program Descriptions

10. There is a full description of the program features, components, and requirements available for inspection by students.

Importance Rating 1 2 3 4 5   Program Rating 1 2 3 4 5

PROGRAM OPTIONS

Reading Specialization

11. Students have the option of completing a specialization program in reading as part of their undergraduate program of work.

Importance Rating 1 2 3 4 5   Program Rating 1 2 3 4 5

(continued)

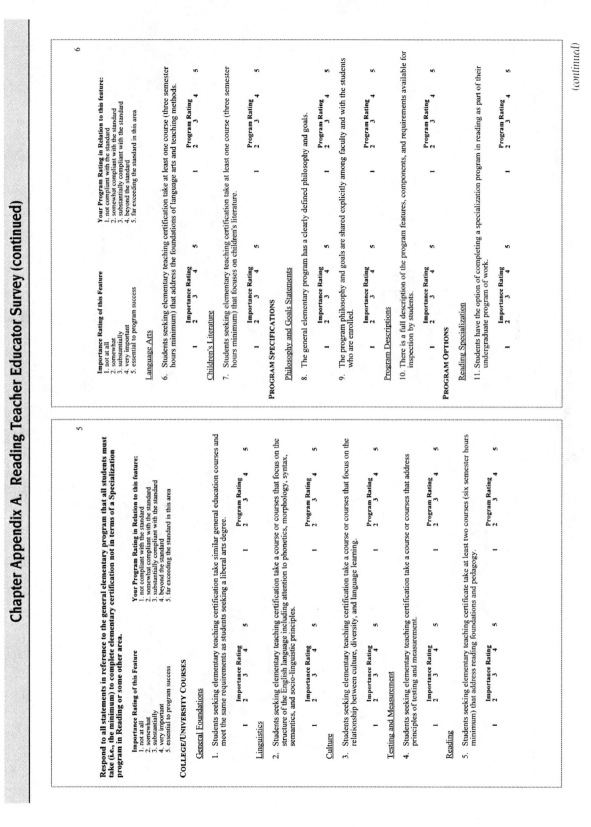

Importance Rating of this Feature
1. not at all
2. somewhat
3. substantially
4. very important
5. essential to program success

Your Program Rating in Relation to this feature:
1. not compliant with the standard
2. somewhat compliant with the standard
3. substantially compliant with the standard
4. beyond the standard
5. far exceeding the standard in this area

RESOURCES/CONTEXT

Class Size

12. Maximum enrollment in organized courses that relate directly to teacher certification is no greater than 25 students.

Importance Rating 1 2 3 4 5
Program Rating 1 2 3 4 5

Classroom (field setting)

13. The program includes opportunities for supervised field experiences in reading with local elementary children.

Importance Rating 1 2 3 4 5
Program Rating 1 2 3 4 5

Budget

14. The program has a discretionary budget for use in program planning and operations.

Importance Rating 1 2 3 4 5
Program Rating 1 2 3 4 5

Teaching Assistants/Assistant Instructors

15. Teaching Assistants are available for supporting course instruction and supervision.

Importance Rating 1 2 3 4 5
Program Rating 1 2 3 4 5

PROGRAM ADMISSION AND REQUIREMENTS

Standards/Requirements

16. Teacher education students must meet minimum requirements for program admission (e.g., grade point average) that exceed the minimum requirements for matriculation and/or graduation.

Importance Rating 1 2 3 4 5
Program Rating 1 2 3 4 5

Procedures

17. Students are personally interviewed before admission into the program.

Importance Rating 1 2 3 4 5
Program Rating 1 2 3 4 5

Importance Rating of this Feature
1. not at all
2. somewhat
3. substantially
4. very important
5. essential to program success

Your Program Rating in Relation to this feature:
1. not compliant with the standard
2. somewhat compliant with the standard
3. substantially compliant with the standard
4. beyond the standard
5. far exceeding the standard in this area

Tests/assessments

18. Students are required to successfully complete a comprehensive examination (written or oral; standardized or local) that goes beyond specific course experiences to complete the program of preparation.

Importance Rating 1 2 3 4 5
Program Rating 1 2 3 4 5

CERTIFICATION

State Assessments

19. Students are required to complete state assessments for certification.

Importance Rating 1 2 3 4 5
Program Rating 1 2 3 4 5

CLINICAL EXPERIENCES

Tutorials

20. Tutorials of elementary students that are directly supervised by the teacher education faculty are a critical part of the preparation in reading methods.

Importance Rating 1 2 3 4 5
Program Rating 1 2 3 4 5

21. Supervised tutorials of adults are a critical part of the preparation in reading methods.

Importance Rating 1 2 3 4 5
Program Rating 1 2 3 4 5

Field experiences

22. Students spend significant time (10-20 hours per week for a full semester) in university supervised field experience prior to the student teaching semester.

Importance Rating 1 2 3 4 5
Program Rating 1 2 3 4 5

Student Teaching

23. Final decisions regarding the placements for student teaching are determined by the university-based program director.

Importance Rating 1 2 3 4 5
Program Rating 1 2 3 4 5

(continued)

Importance Rating of this Feature
1. not at all
2. somewhat
3. substantially
4. very important
5. essential to program success

Your Program Rating in Relation to this feature:
1. not compliant with the standard
2. somewhat compliant with the standard
3. substantially compliant with the standard
4. beyond the standard
5. far exceeding the standard in this area

24. The length of time of student teaching is a minimum of ten weeks with full day work assignments.

Importance Rating	**Program Rating**
1 2 3 4 5	1 2 3 4 5

DIVERSITY REQUIREMENTS

25. Students work in classrooms with a diverse (i.e. ethnic) student background.

Importance Rating	**Program Rating**
1 2 3 4 5	1 2 3 4 5

26. Courses and course content in the teacher education program deal with issues of diversity in schools and teaching strategies.

Importance Rating	**Program Rating**
1 2 3 4 5	1 2 3 4 5

TECHNOLOGY

Instruction

27. Students are instructed in the use of electronic media in the teaching of reading.

Importance Rating	**Program Rating**
1 2 3 4 5	1 2 3 4 5

Use

28. Students use technology in a significant way in their program of studies.

Importance Rating	**Program Rating**
1 2 3 4 5	1 2 3 4 5

READING FACULTY

Background

29. The faculty teaching in the reading program area have an earned Ph.D./Ed.D. degree in Reading Education or Language Arts Education.

Importance Rating	**Program Rating**
1 2 3 4 5	1 2 3 4 5

30. The faculty teaching in the reading program area have a minimum of three years elementary classroom teaching experience.

Importance Rating	**Program Rating**
1 2 3 4 5	1 2 3 4 5

Importance Rating of this Feature
1. not at all
2. somewhat
3. substantially
4. very important
5. essential to program success

Your Program Rating in Relation to this feature:
1. not compliant with the standard
2. somewhat compliant with the standard
3. substantially compliant with the standard
4. beyond the standard
5. far exceeding the standard in this area

Research

31. The faculty teaching in the reading program area are engaged in reading research and active in writing and presenting the findings from their work.

Importance Rating	**Program Rating**
1 2 3 4 5	1 2 3 4 5

EVALUATION

32. Students have an opportunity to evaluate the program (ongoing and at the end).

Importance Rating	**Program Rating**
1 2 3 4 5	1 2 3 4 5

33. Contact is maintained with students and follow-up evaluations of program effectiveness are conducted.

Importance Rating	**Program Rating**
1 2 3 4 5	1 2 3 4 5

NETWORKING

34. Active relationships between the teacher education program and the public schools are maintained.

Importance Rating	**Program Rating**
1 2 3 4 5	1 2 3 4 5

35. Active relationships with other programs of teacher preparation are maintained.

Importance Rating	**Program Rating**
1 2 3 4 5	1 2 3 4 5

OTHER

36. Are there other features of teacher preparation programs that you feel are important but not discussed on this survey? Please attach a note or add your comments on these features on the back of the survey form.

Chapter Appendix B: Table 1. Current Roles by Student Diversity

Current Roles		Student Diversity				Total
		Predominantly Diverse	Substantially Diverse	Somewhat Diverse	Primarily White	
Full-time college/university faculty-tenure track	Count	58	83	262	295	696
	% within STUDDIV	69.9%	72.2%	77.1%	82.1%	77.8%
	% of Total	6.5%	9.3%	29.3%	32.7%	77.8%
Full-time college/university faculty nontenure track	Count	12	15	28	37	92
	% within STUDDIV	14.5%	13.0%	8.2%	10.4%	10.3%
	% of Total	1.3%	1.7%	3.1%	4.1%	10.3%
Part-time college/university faculty	Count	4	9	27	12	52
	% within STUDDIV	4.8%	7.8%	7.9%	5.4%	5.8%
	% of Total	.4%	1.0%	3.0%	1.3%	5.8%
Public school teacher	Count	1		1	1	3
	% within STUDDIV	1.2%		.3%	.3%	.3%
	% of Total	.1%		.1%	.1%	.3%
Public school administrator	Count			1		1
	% within STUDDIV			.3%		.1%
	% of Total			.1%		.1%
Graduate student (full time)	Count	2	2	5	2	11
	% within STUDDIV	2.4%	1.7%	1.5%	.6%	1.2%
	% of Total	.2%	.2%	.6%	.2%	1.2%
Graduate student part time	Count			4	1	5
	% within STUDDIV			1.2%	.3%	.6%
	% of Total			.4%	.1%	.6%
Retired	Count		1		1	2
	% within STUDDIV		.9%		.3%	.2%
	% of Total		.1%		.1%	.2%
Other	Count	6	5	12	10	33
	% within STUDDIV	7.2%	4.3%	5.5%	2.8%	5.7%
	% of Total	.7%	.6%	1.3%	1.1%	5.7%
Total	Count	83	115	540	557	895
	% within STUDDIV	100%	100%	100%	100%	100%
	% of Total	9.3%	12.8%	38.8%	39.9%	100%

Pearson Chi Square 98.957 (24) (N=895), $p=.01$

Table 2. Institutional Mission by Student Diversity

Institutional Mission		Student Diversity				Total
		Predominantly Diverse	Substantially Diverse	Somewhat Diverse	Primarily White	
Research I	Count	16	26	79	37	158
	% within STUDDIV	19.5%	23.6%	24.4%	10.7%	18.3%
	% of Total	1.9%	3.0%	9.2%	3.3%	18.3%
Research II	Count	35	29	105	96	263
	% within STUDDIV	42.7	26.4%	51.8%	27.7%	30.5%
	% of Total	4.1%	3.4%	11.9%	11.1%	30.5%
Teaching	Count	31	55	142	214	442
	% within STUDDIV	37.8%	50.0%	43.8%	61.7%	51.2%
	% of Total	3.6%	6.4%	16.5%	24.8%	51.2%
Total	Count	82	110	524	327	863
	% within STUDDIV	100.0%	100.0%	100.0%	100.0%	100.0%
	% of Total	9.5%	12.7%	57.5%	40.2%	100.0%

Pearson Chi Square 38.855 (6) (N=863), p=.000

Table 3. Institutional Support by Institutional Mission

Institutional Support		Institutional Mission			Total
		Research I	Research II	Teaching	
Associate Degree & BA	Count	131	121	61	313
	% within RSCHTCHG	80.9%	46.6%	15.8%	56.2%
	% of Total	15.2%	14.0%	7.1%	56.2%
Four-year undergraduate	Count	14	67	127	208
	% within RSCHTCHG	8.6%	25.7%	28.8%	24.1%
	% of Total	1.6%	7.8%	14.7%	24.1%
Five-year certification/degree/MA	Count	2	12	29	43
	% within RSCHTCHG	1.2%	4.6%	6.6%	5.0%
	% of Total	.2%	1.4%	3.4%	5.0%
Five-year certification/degree/BA	Count	15	27	27	69
	% within RSCHTCHG	9.3%	10.3%	6.1%	8.0%
	% of Total	1.7%	3.1%	3.1%	8.0%
Alternative program	Count		34	197	251
	% within RSCHTCHG		13.0%	44.7%	26.7%
	% of Total		3.9%	22.8%	26.7%
Total	Count	162	261	441	864
	% within RSCHTCHG	100.0%	100.0%	100.0%	100.0%
	% of Total	18.8%	30.2%	51.0%	100.0%

Pearson Chi Square 303.623 (8) (N=864), p=.000

Table 4. Institutional Support by Student Diversity

Institutional Support		Student Diversity				Total
		Predominantly Diverse	Substantially Diverse	Somewhat Diverse	Primarily White	
Associate Degree & BA	Count	38	52	133	95	318
	% within STUDDIV	44.7%	46.0%	39.6%	27.1%	35.9%
	% of Total	4.3%	5.9%	15.0%	10.7%	35.9%
Four-year undergraduate	Count	18	26	94	78	216
	% within STUDDIV	21.2%	23.0%	28.0%	22.2%	24.4%
	% of Total	2.0%	2.9%	10.6%	8.8%	24.4%
Five-year certification/degree/MA	Count	10	4	9	21	44
	% within STUDDIV	11.8%	3.5%	2.7%	6.0%	5.0%
	% of Total	1.1%	.5%	1.0%	2.4%	5.0%
Five-year certification/degree/BA	Count	6	10	33	25	72
	% within STUDDIV	7.1%	8.8%	9.8%	6.6%	8.1%
	% of Total	.7%	1.1%	3.7%	2.6%	8.1%
Alternative program	Count	13	21	67	134	255
	% within STUDDIV	15.3%	18.6%	19.9%	38.2%	26.6%
	% of Total	1.5%	2.4%	7.6%	15.1%	26.6%
Total	Count	85	113	336	351	885
	% within STUDDIV	100.0%	100.0%	100.0%	100.0%	100.0%
	% of Total	9.6%	12.8%	38.0%	39.7%	100.0%

Pearson Chi Square 62.070 (12) (N=885), p=.000

Table 5. Number of Graduates by Institutional Mission

Number of Graduates		Institutional Mission			Total
		Research I	Research II	Teaching	
<25	Count	6	13	42	61
	% within RSCHTCHG	3.8%	5.1%	9.6%	7.1%
	% of Total	.7%	1.5%	4.9%	7.1%
25–100	Count	42	65	206	313
	% within RSCHTCHG	26.3%	25.4%	47.0%	36.7%
	% of Total	4.9%	7.6%	24.1%	36.7%
100–300	Count	77	107	145	329
	% within RSCHTCHG	48.1%	41.8%	35.1%	38.5%
	% of Total	9.0%	12.5%	17.0%	38.5%
300+	Count	35	71	45	151
	% within RSCHTCHG	21.9%	27.7%	10.5%	17.7%
	% of Total	4.1%	8.3%	5.3%	17.7%
Total	Count	160	256	458	854
	% within RSCHTCHG	100.0%	100.0%	100.0%	100.0%
	% of Total	18.7%	30.0%	51.3%	100.0%

Pearson Chi Square 71.928 (6) (N=854), *p*=.000

Table 6. Number of Graduates by Student Diversity

| Number of Graduates | | Student Diversity | | | | Total |
		Predominantly Diverse	Substantially Diverse	Somewhat Diverse	Primarily White	
<25	Count	4	8	24	30	66
	% within STUDDIV	4.9%	7.1%	7.2%	8.6%	7.5%
	% of Total	.5%	.9%	7.2%	3.4%	7.5%
25–100	Count	57	51	109	141	318
	% within STUDDIV	45.1%	27.4%	32.7%	40.4%	36.3%
	% of Total	2.0%	2.9%	10.6%	8.8%	24.4%
100–300	Count	26	48	121	142	337
	% within STUDDIV	31.7%	42.5%	36.3%	40.7%	38.4%
	% of Total	3.0%	5.5%	13.8%	16.2%	38.4%
300+	Count	15	26	79	36	156
	% within STUDDIV	18.3%	25.0%	23.7%	10.3%	17.8%
	% of Total	1.7%	3.0%	9.0%	4.1%	17.8%
Total	Count	82	113	333	349	877
	% within STUDDIV	100.0%	100.0%	100.0%	100.0%	100.0%
	% of Total	9.4%	12.9%	38.0%	39.8%	100.0%

Pearson Chi Square 29.951 (9) (N=877), p=.01

Table 7. Student Age by Student Diversity

Student Age		Student Diversity				Total
		Predominantly Diverse	Substantially Diverse	Somewhat Diverse	Primarily White	
18–25	Count	40	75	252	292	657
	% within STUDDIV	55.3%	65.8%	77.1%	86.1%	77.1%
	% of Total	4.7%	8.6%	29.6%	34.3%	77.1%
25+	Count	33	34	75	45	185
	% within STUDDIV	44.0%	30.6%	22.92%	12.7%	21.7%
	% of Total	3.9%	4.0%	8.8%	5.0%	21.7%
Other	Count	2	4		10	1.2%
	% within STUDDIV	2.7%	3.6%		3.6%	1.2%
	% of Total	.2%	.5%		.5%	1.2%
Total	Count	75	111	527	559	852
	% within STUDDIV	100.0%	100.0%	100.0%	100.0%	100.0%
	% of Total	8.8%	15.0%	58.4%	39.8%	100.0%

Pearson Chi Square 90451 (6) (N=852), *p*=.000

Table 8. Faculty Degrees by Institutional Mission

Faculty Degrees		Institutional Mission			Total
		Research I	Research II	Teaching	
Missing Data	Count	2	1	5	6
	% within RSCHTCHG	1.2%	.4%	.7%	.7%
	% of Total	.2%	.1%	.5%	.7%
Doctor	Count	152	248	577	777
	% within RSCHTCHG	95.8%	93.2%	84.5%	88.9%
	% of Total	17.4%	28.4%	45.1%	88.9%
Masters	Count	8	17	66	91
	% within RSCHTCHG	4.9%	6.4%	14.8%	10.4%
	% of Total	.9%	1.9%	7.6%	10.4%
Total	Count	162	266	446	874
	% within RSCHTCHG	100.0%	100.0%	100.0%	100.0%
	% of Total	18.5%	30.4%	51.0%	100.0%

Pearson Chi Square 20.080 (4) (N=874), p=.000

Table 9. Faculty Degree Focus by Student Diversity

Faculty Degree Focus		Student Diversity				Total
		Predominantly Diverse	Substantially Diverse	Somewhat Diverse	Primarily White	
Missing Data	Count	8	3	9	15	35
	% within STUDDIV	9.4%	2.6%	2.6%	4.2%	3.9%
	% of Total	.9%	.3%	1.0%	1.7%	3.9%
Elementary Education	Count	4	9	29	17	59
	% within STUDDIV	4.7%	7.8%	8.5%	4.8%	6.6%
	% of Total	.4%	1.0%	3.2%	1.9%	6.6%
General	Count	8	13	47	53	121
	% within STUDDIV	9.4%	11.3%	15.8%	14.8%	13.5%
	% of Total	.9%	1.4%	5.2%	5.9%	13.5%
Language Arts	Count	5	8	24	26	63
	% within STUDDIV	5.9%	7.0%	7.1%	7.3%	7.0%
	% of Total	.6%	.9%	2.7%	2.9%	7.0%
Other	Count	26	19	49	55	149
	% within STUDDIV	30.6%	16.5%	14.4%	15.4%	16.6%
	% of Total	2.9%	2.1%	5.5%	6.1%	16.6%
Reading	Count	30	60	171	173	434
	% within STUDDIV	35.3%	52.2%	50.3%	48.5%	48.4%
	% of Total	3.3%	6.7%	19.1%	19.3%	48.4%
Teacher Education	Count	4	3	11	18	36
	% within STUDDIV	4.7%	2.6%	3.2%	5.0%	4.0%
	% of Total	.4%	.3%	1.2%	2.0%	4.0%
Total	Count	85	115	340	357	897
	% within STUDDIV	100.0%	100.0%	100.0%	100.0%	100.0%
	% of Total	9.5%	12.8%	37.9%	39.8%	100.0%

Pearson Chi Square 32.256 (18) (N=897), *p*=.021

Table 10. Faculty Elementary Teaching Experience by Institutional Mission

Faculty Elementary Teaching Experience		Institutional Mission				Total
		Research I	Research II	Teaching		
None	Count	18	22	26		66
	% within RSCHTCHG	11.5%	8.3%	5.9%		7.6%
	% of Total	2.1%	2.5%	3.0%		7.6%
1–3 years	Count	25	34	45		104
	% within RSCHTCHG	15.6%	12.8%	10.2%		12.0%
	% of Total	2.9%	3.9%	5.2%		12.0%
3–5 years	Count	33	44	65		142
	% within RSCHTCHG	20.6%	16.6%	14.7%		16.4%
	% of Total	3.8%	5.1%	7.5%		16.4%
More than 5 years	Count	84	165	307		556
	% within RSCHTCHG	52.5%	62.3%	69.3%		64.1%
	% of Total	9.7%	19.0%	35.4%		64.1%
Total	Count	160	265	445		868
	% within RSCHTCHG	100.0%	100.0%	100.0%		100.0%
	% of Total	18.4%	30.5%	51.0%		100.0%

Pearson Chi Square 15.812 (6) (N=868), p=.0150

Table 11. Faculty Publication Activity by Institutional Mission

Faculty Publication Activity		Institutional Mission			Total
		Research I	Research II	Teaching	
None	Count	24	54	182	260
	% within RSCHTCHG	15.7%	21.9%	44.6%	52.2%
	% of Total	3.0%	6.7%	22.5%	52.2%
1–5 per year	Count	90	162	196	448
	% within RSCHTCHG	58.5%	65.6%	48.0%	55.4%
	% of Total	11.1%	20.0%	24.3%	55.4%
5–5 per year	Count	24	19	15	56
	% within RSCHTCHG	15.7%	7.7%	3.2%	6.9%
	% of Total	3.8%	5.1%	7.5%	16.4%
More than 5 per year	Count	15	12	17	44
	% within RSCHTCHG	9.8%	4.9%	4.2%	5.4%
	% of Total	1.9%	1.5%	2.1%	5.4%
Total	Count	153	247	408	808
	% within RSCHTCHG	100.0%	100.0%	100.0%	100.0%
	% of Total	18.9%	50.6%	50.5%	100.0%

Pearson Chi Square 81.726 (6) (N=808), p=.000

Table 12. Faculty Publication Activity by Student Diversity

Faculty Publication Activity		Student Diversity				Total
		Predominantly Diverse	Substantially Diverse	Somewhat Diverse	Primarily White	
None	Count	16	57	95	122	268
	% within STUDDIV	20.5%	34.9%	29.6%	36.4%	32.2%
	% of Total	1.9%	4.4%	11.2%	14.6%	32.2%
1–3 per year	Count	52	55	179	179	465
	% within STUDDIV	66.7%	51.9%	57.0%	53.4%	55.8%
	% of Total	6.2%	6.6%	21.5%	21.5%	55.8%
3–5 per year	Count	4	10	29	13	56
	% within STUDDIV	5.1%	9.4%	9.2%	3.9%	6.7%
	% of Total	.5%	1.2%	3.5%	1.6%	6.7%
More than 5 per year	Count	6	4	13	21	44
	% within STUDDIV	7.7%	3.8%	4.1%	6.3%	5.3%
	% of Total	.7%	.5%	1.6%	2.5%	5.3%
Total	Count	78	106	314	335	833
	% within STUDDIV	100.0%	100.0%	100.0%	100.0%	100.0%
	% of Total	9.4%	12.7%	37.7%	40.2%	100.0%

Pearson Chi Square 38.853 (9) (N=833), p=.000

Table 13. Means (SD) for Importance and Program Ratings by Institutional Mission for Ph.D./Ed.D. Faculty Teaching Experience and Faculty Research Activity

Item	Institutional Mission												Total		
	Research I			Research II			Teaching								
	n	X	SD	n	X	SD	n	X	SD				n	X	SD
Ph.D., Ed.D Importance	149	4.31	(.91)	250	4.26	(.95)	427	4.04	(1.05)				826	4.16	(1.00)
Ph.D., Ed.D. Program	139	4.01	(1.03)	240	3.78	(1.11)	414	3.63	(1.27)				795	3.74	(1.19)
Faculty Teaching Importance	148	4.38	(.88)	249	4.47	(.80)	426	4.51	(.83)				825	4.47	(.83)
Faculty Teaching Program	138	3.96	(1.10)	240	3.80	(1.11)	414	4.20	(1.04)				792	4.04	(1.08)
Faculty Research Importance	157	4.05	(.94)	257	3.89	(.97)	435	3.33	(1.14)				849	3.65	(1.10)
Faculty Research Program	147	3.89	(.97)	249	3.25	(1.09)	420	2.77	(1.15)				816	3.12	(1.17)

Table 14. Means (SD) for Importance and Program Ratings by Student Diversity for Ph.D./Ed.D., Faculty Teaching Experience and Faculty Research Activity

Item	Student Diversity															Total		
	Predominantly Diverse			Substantially Diverse			Somewhat Diverse			Primarily White								
	n	X	SD	n	X	SD	n	X	SD	n	X	SD	n	X	SD
Ph.D., Ed.D. Importance	77	4.22	(.84)	108	4.09	(.97)	521	4.18	(1.03)	343	4.13	(1.02)	849	4.15	(1.00)
Ph.D., Ed.D. Program	76	3.47	(1.19)	101	3.76	(1.22)	310	3.76	(1.16)	327	3.76	(1.22)	814	3.75	(1.20)
Faculty Teaching Importance	75	4.45	(.84)	107	4.40	(.89)	521	4.49	(.79)	343	4.48	(.85)	846	4.47	(.83)
Faculty Teaching Program	75	3.64	(1.19)	99	4.05	(1.18)	512	3.96	(1.06)	329	4.17	(1.03)	815	4.05	(1.09)
Faculty Research Importance	82	3.79	(1.11)	113	3.61	(1.11)	528	3.68	(1.07)	349	3.56	(1.13)	872	3.64	(1.10)
Faculty Research Program	80	2.85	(1.08)	105	3.23	(1.15)	517	3.21	(1.14)	355	3.04	(1.22)	857	3.11	(1.17)

Table 15. Means (SD) for Importance and Program Ratings Rated to Networking by Institutional Mission

Item	Institutional Mission									Total		
	Research I			Research II			Teaching					
	n	X	SD	n	X	SD	n	X	SD	n	X	SD
Public School Networks Importance	156	4.54	(.74)	258	4.64	(.63)	435	4.58	(.63)	849	4.59	(.65)
Public School Networks Program	146	4.19	(.93)	249	4.00	(1.05)	423	4.11	(.95)	818	4.09	(.98)
Teacher Ed Networks Importance	152	3.59	(1.06)	255	3.85	(.95)	452	3.82	(.98)	839	3.79	(.99)
Teacher Ed Networks Program	142	2.97	(1.17)	246	3.01	(1.20)	419	3.27	(1.19)	807	3.14	(1.20)

Table 16. Means (SD) for Importance and Program Ratings for Program Resources by Institutional Mission

Item	Institutional Mission									Total		
	Research I			Research II			Teaching					
	n	X	SD	n	X	SD	n	X	SD	n	X	SD
Class Size Importance	157	4.10	(1.01)	255	4.18	(.95)	459	4.17	(.96)	849	4.16	(.97)
Class Size Program	146	2.88	(1.41)	246	5.01	(1.54)	431	5.41	(1.28)	825	5.20	(1.54)
Budget Importance	147	5.73	(1.14)	247	5.96	(.98)	422	5.83	(.99)	816	5.85	(1.02)
Budget Program	155	2.59	(1.28)	257	2.28	(1.14)	410	2.45	(1.15)	782	2.39	(1.16)
Teaching Assistant Importance	156	5.60	(1.25)	255	3.05	(1.55)	429	2.66	(1.32)	858	2.95	(1.56)
Teaching Assistant Program	144	2.58	(1.39)	246	1.76	(1.16)	408	1.67	(1.11)	798	1.86	(1.25)

Table 17. Means (SD) for Importance and Program Ratings for Resources by Student Diversity

Item	Student Diversity															Total		
	Predominantly Diverse			Substantially Diverse			Somewhat Diverse			Primarily White								
	n	X	SD	n	X	SD	n	X	SD	n	X	SD	n	X	SD
Class Size Importance	82	4.25	(.92)	112	4.28	(.91)	528	4.17	(.89)	550	4.11	(1.06)	872	4.17	(.97)
Class Size Program	81	5.02	(1.35)	106	5.42	(1.55)	322	3.12	(1.52)	535	3.27	(1.52)	844	3.21	(1.54)
Budget Importance	82	5.87	(1.04)	108	5.94	(1.01)	311	5.85	(1.05)	556	5.85	(1.00)	857	5.85	(1.01)
Teaching Assistant Program	78	1.51	(.91)	102	1.85	(1.07)	515	1.97	(1.26)	525	1.86	(1.28)	818	1.86	(1.22)
Budget Program	81	2.16	(1.05)	96	2.56	(1.21)	305	2.39	(1.20)	321	2.59	(1.14)	801	2.59	(1.16)
Teaching Assistant Importance	81	3.00	(1.25)	111	3.10	(1.51)	325	2.94	(1.57)	544	2.88	(1.40)	861	2.94	(1.56)

Table 18. Means (SD) for Importance and Program Ratings for Program Structure and Control by Institutional Mission

Item	Institutional Mission																		Total		
	Research I			Research II			Teaching														
	n	X	SD	n	X	SD	n	X	SD	n	X	SD	n	X	SD
Program Admission Importance	153	4.08	(.89)	256	4.06	(.97)	436	4.17	(.95)	845	4.12	(.95)
Program Admission Program	145	3.79	(1.15)	250	3.39	(1.22)	425	3.79	(1.12)	816	3.67	(1.17)
Student Interviews Importance	156	3.51	(1.25)	256	3.57	(1.20)	435	3.70	(1.23)	847	3.63	(1.23)
Student Interviews Program	145	2.55	(1.56)	245	2.44	(1.50)	420	2.93	(1.51)	808	2.71	(1.53)
Comprehensive Exams Importance	147	3.02	(1.30)	241	3.20	(1.33)	422	3.34	(1.34)	810	3.24	(1.33)
Comprehensive Exams Program	156	2.70	(1.56)	253	2.85	(1.56)	409	3.09	(1.53)	778	2.95	(1.55)
State Assessments Importance	149	3.28	(1.39)	245	3.63	(1.27)	424	3.64	(1.24)	816	3.57	(1.28)
State Assessments Program	155	3.75	(1.51)	256	3.76	(1.30)	412	3.75	(1.52)	785	3.74	(1.51)
Follow-up Importance	155	4.05	(.91)	257	4.09	(.91)	434	4.09	(.85)	846	4.09	(.87)
Follow-up Program	145	2.96	(1.23)	247	3.02	(1.22)	421	3.32	(1.18)	815	3.16	(1.21)

Table 19. Means (SD) for Importance and Program Ratings for Program Structure and Control by Student Diversity

Item	Student Diversity												Total		
	Predominantly Diverse			Substantially Diverse			Somewhat Diverse			Primarily White					
	n	X	SD	n	X	SD	n	X	SD	n	X	SD	n	X	SD
Program Admission Importance	82	4.11	(.93)	111	4.07	(.99)	528	4.09	(.95)	348	4.11	(.95)	869	4.10	(.95)
Program Admission Program	79	3.53	(1.01)	105	3.69	(1.24)	521	3.66	(1.20)	352	3.70	(1.15)	857	3.67	(1.17)
Student Interviews Importance	82	3.80	(1.21)	112	3.85	(1.16)	527	3.63	(1.18)	348	3.54	(1.28)	869	3.64	(1.23)
Student Interviews Program	80	2.94	(1.51)	104	2.98	(1.52)	514	2.66	(1.52)	329	2.64	(1.56)	827	2.72	(1.54)
Comprehensive Exams Importance	74	3.20	(1.39)	106	3.31	(1.37)	521	3.15	(1.32)	355	3.28	(1.32)	856	3.25	(1.33)
Comprehensive Exams Program	76	2.62	(1.51)	99	3.11	(1.52)	507	2.86	(1.54)	519	3.04	(1.56)	801	2.94	(1.55)
State Assessments Importance	77	3.66	(1.35)	108	3.76	(1.18)	518	3.57	(1.28)	336	3.49	(1.31)	839	3.57	(1.29)
State Assessments Program	75	4.05	(1.13)	100	4.06	(1.05)	507	3.74	(1.36)	321	3.58	(1.36)	803	3.74	(1.31)
Follow-up Importance	80	4.01	(1.07)	113	4.19	(.76)	527	4.06	(.86)	349	4.11	(.84)	869	4.09	(.86)
Follow-up Program	79	2.81	(1.54)	105	3.50	(1.26)	514	3.11	(1.18)	336	3.25	(1.17)	834	3.16	(1.21)

Table 20. Means (SD) for Importance and Program Ratings for Preparation Process by Institutional Mission

Item	Institutional Mission									Total		
	Research I			Research II			Teaching					
	n	X	SD	n	X	SD	n	X	SD	n	X	SD
Field Experiences Importance	157	4.73	(.59)	256	4.70	(.62)	457	4.65	(.70)	850	4.68	(.66)
Field Experiences Program	143	4.10	(1.10)	249	3.88	(1.20)	429	3.97	(1.06)	821	3.96	(1.11)
Tutor Students Importance	145	3.72	(1.26)	258	4.15	(1.04)	417	3.99	(1.14)	800	3.99	(1.14)
Tutor Students Program	134	2.83	(1.42)	251	3.16	(1.45)	404	3.15	(1.44)	769	3.10	(1.44)
Tutor Adults Importance	138	2.57	(1.37)	253	2.51	(1.39)	400	2.39	(1.29)	771	2.42	(1.33)
Tutor Adults Program	125	1.97	(1.37)	225	1.71	(1.17)	383	1.80	(1.28)	753	1.80	(1.26)
10–20 Hrs. Fieldwork Importance	148	4.25	(1.02)	245	4.16	(1.05)	421	4.04	(1.12)	814	4.11	(1.09)
10–20 Hrs. Fieldwork Program	156	3.94	(1.32)	256	3.46	(1.45)	409	3.33	(1.49)	781	3.47	(1.47)
10-Week Student Teaching Importance	147	4.59	(.81)	243	4.67	(.67)	420	4.64	(.64)	810	4.64	(.68)
10-Week Student Teaching Program	136	4.34	(1.08)	256	4.53	(.88)	408	4.44	(.83)	780	4.39	(.89)
Diverse Classroom Importance	151	4.40	(.80)	249	4.28	(.84)	424	4.25	(.83)	824	4.28	(.83)
Diverse Classroom Program	140	3.78	(1.09)	240	3.40	(1.20)	414	3.55	(1.22)	794	3.54	(1.20)
Use Technology Importance	147	3.86	(.98)	247	3.90	(.99)	427	4.04	(.86)	821	3.97	(.95)
Use Technology Program	157	3.37	(1.12)	242	3.26	(1.09)	414	3.45	(1.15)	795	3.38	(1.12)

Table 21. Means (SD) for Importance and Program Ratings for Preparation Process by Student Diversity

Item	Student Diversity												Total		
	Predominantly Diverse			Substantially Diverse			Somewhat Diverse			Primarily White					
	n	X	SD	n	X	SD	n	X	SD	n	X	SD	n	X	SD
Field Experiences Importance	83	4.55	(.80)	112	4.71	(.61)	330	4.72	(.63)	348	4.67	(.67)	873	4.68	(.66)
Field Experience Program	82	3.79	(1.16)	105	4.04	(1.05)	319	3.96	(1.14)	336	4.00	(1.10)	842	3.97	(1.11)
Tutor Students Importance	72	3.96	(1.22)	104	4.13	(1.10)	313	4.03	(1.12)	333	3.94	(1.14)	822	4.00	(1.13)
Tutor Students Program	71	2.79	(1.55)	94	3.33	(1.56)	304	3.10	(1.43)	320	3.10	(1.49)	789	3.10	(1.44)
Tutor Adults Importance	65	2.46	(1.43)	100	2.66	(1.56)	301	2.47	(1.56)	327	2.28	(1.28)	795	2.41	(1.34)
Tutor Adults Program	64	2.00	(1.39)	94	2.06	(1.31)	285	1.78	(1.25)	307	1.69	(1.22)	750	1.80	(1.26)
10–20 Hrs. Field Work Importance	77	4.32	(1.02)	107	4.26	(1.01)	315	4.11	(1.12)	337	4.00	(1.08)	836	4.11	(1.08)
10–20 Hrs. Field Work Program	75	3.45	(1.43)	101	3.63	(1.39)	303	3.50	(1.47)	323	3.38	(1.49)	802	3.47	(1.47)
10-Week Student Teaching Importance	75	4.64	(.59)	105	4.60	(.67)	317	4.65	(.68)	356	4.65	(.68)	851	4.65	(.67)
10-Week Student Teaching Program	72	4.14	(1.05)	100	4.46	(.82)	305	4.34	(.98)	322	4.49	(.77)	799	4.40	(.89)
Diverse Classroom Importance	76	4.62	(.61)	109	4.42	(.75)	319	4.34	(.75)	343	4.11	(.92)	847	4.28	(.83)
Diverse Classroom Program	74	4.22	(1.06)	105	4.04	(1.06)	309	3.72	(1.10)	328	3.08	(1.17)	814	3.55	(1.20)
Use Technology Importance	75	4.07	(.91)	108	4.01	(.91)	319	3.94	(.97)	342	3.97	(.92)	844	3.97	(.95)
Use Technology Program	75	3.12	(1.10)	100	3.44	(1.17)	311	3.46	(1.06)	328	3.35	(1.15)	814	3.38	(1.12)

Table 22. Means (SD) for Importance and Program Ratings for Program Content by Institutional Mission

Item	Institutional Mission												Total		
	Research I			Research II			Teaching								
	n	X	SD	n	X	SD	n	X	SD				n	X	SD
Foundations Requirements Importance	152	3.82	(1.02)	246	3.91	(.98)	434	3.97	(.95)				832	3.95	(.97)
Foundations Requirements Program	141	3.71	(1.06)	257	3.68	(.99)	421	3.83	(.93)				799	3.76	(.97)
Structure of Language Importance	156	3.57	(1.23)	249	3.71	(1.11)	452	3.60	(1.16)				857	3.65	(1.16)
Structure of Language Program	145	2.47	(1.25)	241	2.50	(1.27)	418	2.57	(1.32)				802	2.53	(1.29)
Language and Diversity Importance	156	4.22	(.99)	251	4.18	(.93)	457	4.05	(.97)				844	4.11	(.96)
Language and Diversity Program	143	3.17	(1.26)	242	3.11	(1.26)	426	3.08	(1.24)				811	3.11	(1.25)
Test and Measurement Importance	155	3.74	(1.08)	250	3.91	(.95)	457	3.86	(1.02)				842	3.85	(1.01)
Test and Measurement Program	143	3.01	(1.21)	245	2.88	(1.11)	425	3.07	(1.25)				809	3.01	(1.19)
Reading Courses Importance	155	4.41	(.94)	252	4.60	(.81)	456	4.59	(.78)				843	4.56	(.82)
Reading Courses Program	145	3.55	(1.43)	244	3.52	(1.39)	425	3.59	(1.29)				812	3.56	(1.34)
Language Arts Importance	155	4.52	(.85)	250	4.50	(.81)	435	4.49	(.84)				840	4.50	(.83)
Language Arts Program	142	3.70	(1.15)	245	3.58	(1.14)	422	3.68	(1.13)				807	3.65	(1.14)
Children's Literature Importance	156	4.29	(.98)	249	4.47	(.74)	454	4.45	(.85)				859	4.42	(.84)
Children's Literature Program	145	3.24	(1.42)	242	3.19	(1.29)	424	3.44	(1.29)				809	3.33	(1.52)
Diversity Strategies Importance	149	4.55	(.70)	250	4.42	(.82)	427	4.35	(.77)				826	4.40	(.78)
Diversity Strategies Program	138	3.88	(1.05)	241	3.62	(1.05)	416	3.67	(.99)				795	3.69	(1.02)
Technology Course Importance	148	3.76	(1.02)	249	3.71	(1.03)	425	3.79	(.98)				822	3.76	(1.00)
Technology Course Program	157	3.15	(1.13)	240	2.89	(1.05)	412	3.14	(1.10)				789	3.06	(1.10)

Table 23. Means (SD) for Importance and Program Ratings for Program Content by Student Diversity

Item	Predominantly Diverse			Substantially Diverse			Somewhat Diverse			Primarily White			Total		
	n	X	SD	n	X	SD	n	X	SD	n	X	SD	n	X	SD
Foundations Requirements Importance	78	3.76	(.98)	112	4.04	(.89)	520	3.80	(1.05)	344	4.04	(.93)	854	3.95	(.97)
Foundations Requirements Program	76	3.58	(1.05)	104	3.65	(.99)	507	3.75	(.96)	331	3.88	(.95)	818	3.77	(.97)
Structure of Language Importance	79	3.63	(1.09)	110	3.95	(.98)	524	3.59	(1.19)	347	3.57	(1.16)	860	3.63	(1.15)
Structure of Language Program	76	2.64	(1.53)	105	2.78	(1.16)	511	2.50	(1.34)	331	2.50	(1.29)	825	2.55	(1.30)
Language and Diversity Importance	80	4.44	(.84)	115	4.21	(.83)	526	4.09	(1.00)	348	4.05	(.99)	867	4.11	(.97)
Language and Diversity Program	79	3.56	(1.16)	106	3.21	(1.34)	514	3.05	(1.26)	353	3.01	(1.22)	852	3.10	(1.25)
Test and Measurement Importance	80	3.91	(1.00)	115	3.88	(.94)	524	3.83	(1.04)	347	3.86	(1.00)	864	3.86	(1.01)
Test and Measurement Program	77	2.69	(1.05)	106	2.94	(1.10)	514	3.02	(1.20)	331	3.08	(1.25)	828	3.00	(1.19)
Reading Courses Importance	80	4.54	(.83)	115	4.65	(.76)	525	4.59	(.80)	349	4.55	(.83)	865	4.57	(.81)
Reading Courses Program	79	3.61	(1.31)	105	3.52	(1.36)	513	3.60	(1.57)	355	3.54	(1.31)	852	3.57	(1.34)
Language Arts Importance	79	4.32	(.99)	112	4.47	(.80)	525	4.55	(.82)	347	4.52	(.82)	865	4.50	(.84)
Language Arts Program	77	3.50	(1.14)	104	3.77	(1.14)	514	3.68	(1.12)	353	3.68	(1.14)	828	3.66	(1.13)
Children's Literature Importance	79	4.18	(.94)	115	4.30	(.95)	524	4.47	(.85)	345	4.45	(.78)	861	4.41	(.84)
Children's Literature Program	78	2.81	(1.30)	106	3.25	(1.37)	512	3.38	(1.29)	353	3.44	(1.31)	829	3.35	(1.52)
Diversity Strategies Importance	76	4.62	(.61)	109	4.58	(.80)	521	4.53	(.76)	345	4.54	(.80)	849	4.41	(.77)
Diversity Strategies Program	75	4.05	(1.00)	105	3.85	(1.11)	510	3.82	(.99)	328	3.45	(.99)	816	3.69	(1.05)
Technology Course Importance	76	3.95	(.98)	108	3.81	(.98)	519	3.79	(.99)	342	3.71	(1.02)	845	3.77	(1.00)
Technology Course Program	74	2.86	(1.05)	101	3.24	(1.14)	508	3.14	(1.09)	527	3.00	(1.10)	810	3.07	(1.10)

Table 24. Means (SD) for Importance and Program Ratings for Philosophy and Commitment by Institutional Mission

Item	Institutional Mission									Total		
	Research I			Research II			Teaching					
	n	X	SD	n	X	SD	n	X	SD	n	X	SD
Philosophy Importance	156	4.31	(.87)	251	4.52	(.76)	454	4.53	(.70)	841	4.49	(.75)
Philosophy Program	144	5.69	(1.09)	245	5.67	(1.11)	423	5.90	(1.01)	812	5.79	(1.06)
Philosophy Shared Importance	156	4.28	(.96)	251	4.41	(.77)	455	4.41	(.82)	842	4.39	(.83)
Philosophy Shared Program	143	5.31	(1.18)	245	5.38	(1.17)	425	5.70	(1.15)	815	5.53	(1.17)
Program Description Importance	156	4.40	(.78)	252	4.46	(.74)	453	4.47	(.76)	841	4.46	(.76)
Program Description Program	144	5.94	(.97)	245	5.80	(1.09)	420	4.10	(1.02)	807	5.98	(1.04)

Table 25. Means (SD) for Importance and Program Ratings for Philosophy and Commitment by Student Diversity

Item	Student Diversity															Total		
	Predominantly Diverse			Substantially Diverse			Somewhat Diverse			Primarily White								
	n	X	SD	n	X	SD	n	X	SD	n	X	SD	n	X	SD
Philosophy Importance	78	4.49	(.70)	115	4.52	(.71)	323	4.47	(.75)	348	4.48	(.78)	862	4.48	(.75)
Philosophy Program	78	5.55	(1.19)	106	5.93	(.93)	315	5.82	(1.05)	355	5.79	(1.08)	832	5.79	(1.06)
Philosophy Shared Importance	78	4.45	(.73)	115	4.42	(.80)	324	4.44	(.78)	348	4.34	(.89)	865	4.40	(.83)
Philosophy Shared Program	78	5.25	(1.25)	106	5.75	(1.04)	315	5.52	(1.18)	354	5.55	(1.18)	835	5.53	(1.18)
Program Description Importance	79	4.49	(.70)	115	4.42	(.80)	325	4.46	(.77)	347	4.44	(.76)	862	4.45	(.76)
Program Description Program	77	5.77	(1.02)	104	4.05	(1.07)	314	4.00	(1.03)	352	5.96	(1.05)	827	5.97	(1.05)

Table 26. Program Ratings by Institutional Mission

Program Ratings		Institutional Mission			Total
		Research I	Research II	Teaching	
Outstanding	Count	53	85	156	294
	% within RSCHTCHG	34.4%	32.9%	36.0%	34.8%
	% of Total	6.3%	10.1%	18.5%	34.8%
Very Good	Count	74	123	234	431
	% within RSCHTCHG	48.1%	47.7%	54.0%	51.0%
	% of Total	8.8%	14.6%	27.7%	51.0%
Satisfactory	Count	25	43	36	104
	% within RSCHTCHG	16.2%	16.7%	8.3%	12.3%
	% of Total	3.0%	5.1%	4.3%	12.3%
Poor	Count	2	7	7	16
	% within RSCHTCHG	1.3%	2.7%	1.6%	1.9%
	% of Total	.2%	.8%	.8%	1.9%
Total	Count	154	258	433	845
	% within RSCHTCHG	100.0%	100.0%	100.0%	100.0%
	% of Total	18.2%	30.5%	51.2%	100.0%

Pearson Chi Square 14.975 (6) (N=845), p=.021

Table 27. Program Ratings by Student Diversity

Program Ratings		Student Diversity				Total
		Predominantly Diverse	Substantially Diverse	Somewhat Diverse	Primarily White	
Outstanding	Count	25	32	117	129	305
	% within STUDDIV	30.9%	28.8%	35.6%	37.5%	35.0%
	% of Total	2.9%	3.7%	15.5%	14.9%	35.0%
Very Good	Count	30	64	175	176	443
	% within STUDDIV	37.0%	57.7%	52.6%	51.2%	51.2%
	% of Total	3.5%	7.4%	20.0%	20.3%	51.2%
Satisfactory	Count	25	15	55	52	105
	% within STUDDIV	28.4%	11.7%	10.6%	9.3%	11.9%
	% of Total	2.7%	1.5%	4.0%	3.7%	11.9%
Poor	Count	3	2	4	7	16
	% within STUDDIV	3.7%	1.8%	1.2%	2.0%	1.8%
	% of Total	.3%	.2%	.5%	.8%	1.8%
Total	Count	81	111	529	344	865
	% within STUDDIV	100.0%	100.0%	100.0%	100.0%	100.0%
	% of Total	9.4%	12.8%	58.0%	39.8%	100.0%

Pearson Chi Square 29.651 (9) (N=865), p=.001

Transitions into teaching: Learning to teach writing in teacher education and beyond

Pamela L. Grossman
STANFORD UNIVERSITY

Sheila W. Valencia, Clarissa Thompson, Susan D. Martin, and Nancy Place
UNIVERSITY OF WASHINGTON, SEATTLE

Kate Evans
SAN JOSE STATE UNIVERSITY

Charles: I think of a workshop as a...place for you to hone a skill you have, whether it's in carpentry or art or writing.... I just think of [writers' workshop] as a...consistent time every day, a structure that provides for the kids to work on the skill of...using written language...and then added to that using minilessons to focus on...skills important for the kids to learn.

Stephanie: That term [writers' workshop] is, it's one of those things that I say, someday I'm gonna do it...when I figure out what it is! When I think of writers' workshop, I think of management. I think of, you know, first draft kids over here, you know, and get the brainstorming kids going over here, and get the final draft going here and I can't do it all in my room.... I'm still at the "what is it?" stage.

Stephanie and Charles, graduates of the same elementary teacher education program, have different ideas about writers' workshop and what it might look like in the classroom. For Charles, it represents a consistent time for honing the skill of writing; for Stephanie, it represents a management nightmare. Both of them first encountered the concept of writers' workshop in their teacher education program. But what accounts for the different ways in which they have come to understand and incorporate this practice into their teaching?

Despite our understanding of the complexity of learning to teach, there are relatively few longitudinal studies of teacher education that look at how beginning teachers adopt concepts and practices in the various settings of professional education and then modify and use them in their first few years of teaching. Most research stops with student teaching; a few studies follow teachers into the first year; fewer still examine how teachers' understanding and practice evolve in the second or third year of practice. Our study of beginning teachers learning to teach writing provides such a longitudinal look.

Specifically, we ask

> What ideas, concepts, strategies, and specific tools for teaching writing do preservice teachers develop during teacher education?
>
> How do their experiences in teacher education and their early experiences in schools shape their understandings and uses of these ideas and tools?
>
> How do beginning teachers continue to develop their understanding and practice of teaching writing over the first few years of teaching?
>
> How do features of the settings of teacher education and the schools affect the ways in which beginning teachers develop their understanding of teaching writing?

Theoretical Framework

We have chosen to explore these questions from a sociocultural perspective, drawing specifically from activity theory (Cole, 1996; Engestrom, 1999; Grossman, Smagorinsky, & Valencia, 1999; Leont'ev, 1981; Tulviste, 1991; Wertsch, 1981). Activity theory starts with the assumption that a person's framework for thinking is developed through problem-solving action carried out in specific settings. This perspective focuses our attention on how beginning teachers develop goals while engaged in activity in particular settings, identify problems they must solve, and choose a set of tools to inform and conduct their teaching. Sociocultural theory would also suggest that individuals' understandings and practices are always shaped by the various settings in which they find themselves. Using the framework of activity theory invites us to look at both the individual's experience, as well as at how settings are structured by historical forces through actions of individuals (Engestrom, 1999), in order to understand the development of an individual's practice.

Activity settings are the social contexts in which learners participate and through which they appropriate knowledge. Learning to teach is comprised of a number of distinct activity settings, including university coursework; field experiences (including student teaching); supervision; and the concentric settings of school, department, and grade level. Each of these activity settings has its own spe-cific motive, structural features, sets of relationships, and resources for learning to teach. Although two teachers may work in the same physical setting (e.g., a school), they may have distinctly different understandings of the school setting based on the teachers' own goals, histories, and relationships within the school arena (Lave, 1988). Furthermore, one activity setting may encompass conflicting goals, creating unique problem-solving situations for the beginning teacher. For example, in the setting of student teaching, preservice teachers must balance the competing goals of demonstrating competence to earn a good grade and trying out new strategies in an effort to experiment and "practice" teaching. Part of our effort in this study is to understand how prospective and beginning teachers and those around them come to understand the problems they face in particular settings, and how they engage in solving these problems, using the resources available to them.

Activity theory, like other sociocultural theories, also focuses our attention on the use of tools (cf. Wertsch, 1991). Teachers use a wide range of pedagogical tools to construct and carry out teaching practices within activity settings. This range of tools encompasses both conceptual and more practical tools. We have defined conceptual tools as principles, frameworks, and ideas about teaching, learning, and English/language arts that teachers use as heuristics to guide their instructional decisions. They can include broadly applicable theories such as constructivism or instructional scaffolding or subject matter-specific concepts such as process writing. Although conceptual tools are useful for a broader understanding of teaching and learning, they do not necessarily solve the problem of what to do in the classroom. We define practical tools as classroom practices, strategies, and resources that do not serve as broad conceptions to guide an array of decisions, but instead have more local and immediate utility. These might include instructional practices such as journal writing or writers' workshop, or resources such as textbooks or curriculum materials that provide such instructional practices. Activity theory provides a framework for examining how teachers understand and use these tools in their teaching. Rather than suggesting that teachers do or do not use a particular strategy or understand a particular concept, activity theory helps us understand the process through which a person adopts, or appropriates, the pedagogical tools available for use in particular activity settings (Leont'ev, 1981; Newman, Griffin, & Cole, 1989; Wertsch; 1981).

Description of Study

For the past 4 years, we have been engaged in a longitudinal study of learning to teach literacy/language arts. As part of the Center for English Learning and Achievement, we have followed beginning teachers from their last year of teacher education into their first 3 years of full-time teaching.[1] We began with 15 preservice teachers—8 secondary and 7 elementary—during their last 2 quarters of teacher education. We have followed 10 of these teachers into their first 3 years of teaching. The teachers teach in eight different districts and in one private school. Five of them teach at the elementary level, two at the middle school level, and three in high school.

Data Sources

This analysis draws from data from the first 3 years of the study. Our data consist of individual and group interviews, classroom observations, and documents. We interviewed each teacher individually on at least 11 occasions and observed them a minimum of 5 times during each of the 3 years of the study. Each observation was accompanied by a pre-observation conversation and a longer post-observation interview. At the secondary level, each classroom observation included instruction in two classes; at the elementary we observed both reading and writing, when possible. We took extensive field notes and wrote detailed analytic memos after each observation. Each year, we also conducted a group interview with the elementary and secondary participants in which they discussed what they were learning about teaching language arts. Group interviews, which were designed to allow us to observe interactions among members of a cohort, often engaged participants in a joint activity. All the interviews were audiotaped and transcribed; the group interviews were both audio- and videotaped.

To capture a fuller picture of the different activity settings, we included several additional data points each year. During student teaching, we accompanied the university supervisor on a supervisory visit, and we also observed and recorded the debriefing between the supervisor and student. We also interviewed the cooperating teachers and observed them debrief a lesson with the student teachers. During the first year of teaching, we interviewed the beginning teachers' mentor teachers, department chairs, and principals. As part of another facet of this research, we also interviewed district administrators about district policies concerning the language arts and support for beginning teachers. During the first and second years, we interviewed teachers at the beginning, middle, and end of the school year, and we collected classroom artifacts, including lesson plans, written materials, and other documents related to teaching.

The design of this longitudinal study afforded us opportunities to explore many facets of the settings in which these teachers worked and to document how they learned to teach across these settings. We were not, however, able to conduct the extensive observational data we would have liked or to videotape classroom interaction. In addition, our data on the methods courses was retrospective, drawn from interviews with professors, teaching assistants, and the participants rather than from direct observation.

Data analysis has been an ongoing and iterative process. We initially identified a wide range of pedagogical tools for each participant from the interview data; we subsequently developed a coding scheme to be used across all the data. Although the focus of the larger study is on language arts in general, we first analyzed the teaching of writing as a way to bound data analysis. In our analyses, we triangulated interview and observational data, as well as data from the beginning teachers with data from their supervisors, cooperating teachers, mentors, and principals. Our first effort has been at un-

---

[1] This study is part of a larger cross-institutional study that ultimately will include data from four different teacher education programs. We would like to acknowledge our colleagues Peter Smagorinsky and Jane Agee, who are conducting similar longitudinal research of beginning secondary teachers.

derstanding the development of each individual's understanding and practice in teaching writing; once we developed the individual cases, we began the process of looking for themes across cases.

Context

Both the elementary and secondary programs from which these teachers graduated are master's programs that emphasize the importance of subject matter preparation for teachers and focus on the preparation of reflective practitioners. We collected extensive data from these courses, including interviews with the instructors and teaching assistants, lesson plans, course readers, and the teaching portfolio of the secondary course instructor. Students in the secondary language arts program took a 2-quarter sequence on the teaching of language arts; over a month of this course was devoted to the teaching of writing. They used the first edition of Nancie Atwell's book, *In the Middle* (1987), in which writers' workshop is described and, in class, they focused on the importance of student ownership and the social construction of meaning through writing. As they discussed the teaching of writing, they were also engaged in writing a lengthy literacy autobiography. The concept of scaffolded instruction (e.g., Bruner, 1960; Langer & Applebee, 1986) was taught in several of the teacher education courses and was further reinforced through discussion and assignments in the language arts methods class.[2] In addition, secondary students were required to complete a course on composition processes in the English department before completion of the program. All the high school teachers in our study shared a common 2-quarter English methods class, but did not necessarily have the same instructors for other required courses in their program.

The elementary program included 3 quarters of coursework on literacy. In the first of these, students studied and personally experienced reading and writing processes, including writing personal literacy autobiographies. The second quarter was devoted to the teaching of reading, and the third quarter was entirely devoted to teaching writing. The primary text, *The Art of Teaching Writing* (Calkins, 1994), emphasized writers' workshop and the importance of student ownership[3] in writing (Atwell, 1987; Au, 1993; Calkins, 1994). In class, preservice teachers discussed adapting the workshop model and explored other approaches for teaching process writing. Instructors emphasized the role of scaffolding and explicit instruction in teaching writing, including the use of modeling and minilessons targeting specific strategies and skills. As part of the coursework, students were required to develop a literacy portfolio for a student in their practicum class and analyze the student's written work. In addition, they taught a multiday process writing lesson that included several minilessons. Two of the elementary teachers in our study, Charles and Stephanie, had graduated from the Special Education/Teacher Education (SPED/TEP) elementary program, which confers dual certification in elementary education and special education. Students in the SPED/TEP program took additional special education coursework in teaching literacy.

We begin by providing brief cases of 3 of the 10 beginning teachers in our study. One teacher, Bill, teaches at the high school level, and two others, Stephanie and Charles, teach elementary school. However, we have drawn from all the case studies of our other participants in our analysis of cross-case themes.

Case Studies

Bill: Going for a Test Drive in Someone Else's Car

Bill entered the teacher education program with strong beliefs about the importance of creativity and communication in teaching writing. Early in his teacher education program, prior to student teaching, he talked about the damaging effects of focusing solely on skills and structure in teaching writing:

[2] Scaffolding, as defined by Langer & Applebee (1986) includes five components: ownership, appropriateness, structure, collaboration, and transfer of control.
[3] In general, the concept of ownership involves students valuing their own abilities, seeing learning as a worthwhile enterprise, and choosing to engage in particular tasks. Specifically, in writing, ownership implies that students view their writing as meaningful, personally satisfying work. They choose to write on their own and are provided opportunities in school to write on self-selected topics.

There's a level of inquiry that needs to be established and challenged and praised and rewarded in elementary school, or else by the time we [secondary teachers] see them, it's just, "What am I supposed to write? Yeah, you want three paragraphs. Here they come. I'm going to give you three paragraphs." And so if you only build skills, you are damaging the students.

Bill's main exposure to the teaching of writing in his English methods course was reading Nancie Atwell's (1987) *In the Middle*. His early comments about not placing the teaching of skills before encouraging creativity aligned with Atwell's approach. But because of his low regard for his English methods teacher, he rejected some of her attempts to model tools for teaching aspects of the writing process in the classroom, such as the use of peer revision groups for engaging students in revision. Expressing great frustration with the lack of practical tools provided in the methods course, Bill had helped start a "shadow" methods course in which students shared materials and lesson plans that they encountered in their field experiences.

After the conclusion of his methods course and prior to his full-time student teaching experience, Bill attended a workshop on the teaching of writing that was offered by the district in which he was to student teach. The teachers in the school district had decided to bring in Jane Schaffer, the developer of a unit plan for teaching writing, for a workshop. Along with other teachers, Bill was wowed by Schaffer: "We were just hook, line, and sinker taken." In response to the workshop, the district adopted the Jane Schaffer materials. Bill was so thrilled with the Jane Schaffer materials that he made copies for his colleagues in the shadow methods course, including several other participants in this study.

Schaffer's method for teaching writing is highly structured; the introduction to the unit terms it "formulaic" (Schaffer, 1995, p. 6). In the unit, students' essays are to have a minimum of four paragraphs, as well as a minimum number of words per paragraph. Paragraphs follow a rigid pattern of topic sentence, followed by a sentence of "concrete detail," followed by two sentences expressing "commentary." The unit is also highly structured for teachers; lessons are tightly scripted, and all materials, including student handouts and quizzes, are included in the packet. While the philosophy on which the unit is built appears to reflect an image of writing by prescription, the unit's introduction, written to the teacher, also articulates a process writing orientation. Schaffer writes that "writing is an act of discovery, a way of clarifying ideas, a social activity that often thrives upon contact with others, and a recursive process requiring time, reflection, feedback, and revision" (Schaffer, 1995, p. 6). She claims that the unit serves to demystify writing, making it "accessible to everyone" (p. 6). Schaffer avows that despite its scripted and formulaic appearance, the unit can be "very flexible" and "easily and successfully modified" (p. 6).

Bill entered student teaching with relatively few strategies for teaching writing. The Jane Schaffer materials filled this void. Presented in terms of equity and ownership, and undeniably representing a form of direct procedural scaffolding, this unit appealed to Bill for a number of reasons. First, the model provided the very kind of pedagogical tool he was seeking. Bill particularly appreciated Schaffer's emphasis on issues of equity, commenting, "at its heart that unit is about parity.... The unit at its heart attempts to place everybody on the same [plane], at least using the same vocabulary." This notion of offering students a kind of cultural capital appealed to Bill's sense of social justice. Second, he justified the model in terms of student ownership. By using the unit, he hoped,

> [S]tudents will learn that they are in charge of their own writing, and it's not something that someone else has to dictate for them...so I hope to give them more power of their own selves, give them more ownership of prewriting strategies.

In his student teaching, Bill followed the Schaffer model very closely, remarking, "right now I'm on a test drive in a new car, and it isn't my car." Although the unit materials claim to be pliable, Bill saw the curriculum as extremely sequential; deviating from the sequence, he believed, might hurt students. He commented, "the unit continually builds on itself and the difficult challenge for me is to not lose anyone at any given part, because if I lose them now, they're gone for the next 9 weeks, and I can't get them back." As the setting of student teaching tends not to encourage improvisation, Bill may have been following the lead of his cooperating teacher or other teachers in the school in his adherence to the model. As Bill said in another context, "it's the building policy, and I live by it. And I can't make my own...rules in the world right now." In addition, Bill lacked a rich subject matter background in writing which might have enabled him to adapt the program.

Despite Bill's initial enthusiasm for the Schaffer model, he began to identify a tension between the very tight structure of the Schaffer model and the issues of ownership that were so central to his initial beliefs about teaching writing. As Bill taught the various prewriting strategies, he did not understand why students had such a difficult time coming up with ideas for their own writing. As he commented about his lower-track class,

> What I have found is that no matter what my subjects were [in my models], their subjects were identical. The first prewrite I did, my topic was sports—basketball, baseball. Well, all their prewrites were about some kind of physical activity.... It didn't make any difference what prompt I gave them—write about anything—pick a subject! "I can't think of anything." Think of any subject whatsoever...any subject! Any subject! Am I speaking English?

Bill's comments suggest that the students did not see the content as particularly important; when what they were learning was a formula, one topic was as good as another.

During this time, Bill's university supervisor was critiquing his teaching as too teacher-centered. Bill seemed to blame this, in part, on the Schaffer unit, commenting,

> "The nature of the writing unit [is teacher-, not student-centered].... But I think it's kind of difficult to establish the modeling part without it being teacher-centered, because the students don't have a clue how to do literature commentary until I work with them."

It became evident in this and other comments that Bill was beginning to critique the Schaffer writing curriculum. Implying that the unit was somewhat unwieldy and outdated, Bill noted that it "uses its own vocabulary," such as "commentary," and that the eight-sentence paragraph model required in the unit "is something straight out of textbooks of the 50s and 60s." Also, part of the Schaffer curriculum requires students not to repeat anything in an essay, which, in Bill's words, was driving the students "bonkers." Bill added, "It's not the way I was taught to write; it's not the way the majority of students are taught to write." As Bill began to realize that his belief in ownership was not being satisfied through his current curriculum, he expressed an interest in talking with a cohort member who had been implementing writers' workshop, to "get her advice on ways of making [the teaching of writing] more writers' workshop oriented, and giving them ownership of the process." He believed that in writers' workshop, the teacher is not the controller; instead, "the kids just take it and they run with it, basically from the first day."

Bill's critique suggests that he was caught in an either-or conceptualization of writing pedagogy—either writing is completely structured and teacher-centered, or it is student-centered and unstructured. This dichotomy reflects, in part, his two primary sources for the teaching of writing—the first edition of Nancie Atwell's book, which downplays the teacher's role in structuring assignments, and the Jane Schaffer materials, which are highly teacher-structured. Despite his budding critiques, Bill stayed with the Schaffer writing unit for the remainder of his student teaching. During his third and exit interviews, he talked about how he believed student writing did improve, commenting, "Anyone who did any work within the writing unit wrote a good essay. [The differences between] the first draft and the second draft are amazing." He talked about intending to teach the unit again, but changing it to incorporate more literature and provide more time. Thus, even though Bill critiqued the Schaffer unit while teaching from it, he continued to espouse its virtues while simultaneously considering how he would change it if he were to teach it again.

Although Bill's university supervisor was critical of the curriculum, she also conceded that it was likely to be effective in its own way. She said, "I don't like that kind of rigid structure, the formulaic approach to teaching. But it does work; you can learn the formula." When pressed to say more about why she might not choose to use the curriculum, she raised her feelings that it was "repetitive and confusing for the students." However, she did not express many of these concerns to Bill, saying that, "It is not the way I would teach writing, but then that's not for me to decide." If the supervisor had elected to talk with Bill about the pros and cons of the writing curriculum, she might have found fertile ground. However, in the supervisor's construction of the activity setting of supervision, there was little room to critique existing school practices. As she saw it, her job was to support the student teacher in adapting to the practices of the school and the cooperating teacher.

Bill was hired by the school district in which he did his student teaching, but he was not assigned to teach ninth grade, the grade in which the Schaffer curriculum was still being used. Instead, he was assigned to teach tenth- and twelfth-grade English; the twelfth grade used the Pacesetter curriculum, a curriculum designed around literature and text. In his first year of teaching, Bill talked little about the teaching of writing. He mentioned that in Pacesetter, the writing students do is generally an "assessment" at the end of the unit. Department policy required tenth graders to write a multiparagraph essay on a universal theme, several creative pieces, and an in-class, timed multiparagraph essay, but did not prescribe any particular curriculum for writing instruction.

In terms of his writing instruction, Bill's first year of teaching was an utter contrast to his student-teaching experience. Instead of focusing on the format of writing, Bill used writing as a way for students to generate and synthesize ideas. For example, we saw him use quickwrites as a precursor to discussion or as a reflective wrap-up. During a lull in a discussion of *Siddhartha* in his tenth-grade class, Bill asked students to write for 5 minutes on a quotation that addressed a theme in the novel. Similarly, he introduced *Waiting for Godot* to his Pacesetter class by first having them write in response to a quotation. Bill also assigned longer writing assignments, which were written at home and turned in to be graded. In his first year of teaching, his conception of the teaching of writing seemed to have shifted to writing as idea-generator and synthesizer (freewrites), and writing as assessment (take-home essays). Bill assigned, rather than taught, writing during this year. We observed little explicit instruction in writing.

In the beginning of his second year of teaching, Bill alluded to having problems with this assign-

and-tell approach to essays and talked about how he was working to change his approach to writing. For instance, in the Pacesetter class, he introduced the essay assignment at the beginning of a unit "so that they [students] had some sense of purpose." Also, instead of treating the essay as a single monolithic assignment, he divided the essay into three distinct parts (the event, the significance of the event, and the large significance), which corresponded to the structure of the Baldwin essay they read in the unit. He also incorporated peer response (guided by teacher-formulated questions) into each of the three steps.

Peer response was not part of Bill's original implementation of the Pacesetter curriculum. When asked where he got the idea to use peer response, Bill reluctantly acknowledged that he had done some peer response in his English methods class. Bill had also incorporated aspects of Schaffer's approach, while dropping the formulaic structure of the unit. Although Bill still professed to revere the Schaffer approach, observations of his teaching reflected a less formulaic approach to scaffolding, which he supported in a variety of ways through various facets of the process. His approach to teaching writing became less prescriptive than it had been during student teaching, but more explicit than it had been during his first year. As he concluded his second year, he continued to experiment with tools for teaching writing in trying to resolve the tension he experienced between providing students with sufficient opportunities for ownership while helping them write well-developed essays.

As Bill concluded his second year of teaching, he was well regarded by colleagues, students, and administrators. An engaging, dynamic teacher, with a passion for teaching, he quickly became a recognized leader within the school. In a surprising turn, his former cooperating teacher transferred to his school, and Bill became her mentor as she began to teach the Pacesetter curriculum.

Stephanie: Writing on the Margins

Stephanie's initial beliefs about writing revealed that, although writing was not difficult for her, it also was not her passion. She valued personal, expressive writing, and through her early athletic experiences, she came to understand the importance of scaffolded learning, a concept further reinforced in her teacher education program.

Stephanie credited the teacher education program (both the Special Education and regular education programs) with helping her to understand and develop strategies for meeting the individual needs of children. She struggled over what she saw as a needed balance between "skills" and "expression," and between "direct instruction" and "writers' workshop," worrying that children need direct instruction in specific skills, but that too much structure might interfere with student ownership. At the end of coursework (before student teaching), Stephanie reconciled these tensions, in theory, by acknowledging that students need different approaches and that it is important for teachers to have "all these different ways to reach kids." In fact, she recalled her language arts professor talking about the importance of having a repertoire of teaching strategies, and she firmly believed her teacher education coursework had provided her with many good ideas for teaching writing.

However, in practice, Stephanie's student teaching experience did not provide her with many opportunities to try out ideas, work out these tensions, or experiment with pedagogical tools for teaching writing. She was not given much responsibility for writing instruction, and at times, her cooperating teacher would change Stephanie's lesson or stop her midlesson and take over. Stephanie felt that she was teaching her cooperating teacher's plan rather than her own. And, in truth, the cooperating teacher's vision of writing instruction was somewhat different from Stephanie's. The teacher described writing instruction as "you develop your skills, you see the progression, skills developing, the modeling.... I look for independent practice as well as guided." In contrast, Stephanie found this approach too tightly controlled and sequenced.

> She [my cooperating teacher] was much more scheduled with the writing, having so many sentences this day, having the draft done this day, having it edited this day, and I was hoping to set up kind of a little more of a writers' workshop format where kids could be at different stages in their writing in the classroom. The first 3 months, we spent a lot of time journal writing and getting the kids focused on the sentence structure, things like that, so we gave them a really good base, I thought, for go-

ing into a writers' workshop format. We had three adults in there for writing, so we had plenty of staff to have different centers and things. But I would have liked to have seen the writing be kind of a more of a free-form kind of thing.

At this point in her professional development, however, Stephanie was philosophical, wondering if writers' workshop would lead to enough productivity. She questioned her own goals in light of her cooperating teacher's push for content coverage and the pressure of fitting into the student teaching context. Feedback from both her cooperating teacher and university supervisor focused on Stephanie's pacing, which only further reinforced her concern about coverage. As the quote above reveals, Stephanie seemed to equate writers' workshop with more student ownership and freedom, and she had trouble reconciling how ownership and structure could coexist. Yet, she seemed quite comfortable with the teacher's explicit instruction framework and focus on writing skills, ideas that were congruent with teacher education.

During student teaching, Stephanie had opportunities to implement the type of structured writing instruction her teacher embraced. She guided students through lessons on story elements, problem/solution, and letter writing. She analyzed student learning, provided students with structured experiences and released them to work on their own. Although she was buoyed by these successful experiences, Stephanie still held on to her concern about student ownership and voice. At the conclusion of her student teaching, she noted that "even at a really young age students have different writing styles, different styles of expression, and that as important as it is to teach basic skills and basic structures of writing formats and stuff, I think that I would like to see some freedom for expression."

Stephanie's first year of full-time teaching was in a diverse, low–achieving school that had recently adopted several highly structured packaged programs, including *Cooperative Integrated Reading and Composition* (CIRC) (Stevens, Madden, Slavin, & Farnish, 1989), the Benchmarks word identification program (Gaskins & Elliot, 1991), and *QUEST 2000* (Charles et al., 1995), a math program. Stephanie was expected to use CIRC for daily reading instruction with her second-grade students. To learn the program, she attended inservice workshops and observed other teachers. For Stephanie, CIRC seemed consistent with many of the ideas she had learned in her teacher education program—alignment of learner outcomes with instruction, explicit instruction, integration of reading and writing, and the structured curriculum programs she studied in the special education program. She seemed comforted to have a program that was so well-structured and in-sync with the state curriculum. She said, "it's so well matched to the state essential learnings [the state's curriculum framework] so it's almost a little brainless for me." On the other hand, Stephanie worried that the structure and whole-class instructional format of CIRC made it difficult to meet the needs of the wide range of student abilities in her classroom, a concern that she had carried since her coursework.

Stephanie's school did not purchase the process writing component of CIRC; instead, they elected to do "Adventures in Writing," the writing portion connected to story reading. This was the only regularly scheduled writing time in Stephanie's weekly plan. Adventures in Writing integrates reading and writing by having students write in response to a prompt drawn from their weekly story (reading instruction). For example, after reading a story about pioneer and Native American children of the Great Plains, students are prompted, "If you could go back in time, which would you rather be—the pioneer or Indian child? Write one day's entry in your pretend journal that tells what you—a pioneer or Indian child—did during the day." The teacher's manual directs students to discuss their ideas with a partner, write their paragraphs, share the writing with their partner and ask what he or she likes, and then "make improvements in the story."

All the Adventures in Writing activities are structured in this way, and Stephanie followed the directions generally as they were specified in the manual. After 4 days of working with a story, Stephanie had the children work on the Adventures in Writing activity. At times, she would talk with the students a bit before writing, building some background, but the other aspects of the writing process and scaffolded instruction evident in her earlier thinking and in some of her student teaching experiences were not evident.

Stephanie liked this section of CIRC because of its structure and the opportunities it provided for students of different abilities to respond in various ways. Stephanie also recognized this activity as one of the only ways she was able to fit writing into her curriculum. There was no other writing scheduled. She viewed the activities as opportunities for students to "go off on tangents that are still related to the story" and to develop their own ideas and to have "ownership" in the story. She felt that when students "personalized and internalized" the story in this way, they would do better on the comprehension test given at the end of the week. So, although this writing fit with some of her beliefs about encouraging student voice and meeting individual student needs, she did the activities, in part to help students pass their weekly CIRC reading tests, and in part to keep pace with the other second-grade teacher using CIRC.

Although Stephanie did not have many opportunities to experiment with writing instruction during student teaching and then found herself in a highly structured program with minimal writing instruction, she still held on to several of the tools she explored during coursework, and she tried to implement them in small ways during her first year of teaching. For example, Stephanie added an "author's chair" to Adventures in Writing, a strategy modeled during her literacy methods course, so students could have more ownership and share their writing. And, a few times during the year, she actually ventured into what she called a "writers' workshop format." She described the process she was planning to use for writing scary Halloween stories:

> We're going to go through as a group really step by step with the brainstorming and then with the sloppy copy and then with the what would you change about this, the revising step. And then the editing—we'll see if we can do that in a week. Ideally, I'd like to get it where they're writing more in a real writers' workshop format where different kids are at different stages and that way I can focus more one-to-one with kids when they get to the revising or editing stage, they'll be more independent with the brainstorming and the prewriting and the drafting.

On one hand, Stephanie's classroom practices and her words revealed her appropriation of tools learned in teacher education and her continuing struggle to balance structure and ownership. She continued to view writers' workshop as a goal that would help her address individual needs of students. On the other hand, writers' workshop and process writing seemed somewhat confounded for Stephanie at this time, and as a result, most of the student writing was first-draft, on-demand writing done in response to reading (CIRC) or in other subject areas.

In her second year of teaching, Stephanie continued to use CIRC and continued not to have a specially designated time for writing instruction. However, the nature and amount of student writing changed, as did Stephanie's willingness to question her programs and implement a wider range of pedagogical tools from teacher education. She scheduled writing journals, both free responses and writing in response to a prompt, more regularly to "encourage writing, to make writing fun, and to personalize it for them so they are not always just writing for an assignment." Similarly, she continued to encourage different genres and purposes for writing, convinced that students should see that writing is connected to real life. In addition, Stephanie engaged her students in several longer writing projects, such as writing second-grade stories and instructions for Amelia Bedelia, each of which was taken through the entire writing process. Stephanie recognized the limitations of her writing program, yet she felt she could not take the time from CIRC to do more. She acknowledged that

> CIRC writing isn't a complete enough writing program for me. We get lots of different genres in, we talk a lot about sentence format...but there's more I would like to do with writing than that—going through the full writing process. Adventures in Writing is fun and really, as useful as it is, [the students] don't create that much of a finished product. And I could change it so that they did, but that's not how I want to use the time schedule.

Stephanie recognized a possible solution to the problem but chose not to act on it. She did, however, take a more active role in shaping her curriculum by making changes inside the CIRC program.

With encouragement from her principal, Stephanie and two colleagues began to work on revisions to CIRC that would eventually be shared with other colleagues. Their aim was to modify this whole-class program to meet the range of abilities in their second-grade classrooms. In the meantime, using strategies from teacher education, Stephanie modified CIRC and Adventures in Writing within her own classroom in an effort to address the problems she had identified in her first year. For example, she did more in-depth prewriting activities before students began their responses to Adventures in Writing, and she sometimes linked CIRC reading and writing activities through skill instruction rather than simply by topic. So, rather than simply using writing to respond to reading, Stephanie tried to create new opportunities to provide explicit writing instruction within the structure of CIRC.

Stephanie clearly struggled with the demands of delivering the CIRC program and, as evident from the chapter-opening quote, she still, in her second year of teaching, felt uncertain about the concept and the management of writers' workshop; in fact, she felt "guilty" not using writers' workshop. Seen as a strong teacher by her colleagues and principal, Stephanie assumed new leadership roles as a CIRC trainer, cooperating teacher, and representative to the district literacy committee. She used those opportunities to reflect on and further appropriate pedagogical tools she had explored in teacher education, clear that it was "good for me to really try to think about and justify why I do what I do and what do the kids need." Although she continued to teach CIRC as it was required, Stephanie began to make important changes both within and on the margins of the program.

Charles: Scaffolding All the Way

Charles came to teacher education with a strong background in writing and positive school writing experiences. Throughout his college experience as an English major and his early school experiences, Charles valued his teachers' high expectations, specific feedback, and concern for him as a writer. Charles carried this vision of teaching into his early work as a tutor and mentor for high school students, and later into his teaching.

Like Stephanie, Charles was also in the Special Education/Regular Education track of the teacher education program. For him, these two tracks seemed to complement each other rather than cause dissonance between the highly structured direct instruction approach he studied in Special Education and the more process-oriented approaches he studied in his literacy classes. In fact, he integrated ideas he learned in both programs rather seamlessly into his vision of good language arts instruction and his early practice. He believed that students need to understand and experience writing for many different purposes and have ownership in their work. At the same time, he acknowledged that without the specific tools of effective writing, his students would be at a disadvantage. And he saw his job in teacher education as learning strategies that would help him maximize each child's abilities.

Although Charles came into the program with a strong background and positive experiences, he emphatically credited his professors and coursework for his conceptualizations about writing and for his understanding of instruction—specifically the concept of scaffolding and the importance of having a range of pedagogical tools. He attributed his understanding to the modeling and practice his professors provided in class.

Charles's student teaching placement in a fourth-grade urban setting supported what he had learned in the teacher education program, and in fact, his cooperating teacher's description of good language arts instruction echoed many of the elements Charles described as part of his coursework. She defines good language arts instruction as

> Very clear direction, very clear instruction, and direct instruction.... This is the concept I'm going to teach...we're going to do some examples of it. You're going to do it on your own, and then you're going to apply it. Actually carry children through the steps so that by the time you've finished the concept, and it may be an ongoing thing for a very long time...the children will be able to reach the highest level of thinking, which is applying what they've learned and making connections.

Elements of modeling, explicit instruction, practice, and release of responsibility were clearly evident in the teacher's explicit instruction model. Less evident, but mentioned in her interviews, were references to giving students meaningful purposes for writing, student ownership, and meeting individual needs, ideas that were very important to Charles. Although the teacher's approach was strongly guided by an explicit instruction model, she supported Charles's experimentation and encouraged him to rely on his conceptual understandings and strategies for good instruction rather than on prescribed curriculum or on one instructional model. She urged him to "just take what's out there already, and from that you can build what you're going to do and be creative. But first you need to start with what's out there...and pick and choose....Then from that develop your own things—things you want to do."

Charles believed this way of thinking about teaching made it easier for him to do what he wanted to do. So, in addition to student teaching with someone who had a similar vision of teaching and who modeled many of the strategies he had encountered in teacher education, Charles was encouraged to experiment with practical strategies from a conceptual basis, and most important, he saw the opportunity and took it. He said, "The best stuff I've had has been being able to try things out and see what works and what doesn't work and having her [the cooperating teacher] to fall back on if I really screw up, or if I really do good, for her to point those things out." With this compatibility between the cooperating teacher's philosophy and the concepts and pedagogy learned in teacher education, Charles taught process writing, conferenced with students, integrated writing into other subject areas, taught lessons on "six-traits,"[4] held writers' workshops, used journals with the students, and experimented with levels of scaffolding. We saw him implement and heard him talk about using task analysis to be sure that teaching was logical and, at the same time, using assessment and knowledge of his students to make sure instruction was at an appropriate level of difficulty. At the

---

[4] Six-trait writing refers to an analytic model of assessing and thinking about student writing. Developed by the Northwest Regional Educational Laboratory, the traits include ideas, organization, voice, words, fluency, and conventions.

end of his teacher education program, Charles had developed a deep commitment to scaffolded instruction and possessed a range of strategies for implementing it in practice:

> I think my goals are still the same [as when I entered the program], but it's how to get to those goals now [that is] different. Whereas now I have this whole idea of scaffolding which is something that probably I had an idea about, but now I have something concrete to think about when I'm planning a lesson.

Charles was recruited and hired at the school where he student-taught. In his first year as a third-grade teacher, he reflected his cooperating teachers' advice as he talked about trying to find a style of teaching that worked for him. But unlike Stephanie, Charles was freer to find his style because there were fewer constraints on what and how he taught. There were, however, two overarching districtwide guideposts for his writing instruction: one was the district curriculum guide, which lists learning outcomes for students at each grade, and the other was the district's emphasis on six-trait writing, which was the basis of the district- and statewide writing assessment. Charles described his curriculum as "basically just that we focus on those six traits—[and] for [the students] to be able to write a personal letter, expository piece, narrative piece and a persuasive piece. Those are the expectations."

Within these general guidelines, Charles implemented many of the pedagogical tools he learned and practiced in teacher education coursework and during student teaching. For example, within writers' workshop, which was scheduled for 40 minutes each day, Charles taught minilessons, held writing conferences, integrated writing with other subject areas, and carefully scaffolded and supported his students' learning. He also made sure to attend to district outcomes for his grade, such as six-traits and specific genres, and to prepare his students for the standardized test given at his grade level. In some ways, these district policies and expectations provided a scaffold to guide Charles's decisions about curriculum, but the rest was up to him. Rather than hampering his instruction, however, such guidelines seemed to provide Charles with some structure within which he could implement the pedagogical tools he had so well appropriated from teacher education.

Even as a first-year teacher, Charles was able to create a cohesive writing program for his students; he strategically pulled from the district curriculum guide, his language arts textbooks, and his bank of pedagogical tools to essentially construct his own program. For example, he developed a writing project based on a play the students had seen, engaging students in developing and publishing their own versions of the play, and using instructional strategies such as story maps, peer editing, and conferencing to guide the students. Even when he felt a need to do Daily Oral Language as other teachers in his school were doing to prepare students for the standardized test, Charles reconstructed the activity as Daily Editing Practice to make it fit with students' experiences with process writing.

Charles retained his reflective stance toward his teaching of writing throughout his first year. Although he did not feel confident about his writing instruction and said that he let it "slide" the first year, he was continually assessing his own instruction and his students' learning. He realized that writers' workshop did not occur every day as he had planned, nor were students writing as much as he wanted. He also worried that he might be too directive in his instruction and wanted to find a balance between what he called "direct instruction" and "exploration." He developed a new goal, to find such a balance, in the context of his teaching—a goal that influenced his decisions in the subsequent year.

In his second year of teaching, Charles continued to develop his curriculum and pedagogical strategies and to act on his concerns from his first year. In keeping with the district's focus on the direct writing assessment and the six traits, Charles set a goal of having his students write well in narrative, expository, and persuasive modes, and demonstrate "control" over three or four of the traits. For him, the emphasis on six traits was more than a district push; he felt it provided diagnostic information, "something to inform your instruction—you have a language, you have a way to think about it, to talk about it.... It means a lot more than the writing section on the ITBS. What does that tell you?"

Charles's second-year goals also included having his students enjoy writing. He felt that he had been inconsistent the previous year about having students write every day and that they needed time to practice and get comfortable with writing. He had students keep two kinds of journals, expanded opportunities to integrate writing with social studies and science, and instituted writers' workshop every day.

As evident from his description of writers' workshop at the beginning of this article, Charles continued to balance his explicit instruction ("mini-lessons") with student ownership and engagement. His writing lessons were quite structured, providing students with strategies and models for writing, yet Charles viewed these models as supports rather than blueprints, encouraging students to "use them or not" as they created their own work. He was proud of how, in his second year, he found better approaches for teaching students skills and strategies for writing so they had the "tools" to help them write well. We observed several sophisticated lessons, part of a 2-week project on poetry in which Charles balanced explicit instruction with student engagement and exploration as students were scaffolded through the entire writing process to final published pieces. Whole-class lessons were supported with small-group and individual follow-up and with many opportunities for students to work collaboratively.

At the end of his second year, Charles had accomplished many of the goals he had set for himself, and in contrast with his first year, he felt more successful at teaching writing than any other subject. He used and adapted what he learned from district inservice programs, his principal, and his own practice to continue to build his vision and repertoire of tools for good writing instruction.

What Teachers Appropriated and Why: Cross-Case Themes

The Power of Ideas, the Need for Practical Tools

Teacher education most definitely provided these teachers with a set of conceptual tools for teaching writing, including the importance of ownership, the concepts of instructional scaffolding and writers' workshop, and a process orientation to writing. Teachers talked fluently about these concepts as they planned and reflected on their lessons,

and we observed classroom practices that supported these ideas. Although few teachers directly attributed their understanding to teacher education, we were able to map the development of these concepts back to coursework. These conceptual tools provided guiding frameworks for the teachers as they began teaching and made decisions about what and how to teach.

Two of the most useful conceptual tools for teaching writing that the beginning teachers appropriated from their coursework were the concepts of instructional scaffolding and writing process. All of the teachers explicitly used the term *scaffolding* to talk about their teaching, and we saw evidence of the principles of scaffolding (as it was presented in the teacher education program) in their teaching. All the teachers also attended to elements of writing process in their instruction. However, the ways in which they appropriated and used the concept varied in response both to the pedagogy of teacher education classes and the various contexts in which they found themselves working. Although the secondary teachers had begun to appropriate some important conceptual tools, they bemoaned their lack of practical knowledge. In contrast, the elementary teachers felt well prepared, both conceptually and practically, for the challenges of teaching writing. However, the classroom context did not always support the practices they had learned.

The concept of scaffolding appears rather prominently in the materials from the secondary language arts methods course. Students were required to read an article on instructional scaffolding (Langer & Applebee, 1986), and the rubric for assessing lesson plans for teaching writing specifically used the language of instructional scaffolding. In their lesson plans, students were asked to provide opportunities for student engagement and ownership and to provide support for student learning. The language also appears in the guidelines for other assignments.

While the concept was initially introduced in the language arts methods course, aspects of scaffolding were also introduced in other courses, such as the courses on learning and assessment. The course on learning theory emphasized the importance of student ownership in learning, and also drew from Bruner's work on instruction (1960). The assessment course provided extensive scaffolding for the development of a unit plan and assessments. However, although the methods course introduced the concept of scaffolding in relation to the teaching of writing, students were not explicitly taught *how* to scaffold student writing. Some students' comments address this directly: "Writing process theory was too much learning about and not enough learning how to implement." Another student commented on the need for more concrete examples, stating, "I crave practical, concrete discussion...deep understanding must include learning how to implement theory and serendipity."

The strategy for teaching writing that the secondary teachers mention most frequently is modeling. One student wrote, "One of the ways learning occurs is by being provided with an authentic example and the modeling of it." Another student teacher commented that "I knew how to model how I read for 'theme' in a novel...and I modeled what they would be doing in writing." Although evidence of students' appropriation of modeling as a strategy continued to be apparent in their classroom practice, they did not seem to have a range of other strategies for teaching writing. Although many of them initially loved Nancie Atwell's workshop approach, but they also began to see the difficulties in orchestrating such complex instruction. One beginning teacher said,

> I still wrestle with the dilemma between letting students write what is meaningful to them, but which may not challenge them, and teaching them to write in ways that push them beyond their comfort zone, but that they may not have any personal connections to. While I admire Nancie Atwell's ability to handle this dilemma brilliantly, I don't feel that I have the experience or energy at this point to resolve it myself.

Perhaps more important, the concepts provided by the student-teachers' methods course were not necessarily buttressed with a range of practical tools. As they criticized the course for not being practical enough, the student teachers eagerly sought materials and methods from other sources. Bill acquired the Schaffer materials in the powerful context of student teaching. The workshop he attended and the written materials for the unit supported many of the concepts Bill had already encountered in teacher education, and the experienced teachers with whom he was working offered an enthusiastic response to the program. Bill's equally enthusiastic endorsement of the curriculum convinced his peers in the program to try out the materials as well.

Nancy, another high school teacher in our study, had a very similar experience with the Jane Schaffer materials. In her first year of teaching, she struggled to find ways to teach writing to her students. Nancy explicitly stated that she did not have the tools she needed to teach writing. Referring back to her teacher education coursework, she claimed, "No one has ever taught me how to teach essay writing, ever.... Methods class wasn't very good." Nancy initially resisted using the Schaffer materials. She commented,

> The older teachers...tend to use Jane Schaffer's write-by-number technique, where they do a paragraph consisting of a topic sentence and they write a topic sentence till they turn blue and then it consists of a chunk, and a chunk is one point of fact or a concrete detail to two points of commentary and you do that, three chunks, and then a concluding sentence, and there's your paragraph...it's like filling in the blanks... My philosophy is that no one writes that way. The way you're going to become a good writer is to just do it—writing is not something that you can necessarily teach, writing is something that you do and then work with from there.

Nancy's comment that "writing is not something that you can necessarily teach" reflects her own uncertainty about what her ideas imply for classroom practice. She ultimately decided to adopt the Schaffer curriculum, in part because it solved a pressing problem for her—how to teach essay writing to her students.

We see the teachers' adoption of the Jane Schaffer materials as evidence, somewhat ironically, of their partial appropriation of certain conceptual tools from the program, including the concepts of scaffolding, process writing, and equity. They use these concepts to explain and critique the materials. At the same time, their adoption of such a structured and formulaic approach seems to suggest an even more partial appropriation of the issues of ownership, and writing as exploration and negotiation that were also addressed in their program.

The materials solved a pressing problem for these beginning teachers, as they struggled to teach writing without a range of strategies. In fact, one interpretation of our data is that the unit plan itself served as a scaffolding for the teachers' learning. The unit plan shaped their understandings of scaffolding and writing process. While Nancy initially rejected the materials because they seemed formulaic to her, they also reinforced her understanding of scaffolding as a step-by-step, linear process. Although all the teachers who used the unit continued to profess their support for its outcomes, they also adapted the model in various ways, taking language and strategies from the materials without necessarily following the blueprint rigidly.

The elementary program (and the dual endorsement program in special education, in particular) strongly emphasized the concept of scaffolding. Like the secondary program, scaffolding was also discussed in courses on learning and assessment, and like the secondary program, the text presented a workshop approach to teaching writing (Calkins, 1994). However, the elementary instructors placed the workshop model along a continuum of approaches to structuring writing instruction, discussing various models and strategies for teaching and engaging students in process writing and directly addressing the pros and cons of writers' workshop. The course assignments required students to teach a multiday writing project with some attention to process writing but not necessarily within a workshop model.

Practical and conceptual tools were intertwined in the pedagogy of the literacy methods course. The instructors introduced a range of strategies such as conferencing, journal writing, peer editing groups, modeling, and author's chair as ways to scaffold students' writing. The instructors modeled these approaches in the classroom and then debriefed the approaches from both a conceptual and practical perspective. Charles argued how important this modeling was for his own learning:

> The first quarter, one thing I really appreciated about the class as a teacher was [the professor] scaffolded and showed us how she was scaffolding. But as a student, just the fact that she scaffolded and the whole process of doing modeling and being really explicit about the modeling and assessing all along the way—doing modeling, doing guided practice,

doing the guided independent work, all the way assessing how students are doing—that whole framework...also changed the way I approach the way I teach.

Of all the teachers, Charles most fully appropriated the concepts of scaffolding and writing process into his teaching. In part, this reflected the context in which he worked. He worked for 3 years at the same school—a school that supported his understanding of writing instruction—as both a student and full-time teacher. Unlike Stephanie and Bill, he did not work within a prescribed curriculum that might conflict with his ideas. He was able to create assignments and curriculum that reflected what he knew. In contrast, the other teachers initially had to work around the edges of a prescribed curriculum. The power of ideas, then, is tempered by the pragmatics of the settings in which teachers work.

The Press of Curriculum Materials

Perhaps one of the most striking findings from the first year of full-time teaching has to do with the power of curriculum materials. The curricular materials that beginning teachers encounter can dramatically influence their learning. The teachers in our study inherited a wide range of curricular materials their first year of teaching, from general rubrics, such as the six traits of writing, to curriculum guidelines, to packaged programs such as CIRC. During the first year of teaching, the beginning teachers generally welcomed curricular materials for teaching writing. As the teaching of writing can be a messy, chaotic endeavor, the appeal of a packaged approach cannot be ignored.

In addition, some of these programs, such as CIRC and the Jane Schaffer materials, included many of the concepts that the student teachers learned in teacher education. The introduction to the Jane Schaffer unit, for example, stresses the importance of explicitly teaching students to write, not just assigning writing and then grading it. So in many ways, the unit seems to support the conceptual tools students had learned. What presents a rather stark contrast, however, is the lack of any ownership for students in their writing. The content or purpose of writing is less important than mastering the formula. In some of the same ways, CIRC also echoed concepts emphasized in the teacher education program. It offered structure and attention to student ownership and voice, concepts learned in the teacher education program. Because Stephanie used only the reading portion of CIRC, she did not expect it to provide guidance for process writing or writers' workshop. Instead she took advantage of the writing prompts to satisfy her desire for student ownership and personal response, albeit in response to reading. However, the time demands of CIRC and its limited attention to writing instruction precluded the possibility of having a fully developed process writing program. Interestingly, the CIRC manual suggests that students spend 3 days responding to a prompt so they can go through the writing process. Ironically, Stephanie did not realize this until her second year when she was preparing to teach a class on CIRC. The CIRC reading manual did not provide enough support for a teacher who had not fully appropriated process writing, and there was not enough time in the schedule to break away from the curriculum materials. These factors, combined with the schoolwide emphasis on reading and Stephanie's partial appropriation and confounding of process writing and writers' workshop, led to a somewhat fragmented writing program.

Bill and Nancy seemed to understand the tension between the Jane Schaffer materials and some of their other ideas for teaching, but their own need for classroom strategies took precedence. Nancy, for example, comments that she has made a deliberate choice to defer thinking about ownership:

> I've chosen my battles, I've set my goals, and right now ownership is not one of the things that I'm working towards. Later on down the road, I might say, OK now let's see if we can incorporate ownership into this mess, but I'm not professionally ready to even think about it. I'm still working on scaffolding writing process, conventions, and integrating all those together. I'm not ready.

This tension between ownership and structure was also reflected in the teachers' reassessment of the texts used in their literacy and language arts methods courses. One of the group interviews revealed that although teachers originally loved the Atwell and Calkins texts used in the program, they eventually saw them as not very useful in their own classrooms. Hannah, one of the other beginning elementary teachers in our study commented,

> What's interesting is Lucy Calkins is big on the ownership, but not huge on the structure, I don't think, in the sense of the scaffolding and the structure part.... I think she believes in all the stages, but it seems like taking the time to scaffold it along the way, teaching the six traits, and all the different things that go along with being a successful writer isn't there, so you need more, I think.

This teacher's comments illustrate her appropriation of a number of concepts from teacher education, including scaffolding, six traits, and the stages of the writing process. She uses these concepts to critique Calkins, couching her critique in the tension between structure and ownership.

This tension between structure and ownership in the teaching of writing has a long history within the field of composition. Different traditions in composition studies resolve this tension in different ways. The expressivist tradition puts the primary emphasis on the writer's voice, while other traditions, such as the current traditional rhetoric, emphasize the importance of mastering fixed rhetorical structures (c.f. Berlin, 1982; Gere, 1986). The struggle that these beginning teachers engaged in, then, is part of a much longer struggle over the definition of the subject matter. The curriculum materials they encountered in the field bear remnants of various movements and theories, but rarely are these made explicit to beginning teachers. They saw their struggles over the tension between structure and ownership as private ones, reflective of their own lack of experience, rather than as larger issues within the field of language arts. This perceived tension between structure and ownership became a problem that the beginning teachers needed to solve. The particular curriculum materials they encountered influenced the ways in which they solved this problem.

By the second year of teaching, there is some evidence that the teachers had begun to critique and repair curriculum materials. Bill confronted the importance of ownership in students' writing and the difficulty of fostering ownership while teaching a formula. The curriculum materials became both a foil for the development of his own thinking, as well as a pedagogical tool he felt he could adapt for different purposes. Allison, another teacher in this study, who remained committed to the Schaffer unit, also began to adapt the materials in her second year of teaching. In using the CIRC materials in her first year of teaching, Stephanie found very few opportunities to engage students in more process-oriented writing. However, by her second year of teaching, she added more journal writing, opportunities for sharing, and process writing projects to her curriculum, and she adapted the CIRC writing prompts to provide more opportunities for her students to write in more open-ended ways.

Pentimento

Perhaps what is most striking across these cases is the teachers' ability to hold on to important concepts, even when they were trying practices that were antithetical in certain ways to their initial conceptions. The pedagogical tools emphasized in teacher education reappeared in the second year of teaching when the teachers talked explicitly about worrying about how to teach *well*. They use concepts from the teacher education program, such as student ownership and voice, to critique aspects of the practices they adopted during their first year of teaching. Other teachers talked of hearing the voices of their teacher educators as they reflected on their teaching. Frank, one of the middle school teachers in our study, commented, "One of [my professors said] 'don't waste students' time...there's a lot better things they could be doing, [so] if you're going to make them sit down and do work, you better make it worthwhile.... I don't use their time wisely, and I wanted to get better at it."

Teacher education provided a vision of ideal practice, an image of how teachers thought their classrooms should ultimately run. As one participant commented, what she got from a course on interdisciplinary curriculum was "that I understood the way it should look like. What an ideal, integrated program should include." Teachers talked of holding themselves to higher standards in their second year of teaching as they tried to get closer to their vision of teaching language arts.

One of the skills these teachers attributed to teacher education is the ability to reflect on their own teaching. In the first group interview, the teachers joked about becoming "giant reflectors" as a result of the constant emphasis on reflective practice. But the habit of reflection, built into their program, endured into their first 2 years of teaching. Reflection provided the catalyst for the reemergence of some of the pedagogical tools in their second year of teaching. Reflective practice depends on having a set of ideas on which to reflect. In the process of rethinking their practice, the teachers used concepts from the teacher education program to help them make sense of their successes and failures. For example, in her first year of teaching, Stephanie did not encourage invented spelling, something that had been suggested in her methods course. She returned to it in her second year, even after attending a workshop where the presenter "blasted" invented spelling, because it struck her that her students "are not going to be writers if they can't do invented spelling. It'll kill them if they have to focus on correctness of spelling. And also, it would kill me." Pedagogical tools developed during teacher education provided a set of frames through which to view teaching and a technical language to make sense of what teachers were experiencing.

Implications for Teacher Education

The Vision Thing

Teacher education can play an important role in helping preservice teachers to construct a set of tools for teaching writing and language arts more generally. The concepts of scaffolding, process writing, and student ownership all help to create a vision of writing instruction toward which beginning teachers can work. Even when the teachers in our study found it difficult to attain this vision in their first year of teaching, they continued to use these tools to critique their own practice and to make sense of their experience.

Conceptual tools, however, need to be exemplified by practical tools and strategies in order for teachers to more fully appropriate them. A vision can seem terribly insubstantial without the concrete strategies to attain it. The success of methods courses for teaching writing seemed to rest, in part, on the extent to which students were able to gain tools for implementing the concepts they were learning.

Theory becomes real only through practice. Without such practical tools and the opportunities to try them, teachers may not continue to develop their understandings of concepts such as ownership or recursive processes in writing. However, if teachers appropriate practical tools that are not grounded in concepts, they may find it difficult to critique new strategies and curriculum materials or to envision alternatives.

Providing teachers with pedagogical tools for teaching is important but not sufficient. Teacher educators must provide opportunities for preservice teachers to experience these tools in practice. Teachers' more refined understandings of the tools emerged through the activity of teaching and learning. Student teaching has traditionally been the way in which teachers experiment with what they have learned in coursework, but our study, as well as the literature on student teaching, would suggest that student teaching can constrain, as well as encourage, experimentation (Dewey, 1965; Zeichner & Gore, 1990). Another widely used approach is for professors to model these tools in the teacher education classroom and then debrief the modeling with students. Yet another approach is to use other materials from practice, including videotapes or hypermedia, to provide experience with a range of pedagogical tools (Lampert & Ball, 1998). Another, still, is for teacher education programs to support teachers in their early years of teaching as they navigate the complexities of learning to teach. This study, in part, provided such an arena for beginning teachers to continue to reflect on their teaching.

Beyond coursework, our data suggest that student teaching continues to be a setting that powerfully influences the ways in which teachers appropriate knowledge. Charles, for example, was able to see a variety of tools discussed in teacher education used in the classroom of his cooperating teacher. However, it is not clear that student teaching placements must be consistent with coursework to be valuable. For some preservice teachers, a contrasting placement encouraged them to think more deeply about the concepts and strategies they had learned in coursework (c.f. Hollingsworth, 1989). In fact, two of the most successful beginning teachers in our study were in student teaching placements that did not exemplify the best of what they had learned. They continued to appropriate knowledge, however, because they were supported in taking a reflective stance toward these experiences.

Predictable Problems

One of the striking findings of this study was the degree to which these beginning teachers, teaching at different grade levels and in different contexts, were struggling with some of the same underlying issues. The dilemma of balancing the need for student ownership with attention to structure in the teaching of writing represents one such problem. Teacher education could play more of a role in identifying predictable dilemmas in the teaching of writing, as well as literacy more generally, and helping preservice teachers negotiate responses to these dilemmas. Teacher educators could showcase curriculum materials that exemplify different responses to these problems. Rather than ignore packaged curriculum materials, teacher education should provide opportunities for students to bring their reflective stance to these materials during coursework. In the throes of the first year of teaching, it is difficult for teachers to question programs or to have the time, support, and confidence to adapt them to their developing conceptions of teaching.

Our study suggests the danger of making claims about what teachers did and did not learn in teacher education based on data from their first year of teaching. Teacher education can affect how beginning teachers think about teaching writing, even if the ideas are not fully appropriated into their classroom practice in the first year. The pedagogical tools provided by teacher education, along with a reflective stance toward teaching, provided these teachers with a vision of teaching writing that has stayed with them. Like paint on a canvas that reemerges with time, concepts and ideas began to resurface in important ways in the second year of teaching. Tools that seemed superfluous during the difficult first year of teaching suddenly found use as second-year teachers reconstructed their understandings and practice.

Context also matters. Aspects of school and district context, including curriculum materials and professional development opportunities, can support or thwart continuing learning and fuller appropriation of ideas and practices for teaching writing. Whether or not Stephanie figures out how to incorporate writers' workshop or process writing into her curriculum will depend as much on her school context as her own developing understanding. Whether or not Nancy reincorporates ideas of student ownership into her practice will undoubtedly be affected by her school district's formal adoption of the Jane Schaffer materials.

All these teachers are off to a strong start in teaching. Now in their third year in the classroom, many of them have taken on leadership positions in their schools and districts, including the roles of team leader, mentor teacher, and professional development facilitator. While they are still very much learning to teach writing, teacher education provided these teachers with a set of tools with which to continue their learning and refine their practice. In the relatively brief amount of time allotted for the professional preparation of teachers, providing tools that enable teachers to continue their development may be the most important legacy of all.

This chapter has been reprinted with permission from the National Reading Conference.

An earlier version of this paper was presented at the annual meeting of the American Educational Research Association, Montreal, Canada, April 1999. We would like to acknowledge our colleagues Peter Smagorinsky and Jane Agee, with whom we are collaborating on a larger study of four teacher education programs. Special thanks to Marsha Buly, Joanne Carney, Jeannine Dingus, Miriam Hirschenstein, and Joelle Jay for their contributions to this research. We would also like to thank Arthur Applebee, Deborah Ball, Mary Kennedy, Judith Langer, George Newell, Susan Florio-Ruane, and Peter Smagorinsky for their helpful responses to earlier versions of this paper. This work has been funded by the Center for English Learning and Achievement and the Center for Teaching and Policy (both through OERI), and the University of Washington, Seattle.

REFERENCES

Atwell, N. (1987). *In the middle: Writing, reading & learning with adolescents.* Portsmouth, NH: Heinemann.

Au, K.H. (1993). *Literacy instruction in multicultural settings.* Fort Worth, TX: Holt, Rinehart & Winston.

Berlin, J. (1982). Contemporary composition: The major pedagogical theories. *College English, 44.*

Bruner, J. (1960). *The process of education.* Cambridge, MA: Harvard University Press.

Calkins, L.M. (1994). *The art of teaching writing.* Portsmouth, NH: Heinemann.

Charles, R., Bennett, D., Brummet, C., Wortsman, R., Hartcourt, L., Barnett, C.S., & Kelley, B. (1995). *Quest 2000: Exploring mathematics.* Menlo Park, CA; Addison Wesley.

Cole, M. (1996) *Cultural psychology: A once and future discipline.* Cambridge, MA: Harvard University Press.

Dewey, J. (1965). The relationship of theory to practice. In M. Borrowman (Ed.), *Teacher education in America: A document of history* (pp. 140–171). New York: Teachers College Press. (Original work published 1904)

Engestrom, Y. (1999). Activity theory and individual and social transformation. In Y. Engestrom, R. Miettinen, & R. Punamaki (Eds.), *Perspectives on activity theory* (pp. 19–38). New York: Cambridge University Press.

Gaskins, I.W., & Elliot, T.T. (1991). *Implementing cognitive strategy instruction across school: The Benchmark manual for teachers.* Cambridge, MA: Brookline Books.

Gere, A.R. (1986). Teaching writing: The major theories. In A. Petrosky & D. Bartholomae (Eds.), *The teaching of writing. 85th Yearbook of the National Society for the Study of Education* (pp. 30–48). Chicago: University of Chicago Press.

Grossman, P.L., Smagorinsky, P., & Valencia, S.W. (1999). Appropriating tools for teaching English: A theoretical framework for research on learning to teach. *American Journal of Education, 108,* 1–29.

Hollingsworth, S. (1989). Prior beliefs and cognitive change in learning to teach. *American Educational Research Journal, 26,* 160–190.

Lampert, M., & Ball, D.L. (1998). *Teaching multimedia and mathematics.* New York: Teachers College Press.

Langer, J.A., & Applebee, A.N. (1986). Reading and writing instruction: Toward a theory of teaching and learning. In E.C. Rothkopf (Ed.), *Review of Research in Education, 13,* 171–194.

Lave, J. (1988). *Cognition in practice.* Cambridge, UK: Cambridge University Press.

Leont'ev, A.N. (1981). *Problems of the development of mind.* Moscow: Progress Publishers.

Newman, D., Griffin, P., & Cole, M. (1989). *The construction zone: Working for cognitive change in school.* New York: Cambridge University Press.

Schaffer, J. (1995). *Teaching the multiparagraph essay: A sequential nine-week unit.* San Diego, CA: Jane Schaffer Publications.

Stevens, R.J., Madden, N.A., Slavin, R.E., & Farnish, A.M. (1989). Cooperative integrated reading and composition: Two field experiments. *Reading Research Quarterly, 22,* 433–454.

Tulviste, P. (1991). *The cultural-historical development of verbal thinking* (M.J. Hall, Trans.). Commack, NY: Nova Science Publishers.

Wertsch, J.V. (1981). The concept of activity in Soviet psychology: An introduction. In J.V. Wertsch (Ed. & Trans.), *The concept of activity in Soviet psychology* (pp. 3–36). Armonk, NY: Sharpe.

Wertsch, J.V. (1991). *Voices of the mind.* Cambridge, MA: Harvard University Press.

Zeichner, K.A. & Gore, J. (1990). Teacher socialization. In W.R. Houston (Ed.), *Handbook of research on teacher education* (pp. 329–348). New York: Macmillan.

CHAPTER 5

"I'm still figuring out how to do this teaching thing": A cross-site analysis of reading preparation programs on beginning teachers' instructional practices and decisions

Amy Seely Flint and Christine H. Leland
INDIANA UNIVERSITY

Beth Patterson, James V. Hoffman, Misty W. Sailors, Marg A. Mast, and Lori Czop Assaf
THE UNIVERSITY OF TEXAS—AUSTIN

Learning to teach is never easy, despite some popular myths to the contrary. "Figuring out how to do it" is a challenge for all who join the profession, as well as for those who guide them in this effort. The challenge level has increased in recent years as the focus on schools and the quality of schooling has become increasingly critical. The crisis rhetoric offered by the media often centers on the "reading problem" and the failure of teachers to help students meet what society regards as reasonable standards for a basic education (Berliner & Biddle, 1995). Such attacks are often not far removed from a causal explanation arguing that most teachers are not receiving the quality of preparation they need to be effective (Brady & Moats, 1997). Although the validity of these attacks has been challenged, there is no question that the policy community and the public at large have accepted them as true and are demanding change. At stake is whether the direction of this change will enhance the quality of reading teacher preparation—or set

the profession back decades. We take the position that the more quality data that can be inserted into this conversation, the more likely change will be truly beneficial to teachers and students.

In the spring of 1999, the International Reading Association (IRA) formed a National Commission to identify the qualities and characteristics of effective teacher preparation in the area of reading. A large-scale research program consisting of a series of smaller, coordinated studies has been initiated. One of these studies is the Beginning Teacher Study, whose research focuses on uncovering the influence and relationship between preparation programs, including reading methods courses and fieldwork, and first-year teachers' decision-making practices regarding reading instruction and pedagogy. More specifically, the Beginning Teacher Study addresses the following questions: (1) How does what first-year teachers report doing in reading instruction compare with their own preparation programs and with their school's beliefs about reading instruction? and (2) What might be some features of preparation programs that are valued and enacted by beginning teachers in their first year of teaching? Graduates from eight universities and/or colleges that reflect a broad range of 4-year undergraduate degree programs are being studied as they enter and work through their first 2 years of teaching. The eight sites identified are Florida International University; Hunter College; Indiana University; Norfolk State University; University of Nevada, Reno; University of Texas—Austin; University of Texas, San Antonio; and University of Sioux Falls.

In this chapter we report on the findings from two of the eight sites, Indiana University (IU) and the University of Texas—Austin (UT). These two sites were selected for this first phase of analysis because of their similarities—both are large public universities that offer students the opportunity to specialize in reading. Both sites identified comparison groups, which consist of graduates at the same institution (at the same time and with similar backgrounds) who did not participate in the reading specialization programs. We are careful in our inclusion of these graduates to not view them as a "control" group in a traditional experimental research design term. Rather, we regard them as offering a possible perspective for interpreting the effects of program content and experiences. This analysis is aimed to provide those involved in teacher education with a greater understanding of how two successful reading specialization programs are shaping the ways in which beginning teachers conceptualize and enact reading instruction in their first few years of teaching.

The findings from these two sites suggest that the beginning phases of teacher practice reveal important information regarding the effectiveness of teacher education programs that specialize in reading instruction. In this chapter, we first describe the programs, the data collection and analysis, and the findings within the two sites. We take a two-case study approach and present the similarities and differences among graduates from each university. Next we discuss how the findings from these two sites relate to the work on identifying critical features of the commission site programs. We conclude with a description of "next steps" in the research, highlighting the specific ways in which our current findings are framing the analysis at the remaining six sites, as well as our questions and procedures for the second year of the study.

Program Descriptions for the University of Texas—Austin and Indiana University

The University of Texas—Austin and Indiana University are two large public universities that offer students choices in content emphasis and in structure in their 4-year, elementary teacher preparation programs; in other words, they offer programs within programs.

UT offers the choice of a general elementary plan as well as a reading specialization cohort plan. Other options (such as bilingual or early childhood) are also offered as specialization options, but graduates of these programs are not being considered in the context of this study. The general elementary education students take 6 semester hours of reading/language arts methods courses. Their professional development program is spread over 2 semesters (one observation and one student teaching). Reading specialization students follow a 3-semester cohort plan that is school-based and involves tutorials with adult literacy students as well as supervised tutorials with children in an elementary school. These reading specialization students complete an additional 6 semester hours of reading courses beyond the regular education students (12 semester hours total).

Indiana University has two campuses involved in the beginning teacher study—Indiana University, Bloomington (IUB) and Indiana University–Purdue University, Indianapolis (IUPUI). One dean supports the two schools of education. The two different campus locations provide for a diverse student population. The majority of students in elementary education programs at IUB are female, Caucasian, and are between the ages of 20 and 24 years old, whereas the IUPUI campus draws from a more diverse population, with many students classified as nontraditional and returning.

The two campuses also offer a range of programs from which the elementary education students may select. At IUB, there are a number of discipline-specific options in which elementary students can minor (such as Reading/Literacy, Math, Science, Music, Art), as well as Bilingual Education, Special Education, and Computer Technology. Students choosing a Reading/Literacy minor are required to take an additional 12 hours of coursework in linguistics, children's literature, and critical reading; they must also complete a student teaching placement with a reading specialist. Students also have opportunities to attend monthly seminars that focus on current issues and concerns related to teaching reading and writing. Reading/Literacy minor students are encouraged to join professional organizations and attend local conferences.

On the IUPUI campus, students enroll in either the cohort or blocked course option of the Learning to Teach/Teaching to Learn program. The cohort option is the program we selected to study. In this program, cohorts of interns complete methods courses together during their junior and senior years, spending 2 years in the same school for field experience and student teaching. A cohort of faculty teaches all the methods courses at a school site, providing interns with optimum observation time, teaching experience, and interaction with teachers.

Participants and Methodology in the Beginning Teacher Study

Study Participants

Graduates from elementary education programs at The University of Texas—Austin and from the two campus locations of Indiana University (Bloomington and Indianapolis) were sent a questionnaire that asked them to indicate whether they were interested in participating in the Beginning Teacher Study. Students with reading specializations and those without were included in the process. The nature of the study—to better understand beginning teachers' decisions and instructional practices—required that participants have teaching positions starting in August/September of 1999.

UT has 26 participants from the two programs: 16 graduates are from the reading specialization cohort, and 10 are in the general elementary program. All of these students graduated from UT in

the spring of 1999 and are teaching in a variety of locales and grades.

Indiana University has 16 graduates from three programs participating in the study. Five graduates are in the Reading/Literacy Minor group from IUB; six are in the Learning to Teach/Teaching to Learn program at IUPUI; and five are in a comparison group at IUB. These students graduated in December 1998 or May 1999. (See Table 1 on page 103 for more information regarding grade level and location of position.)

Data Collection

The Beginning Teacher Study follows graduates of the Commission site programs into and through their first 2 years of teaching. In Year One, the beginning teachers were interviewed at three strategic times in the school year: at the start of the school year (August/September), mid-point (January), and end of the year (May/June). These interviews, conducted over the telephone, focused primarily on reading instruction and the beginning teachers' concerns and practices for teaching reading. Questions were asked that related to concerns, instructional decision making, and support from mentor teachers. We also asked the beginning teachers about their math instruction in order to gain another perspective in addition to our focus on reading. All interviews were audiotaped and transcribed.

The two university sites collected data in similar fashions. Faculty members and graduate students conducted interviews at their respective sites. In an effort to prevent bias, the faculty member and three graduate students who had been directly involved with the reading specialization students interviewed the general elementary education cohort students. A faculty member and three graduate students who had not been involved directly with the reading specialization students conducted interviews with these students. Similarly, at Indiana University, a faculty member primarily associated with the Reading/Literacy minors interviewed the other two groups (IUPUI cohort and comparison), and a faculty member most closely associated with the IUPUI cohort interviewed the Reading/Literacy minor graduates at IUB.

In Year Two of the study, program and comparison teachers will be interviewed and observed.

Table 1. Where Do the Graduates Go?

The University of Texas–Austin

Reading Specialization UT Austin		General Elementary Program UT Austin
Dallas, TX third grade	Fort Bend, TX second grade	San Antonio, TX second grade
Pleasanton, CA fifth	Taylor, TX fourth	Round Rock, TX third
Austin, TX first	Austin, TX first	Plano, TX fourth
Austin, TX fourth/fifth Bilingual	Austin, TX fourth	Austin, TX seventh/eighth Language Arts
Houston, TX second	Leander, TX first	Forth Worth, TX sixth/seventh Science
Austin, TX second Bilingual	Austin, TX first	Round Rock, TX first
Austin, TX second	Houston, TX second	Austin, TX second
Austin, TX second/third	Leander, TX second	Pflugerville, TX fourth
		Austin, TX kindergarten/first
		Not Hired (seeking a teaching position)

Indiana University

Reading Minor IUB	Learning to Teach/Teaching to Learn IUPUI	Comparison Group IUB
Long Island, NY fifth grade	Indianapolis, IN first grade	Rockport, MD first grade
N.W. Indiana Reading Teacher (sixth–eighth)	Indianapolis, IN second/third	Indianapolis, IN Special Education (fifth)
Central Indiana Reading Teacher (kindergarten–second)	Indianapolis, IN fourth	Central Indiana second
Central Indiana Literacy Facilitator (kindergarten–fifth)	Indianapolis, IN fourth	N.W. Indiana ESL (sixth–eighth)
Central Indiana fourth	Indianapolis, IN fourth/fifth	Colorado Springs, CO Reading/Science (sixth–eighth)
	Indianapolis, IN fifth	

Interviews will be similar to those conducted in Year One. We will also interview their mentors and principals once. Student achievement data will be collected, as well. Eventually, all data sources will be combined and analyzed within and across sites to uncover salient themes.

Data Analysis

The data collected for this study are analyzed through a qualitative research methodology (Bogdan & Biklen, 1992; Glaser & Strauss, 1967). To date, transcripts and notes taken during the first and second round of interviews were analyzed. Analysis of the first two interviews sheds light on how critical the first few months are for beginning teachers. The research teams at each institution analyzed their own data. The process was similar for both sites. The first level of analysis involved reading through each interview and noting particular patterns or impressions of the participant as a beginning teacher. These margin notes were helpful when re-reading the transcripts and constructing codes for the individual responses of each participant across all three programs.

The second level of analysis, to analyze each question, involved collapsing the responses from the participants and recording salient quotes and statements. At this level, themes began to emerge that described the experiences of beginning teachers. From here, we began to uncover themes that seemed consistent within the programs at each site, as well as themes that seemed different within the identified programs. These themes contribute to a better understanding of the uniqueness of each program and the commonalities the programs share as preservice teachers are prepared in reading instruction. At each step of the process, discussions were held to confirm the categories, themes, and patterns in the data. Following the analysis, we constructed descriptive narratives to highlight particular themes and experiences of beginning teachers.

Findings of the Beginning Teacher Study

The findings reported are based on themes related to commonalities and differences in prepara-

tion for beginning teachers graduating from the University of Texas—Austin or Indiana University. As we documented the common traits and differences among the graduates at each site, there were some occasions when the themes were quite similar in language and in description from the two commission sites. These included concern about job performance and expectations and strong positive feelings regarding the preparation programs respondents completed. In reporting the findings, then, these themes are present in both cases. There is, however, variation in the themes, including reporting on beliefs about teaching reading, job opportunities, and issues of community. Rather than trying to construct a similar label for these differences, we report them as they were termed originally.

The University of Texas—Austin

The themes highlighted in the narratives are organized around points of commonality and points of difference. The first set of narratives describes themes that we found in evidence for both graduates with the reading specialization (designated with the letter R) and graduates with general elementary education (designated with the letter G) as part of their first-year teaching experiences. The second set of themes is contrastive of the experiences of the two groups. In both sets of narratives, the themes are presented in an order that reflects the clarity and pervasiveness of that theme. In other words, the early themes in each list seem fully substantiated in the data. The later themes are only suggested in the data, and they will require further scrutiny and analysis before we are willing to make claims regarding their salience.

Commonalities Among Graduates of the Two UT Programs

The four common traits or themes that emerged from the UT data include the following: high personal concerns, mentoring relationships, valuing of graduates' preparation programs, and the shock of getting started.

HIGH PERSONAL CONCERNS. Participants within the reading specialization and the general elementary education programs mentioned personal concerns regarding the work and time involved in teaching, self-doubts, and the frustrations in their first-year experiences. As one reading specialization graduate (R) explained,

> I feel like I'm 10 steps behind where I'm supposed to be and I'm getting observed tomorrow.... I dream about school. I've given up staying late. I feel like there's no point except making me more depressed about how bad a job I'm doing.

A fellow beginning teacher (R) described her feelings of inadequacy based on the dissention she experienced with her assigned mentor:

> It's my so-called mentor who hates me and sends me notes every week, if she's not sending them to the principal about how loud I am. And my class is loud because she has a traditional classroom and I don't. I'm feeling pretty inadequate right now.

General elementary education students also described concerns regarding self-doubt and the time they had to invest in teaching. One beginning teacher (G) shared her uncertainty of choosing teaching as her career:

> I have doubted if this is what I really want to do, but it's getting better.... Up until this point, people were telling me during student teaching that the first semester is the worst ever, that if you could get through this you could get through anything. Then they would say the second semester. Then they would say your first year. So I was starting to feel betrayed and lied to. Finally, it's getting better.

Although the following beginning teacher (G) did not voice doubt regarding becoming a teacher, she did articulate her struggles to balance time at school with time at home:

> My concerns are balancing family life and work because teaching will take as much as you will give. I'm dealing with the guilt when you don't give as much as you can or as much as you should give because you want to spend time with your family.

Throughout the first- and second-round interviews, beginning teachers from both groups voiced similar concerns regarding such personal struggles and feelings of uncertainty. We have labeled these concerns as "personal," following Fuller's (1969) developmental conception of learning to teach.

IMPORTANCE OF RELATIONSHIPS WITH MENTORS. We asked each beginning teacher to talk about her assigned mentor. Both groups of participants emphasized the need for support from mentor teachers. Just as the beginning teacher (R) described the difficulties she was having because of clashing with her mentor teacher, others mentioned that their mentor teachers helped make the transition to beginning teaching much more manageable. One participant (R) explained how her mentor's willingness to help her at any time made a big difference in her beginning days of teaching: "When I see her in the hallway, and if I have a question, it's like, 'No problem.' It's like open doors for her.... It's a tremendous amount of support. I just feel very blessed."

Another fellow beginning teacher (R) said that when she interviewed with her school district, the most important thing she looked for was support for beginning teachers through a mentoring system. "That was my number one question. It was really important to me to be in a district that values mentoring, that values the new teacher experience." Those reading specialization participants who did not receive support from their mentors mentioned their disappointment, and those who did connect with their mentors were articulate about how much such mentoring helped them throughout the school year.

General education beginning teachers also emphasized the importance of their relationships with their mentors. Some had not felt much encouragement from their mentors, and these participants wished they had had a better experience with them. Most, though, explained how much their mentors meant to them. One beginning teacher (G) described the ways her mentor gave her space to "be her own teacher," while at the same time always made himself available to her:

> My mentor is there as a resource. He doesn't tell me how to teach. He is letting me figure it out my way. We are very much alike. He told me I was "like a breath of fresh air" for this team.

The idea of mentoring seemed to be one that both groups of participants valued during their first-year experience.

POSITIVE REGARD FOR PREPARATION PROGRAMS (READING AND MATH). Most of the participants expressed general positive regard for their teacher preparation programs. Some mentioned certain methods courses and professors, while others mentioned components such as observations and student teaching. One beginning teacher (R) echoed the sentiments of many of her cohort colleagues when she explained that she felt knowledgeable from the opening days of inservice workshops: "I knew about all of these things that a lot of the teachers I'm working with don't even understand."

Most general education elementary beginning teachers also felt positive toward their preparation programs. One beginning teacher (G) explained how her observation and student teaching experiences in the classroom were valuable to her:

> I appreciated the opportunity that I had to work with children directly because you can teach theory until you're green in the face, but you really need to get out there and experience it and do it. I will always be thankful to have had that experience.

Most participants in both groups described parts of their preparation programs that they felt were highly effective and meaningful in preparing them to become teachers.

Both groups of students felt confident in their ability to teach math, and they regarded their preparation as directly related to what they were expected to do in their schools. One beginning teacher (R) credited her math methods professor with preparing her so well for classroom math instruction: "I like the math program. I'm following the curriculum that AISD has adopted, and the whole program is called Investigations and is standards based. I was really lucky because I had the best methods professor." Another beginning teacher (G) explained how her math preparation taught her a big lesson about children and math instruction:

> At UT, the course I took was strictly CGI...the course packet was CGI, the book we bought was CGI, and I guess that compares since I do a little of CGI...it taught me how to really realize that different children think differently about math.

Most beginning teachers in both groups felt comfortable using what they had learned in their math methods courses and teaching their districts' chosen math curriculum.

RUDE AWAKENING: THE SHOCK OF GETTING STARTED. Most of the first-year teachers expressed shock at the requirements of classroom management. Many also described their surprise at just how demanding the first year of teaching can be. Even those who thought they were prepared for such demands experienced this element of surprise. One beginning teacher (R) reported, "My biggest concern is effective classroom management skills. I think with the classroom that I have, meeting everyone's needs is a challenge. You hear it when you're studying and you see it during student teaching, but...." Such concern for effective classroom management showed up across the groups of beginning teachers.

Another beginning teacher (R) explained how she thought she was well-prepared for the time commitment because her reading specialization program had required a great deal of her time. She was surprised to discover, however, that "even though Dr. Hoffman's program is really demanding in terms of time, I was not prepared for the amount of time that teaching takes." Many teachers from both groups were shocked by the demands of first-year teaching.

Differences Among the University of Texas—Austin Graduates

Themes reflecting significant differences were found between those students completing the general program and those completing the reading specialization program. These themes included perceptions of job qualifications and opportunities; confidence in teaching reading; application/connection; valuing learning communities; and impact concerns for students.

JOB QUALIFICATIONS AND OPPORTUNITIES. When asked early in the school year why they thought they were hired, clear differences were found between the reading specialization group (R) and the general teaching group (G). The reading specialization group viewed their specialization in reading as a critical factor in their acquisition of a first teaching position.

As one teacher shared with us, "I feel like I'm bragging. I think that was the biggest reason they hired me because I have a major in reading; it was why I was offered a job in this district." Not only did they view themselves as having the most current knowledge about literacy instruction, but they also felt their experiences during their student teaching spoke volumes for who they were as beginning teachers. As one student (R) stated, "I had done a lot of things in my student teaching classroom that he [the principal] was interested in, and is interested in having his teachers…learn how to do."

Without sounding too boastful, one new teacher (R) told us she "already knew the stuff that the experienced teachers were struggling to learn." Many of the members of the reading specialization group had knowledge of the direction in which reading instruction was moving within their new schools and felt that they were already there, knowledge-wise.

The general education teachers tended to express their strengths that led to their hiring in terms of personality traits, such as "excitement and enthusiasm." In addition, one shared that she thought her hiring was due to the fact that both she and the principal were graduates of UT: "So basically, she didn't ask me a lot of questions, she just went OK, go ahead, so you got the job. We are both graduates of UT."

CONFIDENCE IN TEACHING READING. The reading specialization group vocalized a confidence in their ability to implement strategies and teach reading in a way that was different from what the other teachers in their new schools were doing or moving toward. One beginning teacher (R) made sure her school was one in which she wanted to spend her first year. She knew she wanted to teach at this school because she "knew that the principal's goals were very much in line with what I was hoping to be able to do in the classroom." In addition to these feelings, the reading teachers seemed to perceive themselves as seeming knowledgeable to the other teachers: "My teammates are just flabbergasted when I come up with reading ideas." One new reading teacher spoke about helping a teacher who began teaching 4 months after she had, stating, "I feel like it's coming to me now…. Even though I'm new I still have those 4 months that I can offer her some help and perspective." This confidence in teaching reading has spilled into the area of teaching math; another teacher (R) spoke of the scaffolding that goes on in both math and reading instruction, noting, "[math] is a lot like reading because you take what a child knows and go a step further each time."

With the exception of one, all the teachers in the (R) group were pleased (mid-year at the time of the second interview) with the reading instruction in their classrooms. Interestingly, the one unhappy reading teacher was dissatisfied with her reading instruction because she felt she was being forced to teach a program that was not in keeping with her philosophy of reading instruction. The other teachers from the reading specialization group, however, were generally pleased with the way their teaching was going, noting that their reading expertise enabled them to choose how and what to teach. This intellectual freedom appeared to be a major source of their teaching enjoyment: "I feel very lucky. I didn't want to be stuck in a district where I wouldn't be free to do some of my own things and try new things."

Although many of the teachers in the general program group were pleased with their instruction, they did not display the confidence level that was discovered in the reading specialization group. As one participant (G) stated,

> I'm so scared about adventuring out on my own. I'm really kind of playing it very safe. And I hate it…I would like to have my kids not have to do stupid unit chapter questions. I can't stand those things. My kids can't stand those things.

She did not indicate, however, that she felt able to make changes to her reading program to meet the needs and interests of her students.

The reading specialization teachers, although they feel confident in teaching reading early in their career as teachers, recognize the fact they still face challenges, "It's been very challenging trying to address all the different diverse needs of these first graders, but I'm real happy. I've seen some successes, but I know I still have more to learn," (R). Here we think these kinds of comments from the beginning (R) teachers reflect a stance of "constant learner" that was encouraged and nurtured through their cohort experiences.

A clear distinction between groups (R and G) can be seen when looking at the types of professional development the new teachers experienced throughout their first year of teaching, both in inservices offered by their district and self-imposed learning tasks. The general group spoke of professional growth in terms of what the district was providing them (for example, reading, writing, science, technology, and math "training"). They tended to rely on their district-provided inservices as the main means of professional preparation the summer before they began teaching. In addition, half the general group (G) mentioned reading as the type of inservice they sought out as part of their professional development throughout the school year. Many of them commented on the usefulness of these inservices, saying, for instance, "…I just felt like that literally prepared me for what I was getting into."

The reading specialization teachers also mentioned how they chose certain workshops based on their own teaching needs; several mentioned attending math workshops as "…where I felt I needed the most support." While they attended mandatory district inservices, many felt that the material provided to them in the reading-oriented workshops was material they had encountered and learned in their methodology courses and was not "rigorous enough." In addition to the mandated inservices, many teachers from the reading specialization (R) group were increasing their knowledge of teaching by reading new professional materials (many mentioned current issues of *The Reading Teacher*). In addition, they mentioned looking to the material used in their reading/language arts (methodology) courses at the university as a way of "refreshing" their knowledge. These titles included, *Classrooms That Work* (Cunningham & Allington, 1999), *Guided Reading: Good First Teaching for All Children* (Fountas & Pinnell, 1996), and *And With a Light Touch: Learning About Reading, Writing, and Teaching With First Graders* (Forseth, 1993).

From these interviews, it seems as though the teachers from the reading specialization group felt that their university courses prepared them to teach reading. The general elementary teachers felt the district-provided inservices prepared them to teach reading.

APPLICATION/CONNECTION. When asked about the value of their preparation program on their beginning teaching experiences, both groups of teachers commented on the theoretical and practical sides of their preparation. The levels of satisfaction, however, were very different. As one teacher (R) stated, "The knowledge that I have of methods for teaching reading are invaluable. So, what do I value the most? It's the time that was spent on really focusing on ways to teach reading."

The teachers from the reading group found immediate opportunities within their new schools to apply the strategies they had learned in their university training. They felt right at home, as the strategies implemented in the schools in which they taught were strategies similar to those they learned in both the theoretical and practical aspects of their coursework. A high value was placed on the experience provided by "great teachers and children" (referring to their cooperating teachers' classrooms) as these new teachers have come to appreciate the depth of knowledge they received from their field-based methodology courses. One teacher (R) spoke glowingly about the theoretical experiences she had:

> There is so much. It gave me a background on which to draw. I don't have to go and look up everything. The rigor that we were put through is so preparatory for this first year. I didn't get blindsided. The discussions that we had about the different articles [during coursework] solidify the knowledge so that I can tell my teammates.

Teachers in the general elementary group expressed an appreciation for the theories they had learned, but could not begin to apply that knowledge in their schools. One teacher (G) reflected, "I learned a lot of names, all about phonics approach, what a whole language approach is, but no one actually said that you give a child a book and you sit down with them and this is how you teach them to read."

Another teacher (G), admitting that she felt reading was her "biggest weakness," attributed that to the politics of the "reading wars." Not knowing if "it was the district's fault or the university's fault," she felt,

> I don't know if I'm doing it the right way or if there is one right way. And I feel that in my methods classes, they were very scared to tell us how to do

anything, because of the debate on whole language and phonics approach and which way you should do it. They never said, "Okay, this is how you can help a kid when he gets stuck on a word...." They didn't give us any practical things that we can apply in the classroom.

Many of the general elementary teachers wished that they had had more experience with these theories in a practical way during their university experience. With the notion that at some point and with some experience, they could begin to build on their own philosophy, they were left to follow the plan that is in place in their school.

Teachers from the reading specialization group attributed their successes with their students and knowledge in their reading instruction to the "opportunity to tutor and work with students" that was part of their preparation program. They appreciated the fact that they worked with one student over the course of a year and the influence this experience had in their own classroom: "It really gave me a lot of practice in doing these assessments and thinking about the mistakes that the students were making and thinking about why they were making them.... It's not just recognizing the problem, but why it's happening."

The tutoring experience these teachers received throughout the final year of their program was described as "invaluable," and is seen to have "prepared" these new teachers for teaching in a class of their own. This tutoring experience added to the feelings of competency discussed earlier including, "...through the tutoring experiences, I already knew a lot of stuff that the principal wanted his teachers to learn about."

In addition, the reading specialization group also attributed their success with their students during their first year of teaching to the field experiences they encountered with their cooperating teachers:

> I feel like I was the luckiest person in the world because she was so good. I learned so much from her and the others and that's why I was a little disappointed when I got into this school because it [the reading program in place] is so structured. They just had set me up with a good teacher to be under for my student teaching.

These cooperating teachers share a similar vision for children and their reading instruction is very much in line with the way the theory in the methodology courses is structured, making the transition from university coursework to teaching a very easy one. Speaking of the inservice experiences she had during her first year and how it compared to the rigors of the reading program, one new teacher (R) stated, "We just got tons of ideas on the centers and the guided reading. Nothing to the degree, though, that we went through in our reading specialization."

COMMUNITY. Reading specialization graduates talked about the ways they continued to collaborate with their former cohort members, UT faculty (field supervisors and professors), and cooperating teachers in their planning. "Teachnet"—the computer-mediated communication software used by the graduate and undergraduate students, faculty, and staff of the College of Education at UT—plays an important role in forming and maintaining contact between these new teachers and the members of their university community. Because the reading specialization teachers were required to use Teachnet during their 3-semester coursework program, they seemed more comfortable communicating with their peers and reaching out to others for help. Many reading specialization teachers mentioned that Teachnet continued to be a vehicle for them to stay in touch with and support one another as they began teaching. As one teacher (R) stated, "so once I get a connection to the Internet, I would like to download Teachnet again. Be able to, you know, [because] everyone else is in the same position as me."

Although electronic means played an important role in maintaining contact with members of the university community, the physical act of calling on those who supported them during student teaching was mentioned often. At the time of the second interviews, many of these new teachers had made contact with either their university supervisor or professor of their literacy classes. One teacher (R) mentioned calling her professor from the reading cohort:

> I called him at home last night. Could you believe that, because I called the office and...he wasn't there.

So, I was ahhhh! So, I called his house and talked to his wife, and she said he was in Portland. But, I mean, he's so used to it…it's so comfortable going back to the office.

In addition to the university support they sought, these new teachers also looked to another member of their past community (such as their former co-operating teacher) as a way of gathering answers to questions.

As a possible extension from the support they felt from their university community, these new teachers have turned to teammates (as well as mentors) with questions and concerns, and to ask for help with their planning. "My whole team is aware of the challenges I have," said one. Another "brainstorms and thinks with her teammates," for whom she has a "great deal of respect." These new teachers describe their teams as "awesome," "wonderful," and "so supportive." However, although they sought out these types of relationships, they were not always successful in their endeavors, for a variety of reasons.

It is clear from the following excerpts from both the first and second interviews that the idea of "community" is significant to these new teachers. One new teacher, in her quest to have some puzzling questions answered, sought out the members of her second-grade teaching team. She was overwhelmed with disappointment, saying "They're trying to help me, but I don't think they remember what it's like to be a first-year teacher because they've been teaching for a while." As another teacher turned to her teammates to help and support her in her first year, she found it interesting that all the colleagues on her team were new to the school or grade level, although she found them to be supportive. She admitted that it was difficult, much more so "than the people who have mentors on their grade level." And finally, another new teacher who sought to belong to the grade-level community found that she had violated her acceptance into one through an unintentional behavior, and this mistake cost her the support of her colleagues. She talked about her concerns to her personal friends, but thought "it would make a huge difference" if she had someone at school to talk to. Acceptance into the new community of teachers is very important to these reading specialists.

A small percentage of the general education elementary group voiced looking to their team (in addition to their mentors) for help, but added that they only met with their teammates at "regularly scheduled team meeting times." Twice as many reading participants found encouragement, support, and assistance from supportive teammates at their grade level than did those from the general preparation program. We see the efforts of the reading specialization graduates to surround themselves with new learning communities as an outgrowth of their "community" learning experiences in their preparation program.

IMPACT CONCERNS. Many beginning teachers are concerned with how they perform as teachers. We found in the reading specialization group that this was not as clearly the case; these new teachers appeared more concerned with the impact they were having on their students' learning, rather than how they were doing as a teacher. For example, in the second interviews, one teacher in the reading specialization group shared with us that her most important teaching experience was realizing the role she played in the climate of the classroom: "I had to stop putting the blame on the kids and really start looking at myself as a teacher and how do I react. It took me a while to realize that."

Coming to realize that the children in the class were individuals and should be taught as such was an important one for many of the teachers, as voiced by one (R) who said, "Being able to modify what I'm doing…to reach all of them.… It's so diverse. I'm thinking about how I'm going to meet everyone's needs; it's so overwhelming."

When explaining her vision for her students, one beginning teacher (R) questioned, "Am I giving the best to them? What can I do to make it better? Am I preparing them not only for second grade, but also college? I've already told them they're my little Longhorns; they're going to UT."

Overall, in our data from the UT site, there is clear evidence of some of the specific ways in which the entry into the first year of teaching has been affected by the qualities of the preparation program. The concerns, frustrations, and successes of these first-year teachers reflect the features of their preservice program.

Indiana University

The themes established at the Indiana University site represent both similarities and differences among graduates. This section describes similar traits and characteristics of each theme and offers teachers' voices sharing their experiences as beginning teachers. Within the descriptions, teachers graduating with a Reading/Literacy minor are referred to as R/L; teachers from the IUPUI cohort program are referenced as C; and the comparison group is referenced as O (for other). These designations enable readers to gain a greater sense of the common traits and differences among the graduates. The following are descriptions of the themes and quotes from various beginning teachers to further substantiate the theme.

Similarities Among Indiana University Graduates

Beginning teachers from all three programs expressed common sentiments regarding their concerns about job performance, establishing relationships with those in the school community, and valuing their preparation programs.

CONCERNS ABOUT JOB PERFORMANCE. This theme emerged from the ways in which the teachers talked about their roles as teachers. They expressed concern and anxiety as reality hit and the school year approached. After 4 years of learning strategies for teaching, they were now in roles as teachers. Concerns ranged from planning and creating curriculum to establishing room environment and routines. Many were worried about being "on task" and teaching what was appropriate and expected. These initial concerns seem to be grounded in what teachers' expectations were for job performance–constructing curriculum, meeting students' needs, and performing their roles as teachers.

The expressed self-doubts are quite common for those first starting in the field. One beginning teacher (C) questioned, "Am I going to be able to do this?" and then followed with, "I'm confident, but it might be a little rough at first." Although she felt confident overall, there was still a bit of apprehension about whether or not she would succeed. Another teacher (O) expressed her anxiety about a variety of issues: "I was nervous about curriculum. I didn't know where to begin. How do you know what to teach the first day? What do you expect the first day?" She continued, "It was scary knowing I was going to have my own classroom and no lesson plans planned for me. I didn't know how to start the curriculum. I didn't know what to do the first day."

A teacher assigned to an ESL position (O) worried about communicating with her ESL students and about discipline:

> I was really nervous. I was concerned about discipline, classroom management, and I was really scared that I wasn't going to be able to communicate with the kids because I didn't know the new students. All of the students I teach are Hispanic, and I sort of know how to speak Spanish, but not really, so that made me really nervous. I was also nervous about the staff, getting to know everyone, and it was a new school. I felt a lot of pressure just about everything. It's a new job.

Yet another teacher in the R/L group alluded to the fact that her position as a literacy facilitator is a bit overwhelming in that she has many students and has to create a curriculum that meets certain expectations:

> This position is difficult because I don't just have one grade level and 25 kids to deal with. I have 15 classes and over 300 kids. And there is no set curriculum for me, so that I have to create the curriculum totally on my own, based on what the other teachers want and the principal wants and what fits the state standards and the school standards and all of that. So I was nervous because I didn't have a textbook to follow or anything like that. Everything I teach is something I created on my own.

Apprehension about job performance and expectations was a salient theme in all three groups. All the participants had something to say regarding their roles as teachers and what the job entailed as they established themselves at various school sites.

RELATIONSHIPS WITHIN THE SCHOOL COMMUNITY. The first-year teachers began to establish relationships with those in the school community. Many were assigned mentor teachers within the school building. These mentoring arrangements varied greatly from school to school. At the time of the first interview, many of the teachers briefly met their mentor, became familiar with district mentoring plans (such as specified number of observations, meetings, etc.), and, in general, looked forward to the experience. A few of the beginning teachers in each of the programs viewed their mentors as valuable resources for curriculum, materials, and strategies. One teacher (O) commented, "The teacher across the hall is my mentor. She's also a second-grade teacher. She's been a lot of support and encouragement. We see eye-to-eye on things, but she also has 15 years ahead of me, so she has a lot of wisdom to pass on." By the second interview, however, first-year teachers were less positive about their relationships with the mentors and used them more for procedural types of concerns or questions.

The new teachers found a tremendous amount of support from other colleagues at their schools. When asked who they shared concerns with, most mentioned fellow grade-level teachers at their site, other teachers they knew in different schools, or in the case of the cohort program, fellow cohort members with whom they maintained contact. One teacher (O) stated, "I would talk to the other first-grade teacher. I would talk to the second-grade teacher. I would talk with my coworkers. I talked to my mother. I would talk to anybody who would listen." Four beginning teachers shared concerns with their mothers who were also teachers, which seemed to provide them with an additional layer of support.

Initially, the new teachers wondered how others in the school community would view them. They saw themselves as "change agents" and were concerned that they might not fit in, or might have a more difficult time establishing themselves at the school site. In particular, teachers from the IUPUI cohort program were cognizant of how they may "rock the boat." According to one teacher (C), "It is difficult to talk with people at my school because we had a new principal that came in when I came aboard, and a lot of people don't like her and her style, and I really like her. So it's like, if I say things it kind of rocks the boat with them, whereas I might support something that she's doing and they're totally against it." A teacher (O) who initially stated she would speak to "anybody that would listen" ran into difficulties when another teacher expressed concerns to the principal about this beginning teacher's level of knowledge and preparedness:

> I was asking her questions, but then she went to my principal and was saying that I was asking all these questions and she didn't think I understood and she said she was really concerned about me. My principal called me into her office and said she was concerned about me and she heard that I was asking a lot of questions and that I wasn't sure what I was supposed to be doing and that made me really mad. I'm a first-year teacher. What was I supposed to be doing if I can't go to my teammates?

When asked how the issue was resolved, the teacher continued,

> I was very upset. I was working from 6:50 in the morning at school until 6:30 in the evening, then coming home, eating dinner, and working until 10 or 11 at night. So from then on, I was very sad. I put my heart and soul into teaching these kids and I worked really hard. It was really hard for me.... With my principal, it's really hard on me, and now I don't speak...well I talk to the teacher and we are friendly, but I don't ask her anything and I don't trust her and that stinks.

Along with colleagues and administrators, the beginning teachers were also trying to establish relationships with parents. Those in the Reading/Literacy minor program and the comparison group worried about how to include parents in their classrooms. One teacher (O) explained, "I'm pretty worried about parents. I have a couple of parents that have called the school. One is happy and one is not happy. So I guess it's starting to dawn on me more how important parent communication is." An R/L teacher working in what she says is a "demanding" district also shared similar concerns about parents at the beginning of the year, stating, "I had three parents call today, and I haven't even met them yet. All they know is that I'm taking over for this teacher and just a little bit about my background. Three parents called to say they don't want their child to have a first-year teacher."

As the new teachers established themselves in their school sites, they were learning to negotiate and participate in a variety of relationships with mentor teachers, other colleagues (both novice and veteran), administrators, and parents. These relationships, while often tenuous and fragile, are an important part of a new teacher's professional identity.

POSITIVE REFLECTIONS OF TEACHER PREPARATION PROGRAMS. The participants in this study maintained high regard for the teacher preparation programs they completed. Many of them talked of favorite professors, courses, readings, or experiences they had as a preservice teacher. As they reflected on the programs, what seemed to stand out were their positive comments in all that they learned regarding literacy and teaching. One beginning teacher (C) summarized her experience by saying,

> I would not trade my college experience for anything. The first 3 years were normal, and then the last 2 I was in a cohort program. It really changed my attitude, changed my view of what teachers do and how teachers teach. And really about students and how they learn and I would not trade that for the world. I am so thankful that's the way I went through college.

Another in the same program (C) explained,

> I'm just really thankful for the experiences that I had at CFI [Center for Inquiry] and actually being able to see—they do the self-selected reading and the literature circles—actually seeing it done as opposed to just reading it a book. Seeing it work gave me the confidence that I could do it and that I wanted to do it.

Although the cohort students were quite complimentary about reading methods, they felt as though not enough time was spent on math. Many were less sure of what to do in math instruction.

The Bloomington campus students (R/L and O) also felt positively about their preparedness as a result of their teacher preparation program. A teacher in the Reading/Literacy minor group (R/L) talked about how she valued learning the various reading approaches and strategies, and how without this knowledge, she would feel quite lost. The comparison teachers talked mostly about issues related to reading assessment: They were glad to have learned how to assess children in a variety of ways. One teacher (O), however, believes she left IU under-prepared, because she did not know as much as she needed to teach reading, and she felt that

what she had learned was from other teachers at her school.

The similarities in the three groups of teachers from Indiana University were related to issues of job performance, the way in which they valued their preparation programs, and the relationships formed with those in the school community. These similarities help to better understand some of the issues beginning teachers face as they enter this profession. The next section focuses on what emerged as differences among the programs offered by Indiana University.

Differences Among Indiana University Programs and Graduates

Differences among those in the three different programs include having strong a belief system in place related to reading instruction, applying methods, and assuming leadership roles within the school culture.

STRONG BELIEF SYSTEMS ALREADY IN PLACE. This theme signifies an important difference among graduates in the three programs. Knowledge and beliefs about how children learn to read influence every aspect of one's instructional decisions and practices. As the beginning teachers reflected on their perceived strengths and the ways in which they believe students learn to read, it became evident that those in the cohort option had a more grounded philosophical base than those teachers graduating from the other two programs. Three teachers in the IUPUI cohort group explicitly linked their ability to articulate a philosophy regarding teaching and reading with being offered a position. One teacher (C) said, "being able to express my philosophy and give examples—I think that helps." Another teacher (C) talked about how having a philosophy and knowing what she stood for was critical and that "you can't just go into an interview and fake anything." She then went on to say,

> I feel very strongly that I'm happy that I have a strong philosophy and that I know what I'm doing, as opposed to not having a philosophy and not know what I'm doing. I can pretty well discuss my point of view with other professionals and other teachers here in the building. I can stand behind them [beliefs] and tell them [teachers] why…if you

don't know your philosophy or what is your driving force or what you believe in, I don't know how you can figure out where you are going.

Three of the six teachers in the IUPUI cohort option brought to their teaching a strong sense of who they were as teachers and what they believed about teaching. Making explicit the connections between beliefs and decisions was an aspect found only within the cohort group. This seems to indicate that the teachers' education program strongly addresses the critical nature of belief systems and the impact on instruction.

Those in the Reading/Literacy minor (R/L) and comparison groups (O) did not make mention of their philosophy in teaching. Rather, they talked about being knowledgeable and prepared to teach. An R/L teacher explained, "I have a strong reading and writing background," while a comparison teacher (O) commented that in her interview, she was able to share with the principal some of her ideas regarding curriculum.

APPLICATION OF READING METHODS AND APPROACHES. Closely associated with establishing a belief system is the way in which the graduates in these programs chose to apply their knowledge and understandings of the reading process. All the graduates describe their preparation programs as holistic, whole language oriented, and emphasizing meaning making. They talked about the various strategies they learned, including how to conduct literature discussions, use texts sets and literature, incorporate writing, and engage children in a variety of reading invitations. What became a salient difference, then, was the application of reading approaches. Not surprising, the cohort teachers were more grounded in their beliefs and were also willing to teach "against the grain." These teachers frequently commented on how they taught reading differently than what the overall school approach to reading was. The schools, in general, seemed to have adopted various basal programs. Rather than assuming this was the program to use and follow, one beginning teacher (C) stated, "I feel real cautious about it [the basal program]." Another teacher, who was required to use Open Court, a prescribed reading curriculum, in her classroom, said, "Most of the first-grade teachers go strictly by Open Court and

they do everything that the manual says to do. I'm different because I pull in real literature to pair with whatever they're reading from Open Court. I try to do a variety...I hope that next year I'll be able to pull in more of what I learned in college and use less of the teacher's manual."

The Reading/Literacy minor teachers were also somewhat hesitant in going along with the prescribed programs in place. Although they were less confident in their stance, they were trying to construct possibilities that made sense for them and their students. As one R/L teacher explained,

> It's actually a really good foundation for me to use a lot of the more progressive ideas that I got from IU. I'm starting off with my reading program with our trade books. It's pretty basic right now. But I'm working on trying to bring in more aspects such as literature circles and sharing; more small-group things with my fourth graders.

Another R/L teacher was less satisfied with her preparation and commented, "I wish they [instructors] would have talked more about how to integrate whole language and phonics.... I would have liked to have also learned about different programs that are available for kids. I know Pat Cunningham has a four-block program. I didn't learn about that until I student taught." For this teacher, she felt that her preparation program lacked in providing the knowledge she needed to teach more effectively.

The comparison group teachers (O), however, felt as though there were limited, if any, possibilities of using ideas learned in the preparation program. They were much more likely to follow the school program. There was also a sense that by not using the basal or other prescribed program, children would not learn all that they need to learn. One teacher in this group (O) commented on how she liked the structure of the basal:

> I like using it [basal]. I do other things, like literature units and activities, but sometimes I think because I am a new teacher, especially, it's nice to have a book there and it has the pages that you can read and all the ideas of what to do with it; sometimes I think that helps me because it's a lot of structure. Sometimes I really need that because I kind of find all the work overwhelming. It's nice to have something written out for me. I like it.

This same teacher continued to talk about how using the basal did not really "fit" with what she learned in the teacher education program:

It kind of does [fit], in a way, but not really, because mostly everything I learned in my methods courses was...you would have the kids read a book, and then you would create different activities and nothing was really set.... The way we learned in school was like the whole language approach—if you keep having the kids read, they'll eventually get it and the skills and everything—but I never really bought into that idea. I think that the basal is sort of like that, but you should have the workbooks that go along with it that cover the skills. In a way it's a little bit safer because I know it is all there.

Another teacher (O) shared reasons why she does not use some of the strategies learned in her preparation program:

I think it [reading program] is a lot more basic than what I learned. I don't get to do a lot of the creative lesson plans, projects, and activities that I'd like to. It is more come in, do the vocabulary, read the story, take the quiz, and we leave. It's not fun, active, and lots of projects and things going on because I can't have all that noise and activity. I share a classroom and I don't have a lot of time with my kids to do that. I don't see them for very much of my day. I only have an hour to get the reading in, so we just do what we can for that hour.

The most striking difference noted as these teachers talked was that the cohort group was willing to find ways to teach more integrated and holistic lessons, regardless of the school approach, while the Reading/Literacy minor students took less drastic measures, and the comparison group was satisfied with the school approach and had reasons why they were not able to do something beyond or different than the prescribed curriculum.

ASSUMING LEADERSHIP ROLES WITHIN THE SCHOOL CULTURE: ONGOING LEARNING ABOUT LITERACY. The third significant theme in which we found differences among the study participants relates to assuming leadership roles within the school culture and taking a proactive stance toward ongoing professional development. Most of the participants were active in some kind of professional development, whether it was reading a professional journal or book, attending district inservices and workshops, or attending regional and national conferences. The difference, however, seemed to be in what was done with the information. For example, in the comparison group, the teachers who attended conferences viewed them as opportunities to gather strategies and ideas. As one teacher (O) stated, "I went to a couple of seminars and they were really interesting and gave me a lot of good ideas about how one responded and participated in the professional development." A second teacher (O) stated, "I'm signed up to go to a writing course in February, the Six Trait Writing Course." When asked more about it, the teacher indicated that it was district-sponsored. Professional development opportunities were for gathering strategies and ideas. Conferences were for "toolbox stocking"— these teachers wanted more strategies for their teaching toolbox.

The Reading/Literacy minor group reported less choice and participation in professional development. Teachers attended district-mandated inservices on various programs or designed specifically for new teachers: "We are a C.L.A.S.S. school, so we have professional development that we have to go to, so I've been to those. As far as other classes, I've gotten to all the things that are required." A second R/L teacher mentioned, "I went to a conference in Indianapolis called 'Leave No Child Behind,' and they had a really wide variety of sessions that you could attend, but mostly I went to the reading ones.... Also, I went to [a session] on how to write behavior plans." There was not a sense of a lack of time for professional development among the comparison or cohort group. Two teachers in this group commented that they are too busy with daily teaching responsibilities to attend professional development. One of these teachers, however, said she tries to read as much as possible on various topics and issues.

Finally, the cohort group had a more intense experience with and reaction to professional development. Not only did group members attend various workshops and the like, they presented and took on more leadership in professional development at their school sites. Four of the teachers attended the National Council of Teachers of English (NCTE) annual fall conference, and three of the four presented. This seemed to strengthen their practices and belief systems. As one teacher (C) commented,

> I'm just preparing for NCTE, taking notes in my classroom, trying to create different engagements for the kids and see where they're going with it and if I can use that for my research as well…. I'm a firm believer in that [professional development] because I think that's part of the job. I think if I sat here and did the same thing day after day after day after day without any changing whatsoever or any type of challenges, I think I wouldn't be in this position anymore.

This same teacher also shared her involvement with the professional development committee at her school, with whom she has been observing classrooms using differentiated instruction.

Other teachers in this group attended meetings of local organizations (such as Teachers Applying Whole Language [TAWL]), led study group meetings and book talks with colleagues, and had opportunities to return to their preparation program and discuss a professional book with the new group of cohorts. A teacher who was also involved in differentiated instruction commented, "Our principal is into this differentiated instruction stuff, so I've volunteered to one of the first groups to go out and get this training and learn more about it." Evidence of all these opportunities indicated how these teachers are doing more than collecting strategies or attending district-mandated workshops. For them, professional development, and ultimately teaching, is a lifelong process of learning.

Similar to the University of Texas site, there is clear evidence in our data from Indiana University about specific ways in which entry into the first year of teaching has been affected by the qualities of the preparation program. The interpretations of these beginning teachers about their first-year experiences reflect the features of their preservice programs.

Discussion

The organization and structure of the reading specialization program at UT and cohort option of the Learning to Teach/Teaching to Learn program at IUPUI significantly affected the ways in which these graduates entered the teaching profession. Both programs provided extended opportunities to work with children, peers, teachers, and a common core of faculty. Working overtime with a core group of faculty, teachers, peers, and children facilitated the building of a community of learners. Building community enabled everyone to take risks in learning and teaching. In doing so, new ideas were presented, examined, challenged, and interpreted in multiple ways.

These programs seemed to have considerable influence on the beginning teachers' frame of reference for teaching reading. The teachers graduating from the reading specialization programs expanded their own knowledge base and were willing to enact alternative approaches to teaching reading, instead of following what was being prescribed by the individual school sites. This notion of "teaching against the grain" is in many ways a byproduct of feeling supported and encouraged in their professional communities. The structure and organization of the programs fostered both knowledge building and entry into supportive professional communities. The professional communities many of the graduates sought out led to greater satisfaction and confidence. They did not automatically socialize into what everyone else was doing. Part of this may be due to the specialized focus and the cohort structure—the graduates had a sense of belonging and connections to like-minded people.

The themes revealed in the data also suggest that large public universities value quality instruction and experiences. Graduates of the reading specialization programs were more conceptually and theoretically grounded in their beliefs about the reading process and teaching reading. As a result of their strong belief systems, they were able to enact practices to which they were committed. Many of the graduates talked of specific reading strategies that they were putting into action. In a great number of cases, there was a sense of trial-and-error as new teachers attempted to implement a more responsive program. And although frustrations were common, the graduates did not abandon their ideas for what seemed to be an easier way of teaching. This does not imply, however, that the program graduates were inflexible or unable to reconsider approaches and strategies. It does mean that when teaching was difficult, graduates with a reading specialization or minor were more likely to consider a variety of alternatives and possible solutions to facilitate reading instruction in their classrooms.

Our findings contribute to the limited research literature on reading teacher preparation in relation to effectiveness in teachers' first few years of teaching (Anders, Hoffman, & Duffy, 2000; Hoffman & Pearson, 2000). Previous reports from beginning teachers indicate that their overall elementary education preparation programs were not valued as contributing to their development as teachers (Feiman-Nemser, 1983; Lortie, 1975). Our findings describe something very different. The themes we identified suggest that this study may tell us something about the influence of organization and structure of reading specialization programs and the relationships between beginning teachers' beliefs and what is enacted in classroom practice.

As we continue to move forward on this project and analyze the third round of interviews as well as Year Two, we hope to further uncover those features of various teacher preparation programs that make a difference in the quality of beginning teachers' experiences and decisions. Such features may include articulating and enacting mission statements, personalizing teaching to meet individual needs, building community with various constituents, and developing preservice teachers' professional identities. These features may have lasting impact on beginning teachers' instructional practices and decision making, and may ultimately influence the learning and achievement of the children in their classrooms. Moreover, by highlighting those features that appear essential to preparing preservice teachers to teach reading effectively, we may begin to quiet the rhetoric that says teachers are entering the field under-prepared and without direction. The insights and reflections of beginning teachers from two of the eight commission sites demonstrate that in many ways, these new teachers are prepared to meet the challenges and demands of teaching reading in the 21st century.

Our findings suggest that quality programs of preparation exist and that the shape of these programs is complex. Indeed, our findings are very much in line with the kinds of recommendations for improving reading teacher education reported in a number of recent research syntheses (Anders, Hoffman, & Duffy, 2000; Hoffman & Pearson, 2000; National Reading Panel, 2000; Snow, Burns, & Griffin, 1998). Whether the qualities of excellence we have uncovered are representative of most teacher education programs in the United States is a matter for inquiry. The findings from the IRA Commission's national survey study (see Hoffman, Roller, & the National Commission on Excellence in Elementary Teacher Preparation for Reading Instruction, Chapter 3 of this volume) suggest that many programs are moving in the directions identified in our follow-up study.

No doubt, the assaults on the quality of reading teacher education will continue (see Moats & Lyon, 1996), despite the lack of empirical evidence to support such attacks and in the face of the kind of evidence we offer to the contrary. We are confident that the challenge to improve the quality of reading teacher preparation will not be solved through some simple mandates related to course content or "adding a course" to programs of preparation. Indeed, the pursuit of such simplistic solutions may only degrade our genuine efforts for substantive reform. What is needed is nothing less than a major investment in the education of teachers for a lifetime of learning. Such a commitment will require resources, vision, expertise, effort, and time. The research evidence is clear that such an investment in reading teacher education will result in improved learning in schools for all children (see Pearson, Chapter 1 in this volume).

REFERENCES

Anders, P., Hoffman, J.V., & Duffy, G. (2000), Teaching teachers to teach reading: Paradigm shifts, persistent problems, and challenges. In M. Kamil, P. Mosenthal, P.D. Pearson, & R. Barr (Eds.), *Handbook of reading research: Volume III* (pp. 719–742). Mahwah, NJ: Erlbaum.

Berliner, D., & Biddle, B. (1995). *The manufactured crisis: Myths, fraud, and the attack on American's public schools*. Reading, MA: Addison-Wesley.

Bogdan, R., & Biklen, S. (1992). *Qualitative research for education: An introduction to theory and methods*. Boston: Allyn & Bacon.

Brady, S., &. Moats, L. (1997). *Informed instruction for reading success: Foundations for teacher preparation. A position paper of the International Dyslexia Association*. Baltimore: International Dyslexia Association.

Cunningham, P., & Allington, R. (1999). *Classrooms that work*. New York: Longman.

Feiman-Nemser, S. (1983). Learning to teach. In L. Shulman & G. Skyles (Eds.), *Handbook of teaching and policy*. New York: Longman.

Forseth, C.A. (1993). *And with a light touch: Learning about reading, writing, and teaching with first graders*. Portsmouth, NH: Heinemann.

Fountas, I.C., & Pinnell, G.S. (1996). *Guided reading: Good first teaching for all children*. Portsmouth NH: Heinemann.

Fuller, F. (1969). Concerns of teachers: A developmental conceptualization. *American Educational Research Journal, 6*(2), 207–226.

Glaser, B., & Strauss, A.L. (1967). *The discovery of grounded theory: Strategies for qualitative research*. Chicago: Aldine.

Hoffman, J.V., & Pearson, P.D. (2000). Reading teacher education in the next millennium: What your grandmother's teacher didn't know that your granddaughter's teacher should. *Reading Research Quarterly, 35*(1), 28–45.

Lortie, D. (1975). *Schoolteacher: A sociological study*. Chicago: University of Chicago Press.

Moats, L.C., & Reid, G.L. (1996). Wanted: Teachers with knowledge of language. *Topics in Language Disorders, 16*(2), 73–86.

National Reading Panel. (2000). *Report of the national reading panel: Teaching children to read*. Washington, DC: National Institute of Child Health & Human Development.

Snow, C.E., Burns, M.S., & Griffin, P. (1998). *Preventing reading difficulties in young children*. Washington, DC: National Academy Press.

CHAPTER 6

Social reconstructionism as a framework for literacy teacher education

Rosary Lalik and Ann Potts
VIRGINIA POLYTECHNIC INSTITUTE AND STATE UNIVERSITY

As Pearson (2000) pointed out in his keynote address to the Reading Research 2000 Conference, language is a system in use. It serves human needs and desires, and it can fulfill a wide array of functions. In the United States, there has been a longstanding dispute about what purposes schools, and by extension school-based literacy, should serve (Mosenthal, 1999). Thus, numerous competing positions have been developed and disseminated. One, in particular, has used the concept of democracy as the fulcrum for educational theory and practice. For example, John Dewey (1944) argued that schools should prepare each new generation to participate as active members of a democratic society. In presenting this position, Dewey emphasized the power of responsiveness in human relationships:

> A democracy is more than a form of government; it is primarily a mode of associated living, of conjoint communicated experience. The extension in space of the number of individuals who participate in an interest so that each has to refer his [sic] own action to that of others, and to consider the action of others to give point and direction to his [sic] own, is equivalent to the breaking down of those barriers of class, race, and national territory which kept men [sic] from perceiving the full import of their activity. (p. 87)

Dewey believed that the capacity for democratic life was learned through experience in the activities of democratic action. He argued persuasively that the school is one ideal place where children may appropriately gain such experience, and he questioned the worthiness of more limited goals for public schooling (Dewey, 1944).

More recently Maxine Greene (1988, 1995) furthered this tradition by describing the role that school curriculum can play in helping children develop agency by working together, critiquing current conditions, and transforming unacceptable conditions toward ideals of equity and justice. Greene has written emphatically of the place of the language arts—reading, writing, speaking, and listening—in these processes. In particular, she has found hope in giving learners opportunities to share stories:

> We are appreciative now...of the connection between narrative and the growth of identity, of the importance of shaping our own stories and, at the same time, of opening ourselves to other stories in all their variety and their different degrees of articulateness. (Greene, 1995, p. 186)

Greene's views are consonant with a perspective on literacy described and developed by Paulo Freire (1970) and others (such as Adams, 1975; Luke & Gore, 1992; Shannon, 1992; Shor, 1992; Weiler, 1988). Within this tradition, sometimes called social reconstructionism (Shannon, 1990; Stanley, 1992), literacy is understood as the ability to read and write the world. That is, it is understood as the ability to critique the contexts in which we live in terms of equity and justice and to change those circumstances that are unjust. Understanding and changing one's self and one's role in oppressive relations and structures is an essential genesis for such work.

Within this framework, becoming literate means acquiring facility with language, including decoding and other conventional linguistic abilities associated with school-based literacy that Snow and her colleagues (Snow, Burns, & Griffin, 1998) have called "real reading." It also requires the acquisition of a wide range of other skills and abilities necessary in accomplishing transformative purposes—skills and abilities such as questioning assumptions, conducting research, weighing evidence, arguing persuasively, lobbying, and designing and preparing technical documents, to name just a few. Human qualities such as hope and moral courage are also vital human capacities within this framework. Such qualities are often required when acting in the face of opposition from entrenched groups (Zinn, 1995).

Several interpreters of social reconstructionism (Adams, 1975; Luke & Gore, 1992; Shannon, 1992; Shor, 1992; Weiler, 1988) have been critical of school literacy education, claiming that it supports the development of complacency or domestication among students (Freire, 1970). Thus they have called for the development of alternative pedagogy (Gore, 1993; McCaleb, 1994; Weiler, 1988) such as the work done by Ira Shor (1992) at City University of New York (CUNY). Shor has developed an extensive curriculum in which college students raise and explore questions about equity while examining issues and developing skills in journalism. Along these lines, Edelsky (1999) has highlighted the practices of a group of teachers who are developing classrooms within which learning literacy centers on systemic critique and social transformation.

Since the decade of the 1930s, social reconstructionism, coalescing with the critical tradition in education, has been elaborated by theorists who have addressed the intersections of gender, race, and class in schooling and society (see Collins, 1991; Delpit, 1995, 1998; hooks, 1990, 1994; Ladson-Billings, 1994). These theorists have been especially articulate in their critique of inequities within existing practices as well as in their description of alternative ways of understanding and acting in the world. Several have "incorporated the insights of the new sociology, Critical Theory, neo-Marxism, feminism, cultural studies, neo-pragmatism, post modernism, and post structuralism" (Stanley, 1992,

p. 218). Collins (1998) explained the "critical" in these theories:

> Critical social theory encompasses bodies of knowledge and sets of institutional practices that actively grapple with the central questions facing groups of people differently placed in specific, political, social, and historical contexts characterized by injustice. What makes theory "critical" is its commitment to justice, for one's own group and/or for others' groups. (p. xiv)

According to many current critical theorists, an important goal of education is to understand how various socially constructed categories, including race, class, gender, age, religion, sexual orientation, physical ability, region, and ethnicity, shape systems of privilege and inequality (Andersen & Collins, 1995).

Research Focus and Method

While the tradition of social reconstructionism has been critiqued, reworked, and allied with critical theories of education, its commitment to social justice and societal transformation as goals of education and literacy has persisted in academic conversations (Edelsky, 1999; Shannon, 1990; Stanley, 1992). What is less sure is whether this theoretical perspective remains a viable framework for literacy teaching and teacher education in the face of the persistent and widespread trend toward narrowing discussions about the purposes of literacy (Allington & Woodside-Jiron, 1999; Coles, 2000; Gee, 1999). Recently, discussions of literacy have become increasingly riveted on controversies about competing methods for helping children decode U.S. English orthography. As Luke (1998) explains, "In Canada, Australia, New Zealand, U.S., and England the 'great debate' over literacy education has taken the form of a near-continuous debate over which instructional approach is best able to 'solve' student reading and writing problems" (p. 365).

Further the standards movement has exacerbated our cultural myopia with respect to literacy and schooling (Apple, 1998). The movement has been fueled by persistent though questionable reports of declining literacy in the United States and the failure of public schools (Berliner & Biddle,

1995). One might expect such a movement to include great attention to ways of understanding, supporting, and more equitably funding (Kozol, 1991) literacy learning. Nevertheless, the lion's share of the work has focused on the development of high-stakes tests (McLaughlin & Shepard, 1995). To assist students in producing high scores on these tests, school administrators and teachers have increasingly described curriculum as accumulations of facts and isolated skills and teaching as skill-and-drill routines (Kohn, 1999; Whitford & Jones, 2000). Within this milieu, we questioned whether issues of equity and justice so prominent in social reconstructionism and allied critical theories of education would find a place in the considerations and practices of literacy teacher educators and practicing literacy teachers, especially as the sense of urgency about focus grows (Pearson, 2000).

To examine our research question about the viability of social reconstructionism, we relied on one definition of the word *viable*. That is, viable as "capable of actualization, as a project; practicable" (Morris, 1975, p. 1427). Using this definition as our guide, we talked with two literacy education faculty members and eight practicing teachers who had participated in a graduate level initial teacher preparation program at the university where we work. We wanted to know whether themes of social justice and societal transformation were evident in their descriptions of their work, and if they were, did participants feel able or prepared to use these themes in their teaching. We felt that attention to informants' talk was a reasonable first step in our research project, given that talk is a common form of discourse through which meanings are circulated, thus shaping culture and positioning and defining human subjects (Dyer, 1997; Fairclough, 1992; Hicks, 1995–1996; Luke, 1995–1996).

The two faculty members we interviewed had taught and supervised many students in the program. To guide our conversation with faculty, we asked three interview questions: (1) What are the most important outcomes that you hope teachers will gain from your work with them? (2) What role, if any, do social justice and societal transformation have in your efforts at preparing literacy teachers? and (3) To what extent do you help beginning and/or experienced literacy teachers develop practices that support social justice and societal transformation?

We interviewed teachers who had already completed or were about to complete the program. Those six teachers who had already completed the program were teaching full-time. Five worked at one elementary school near the university; the sixth worked in a more rural middle school division. The two teachers who were nearing the completion of their programs were employed as substitute teachers at the local school division where the other five teachers worked.

All the teachers had been students in the teacher education program, completing the program across an 8-year time span—the period during which program documents suggested a commitment to ideals of social reconstructionism. Jean and Carrie were nearing completion of the program when we spoke with them. Jo Ann had graduated one year before this study began; she was completing her first year of teaching. Dianne was completing her fourth year of teaching. Christine was completing her fifth, Paula and Jennifer their sixth, and Mary her eighth. We talked with all teachers during one week in the spring of the year.

We asked practicing teachers to address four interview questions: (1) How did you come into teaching? (2) What were the major themes developed by your teacher preparation program? (3) How useful was the preparation program to you as a practicing teacher? and (4) What are your current views, practices, and concerns?

We transcribed all nine interviews, producing 130 transcription pages. Using constant comparison (Glaser & Strauss, 1967), we read and reread data to determine themes that were reflected within and across various data segments. We then drafted interpretations in the form of assertions, describing themes and their relationships. We reexamined the data in line-by-line fashion to identify confirming and disconfirming evidence pertinent to each assertion (Erickson, 1986). As part of this process, we developed a table within which we recorded pertinent data lines by theme and respondent. We used the identified evidence to correct, elaborate, and discard assertions. As literacy teacher educators we had become sympathetic to perspectives allied with social reconstructionism, thus our research should be understood as committed (Frankenberg, 1993). That is, as researchers, we do not claim neutrality with respect to the issues under study. Yet it is important to note that we see ourselves as practitioners working to increase the life chances of children (New London Group, 1996). This goal, more than ideology or method, inspires our practice. Our hope is to develop literacy teacher education programs that are highly effective for promoting those life chances.

Interpretations

In this section, we present our interpretations by focusing on the two faculty members we interviewed. One faculty member, Beth, had served on the faculty for 2 years as a leader for students in one section of the program, teaching courses and assisting their student teaching. She had also earned a doctoral degree from the program several years earlier, during which time she worked as student teacher supervisor for 4 years before leaving to take a position at a nearby college. The other faculty member, Bradley, had been a faculty member for over 20 years, teaching most of the students in a required literacy methods course and advising many student teachers. Both considered literacy to be their primary area of specialization in teaching and scholarship.

Faculty Member Profile: Beth

CONCERN ABOUT SCHOOL LITERACY INSTRUCTION. Beth expressed a concern that school literacy practices often exacerbate problems for those children struggling for school success. She described the actions of a student teacher whom she believed had counter-balanced the existing phonics program by introducing several of her favorite books by Eric Carle to struggling fifth-grade readers:

> She [the student teacher] was inviting those students into her own personal literacy club. They were now reading the same books that Ms. Hinton read.... These were fifth graders, but they never experienced Eric Carle when they were in early grades. They were in the phonics readers, and the phonics reader is the most horrible reader of all. There's nothing worse. What is it Gentry says, "kneeling on hard rice"?

ROLE IN LITERACY TEACHER EDUCATION. Beth described her teaching of a course as only a small part of what she is about—as only a "bit" of her work. Nevertheless, she described her work to transform literacy education courses as "naughty," expaining that she "takes courses like that and [turns] them into courses in which we read interesting things about school change, and innovation, and really look hard at issues of social change and justice."

Beth expressed pride in the times in her teaching when classroom dialogue occurred among diverse members of the classroom community. She recalled one such occasion:

> It was the best discussion of race in a mixed-race group I had ever witnessed.... But to have minority teachers talk about their experiences, as members of a minority, and their understanding of students... and to talk straight—they were not talking like talking to white people, they were talking like talking to each other. Those are the kinds of outcomes...that really interest me.

Beth explained that she was concerned that the population of university students at her current institution was too homogeneous to allow for good dialogue and multiple perspectives. She illustrated her concern by reporting that one white student teacher had complained about her student teaching placement in a predominantly African American urban school, saying, "I don't have anything in common with these children. I don't know how to understand them." Beth confided, "My secret feeling in my heart was, 'That's why I want you here.'"

Besides nurturing dialogue about issues of equity such as those related to race, Beth explained her efforts to evoke and sustain inquiry as a primary learning process for beginning and experienced teachers. She generally invited students to develop inquiries that held personal significance. For example, she told us of one student who became interested in the Ku Klux Klan because of family connections. As a project in her literacy education course, he interviewed family and community members in his hometown, ultimately transforming his formerly positive thinking about the organization. Beth commented, "That was exceedingly powerful for that young man—maybe a life-changing experience."

Beth also frequently asked students to identify and study issues that arose in the school settings where they worked as student teachers or full-time members of the teaching faculty. Often she created assignments that encouraged students to address what they saw as obstacles to good practice— obstacles such as high-stakes testing. To illustrate her approach, Beth described a two-course summer school experience she had designed for practicing teachers: "I invited those folks to look at their teaching and find where their biggest challenges were and to try and use the two courses as a means of addressing those challenges in their teaching."

Beyond teaching courses and giving assignments, Beth described her pedagogy as strategic activity aimed at developing a network of people and resources for addressing inequity in literacy teaching and schooling. When one African American student teacher complained about feeling alone in her school placements, Beth found a second-year African American teacher for her to work with at school. Similarly, Beth brought people together to develop long-term curriculum projects designed by teachers. Beth described one such project in which teachers were identifying community sources of knowledge pertinent to the statewide barrier tests, as one means of highlighting strengths of the local community.

These projects typically lasted several years and involved preservice and practicing teachers in a variety of activities including creating curriculum, teaching, examining classroom learning, and sharing learning at local, national, and international meetings. To fund these activities Beth collaborated with teachers to write grants, and she contributed professional development resources from her position as university faculty member.

EARLY INFLUENCES ON BETH'S TEACHING. Beth reported that early influences on her teaching included awareness of inequitable conditions at school. For example, she told us that when she worked as a teacher's aide she noticed that those children in dire need of skilled literacy teaching were assigned to her—at the time a relatively inexperienced newcomer to education. She explained, "...And then at that same time being just totally shocked at the bottom quartile [children] who got all their reading and math from me with one year of college English. No one checked my plans, and these were children who could learn." Even this many years later, on the day we talked with her, the experience of inequity lingered, fueling Beth's sense of outrage.

PHILOSOPHY OF LITERACY LEARNING. Beth described literacy learning as a sociopolitical process that occurs across time and space:

> It's not so much the little bits that we're taught here and there as [it is]: What is the social milieu? What were the literacy communities that they had access to? And how can you help them have access to many different ones so that they could have some real choices? So yes...social justice is the most important thing.

SUCCESS AS A LITERACY TEACHER EDUCATOR. Beth questioned her success as a literacy teacher educator, again invoking concepts of time and space. She told us that she is unable to tell whether she is doing a good job until after her time with learners: "You only know when you look over time and see what happens. And sometimes you have to look over a long period of time and [you know success] only in terms of how they work with students in the classroom."

Beth judged the dominant propensity in literacy teaching to be an overriding focus on text, and she warned that this approach would ultimately interfere with success for many children:

> If we only put our focus on text, then they [children] will not have any ability to understand that they are moving through a politically charged system. They will only understand themselves in terms of their test scores, in terms of their grades. They will begin to believe they can't learn or that they can't do school.

Even while rejecting current teaching as overly text-oriented, Beth emphasized her appreciation for including textual skills of reading and writing within a more robust interpretation of literacy. She explained, "I think we need to help them get good at text. I think we need to help them have success with many different kinds of semiotic systems, different codes, different ways of interacting."

Faculty Member Profile: Bradley

CONCERN ABOUT SCHOOL LITERACY INSTRUCTION. Bradley described school literacy as one part of a larger social structure that he assessed to be fundamentally corrupt: "I am really trying to go down deep…at least invite them to be suspicious that the system is messed up top to bottom, not just education. We are just the poor people on the side who get dumped on." Even while Bradley saw teachers as an oppressed group, he held them partially responsible for many of the inequities he saw in conventional literacy teaching.

ROLE IN LITERACY TEACHER EDUCATION. For Bradley, teaching university courses was a rich context for his work as a literacy teacher educator. He saw his teaching goals as overriding the particular course that he happened to be addressing. He explained, "It doesn't make any difference whether it's foundations, or language arts, clinical assessment, content, independent studies…. [I'm] hoping that I can create some anger in some, and really some outrage in some others."

Besides helping students learn about corruption in the social system, Bradley held other goals for his teaching. For example, he explained his interest in helping students learn how to connect curriculum and communities, saying, "There has to be that partnership…. And just as we have to quit disembodying our [school] subjects, we have to quit disembodying what we do in school from what we do in the community."

Bradley also expressed considerable interest in helping students understand the power of language to shape their world. "I want those people to know how language can both free you and imprison you," he said. "And it's your choice when you are in front of that class." This sense of moral responsibility was a persistent theme in Bradley's conversation about literacy teaching.

During class Bradley challenged and confronted students. To illustrate his approach, he reported one line of questioning he used in class to highlight the inequities of tracking students in high school:

> I ask them [students], for example, to remember when they went [through] their high school door, which way did they go? And they could tell you. "Did you ever go in the other direction?" "No!" "Who

went that way?" "I don't know!" "What was down there?" "I don't know…." And we've got those people there [in class, also as university students], and they will say, "Yeah! We went the other way…. Let's tell you what's down there. We also know that you didn't dance with us. You didn't sit with us at the athletic events. You didn't date us. You paid no…attention!" That's anger I create in my classroom. That's exactly what I want!

Anger is an important teaching tool for Bradley—one he viewed as necessary for the learning process. Though he described himself as confrontational, Bradley also pointed to his interest in helping his students understand that when addressing issues of equity, making mistakes is one vital aspect of learning. "[We] have to get over this business of being so…walking on eggshells about everything—about culture, about literature, about gender, about being politically correct…. I tell my students, 'I expect you to screw up. If you don't, I'll fix it so you do.'"

Bradley reported that courses in content area literacy were a particularly rich venue for his pedagogy. He described using content area knowledge as one means for helping students identify contradictions in their thinking:

> Content can be addressed when we talk about classroom management, trying to create justice and fairness and humanness…. We can talk about it from a constitutional point of view: what a contract means, what would business do, what would it mean…for management styles.

It was important to Bradley to bring teachers together from across grade levels and content areas, as was his practice in content area reading courses. In such diverse groups, Bradley believed that students would be more likely to discuss issues and recognize inequities in the educational and social systems. He explained his view that the separation of teachers along various lines supports a system of blaming that solidifies inequity.

EARLY INFLUENCES ON BRADLEY'S TEACHING. When discussing the influences on his teaching, Bradley pointed to his life as a young adult in the 1960s, as well as to his doctoral education—an experience that changed the course of his thinking and his understanding of literacy and schooling. The doctoral experience influenced Bradley's personal life as well. He talked emphatically about his relationship with his father, who he described as rather conservative in his views and practices. With respect to this relationship, Bradley described his horror and pain when he discovered a document that indicated that the family had at one time owned slaves. He explained the tension created from the differences between his university experience and his familial ones:

> [It was difficult] going home to visit my parents after I was involved with [the] programs I was involved with. How could I sit there and listen to my Dad talk as he'd been talking? I knew it was wrong to begin with, but I was given knowledge now. So I challenged him.

PHILOSOPHY OF LITERACY LEARNING. Bradley was adamant that learning language is a whole-to-part process—a process he saw as inconsistent with typical school literacy instruction. He frequently mentioned his concern:

> So there's the linguistic model for the curriculum— a thematic, integrated kind of thing. I think it does come out of that in terms of when and how kids learn language. They don't learn it word-plus-word. They learn it as concepts, and then we [educators and researchers] took it apart and made it miserable for them.

Bradley explained that language skill develops when people have important goals as well as opportunities to learn the skills necessary to accomplish those goals. "If we are going to stand in front of people and talk about why we should not have the Confederate flag on the top of South Carolina's capital building…it behooves us to give them a [code that is acceptable to those in power]." He explained further his belief that learners should maintain their primary discourses while learning additional discourses necessary for achieving various life goals.

Developing trust with learners at the margins of society is an important element in literacy teaching for Bradley. He described an experience he had as a tutor when he tried to convince an incarcerated young adult that learning conventional reading and writing was worth the effort. Bradley explained, "If we get you to put some things on paper and get you to look at some of the kinds of texts, that [learning] might be of interest to you in your own defense in the future."

SUCCESS AS LITERACY TEACHER EDUCATOR. Bradley remained equivocal when we asked him to discuss his influence on students. In response, he pointed to the effect his teaching had on his own life and development:

> Have I transformed anybody? That's where that kind of question started. I've done a lot for myself. So for one, it has been successful! That's the only certainty that I have. That I am less racist, less unjust, less unfair…today because of my teaching and learning than I was. But I've got a long way to go! And I let students know that. I let them know that right off!

Bradley pointed to continued racism and injustice as lingering educational and societal problems, saying, "But those white teachers are carrying still the racism and bigotry from their parents. We have got another generation or two to go before we will ever get down to being able to deal with that [racism], I think."

Practicing Public School Teachers

In the following section, we describe and illustrate the patterns we observed in what practicing teachers had to say, pointing as well to variations within each pattern. An overview of the teachers' responses is presented in Table 1 (see page 126).

Entry Into Teaching

Teachers described their backgrounds and reasons for entering the teaching profession largely in terms of child advocacy. Though different in content, five teachers shared explanations in which they placed themselves in the role of advocate for children. Dianne's explanation is illustrative: "I think the thing that made me really decide [on teaching as a career] was having a child of my own and realizing that children need more advocates than they get."

Teachers often characterized their advocacy role as nontraditional or counter-cultural. Jean drew from her personal experiences as a child

Table I. Themes Appearing in Teacher Interviews

Assertations	Jean	Carrie	Jennifer	Mary	Paula	Jo Ann	Debbie	Christina
Entry Into Teaching								
Child Advocacy	●	●	●		●	●	●	
Counter Cultural	●		●		●	●	●	
Program Characteristics		●						
Self-Development	●		●	●	●	●	●	●
Peer Groups		●	●	●	●	●		●
Interactions		●	●	●	●	●	●	
Principles and Strategies	●	●	●	●	●	●	●	●
Diversity			●	●	●	●	●	●
Program Usefulness	●							●
Practices and Views								
Concerns								
High-Stakes Testing	●	●	●	●	●		●	●
Competing Responsibilities				●	●	●	●	●
Adequate Support for Teaching					●			

struggling with the reading process to frame her characterization of herself as a change agent:

> I guess in terms of literacy I always struggled with reading. Reading was something that was always difficult for me…. So that's been a great challenge for me to look back and to see why I had problems and then to change from the way that I was taught to help the children I will be teaching.

For Jean the reading curriculum was a focus of consideration and development. As a substitute teacher completing her graduate program and eager to begin her first year as a full-time teacher, Jean wanted to help children avoid experiencing feelings of difficulty and frustration she had endured as a youngster struggling with school-based literacy.

Also describing herself as a child advocate, Jo Ann highlighted her approach to teaching as atypical, as having "so many things I wanted to do with the kids, and so many ways that I wanted to teach in a different way than the other teachers were teaching." Jennifer explained that her atypical style had been inspired by her first-grade teacher, saying, "I thought about my first-grade teacher and how she was just way ahead of her time—I mean, she taught the way I teach now."

Characterization of the Program

Teachers pointed to numerous themes in their teacher preparation program, including self-development, interactive learning opportunities, the peer group, principles and strategies for teaching, and diversity.

SELF-DEVELOPMENT. Seven teachers highlighted their experience of emerging from their preparation program with a strong sense of self-development, including development of a personal philosophy and belief system. For example, Jennifer explained learning from the program "your own way, what you thought was your own style, or what you thought was important, and how you could get that across to the children…there are many ways to teach." Christine echoed this theme, saying the program allowed beginning teachers to "develop our own philosophy." She continued, "A lot of it was forming our own opinions and our own educational backgrounds."

Christine expanded on her idea of self-development to include a personal dimension. "It helped me learn who I am as a person, and I think that helped me come into teaching and understand…my strengths, my weaknesses, my interests, my goals."

Paula also reflected on her self-development experience, commenting, "I feel like I expanded my knowledge and my ability to learn. I have come away with a blending of ideas and perspectives and research and practice that I have been able to continue to reflect on. And I've been able to pull out what I want from it, and it helps me."

INTERACTIVE LEARNING OPPORTUNITIES. Teachers also pointed to interactive learning opportunities as a theme of the program. For example, Paula described classroom discussions, highlighting the sense of freedom that she experienced: "I think one of the biggest parts of the program was that we were allowed to speak openly and disagree, to argue, debate, and come up with different ideas. I didn't feel I had to fit into a certain mold."

Jean explained that not all her classes provided such opportunities, though when they occurred, she noticed their positive influence on her. This opportunity for comparison influenced her teaching methods. She said, "I believe in a lot in group work and working with each other because I see what a difference it's made in my life in classes that were based on discussion and group dynamics."

THE PEER GROUP. Six teachers described the influence of the peer group. Paula highlighted the theme of activism and connected it to her peer group:

> That's one of the things I think so much about when I think about the program, is the active, an activist, being an advocate for learning…. It was a huge theme within the program, but that may have been associated to the group of people in the program. I felt like we were a politically active group.

Paula connected this theme with her work as child advocate. "I'm glad I developed that political awareness and responsibility to be an advocate for children."

Christine pointed to the salience of the peer group, crediting it for much of her learning. For Mary, friendship was an important dynamic within the peer group. "[The peer group became] friends and colleagues that were a support system to me," she said. "I found [them] very helpful both through school and afterwards in my first year of teaching."

Jo Ann explained how she admired the group of which she was a member and how she transferred those feelings to her students:

> The people that were in that program with me…were absolutely incredible. I learned so much…. I remember saying to someone, "We are the best group that has ever been through the program!" And I began saying that to my second graders, too! "You're the best second graders I've ever had ever!" And I really mean it. I know that if I have second grade next year, I am going to say the exact same things to those kids and mean every single word of it.

PRINCIPLES AND STRATEGIES FOR TEACHING. Each teacher highlighted the development of teaching principles and strategies as a program theme. Most of the examples they gave related to literacy instruction. Several discussed the importance of providing authentic learning experiences for the children and the significance of knowing a variety of ways to assess children's literacy learning as examples of this theme. Mary told us that the courses allowed her to explore assessments alternative to multiple-choice or essay tests.

For Jean the program promoted meaningful activities to enhance literacy for young children with a particular focus on using children's literature and spending time reading and writing.

> I think it was emphasized all along [in the program]…getting children into books and having authentic experiences in the classroom. Working a lot of hands-on and really getting involved in their literacy, rather than being told how to read…. They are actually doing, not being told how to do it…. Also it's been stressed numerous times that you can't teach reading without writing…. [Reading and writing] are interactive, and children need to see the relationship between the reading and the writing through their own experiences.

Jo Ann explained how pleased she was that the courses emphasized developing authentic experiences for children, saying, "I think that's the one theme that was through all the classes that I took,

the authenticity of the learning, and I was very, very pleased with that."

Jean explained that teaching strategies were a salient feature of the program for her, pointing particularly to the technique she called guided reading:

> I have done a lot [with]…guided reading…. So that was nice to have the background of that, to understand the philosophy behind it, and the reasons for doing that in a classroom…. The techniques described in the guided reading book are beneficial to children because it gets their attention. They are reading it together they are discussing it, and it's a lot more authentic than the old reading groups.

For Jean, the focus on teaching strategies contributed to her sense of readiness for teaching.

These teachers' language often revealed a sense of personal autonomy for selecting strategies that they found useful, while rejecting those they assessed as unhelpful. Paula's discussion of cooperative learning illustrates this pattern:

> One of the themes that comes to mind is cooperative learning, and while I'm an advocate of cooperative learning…I didn't take it with me. Well, I know I took it with me the first year I taught, and then I realized it wasn't useful. It wasn't practical as a teacher in a classroom…. It [was] something that I use, but I use very carefully.

In contrast, Jennifer described using cooperative learning extensively in her third-grade classroom. When we asked what she liked to do in her practice, she responded, "Lots of cooperative learning, experiments, inquiry—let them come up with their own questions about a topic and research that… sometimes as a group…lots of hands-on…almost everything I do is cooperative learning."

DIVERSITY. Only two teachers identified diversity as a program theme. Carrie noted the work of Beth, one of the instructors we interviewed, with respect to diversity. "Beth brought more trade books than I could ever imagine, dealing with diverse populations, and that really helped," Carrie explained. Carrie also pointed to a continuation of the theme of diversity throughout the program, providing as an example her study of a course text that highlighted ways to assist second language learners in acquiring school literacy. She attributed her increased understanding of diversity to her graduate literacy classes, where the student population was more diverse than the undergraduate student population.

Christine credited her social studies professor with helping her appreciate diversity, remarking,

> [I remember] his multiculturalism and his elementary education in kindness. I think that just came out as being one of the themes that I learned most from him, as being kind and tolerant and learning to laugh and to understand each child's background and what they bring.

Even while diversity was identified as a theme, one teacher, Jean, questioned the adequacy of its development through the program. In particular she worried about having the knowledge to work in the much more diverse northern section of the state—the area where she planned to seek a teaching job. "So teaching children that are learning English as a second language was something that is definitely going to be challenging, and I don't necessarily know that I've experience to handle it." To address this lack, Jean planned to complete an independent study especially tailored to this need.

Usefulness of the Teacher Education Program

All the teachers we interviewed described the program as quite useful to them. Their comments tended to be both laudatory and enthusiastic. Jennifer's response—"I thought the program was wonderful; it was wonderful!"—was characteristic of the group. Christine expressed a similar reaction, pointing to the self-knowledge the program helped her develop. Jo Ann appreciated the program as one that personally suited her, insofar as it did not force her to attend primarily to procedural aspects of teaching, such as attendance taking.

Mary expressed the view that the program was helpful because as an "older" student, she had scholarly interests that the program helped her pursue:

> I found it really helpful. I think…being older was an advantage, for I was coming, looking for more in-depth knowledge…. I found it really helpful in looking at new research that had been done in the last 10 years.

Dianne elaborated on her appreciation for the program in terms of how it helped her learn to resist approaches that she saw as antithetical to children's interests:

> [It helped me] to try to fight against movements that would tell us that children need to just memorize facts and just regurgitate those facts. You know children are intelligent and vibrant and full of ideas and knowledge…. From the professors, I was able to feel their strong conviction on these issues—not that there is one way to do it, but that there are many ways to teach, many excellent methods of teaching—but to always keep in the forefront the child. And the fact [remains] that the child needs to have a voice in the classroom. Whether it's a choice—"Will I do this project, or this project?"—or "I have question I really want answered." The child needs to be able to feel they have some say in the classroom…and it gets harder to do that. I think we really have to fight for that.

Though as a group, teachers were uniformly enthusiastic about the overall usefulness of the program, they varied in terms of how prepared they felt when they initially completed the program. Most felt well-prepared for their day-to-day teaching responsibilities. Mary explained that she felt capable of helping children become learners, "how to help children build their own structure, their own learning in future years." Jean felt generally quite confident about beginning her career. She attributed the confidence to the emphasis on the practical implementation of theory that she saw as one feature of the program.

In contrast to the confidence expressed by these teachers, Dianne explained her initial dissatisfaction and frustration:

> It was an extremely useful program. You didn't give me a lot of real specific strategies, and at first when I got out of the program, I was…thrown into a classroom. I was really a little upset about that. As I've taught more, I've realized how smart that is. While it's difficult the first year, you have such a strong foundation coming out of the program of beliefs and convictions. That's what carries you through the difficult times. It's not the strategy you pull out of your back pocket…. You search out strategies, strategies you feel will work for you, [strategies that] will best support your philosophy.

For Dianne, the learning process was worth her effort, even though she experienced a difficult initial period.

Practices and Views

All eight teachers identified various approaches to child-centeredness as an important characteristic of their practices. Their descriptions of child-centered engagements took several forms, including classroom activities in which the children were encouraged to adopt active roles in learning; programs tailored to children's particular learning needs; inquiry instruction in which children were helped to raise questions and consider conflicting viewpoints; activities that assisted children in learning how to learn; and assistance for socially marginalized children.

For Mary, for example, child-centeredness came in the form of sharing control, giving children some influence on classroom activities, and focusing on what children can do:

> I'm learning to do more open-ended activities. And that is a growth area for me that I've come to realize working with young children…. But having done several of them [open-ended activities], realizing that I like the results, and seeing the children's excitement about that is reinforcing for me.

Mary's words convey a sense of struggle to work in the ways she sees as helpful for children, as well as a sense of commitment to grow in those directions.

Jo Ann explained child-centeredness in her practice in terms of responding to the variability she saw in children's learning needs. She explained,

> I have 16 kids in my class. I have 16 math programs. I have probably 12 reading programs…. And the reason I do that is that every child that comes into the classroom is different, and they have to be taught in a different way.

For Jennifer, child-centeredness came in the form of children's inquiry during content instruction. To give an example, she talked about a particular project:

> As a group we'll do experiments to try and find out answers and…lots of hands-on. We had clay, silt, and sand in there. We did them dry and wet, and

so [the children] were all muddy. I think they could see the difference. And then they had to decide what would be best for a plant to grow.

Also interested in inquiry teaching, Jean described how children's classroom responses to an opportunity for inquiry fueled that interest:

> I was doing a unit on plants, and I brought in a plant. And we were all sitting around and taking apart this plant, and looking at the roots, and looking at the leaves and the flowers and everything…. So [the children] were sitting there with this plant, and I mean, I just expected them—they're in kindergarten—to look at the leaves…. And the next thing I know they are…peeling their geranium…. They are peeling the outside of the leaves off. It was interesting to see how you give them one thing, and they can do so much more with it.

Dianne described her work with an inquiry-based unit on the rain forest that included helping children raise critical questions as they read texts. During this unit, it was reinforced for Dianne that "children have so much more that they are capable of doing than we give them credit for." Dianne's explanation suggested an emerging skill in helping children question texts and weigh alternative claims.

Several teachers explained child-centeredness in their practice in terms of helping children learn to learn. Dianne emphasized her need for the children to learn how to be learners through their inquiry. Learning to be learners was also a focus for Jo Ann, who said,

> I hate to use the words *hands-on*, because we use the term *hands-on* all the time, and most of what we do is not hands-on…. I wanted the kids to actively learn for themselves and to get in there and create their own knowledge, instead of me pouring stuff into their heads and thinking that was teaching.

Paula described her child-centered focus in terms of her work with children at the social margins of the classroom or school:

> This year I have a young man who is so different from everybody and is probably the most intelligent youngster I have been around, but he doesn't fit in with anybody…. Granted, it took several weeks for me to develop a rapport with this child. So I just had him come back into the classroom with me and work with me on developing social skills…. You

know it bothers me so, not just social interactions with peers but that child being so ostracized by adults because he is different.... He's like, "Well you know I feel like everybody else has a whole road, and all I have is the tight rope." And he's right; it's true you know; so many other kids, because they are considered to fit into the norm, can push the limits and be okay. Whereas he's already considered outside the limits, so anything else he does is considered extreme. And so I guess that's where my activism comes from. [It] is fighting for those kids who don't fit in, who don't get the opportunity to fit in.

Paula saw the dynamics of schooling work against some children, and she "fought" to support those youngsters.

Concerns

Teachers expressed several concerns. These included concerns about the impact of high-stakes testing, conflicting demands of teaching, and inadequate support. When expressing concerns, teachers' language was generally upbeat and hopeful; they seemed anxious but not defeated.

Seven reported concerns about the Standards of Learning (SOL) Tests, the high-stakes tests currently used by the state to hold teachers and schools accountable for children's learning. Most vocal were the teachers most directly responsible for giving the tests. For example, Jennifer, who taught third grade, talked at length about how the test promoted questionable assessment practices, saying, "I don't feel testing is the best way to assess; I feel like observation is more accurate.... I try not to do a whole lot of testing.... My biggest concern, as a teacher, is where this SOL test is trying to take us." Jennifer related her recent visit to an accredited school touted as a model of success because of its high SOL scores. She told us that teachers there had described their efforts as "skill and drill, skill and drill, we pound it in." She reported her horror in learning that children in that school, according to their teachers, had no opportunity for cooperative learning, science experiments, or "anything fun."

> All it was, was whole-class, every seat was in a row; every teacher was at her desk with her feet in front of her with her book open. Everyone was at their desk with their book open, and she'd read and point and someone would answer, and then she'd read and point and someone would answer.

Reflecting on teaching style, Jennifer concluded, "I could never come to work each day if I had to teach that way."

In spite of her disapproval of much of what she saw, the school visit prompted Jennifer to reconsider her own teaching. "What I came away from that [visit] with was the understanding that I am teaching the content, and it is meaningful." She pointed out that she needed to work on finding ways to "tie in some [test taking] skills, to show the people who are creating these tests that they [her students] know the material." Thus, she concluded that she would continue to teach in meaningful ways, while also helping the children develop "test-taking skills."

Five teachers told us that they felt concern about the increasing and often conflicting responsibilities of teaching. Christine was among those who described this concern. When entering the profession she never realized the need to "teach values, morals, and ethics, and all those good things that I expected to come from home." She reiterated how hard it was to accommodate all these issues and also accommodate inclusion of children with special needs within her classroom:

> The inclusion student has rights and needs, and his [] needs are different than everyone else's. But that's not to say that Joe's rights and needs are not just as important as Susie's needs. So how do I meet all these needs in the classroom? I care about that; I care about making everyone's experience successful.

Christine's language suggests her effort to address needs she saw as conflicting.

Though generally satisfied with her teaching, Jo Ann worried that the questioning attitude she encouraged could interfere with future school success for some of the children.

> When I give them information, if they don't think that [the information] sounds right to them, they will ask why. They will ask where I found the information, and sometimes, I will have to get a book out and show them this is where I got the information. So they question everything in the classroom. That might not go over well in later classes, but then,

in the long run in their lives it will be better for them.

Although Jo Ann was concerned about future difficulties for children who question teachers, her concern did not extinguish her practice because of the long-term benefits she saw for students.

Paula expressed concern about conflicts between her responsibility as a teacher of academic content and her responsibility to promote the well-being of children who struggle at school.

> You know…she [a student in Paula's class] is so abrasive and so belligerent, yet we can't take those skills away from her. We can't because she needs them to survive in the environment she's in [outside of school]…. And it's so hard for me to keep this child in a learning environment that doesn't support her needs…. She needs an alternative program that can really help her with life skills and social skills and taking care of herself.

Lack of support for her child advocacy was also a salient concern for Paula. In particular, she wanted support from university faculty whom she saw as allies and supporters of her philosophy and practice. Paula's comments suggested that she was experiencing a sense of abandonment at her rural school, where unlike the experiences of the other teachers we interviewed, she did not have frequent opportunities for conversations with university-based literacy faculty. Notably, none of the other teachers expressed a concern about isolation.

Discussion

To initiate our study of the viability of social reconstructionism as a framework for literacy teaching and literacy teacher education, we interviewed literacy teacher educators and practicing literacy teachers who participated in a graduate level teacher preparation program on our campus. We wanted to learn whether the themes of social justice and societal transformation, so prevalent in social reconstructionism, were part of participants' conceptions of their work, and if so, did participants feel able and prepared to use these themes in their teaching.

Both literacy teacher educators said that social justice and societal transformation were significant themes in their work. Nevertheless, their approaches to implementing these varied. Beth focused on teacher-generated questions and inquiry-based instruction through which teachers raised and explored questions that emerged as salient for them within the confines of their courses and professional associations with Beth. She taught by providing a wide range of materials to support a critical perspective and by designing inquiry-based assignments in formal coursework. Beth also nurtured many informal learning opportunities for literacy teachers by providing information, encouragement, and other resources for teacher-generated projects.

Bradley taught using a combination of lectures, class discussions, and debates. He raised issues focusing on equity in literacy teaching, schooling, and society, and he created numerous classroom opportunities for his students to present and argue about views and practices. The course assignments he designed gave students further opportunities to describe and support their views, as well as critique the views of others.

Through their verbal explanations of literacy and through their course assignments, both faculty members constructed a complex view of literacy. For both, literacy is tied to larger social issues and is best understood as a range of often competing and conflicting agendas for society. Issues related to injustices of social class and race were particularly salient in the discussions of both teacher educators. To work with their students with these and other similar issues, both expressed an appreciation for a diverse student population. Beth complained about the difficulties in sustaining critical dialogue among the homogenous white, middle class students in this program. Bradley was more sanguine on this issue, explaining that he benefited from classes that drew students from various teaching majors, thus allowing for differences of perspective.

Even while construing complex notions of literacy and literacy teaching, neither Beth nor Bradley rejected the importance of "real reading" (Snow, Burns, & Griffin, 1998). Rather, both teacher educators saw text skill as a critical feature of literacy learning. Though they may not have agreed with more mainstream literacy educators on how to develop text skill, both saw it as a necessary yet insufficient aspect of literacy. For Beth, skill with text was among the many abilities within a range of semiotic systems she believed children should develop in order to liberate themselves from demeaning social constructions, such as those produced through school failure. For Bradley, text skill was a tool that could help people achieve important goals, such as getting out of jail or changing an unjust public display.

Both teacher educators had developed their perspectives over a long period of time. In tracing their development, they assigned special significance to particular past experiences. For Beth, her experience as a teacher aide allowed her to view one way through which school resources were withheld from certain children, unjustly limiting their chances for school success. For Bradley, the contradictions between the knowledge he developed in his doctoral program and the circumstances and views produced within his family unit inspired his desire to work in ways he construed as counter-cultural.

Though neither teacher educator could point to evidence of great success, both seemed convinced of the wisdom of their pedagogies. Bradley seemed to use his teaching as one means of improving himself as a person, even if he could not be sure it made the teachers with whom he worked any different. For Beth, the question of influence on students could not reasonably be answered in the short term; she seemed content to wait it out.

The practicing literacy teachers constructed themselves as child-centered and counter-cultural literacy teachers. Our conversations with these teachers did not uncover explicit references to the terms *social justice* or *societal transformation*—words that, we assumed from our earlier conversations, they would have considered esoteric. Yet the practicing teachers expressed concerns about the ways in which the curriculum, as well as conventional teaching and assessment practices, conspire against students as a group and as individuals. In their conversations with us, teachers pointed out numerous efforts they made so that the school experience would be more fair and just for children. These teachers created specially designed programs, employed cooperative groups, provided a range of choices for students, used inquiry teaching, sup-

ported students' questioning of classroom materials and activities, considered various perspectives presented in texts, and supported marginalized students in order to create more just classrooms. In describing these efforts, teachers expressed confidence in their professional judgments and classroom practices, although they saw their approaches as inconsistent with the current press toward more conservative approaches.

Commitment to equity was evident in teachers' responses to state-supported high-stakes testing. Thus, even while refusing to adopt teaching strategies they felt were insensitive to children's interests and abilities, the teachers did not dismiss the importance of helping students perform well on high-stakes tests. Rather, they searched for ways to do both. For example, Jennifer planned to increase attention to test-taking skills while retaining her commitment to inquiry learning and group work. Dianne designed inquiry units so that students could learn the information listed in the state curriculum, while she could address children's questions about the world's ecology and explore with students the intersections of opinion and knowledge.

Developing one's own beliefs and style of teaching was an important element of the teacher preparation program as experienced by these respondents. The teachers seemed to feel that they had responsibility for their practice. This aspect of the program may have contributed to teachers' willingness to find a resolution to their current challenges. That is, if their practice belonged to them and was part of them, it could not be simply discarded to accommodate some external pressure. Nevertheless, it could be altered and shaped with changing conditions.

The teachers assessed the preparation program as extremely useful; even the teacher who told us that she had experienced a difficult time developing teaching strategies during her first year of teaching assessed the program as useful. For her, in the long run, it was the personal and professional beliefs and principles she had developed that sustained her through difficult times. Those teachers who told us that they had learned many teaching strategies explained that they had done so within a programmatic context of reflection and consideration.

One teacher told us of her sense of abandonment from university faculty since completing the program. She constructed the lack of interaction as a detriment to her pedagogy. Her description was poignant, although she had graduated over 8 years prior to the interview. It caused us to note that unlike this teacher, the other seven respondents had experienced frequent opportunities to interact with university faculty. This contrast caused us to wonder whether, as Paula noted, those interactions were a resource for teachers in sustaining their counter-cultural approaches to literacy teaching. This interpretation is consistent with the recent findings about the significant role of teachers' learning communities in supporting the long-term professional development of teachers (Pearson, 2000).

We began this exploration by asking whether social reconstructionism remains a viable framework for literacy teacher education and literacy teaching in light of the current trend toward explaining and supporting a narrow conception of literacy, operationalized largely in terms of students' standardized test scores produced within a context of school and teacher accountability (Shepard, 2000). Given our conversations with teacher educators and practicing teachers, it seems that, at least in the program we studied, the framework remains viable. That is, the particular version of social reconstructionism in practice seems to help literacy teachers and teacher educators raise issues of social justice and transformation and find practices consistent with their understandings of those issues. Nevertheless, to say that a theoretical framework is viable does not address questions about where its shortcomings lie or how it can be improved. For example, we want to know what the first year of teaching looks like for program graduates and what resources new teachers make use of to successfully transition into full-time teaching, while maintaining the progressive perspectives they develop in their preparation program. This and other questions are among those that shape our research agenda as we continue to examine our teacher preparation program.

REFERENCES

Adams, F. (1975). *Unearthing seeds of fire: The idea of highlander*. Winston Salem, NC: John F. Blair.

Allington, R., & Woodside-Jiron, H. (1999). The politics of literacy teaching: How "research" shaped educational policy. *Educational Researcher, 28*(8), 4–13.

Andersen, M., & Collins, P. (1995). *Race, class, and gender: An anthology*. New York: Wadsworth.

Apple, M. (1998). Are markets and standards democratic? *Educational Researcher, 27*(6), 24–28.

Berliner, D.C., & Biddle, B. (1995). *The manufactured crisis: Myths, fraud, and the attack on America's public schools*. Reading, MA: Addison-Wesley.

Coles, G. (2000). *Misreading reading: The bad science that hurts children*. Portsmouth, NH: Heinemann.

Collins, P. (1991). *Black feminist thought: Knowledge consciousness and the politics of empowerment*. New York: Routledge.

Collins, P. (1998). *Fighting words: Black women and the search for justice*. Minneapolis, MN: University of Minnesota Press.

Delpit, L. (1995). *Other people's children*. New York: New Press.

Dewey, J. (1944). *Experience and education*. New York: Macmillan.

Dyer, R. (1997). *White*. New York: Routledge.

Edelsky, C. (1999). *Making justice our project: Teachers working toward critical whole language practice*. Urbana, IL: National Council of Teachers of English.

Erickson, F. (1986). Qualitative methods in research on teaching. In M.C. Wittrock (Ed.), *Handbook of research on teaching* (3rd ed., pp. 119–161). New York: Macmillan.

Fairclough, N. (1992). *Discourse and social change*. Malden, MA: Blackwell Publishers.

Frankenberg, R. (1993). *White women, race matters: The social construction of whiteness*. Minneapolis, MN: University of Minnesota Press.

Freire, P. (1970). *Pedagogy of the oppressed*. New York: Seabury.

Gee, J.P. (1999). Critical issues: Reading and the new literacy studies: Reframing the national academy of sciences report on reading. *Journal of Literacy Research, 31*, 355–374.

Glaser, B.G., & Strauss, A.L. (1967). *The discovery of grounded theory: Strategies for qualitative research*. New York: Aldine.

Gore, J.M. (1993). *The struggle for pedagogies: Critical and feminist discourses as regimes of truth*. New York: Routledge.

Greene, M. (1988). *Dialectic of freedom*. New York: Teachers College Press.

Greene, M. (1995). *Releasing the imagination*. San Francisco: Jossey-Bass.

Hicks, D. (1995–1996). Discourse learning and teaching. In M.W. Apple (Ed.), *Review of research in education* (Vol. 21, pp. 49–95). Washington, DC: American Educational Research Association.

hooks, b. (1990). *Yearning: Race, gender, and cultural politics*. Boston: South End Press.

hooks, b. (1994). *Teaching to transgress: Education as the practice of freedom*. New York: Routledge.

Kohn, A. (1999). *The schools our children deserve: Moving beyond traditional classrooms and "tougher standards."* New York: Houghton-Mifflin.

Kozol, J. (1991). *Savage inequalities.* New York: Crown.

Ladson-Billings, G. (1994). *The dreamkeepers: Successful teachers of African-American children.* San Francisco: Jossey-Bass.

Luke, A. (1995–1996). Text and discourse in education: An introduction to critical discourse analysis. In M.W. Apple (Ed.), *Review of research in education* (Vol. 21, pp. 3–48). Washington, DC: American Educational Research Association.

Luke, A. (1998). Getting over method: Literacy teaching as work in "New Times." *Language Arts, 75,* 305–313.

Luke, C., & Gore, J. (Eds.). (1992). *Feminisms and critical pedagogy.* New York: Routledge.

McCaleb, S.P. (1994). *Communities of learners.* Hillsdale, NJ: Erlbaum.

McLaughlin, M.W., & Shepard, L.A. (1995). *Improving education through standards-based reform: A report of the National Academy of Education panel on standards-based educational reform.* Stanford, CA: National Academy of Education.

Morris, W. (Ed.). (1975). *The American Heritage dictionary of the English language.* Boston: Houghton Mifflin.

Mosenthal, P. (1999). Critical issues: Forging conceptual unum in the literacy field of pluribus: An agenda-analytic perspective. *Journal of Literacy Research, 31,* 213–254.

New London Group. (1996). A pedagogy of multiliteracies: Designing social futures. *Harvard Educational Review, 66,* 60–92.

Pearson, P.D. (2000, April). *Learning to teach reading: The status of the knowledge base.* Paper presented at the meeting of the International Reading Association, Indianapolis, IN.

Shannon, P. (1990). *The struggle to continue: Progressive reading instruction in the United States.* Portsmouth, NH Heinemann.

Shannon, P. (1992). *Becoming political: Readings and writings in the politics of literacy education.* Portsmouth, NH: Heinemann.

Shepard, L.A. (2000). The role of assessment in a learning culture. *Educational Researcher, 29*(7), 4–14.

Shor, I. (1992). *Empowering education: Critical teaching for social change.* Chicago: University of Chicago Press.

Snow, C.E., Burns, M.S., & Griffin, P. (1998). *Preventing reading difficulties in young children.* Washington: National Academy Press.

Stanley, W.B. (1992) *Curriculum for utopia: Social reconstructionism and critical pedagogy in the postmodern era.* Albany, NY: State University Press.

Weiler, K. (1988). *Women teaching for change: Gender, class & power.* New York: Bergin & Garvey.

Whitford, B.L., & Jones, K. (2000). Kentucky lesson: How high stakes school accountability undermines a performance-based curriculum vision. In B.L. Whitford & K. Jones (Eds.), *Accountability, assessment, and teacher commitment: Lessons from Kentucky's reform efforts.* Albany, NY: State University of New York Press.

Zinn, H. (1995). *A people's history of the United States: 1492–present.* New York: Harper Perennial.

CHAPTER 7

Teacher education, diversity, and literacy

Kathryn H. Au and Margaret J. Maaka
UNIVERSITY OF HAWAII

In this chapter we look at the intersection of three topics that are each complex in and of themselves: teacher education, diversity, and literacy. We want to ground this discussion in the work we have been conducting in Hawaii. Like many literacy researchers, we are also teacher educators. At the University of Hawaii, we have had the opportunity to conduct an effort called the Ka Lama O Ke Kaiaulu Teacher Education Initiative (Ka Lama, for short), which aims to increase the number of Native Hawaiian teachers in schools in their own communities. The research findings and experiences from our work on the Wai'anae Coast of O'ahu provide the examples for this discussion of teacher education, diversity, and literacy.

Trends and Issues of Diversity in the United States

Issues of diversity are particularly salient in Hawaii, which is the first of the 50 U.S. states to have no majority group. An increasing diversity is evident, however, in the U.S. population as a whole and in the student population in particular. In the 1990s, 35% of students in the United States were members of minority groups: 16.7% black, 13% Hispanic, 3.6% Asian and Pacific American, and 1.1% Native American (National Center for Education Statistics, 1998). U.S. census projections for 2025 indicate that the student population will become even more diverse. At that time, 23% of students will be Hispanic, 17.3% black, 7.4% Asian and Pacific American, and 1.3% Native American (U.S. Bureau of the Census, 1997). These changes are of great significance for literacy educators be-

cause of the continuing gap between the achievement of mainstream and nonmainstream students.

In contrast to the student population, which has become increasingly diverse, the population of teachers in the United States has become somewhat less diverse in recent years. In 1993–1994, only 7.4% of U.S. teachers were black, 4.2% were Hispanic, and 1.9% were of other minority backgrounds (National Center for Education Statistics, 1997). The population of teachers is not shifting in parallel with the dramatic changes in the student population.

These trends highlight the urgency for addressing two issues in teacher education. The first centers on the recruitment of many more individuals of diverse backgrounds into the teaching profession. The second centers on the preparation of all teachers to bring students of diverse backgrounds to high levels of literacy in school. Both of these issues are addressed in this chapter.

Context of Our Work in Hawaii

About 24% of the students enrolled in Hawaii's public schools are of Native Hawaiian ancestry. However, only 8% of the teachers in the public schools are of this same ethnicity (Office of Accountability and School Instructional Support/ Planning and Evaluation Group, 1997). The Wai'anae Coast, Ka Lama's home base, is a low-income, rural area about a 45-minute drive from downtown Honolulu. About 67% percent of the students in the public schools on the Wai'anae Coast are of Hawaiian ancestry (Office of Planning and Evaluation, 1995). In contrast, even in this area heavily populated by Hawaiians, only 9% of the teachers are Hawaiian (Tikunoff, Ward, &

Broekhuizen, 1993). It is quite possible, then, for a Hawaiian student on the Wai'anae Coast to go through schooling without ever having a Hawaiian teacher to serve as a role model.

In our years of working on the Wai'anae Coast, we have observed a phenomenon that may be called the "revolving door." This phrase best describes the dramatic turnover of teachers that can take place in area public schools every 3 years. Kathy, in particular, has observed this prevalent trend during her 20-year association with Wai'anae Coast schools.

Approximately two thirds of the graduates of the College of Education at the University of Hawaii, the state's major teacher preparation institution, receive their first teaching assignments on the Wai'anae Coast. However, after 3 years, when they have received tenure, many of these teachers move to schools closer to the city. It is natural for them to want to teach in schools close to their homes, usually in the suburbs west of Honolulu. As a result, schools on the Wai'anae Coast can experience a faculty turnover of up to 50% in a given year. One elementary school principal stated 3 years ago that she would have to hire 18 new teachers, or about half of her staff. In the present school year, this same school needed about a dozen teachers. Needless to say, the revolving door must be of concern to those seeking to improve the quality of education on the Wai'anae Coast.

Schools on the Wai'anae Coast, like those in other diverse, low-income communities, have their own unique characteristics as cultural and educational environments. The Wai'anae Coast schools all qualify for the federally funded Title I program, with over 75% of the students from low-income families. Many of the students score in the lowest three stanines on standardized tests of reading achievement, and almost none score in the top three stanines. In other words, students in schools on the Wai'anae Coast show social and academic difficulties similar to those of students in comparable communities on the U.S. mainland.

As might be expected, beginning teachers from outside the community are likely to experience a form of culture shock when they start teaching in Wai'anae Coast schools (Au, in press). In common with beginning teachers throughout the United States, they are likely to be from middle-class backgrounds and unfamiliar with diverse, low-income communities. These teachers usually require a period of 2 or 3 years to make the adjustment to this new cultural context and to acquire effective strategies for classroom management and instruction. Typically, they acquire these strategies right about the time that they transfer from the Wai'anae Coast to schools in the middle-class suburbs. Thus, the Wai'anae Coast continues to be a training ground for beginning teachers, with the benefits of this training accruing to students in more affluent communities.

It is difficult to imagine how schools with such high rates of teacher turnover can successfully sustain innovations in their literacy curricula or carry out other reforms likely to make a significant difference in student achievement. In fact, the two Wai'anae Coast elementary schools that have been successful in implementing strong, home-grown balanced literacy curricula are led by principals who have significantly reduced the turnover of teachers at their schools.

In short, the revolving door creates a serious obstacle to improving the literacy achievement of students on the Wai'anae Coast. One solution being explored is the recruitment of residents of the Wai'anae Coast to become teachers. This effort is addressed later in this chapter.

Teacher Education to Serve Diverse Communities

The job of teacher education resides with colleges, universities, and school systems. These institutions, such as the University of Hawaii and the Hawaii State Department of Education, often see their missions in terms of broad, statewide responsibilities. For this reason, teacher education is usually viewed as a generic process, in the sense that the goal is to prepare teachers to work effectively in a broad range of settings (for example, what Haberman, 1996, terms the universal approach). Christensen (1996) presents an analysis showing the 83 knowledge-based instructional models used by faculty at 42 teacher education institutions. Only one institution identified multicultural education as one of its models. In general, the focus in teacher education programs is not to prepare teachers specifically to teach in schools in diverse, low-income communities, as these are just one subset of schools in the state. The upshot of this generic approach to teacher education is that most graduates do not receive specialized preparation for teaching in communities such as the Wai'anae Coast. As a result, they are generally better prepared to teach in schools in middle-class, suburban settings, similar to those in which they attended school.

In our work on the Wai'anae Coast, we have tried to look at teacher education from a different perspective. We are not viewing teacher education as a generic process, but as a process specifically aimed at preparing excellent teachers for this particular community (Au, in press). Because of this perspective, one of our challenges is to make sure that our efforts in teacher education build on resources in the community and are consistent with long-term community development efforts. As teacher educators who are non-Hawaiian and outsiders to the Wai'anae Coast, we depend on insiders, particularly those of Hawaiian ancestry, to give us the guidance we need. We have a community advisory board that consists of community leaders, principals from area schools, preservice teachers from the community, and colleagues at the local campus of a community college. Many of the community advisory board members have children or grandchildren currently attending public schools on the Wai'anae Coast. This advisory board meets every semester to hear updates on the teacher education initiative and to provide us with feedback about our work.

The contributions of advisory board members have been central to the success of our efforts. When we needed a place to hold our courses, one of the advisory board members offered the use of a meeting room at his organization's headquarters. After a semester, we moved our courses to the community college, an idea proposed by another advisory board member. A third advisory board member, who works in an award-winning drug rehabilitation program, pointed out the need for teachers to understand how drug abuse affects students and their families. Subsequently, we incorporated this topic into our classes. Finally, advisory board members came up with the idea for the Education Academy (discussed later in this chapter). This idea was generated by the preservice teachers who had grown up in the community and knew the hardships faced by those aspiring to become teachers.

We involve instructors from the community in the teacher education courses. These instructors, most of whom are of Hawaiian ancestry, play important roles in helping the preservice teachers to become aware of and value opportunities for learning that connect children to the community and to their cultural heritage. Because a sense of place is so important in Hawaiian culture (Kanahele, 1986), it is essential for the preservice teachers to see connections to the community as central to their curriculum development efforts on behalf of Hawaiian children. One of the community instructors directs a cultural learning center that children can visit to learn about traditional agriculture and crafts, as well as legends and geology. In addition to familiarizing the preservice teachers with the work of this center, he showed them archaeological sites that children would soon be able to tour. Three of the community instructors are artists. One specializes in kapa making, the traditional Hawaiian bark cloth. She showed the preservice teachers how to engage children in this craft as a way of teaching them about the ingenuity, artistry, skill, and effort required to make clothing in traditional times. The other is a local school teacher who conducted a course called Hawaiian Art for the Elementary Classroom. In this course, the preservice teachers explored strategies to implement a culturally responsive elementary art curriculum in which forms, ideas, and concepts derived from Hawaiian culture, language, and history were integrated with Western visual arts. Still another community instructor is a published poet, and she demonstrated how teachers could use poetry to encourage children to write about their life experiences.

The point of these examples is to suggest that the job of preparing teachers to teach in a diverse, low-income community is not best handled by university-based teacher educators working alone. Colleagues from the community should play an influential role and, in the true spirit of community ownership, eventually come to direct these efforts. As outsiders to the community, we can offer our expertise as teacher educators and literacy researchers. However, we believe it is important in our work to follow the policy directions set by our advisory board, which represent the broader interests of the community on the Wai'anae Coast.

First Issue: Recruiting Teachers From the Community

We hypothesized that the difficulties created by the revolving door described earlier in this chapter could be solved—or at least greatly reduced—by recruiting residents of the Wai'anae Coast, especially Native Hawaiians, to become teachers in Wai'anae Coast schools. Residents already have a commitment to the community and are likely to remain in the area for a long time. A school with a stable core of teachers—who reside in the community and who have received the professional development necessary to achieve excellence in teaching—is likely to provide students with higher quality educational experiences than a school lacking this core. The core group of teachers can provide the school with leadership, in the literacy curriculum and other areas, and help to socialize teachers new to the school. They can sustain an ongoing program of professional development at the school. They can build relationships with community leaders and students' families. In the classroom, they can set high expectations for students' achievement and serve as role models, showing that members of the community can achieve success as teachers and as educational leaders. They can raise students' aspirations and encourage them to go on to higher education.

Recruiting residents proved extremely difficult with the first two cohorts of preservice teachers. Our goal is to have about half the members of each cohort be residents of the Wai'anae Coast, and we fell far short of this goal with these cohorts. The first cohort began with 29 students, but only six of these were residents of the Wai'anae Coast. The second cohort began with 26 students, of whom only four had ties to the Wai'anae Coast. By the time the second cohort had been admitted, it was clear that we needed a new approach. Kathy raised this problem at an advisory board meeting held in June of 1998. In the ensuing discussion, the source of the difficulty became obvious: In order to be admitted to the preservice cohort, students had to have sufficient college credits to be enrolled as juniors in the College of Education. The Wai'anae Coast is an area with a high rate of high school dropouts, only a small number of students who enter college, and a smaller number still who succeed in advancing past the first few courses.

The advice from the community advisory board was clear. The situation was too urgent to wait for students to come through the existing pipeline. Instead, we had to create our own pipeline. We needed to find residents interested in becoming teachers and help them to earn associate's degrees from the local community college. With these degrees in hand, they could then gain admission to the College of Education and our preservice cohort. To accomplish this goal, Kathy wrote a grant for the Ka Lama Education Academy, modeled after a health academy already in place at the local community college. In October 1998, the Education Academy opened its doors. The third Ka Lama cohort includes six community residents who came through the pipeline created by the Education Academy, in addition to two other students with ties to the Wai'anae Coast. We have not yet achieved our goal of having half the cohort come from the coast, but we are moving closer to it. It is expected that the fourth cohort, which will begin in the 2002 fall semester, will see our goal accomplished.

Second Issue: Preparing All Teachers for Diversity

The Ka Lama teacher education cohort is one of several cohorts in the elementary education program conducted by the College of Education at the University of Hawaii (Stephens, Zilliox, & Deering, 1998–1999). This is a full-time, 2-year program. Preservice teachers enter as juniors and graduate with bachelor's degrees in education. Courses in the program are a typical mix of foundations and methods courses. In the first 3 semesters, the preservice teachers spend 10 hours per week in the classrooms of mentor teachers; the fourth semester is spent in full-time student teaching. Students in the Ka Lama cohort have their field experience, including student teaching, in the classrooms of mentor teachers on the Wai'anae Coast. Continuity is provided by having one or two faculty members (in the case of the Ka Lama cohort, the two of us) who remain with each cohort over the 2 years, coordinating arrangements, teaching courses, and supervising the preservice teachers' work in the field.

The overall perspective that we present in courses to the Ka Lama preservice cohort is that education should be seen as a process of social change, not as a process of reproducing the existing social order (e.g., McLaren, 1989). Many of the preservice teachers, including some of those from the Wai'anae Coast, have not thought broadly about how education can facilitate the process of social change in a particular community. However, it does not take much experience in Wai'anae Coast schools for most of the preservice teachers to be convinced of the need for this approach.

Under this overarching theme, the additional themes of literacy, multicultural education, and Hawaiian studies run through our courses. The theme of literacy is appropriate because of the importance of literacy for success in school as well as in the workplace. Furthermore, as mentioned earlier, students in classrooms on the Wai'anae Coast typically need a great deal of powerful instruction to become good readers and writers. The theme of multicultural education is appropriate because of the diversity within the U.S. population, the population of Hawaii, and the population of the Wai'anae Coast. The theme of Hawaiian studies is appropriate because the majority of students and residents of the Wai'anae Coast are of Hawaiian ancestry. Hawaiian studies is an area of high interest for elementary students on the Wai'anae Coast, and in an integrated approach, can be a vehicle for teaching concepts in all the academic subjects. About one third of the Ka Lama preservice teachers have academic majors in Hawaiian studies, so this is obviously an area of high interest for them, as well.

EDUCATIONAL FOUNDATIONS. In place of a typical foundations course, Kathy teaches a course on Hawaiian and American foundations of education. This course includes several sessions at the Cultural Learning Center at Ka'ala, in which the preservice teachers study traditional crafts and archaeological sites under the direction of community instructors. The preservice teachers learn the history of education in Hawaii and compare and contrast these trends and events with those that took place on the U.S. mainland. They gain an understanding of the relationships among Hawaiian ways of knowing (Meyer, 1998) and Dewey's vision of progressive education (Dewey, 1944).

The main project is the writing of a family educational history. Kathy uses the educational history of her own family as an example. So far, all the preservice teachers have entered the course expressing a dislike of history as an academic subject. However, Kathy finds that this attitude can be changed if she succeeds in helping the preservice teachers to see themselves and their families as part of history. She raises questions she hopes will provoke critical thinking. For example, she asks the Hawaiian preservice teachers to consider the influence of language and politics in the educational histories of their families. In all likelihood, until the 1880s, members of their families attended schools taught by Hawaiian teachers in the Hawaiian language. At what point did their families cease speaking, reading, and writing the Hawaiian language? What influenced this change and the shift to English? Why have Hawaiians as a group not shared the same educational successes as Asian immigrant groups, such as the Japanese Americans? Similarly, she asks the Japanese American preservice teachers to consider the influence of language and politics in their families' educational histories. When and why did their families immigrate to Hawaii? How have family members' educational opportunities and accomplishments changed across the generations? What was the effect of World War II, which disrupted families but also brought the educational benefits of the G.I. Bill to men who had served in the armed forces?

The preservice teachers prepare written reports on their families' educational histories and present their main findings to the class. These presentations enable members of the class to gain insights into similarities and differences in educational experiences within and across ethnic groups.

Through these activities the preservice teachers gain a sense of how larger social, political, and economic forces have shaped their own educational histories and those of their classmates. A good number of the Hawaiian and Filipino preservice teachers in these cohorts are first-generation college students, and it is especially important for these students, from groups underrepresented in the teaching force, to appreciate the significance of having reached this new level of education.

The culminating activity in this course is an interesting one, as well. The preservice teachers are asked to work with a partner to present their vision of Hawaiian education. The view most often presented is that the setting for education should be the *ahupua'a*, the traditional Hawaiian land division that extends from the mountains to the sea. In short, the preservice teachers come to see the setting for education as not just the school, but the community.

Unlike many foundation courses on educational psychology, which emphasize theories or topics examined in isolation and out of context, Margie's course focuses on helping preservice teachers to develop theories of learning and teaching that are appropriate for schools in diverse communities—in this case, schools on the Wai'anae Coast. Like Kathy's foundation course, this one also rejects the notion of teacher preparation as a generic, prescriptive process.

Early in the semester, Margie asks her preservice teachers to write about what motivated them to become educators. This exercise is the first important step in helping them gain an awareness of themselves as they develop as teachers. Several explain that their own school experiences were the impetus for choosing careers in teaching. For many, these experiences were marked by discrimination, a lack of role models, and a lack of connection to the school system. The desire to make quality education accessible to all children is what drives many Ka Lama preservice teachers.

As they consider their own developing teaching stances, the preservice teachers are asked to consider one essential question, What is important and why? With this as the anchor, the course promotes two important imperatives: (1) teaching must be a process of inquiry, experimentation, reflection, and refinement; and (2) school success must be an expectation for all children. In short, the focus of this course is the development of teachers who are well-informed professionals able to reflect critically on their own theories and practices, and who are accountable to students, parents, and the community.

Because conventional wisdom about learning and teaching may be the very thing that is responsible for the poor school performance of Hawaiian children, the Ka Lama preservice teachers are encouraged to question the status quo. As their studies progress, the preservice teachers critically examine the works of other educators, including Gardner's (1983) theory of multiple intelligences, Purkey and Novak's (1996) theory of invitational education, Piper's (1998) work on language and learning, Hirsch's (1987) cultural literacy curriculum, Kohn's (1998) provocative commentaries on U.S. schooling, and Au's (1997a, 1997b) research on schooling for children of diverse cultural backgrounds. Opportunities to critique different theories and approaches, especially those that do not place the interests and educational well-being of each learner as paramount concerns, enables the preservice teachers to become confident in their abilities to make sound decisions regarding their own teaching stances. Throughout the course, Margie bombards the preservice teachers with critical concerns and considerations: What should be the aims of an effective learning and teaching program? Is it possible to provide a range of learning programs, supported by innovative teaching methods and quality resources? What questions need to be asked about teacher development? What questions need to be asked about children's learning? Is it acceptable for education programs to ignore the multicultural nature of Hawaii's society? What does successful teaching in culturally diverse classrooms entail? How are children "turned on" to school?

The end-of-semester goal is to have the preservice teachers understand the importance of recognizing, respecting, and responding to the educational needs, experiences, and values of all children—both female and male, children of all ethnic groups, children of different abilities, and children of different social and religious backgrounds. By providing opportunities for personal and professional self-discoveries and by modeling culturally responsive teaching practices, Margie encourages the Ka Lama preservice teachers to accept the challenge to develop their own gender-inclusive, nonracist, and nondiscriminatory classroom practices.

LITERACY LEARNING AND TEACHING. The elementary education program in our college calls for a two-semester sequence in methods for teaching literacy. Kathy teaches the first-semester course, while Margie teaches the second. Kathy's course draws from the research she conducted while employed at the Kamehameha Elementary Education Program (KEEP), a long-term educational research and development effort. This research identified the features of classroom instruction used by teachers effective in bringing Hawaiian students to high levels of literacy (e.g., Au & Carroll, 1997). A substantial portion of the data for this research came from classrooms on the Wai'anae Coast. The findings point to the importance of ownership of literacy as the overarching goal in the literacy curriculum. Students who have ownership of literacy use reading and writing in school as well as in the community, for purposes they have set for themselves (Au, 1997a). Literacy instruction centers on the writers' workshop and the process approach to writing (e.g., Graves, 1983), and the readers' workshop and literature-based instruction (e.g., Raphael & Au, 1998).

Most preservice teachers have not previously had the opportunity to participate in the readers' and writers' workshops, so Kathy's first task is to provide them with this experience. She conducts a writers' workshop to engage the preservice teachers in the process approach to writing. They create topic lists, draft, receive feedback through conferences with peers and with Kathy, make revisions, and edit personal narratives. They share their narratives through the Author's Chair (Graves & Hansen, 1983). Similarly, Kathy conducts a readers' workshop to engage the preservice teachers in literature-based instruction. She has the preservice teachers join Book Clubs (Raphael & McMahon, 1994) in which they read, prepare written responses, and engage in open-ended discussions of novels. While conducting the workshops, Kathy models how a teacher goes about teaching minilessons, conducting conferences, selecting novels for students to read, and discussing adaptations appropriate for different grade levels.

Our goal is not just to teach the preservice teachers the instructional strategies associated with these approaches—our goal is also to build their ownership of literacy. Our research shows that a surprising number of our preservice teachers do not enjoy reading and writing and do not see themselves as readers and writers. Sometimes this dislike or indifference to reading and writing is a matter of personal preference, for example, in the case of a preservice teacher who has always had a greater interest in the visual arts. More often, however, this negative attitude has developed through boring or painful school experiences with literacy. An example is the preservice teacher who reported that she had disliked writing since an incident in which a teacher had criticized her writing in front of the class. As literacy educators, we have come to appreciate that the teacher must be a reader and writer to inspire students to love literacy and to read and write well (Graves, 1990).

Kathy finds that having the preservice teachers prepare literacy portfolios is another way to build their ownership of literacy. She follows the model developed by Hansen (1992), asking the preservice teachers to answer the question, Who am I as a reader and writer? The assignment involves having the preservice teachers choose four artifacts (some always end up including more), accompanied by half-page reflections stating why they chose each artifact and what it shows about them as readers and writers. The preservice teachers are also asked to write about their strengths and challenges as readers and writers, their goals for themselves as readers and writers, and the steps they can take to meet these goals. As with the personal narratives, the literacy portfolios are shared in the Author's Chair.

POLITICS OF LITERACY. In recent years, we have found it increasingly important to teach preservice teachers about the politics of literacy. The schools on the Wai'anae Coast are subject to the pressures seen in schools in other diverse, low-income communities across the U.S. mainland. The problem is typically posed as that of needing to raise scores on standardized tests. Particularly at the primary grades, most standardized tests emphasize the testing of lower level reading skills in isolation. The push to improve children's performance on such items frequently results in the adoption of reading programs focused on the teaching of skills in isolation, through rote learning activities. Such programs reflect a vision of literacy and instruction very different from the one we present in our language arts methods courses.

Margie's literacy course follows Kathy's. It is designed to establish a context and pull pieces together. In keeping with the focus of other Ka Lama courses, this one encourages the preservice teachers to develop approaches to literacy learning and teaching that are applicable for classrooms on the Wai'anae Coast.

The course begins with an examination and a reconceptualization of *literacy*. As a continuation of a course on multicultural issues in education, the preservice teachers examine the impact of European and American colonialism on the indigenous peoples of Hawaii and how this has informed literacy learning and teaching in schools. From visiting speakers and assigned readings, the preservice teachers learn about colonization and how it has stripped away the fundamental markers of Native Hawaiian cultural identity—sovereignty, ancestral lands, language, and traditional knowledge.

In class activities, preservice teachers of Hawaiian ancestry have spoken and written about what it is like to have their cultural literacy dismissed as a record of legitimate knowledge. Bearing the labels "primitive," "uncivilized, " and "ignorant" has been an overwhelming burden for many generations of Hawaiians. Ka Lama preservice teachers from other underrepresented groups also tell similar stories of degradation. From these experiences, the preservice teachers learn that, for some groups, regaining and developing positive identities and strong cultural bases involve constant struggles to recover or discover that which has been stripped away (see Giroux & McLaren, 1994; Rosaldo, 1989).

After bringing her preservice teachers to an understanding of both the power and politics of literacy, Margie spends the remainder of the semester providing opportunities for them to develop literacy curricula that reflect the unique culture of the Wai'anae Coast. When asked to state their beliefs about children's literacy learning, preservice teachers begin to formulate philosophies and goals for student learning. To help the preservice teachers make sense of the politics of literacy, Margie acquaints them with critical theory, including Shannon's (1989) analysis of the tensions between the dominant scientific-managerial tradition and the progressive tradition. Later, the preservice teachers work in small groups to identify literacy-related issues worthy of research. In the past, these issues have focused on the effectiveness of standardized assessment, conflicts between the home culture and the school culture, structured play in preschools and kindergartens, culturally responsive literacy curricula, prepackaged versus "home grown" curricula, and direct skills instruction.

At the end of the semester, each student is required to submit a language arts portfolio. This usually includes detailed notes on classroom management; the implementation of writers' and readers' workshops; integrated curriculum development, including the integration of the language arts (such as reading, writing, speaking, listening, shaping, viewing, moving, and watching) and the integration of language arts across the curriculum; provisions for students with special needs (with a major focus on diagnostic reading and writing programs); methods for assessing children's learning; culturally responsive teaching; and balanced literacy curricula.

While the Ka Lama preservice teachers are well aware that there is no single or simple solution to improving the literacy achievement of Hawaiian children and others from underrepresented groups, they understand that the push in Wai'anae Coast schools for commercial programs favoring the teaching of lower level skills in isolation is no accident. They recognize this push as a systematic result of institutional forces that tend to limit the literacy learning of Hawaiian and other students of diverse backgrounds, by reducing their opportunities to receive instruction in higher level thinking. Once they have classrooms of their own, Ka Lama graduates must have strategies for promoting students' ownership of literacy and higher level thinking, following approaches such as the process approach to writing and literature-based instruction, while working around and against forces promoting an overemphasis on the teaching of lower level skills in isolation.

At the same time, the Ka Lama preservice teachers receive extensive preparation in the teaching of word identification skills. They are presented with research on decoding by analogy and are taught the Cunninghams' (1992) strategy, Making Words. They learn how to build word identification instruction into shared and guided reading lessons (Fountas & Pinnell, 1996). In addition, they learn to assess children's development of word identification skills through running records (Clay, 1993). The emphasis is on teaching word identification skills in a meaningful manner that connects with children's existing knowledge.

In short, their literacy courses charge the preservice teachers with the responsibility of developing literacy curricula that acknowledge and respect the culture and life experiences of children in schools on the Wai'anae Coast.

EXPLORING CULTURAL IDENTITY. In Kathy's literacy course, she introduces both the personal narratives and literacy portfolios by sitting in the Author's Chair and sharing her own work (Au, 1998–1999). She does not tell the preservice teachers that they should explore issues of cultural identity through these assignments, but she models by example how she has chosen to do so in her own writing. Kathy often reads aloud narratives about her two grandmothers, part of a larger piece she wrote exploring the roots of her research interests in personal experience (Au, 1997b). Her literacy portfolio includes a biography of one of her grandmothers, based on oral history interviews; a poem written in Hawaii Creole English (Kathy's first language); and a book of poetry by her friend Wing Tek Lum (Lum, 1987), a Chinese American poet. The reflections reveal her interest in using literacy to explore, understand, and preserve her Chinese American heritage. Many of the preservice teachers choose to follow this example. They have written about the lives of their Hawaiian, Filipino, Japanese, and Native American relatives; about the tensions of growing up in immigrant families; and about the pressures of raising one's younger siblings in a large Hawaiian family. Their literacy portfolios contain artifacts including chants written in the Hawaiian language, family histories written for ethnic studies courses, and religious or inspirational texts.

Teacher educators at other institutions tell us that most of their students are young, white females from affluent suburban communities who have little experience with issues of cultural diversity. We feel fortunate as teacher educators to work with preservice teachers of different ethnicities and cultural identities, because we can design our courses to take advantage of this diversity. We can give these preservice teachers opportunities to hear presentations of personal narratives, literacy portfolios, and family educational histories by classmates with cultural identities both similar to and different from their own. Through these presentations they can arrive at generalizations while still appreciating individuality, and the simplistic stereotyping of ethnic and cultural groups is more likely to be avoided.

Margie's course on multicultural issues in education focuses on the themes of cultural identity, schooling, and literacy. Throughout the semester, the preservice teachers develop understandings of their own cultures, as well as understandings of the diverse cultures of others. Course activities encourage the preservice teachers to discuss their experiences with a range of issues, such as family histories, stereotypes and discrimination, celebrations of diversity, and literacy instruction in a Hawaiian setting, including the qualities of an effective teacher.

A course on Hawaiian art also places cultural identity at the center of discussion. Taught by a local Hawaiian artist, the course inspires preservice teachers to explore the indigenous art of Hawaii as a framework for viewing the art of other cultures. This unique perspective places Hawaiian art, language, and culture at the center of study rather than on the periphery. This stance is reflected in the Coollongatta Statement on Indigenous Rights in Education (1993), which states that indigenous people across the world have the right to establish education systems that reflect, respect, and embrace indigenous cultural values, philosophies, ideologies, and practices. Through this course, the preservice teachers develop deeper understandings of and appreciations for the role of art in both traditional and contemporary Hawaiian and Western societies.

Literacy is also connected to the preservice teachers' exploration of cultural identity through reading literature in which authors of diverse backgrounds address issues of cultural identity. In this way, literacy becomes a tool in the preservice teachers' examination of the meanings, values, and beliefs that they share with members of the same cultural group; the beliefs they have about members of other cultural groups; and the beliefs they have about effective ways to teach children, especially those of diverse backgrounds. Through these experiences, Ka Lama preservice teachers also learn how to use literacy to help children explore their cultural identities.

While encouraging the preservice teachers to formulate their own ideas about multiculturalism and multicultural education, Margie requires them to examine issues such as inequity in educational opportunities, the origins of minority group status, the language achievements of children of diverse backgrounds, and how literacy is used as a tool of empowerment and disempowerment.

Issues of Hawaiian identity, autonomy, and self-determination have important implications for teachers in Hawaii, especially non-Hawaiian teachers. Initiatives for the educational advancement of Hawaiians must include decision making that reflects Hawaiian realities and aspirations. The role of Hawaiians, therefore, is critical.

CULTURALLY RESPONSIVE INSTRUCTION. In our view, culturally responsive instruction should enable students to learn challenging academic content that is relevant in mainstream contexts as well as the students' own community (see, for example, the view of culturally responsive pedagogy presented by Ladson-Billings, 1995). Four aspects of culturally responsive instruction play an important role in the courses we conduct with the preservice teachers.

First, the work of the anthropologist John D'Amato plays an important part in the way we teach the preservice teachers to address classroom management. D'Amato (1986) found that Hawaiian children valued two qualities in their friends: niceness and toughness. Leaders or popular children were those judged by their peers to be kind and generous to those around them, yet they could not be pushed around. D'Amato noted that teachers who showed the most effective management in classrooms with Hawaiian children exhibited these same qualities of niceness and toughness. To the

children, niceness meant that the teacher treated everyone fairly and did not have favorites. Toughness meant that the teacher could command respect and keep the class firmly under control. D'Amato used the metaphor of a "smile with teeth" to describe this management style. We use the same metaphor of a smile with teeth to explain classroom management to the preservice teachers. The majority of preservice teachers begin their work in classrooms by showing a great deal of smile and not enough teeth, but they usually reach the right balance by the end of the second semester.

The second aspect of culturally responsive instruction is peer teaching-learning interactions, based on research conducted by the anthropologist Cathie Jordan (1985). Anthropological research has shown that many Hawaiian children grow up in families with sibling caretaking (Gallimore, Boggs, & Jordan, 1974). This means that while parents provide overall supervision, older children have major responsibilities for taking care of their younger brothers and sisters. These responsibilities may include seeing that their charges are fed and dressed for school in the morning, are given baths in the evening, and do their homework. These experiences with sibling caretaking mean that many Hawaiian children come to school prepared to teach and learn from peers and near-peers. Teachers do well in classrooms with Hawaiian children when they understand how to take advantage of this preference for peer teaching-learning interactions, for example, by allowing children to complete assignments in peer work groups. Within the writers' workshop, the preservice teachers are taught to encourage children to help one another through peer conferences. Within the readers' workshop, they learn to use partner reading as well as literature discussion circles or Book Clubs.

The third aspect, which is based on Kathy's research, involves talk story-like participation structures. Many studies have documented cultural differences in the patterning of face-to-face interaction, including differences in speaking, listening, and turn taking (e.g., Trueba, Guthrie, & Au, 1981). Most common in schools is a speech event known as classroom recitation, in which the teacher asks a question and calls on a student to answer (Cazden, 1988). The teacher then evaluates the student's response, and the cycle of teacher initiation-student response-teacher evaluation (IRE) begins again. The IRE pattern reflects the value attached to individual achievement in many schools; in these cases the teacher spotlight shines on the one student who knows the answer.

In general, young Hawaiian children perform poorly when teachers conduct discussions following the IRE pattern (Boggs, 1972). They tend to be more engaged, cover more ideas from the text, and make more logical inferences when teachers conduct discussions following a different pattern—talk story, a Hawaiian community speech event (Au & Mason, 1981). In talk story, participants recount events or convey ideas by speaking in rhythmic alternation. Talk story reflects the value attached to cooperation in Hawaiian culture. In reading lessons conducted with talk story-like participation structures, the point is not to shine as an individual but to work together with other students to interpret the story.

The fourth aspect centers on Hawaiian studies, and it differs from the first three in focusing on the content as well as the process of instruction (cf. Dei's [1994] discussion of Afrocentric pedagogy). Hawaiian studies provide a vehicle for the learning of rigorous academic concepts, through the medium of culturally relevant content. For example, in the language arts, stories of ancient Hawaii can be used to convey the idea that man has always sought to explain natural phenomena, such as why the sun rises and sets. Students find these ancient Hawaiian stories of interest and can move from culturally familiar content to the pourquoi tales of other cultures. Hawaiian studies content offers students a double benefit: They receive learning experiences that help them to feel pride in their own culture, while at the same time they learn important, generalizable academic concepts. Hawaiian studies also prepare students to participate in the social, cultural, and political revitalization of the Hawaiian people after many years of foreign domination (see Kame'eleihiwa, 1992).

Conclusion

Practical implications of our work with the Ka Lama Teacher Education Initiative may be sum-marized in terms of five lessons learned. First, to prepare teachers to be successful in schools in diverse, low-income communities, teacher education should be viewed as serving these particular communities. Teacher education cannot be viewed in a generic manner, as preparing teachers to teach in any and all communities, because in practice this approach results in teachers who are prepared to teach only in mainstream communities. Viewing teacher education as serving a community such as the Wai'anae Coast means tailoring efforts to meet particular needs, identified in collaboration with community leaders. Other steps involve providing preservice teachers with extensive field experience in area schools and working with instructors from the community.

Second, if one of the goals is to help residents of the community enter the teaching profession, it may well be necessary to create a pipeline for this purpose. This pipeline may consist of services such as those provided by the Ka Lama Education Academy, which enable residents first to graduate with associate's degrees from a local community college, and then to gain admission to a university preservice program.

Third, the content of the teacher education curriculum should be aimed at helping preservice teachers to see themselves as change agents. With the Ka Lama preservice cohort, several courses emphasize the overall theme of education as a process of social change. In the literacy courses, instructors highlight the importance of students' ownership of literacy and higher level thinking about text, including critical evaluation. Culturally responsive instruction, including Hawaiian studies content, is seen as building students' pride in their own cultural identity and as a vehicle for promoting higher academic achievement.

Fourth, preservice teachers should be offered numerous opportunities to reflect on issues of culture. They benefit from exploring their own cultural identities, as well as from learning about the cultural identities of others. Assignments that serve this purpose include personal narratives, literacy portfolios, and family educational histories. Instructor modeling of how these assignments may be used to explore issues of cultural identity is critical in encouraging preservice teachers to go beneath the surface of these issues.

Fifth, preservice teachers being prepared to teach in schools in diverse, low-income communities need to learn about the politics of literacy. Through their field experiences in these communities, preservice teachers quickly become aware of inequities in funding for education. They often see the narrowing of the curriculum that results when schools feel the pressure to raise scores on standardized tests. They need to understand how raising test scores, when those scores are based on the evaluation of skills in isolation, differs from bringing students to high levels of literacy. They should be guided to think about how they will provide excellent instruction oriented toward developing students' ownership of literacy and higher level thinking about text, when they may be working in school settings that create obstacles to their goals.

It is too soon to tell if the Ka Lama teacher education initiative will succeed in its aims of improving education and raising the literacy achievement of children on the Wai'anae Coast. At present we can only say that we take pride in the graduates of the Ka Lama preservice cohort who are now in classrooms of their own, and we believe that their performance provides validation for the ideas discussed in this chapter. A few graduates are already serving as mentor teachers for our present Ka Lama preservice teachers. This is a story in progress, which we hope will continue to inform literacy educators' ongoing discussions of the critical issues of diversity and teacher education.

REFERENCES

Au, K.H. (1997a). Ownership, literacy achievement, and students of diverse cultural backgrounds. In J.T. Guthrie & A. Wigfield (Eds.), *Reading engagement: Motivating readers through integrated instruction* (pp. 168-182). Newark, DE: International Reading Association.

Au, K.H. (1997b). Schooling, literacy, and cultural diversity in research and personal experience. In A. Neumann & P.L. Peterson (Eds.), *Learning from our lives: Women, research, and autobiography in education* (pp. 71-90). New York: Teachers College Press.

Au, K.H. (1998-1999). Personal narratives, literacy portfolios, and cultural identity. *National Forum of Teacher Education Journal, 8*(1), 14-20.

Au, K.H. (in press). Literacy education in the process of community development. In T. Shanahan & F. Rodriquez-

Brown (Eds.), *Forty-ninth yearbook of the National Reading Conference.* Chicago, IL: National Reading Conference.

Au, K.H., & Carroll, J.H. (1997). Improving literacy achievement through a constructivist approach: The KEEP Demonstration Classroom Project. *The Elementary School Journal, 97*(3), 203-221.

Au, K.H., & Mason, J.M. (1981). Social organizational factors in learning of read: The balance of rights hypothesis. *Reading Research Quarterly, 17,* 115-152.

Boggs, S.T. (1972). The meaning of questions and narratives to Hawaiian children. In C. Cazden, V. John, & D. Hymes (Eds.), *Functions of language in the classroom* (pp. 299-327). New York: Teachers College Press.

Cazden, C.B. (1988). *Classroom discourse: The language of teaching and learning.* Portsmouth, NH: Heinemann.

Christensen, D. (1996). The professional knowledge-research base for teacher education. In J. Sikula, T.J. Buttery, & E. Guyton (Eds.), *Handbook of research on teacher education* (2nd ed., pp. 38-52). New York: Macmillan.

Clay, M.M. (1993). *Reading recovery: A guidebook for teachers in training.* Portsmouth, NH: Heinemann.

Cunningham, P.M., & Cunningham, J.W. (1992). Making words: Enhancing the invented spelling-decoding connection. *The Reading Teacher, 46,* 106-115.

D'Amato, J. (1986). *"We cool, tha's why": A study of personhood and place in a class of Hawaiian second graders.* Unpublished doctoral dissertation, University of Hawaii, Honolulu.

Dei, G.J.S. (1994). Afrocentricity: A cornerstone of pedagogy. *Anthropology & Education Quarterly, 25*(1), 3-28 .

Dewey, J. (1944). *Democracy and education: An introduction to the philosophy of education.* New York: Free Press.

Fountas, I.C., & Pinnell, G.S. (1996). *Guided reading: Good first teaching for all children.* Portsmouth, NH: Heinemann.

Gallimore, R., Boggs, J.W., & Jordan, C. (1974). *Culture, behavior and education: A study of Hawaiian-Americans.* Beverly Hills: Sage.

Gardner, H. (1983). *Frames of mind: The theory of multiple intelligences.* New York: Basic Books.

Giroux, H.A., & McLaren, P. (Eds.). (1994). *Between borders: Pedagogy and the politics of cultural studies.* New York: Routledge.

Graves, D. (1983). *Writing: Teachers and children at work.* Exeter, NH: Heinemann.

Graves, D. (1990). *Discover your own literacy.* Portsmouth, NH: Heinemann.

Graves, D., & Hansen, J. (1983). The author's chair. *Language Arts, 60*(2), 176-183.

Haberman, M. (1996). Selecting and preparing culturally competent teachers for urban schools. In J. Sikula, T.J. Buttery, & E. Guyton (Eds.), *Handbook of research on teacher education* (2nd ed., pp. 747-760). New York: Macmillan.

Hansen, J. (1992). Teachers evaluate their own literacy. In D.H. Graves & B.S. Sunstein (Eds.), *Portfolio portraits,* (pp. 73-81). Portsmouth, NH: Heinemann.

Hirsch, E.D. (1987). *Cultural literacy: What every American needs to know.* Boston: Houghton Mifflin

Jordan, C. (1985). Translating culture: From ethnographic information to educational program. *Anthropology and Education Quarterly, 16,* 105–123.

Kame'eleihiwa, L. (1992). *Native land and foreign desires.* Honolulu, HI: Bishop Museum Press.

Kanahele, G.H.S. (1986). *Ku kanaka, stand tall: A search for Hawaiian values.* Honolulu, HI: University of Hawaii.

Kohn, A. (1998). *What to look for in a classroom...and other essays.* San Francisco: Jossey-Bass.

Ladson-Billings, G. (1995). Toward a theory of culturally relevant pedagogy. *American Educational Research Journal, 32*(3), 465–491.

Lum, W.T. (1987). *Expounding the doubtful points.* Honolulu, HI: Bamboo Ridge.

McLaren, P. (1989). *Life in schools: An introduction to critical pedagogy in the foundations of education.* New York: Longman.

Meyer, M.A. (1998). Native Hawaiian epistemology: Sites of empowerment and resistance. *Equity & Excellence in Education, 31*(1), 22–28.

National Center for Education Statistics. (1997). *The condition of education 1997.* Washington, DC: U.S. Department of Education, Office of Educational Research and Improvement.

National Center for Education Statistics. (1998). *The condition of education 1998.* Washington, DC: U.S. Department of Education, Office of Educational Research and Improvement.

National Organizing Committee of the World Indigenous Peoples' Conference on Education (1993). *The Coollongatta statement on Indigenous rights in education.* Coollongatta, Australia: Author.

Office of Accountability and School Instructional Support/Planning and Evaluation Group. (1997). *The superintendent's seventh annual report on school performance and improvement in Hawaii, 1996.* Honolulu, HI: Department of Education, State of Hawaii.

Piper, T. (1998). *Language and learning: The home and school years.* Upper Saddle River, NJ: Prentice Hall.

Office of Planning and Evaluation. (1995). *Hawaiian students in the Hawaii State Department of Education 1994–1995.* Honolulu, HI: Kamehameha Schools, Bernice Pauahi Bishop Estate.

Purkey, W., & Novak, J.M. (1996). *Inviting school success: A self-concept approach to teaching, learning, and democratic practice.* Belmont, CA: Wadsworth.

Raphael, T.E., & Au, K.H. (Eds.). (1998). *Literature-based instruction: Reshaping the curriculum.* Norwood, MA: Christopher-Gordon.

Raphael, T.E., & McMahon, S.I. (1994). Book Club: An alternative framework for reading instruction. *The Reading Teacher, 48,* 102–116.

Rosaldo, R. (1989). *Culture and truth: The remaking of social analysis.* Boston: Beacon.

Shannon, P. (1989). *Broken promises: Reading instruction in twentieth century America.* New York: Bergin & Garvey.

Stephens, D.L., Zilliox, J.T., & Deering, P.D. (1998–1999). Learners' perspectives on learning to teach. *National Forum of Teacher Education, 8*(1), 28–35.

Tikunoff, W.J., Ward, B.A., & Broekhuizen, L.D.V. (1993). *KEEP evaluation study: Year 3 report.* Los Alamitos CA: Southwest Regional Educational Laboratory.

Trueba, H.T., Guthrie, G.P., & Au, K.H. (Eds.). (1981). *Culture and the bilingual classroom: Studies in classroom ethnography.* Rowley, MA: Newbury House.

U.S. Bureau of the Census. (1997). *Current population reports.* Washington, DC: United States Bureau of the Census

INSERVICE TEACHER EDUCATION

CHAPTER 8

What do we know about effective fourth-grade teachers and their classrooms?

Richard L. Allington
UNIVERSITY OF FLORIDA

Peter H. Johnston
UNIVERSITY AT ALBANY-SUNY
AND THE NATIONAL RESEARCH CENTER ON ENGLISH LEARNING AND ACHIEVEMENT

What teachers know and understand about content and students shapes how judiciously they select from texts and other materials and how effectively they present material in class. Their skill in assessing their students' progress also depends upon how deeply they understand learning, and how well they can interpret students' discussions and written work. No other intervention can make the difference that a knowledgeable, skillful teacher can make in the learning process. (National Commission on Teaching and America's Future, 1997, p. 8)

Schools in the United States have been directed to achieve a new standard: All children will attain thoughtful literacy proficiencies. This standard represents two challenges. First is the challenge to educate all children well. For most of the past century, U.S. schools were organized to educate only some children well (Allington, 1991). Thus, schools set different goals for different children; the traditional three-reading group model in elementary schools and the three-track high school were the result of this differentiated education model. Second, in most schools the focus was on developing basic literacy, not thoughtful literacy. Basic literacy is perhaps best characterized as a read-and-recall, write-neatly-and-spell-accurately model of performance. Thoughtful literacy, on the other hand, is characterized by students who can read, write, and think in the complex and critical ways needed in a post-industrial democratic society.

Stimulated by various federal initiatives, individual states have moved to create achievement benchmarks that reflect the new goal: All students will attain thoughtful literacy. Fourth-grade achievement has been a popular target, perhaps because it is at fourth grade that the NAEP assessments and state-by-state comparisons begin. Thus, we see "fourth-grade guarantees"—all fourth graders required to attain some specified level of reading proficiency on some new state-sponsored assessment to be promoted to the fifth grade—and considerable media attention is devoted to publicly ranking schools based on fourth-grade assessment results. Some states are even rewarding teachers whose students perform well on the chosen assessments, increasing the stakes considerably.

Most assessment pressure is focused on reading, and there is substantial variation among states in how performance is assessed. Some state assessments focus quite narrowly, while others attempt to provide a broader picture. However, Bob Linn (2000) captured the current state of affairs quite well when he concluded that "in most cases the instruments and technology have not been up to the demands that have been placed on them by high-stakes accountability" (p. 14).

In most U.S. elementary schools these days, fourth grade is the high-stakes teaching assignment, although fourth grade has long been considered a critical point in the elementary school experience. Chall (1983) wrote of the "fourth-grade hump"—the point at which some children who had been previously successful begin to experience difficulties. With today's high-stakes assessments focused on fourth grade, the "hump" has become a mountain for some children, even without the increased expectation for a more thoughtful literacy.

Despite all the recent attention focused on fourth grade, there has been relatively little research on the nature of instruction in fourth-grade classrooms. Although a number of such studies of primary grade classrooms have been reported in recent years, only a scant few studies of fourth grade (or third grade or fifth grade) have appeared, and these have typically been small and local (see Pressley, Wharton-McDonald, Mistretta-Hampston, & Echevarria, 1998; Sosniak & Stodolsky, 1993). Likewise, although much reform attention has been directed toward enhancing early literacy instruction, few broad efforts to improve the quality of reading instruction in the upper elementary grades have been undertaken.

Because effective classroom instruction has been identified as the critical variable for fostering student achievement (National Commission on Teaching and America's Future, 1997; Snow, Barnes, Chandler, Goodman, & Hemphill, 1991), we set out to find out more about the nature of effective fourth-grade classroom teaching. Until we can better articulate the qualities of effective upper elementary teachers, efforts to enhance the quality of the instruction at that level will be hindered.

Thus, in this chapter we begin with a review of studies of effective upper elementary grade teaching and an attempt to identify core constructs that were used to characterize effective teaching in those studies. We then discuss at some length a larger scale study of exemplary fourth-grade teaching that we have completed recently, accompanied by our analysis of how this study "fits" with the previous research. This analysis leads us to propose that if we are to understand instruction that successfully fosters thoughtful literacy, future research will need to be designed to more carefully and thoroughly document classroom discourse.

A Review of Research on Effective Fourth-Grade Teaching

Our work was guided, in part, by that small body of studies of upper elementary grade classrooms, especially by the few available studies of exemplary upper elementary teachers. We were less interested in the studies that compared different curricula and more interested in studies that attempted to delve into the complicated arena of good teaching. We agree with Duffy and Hoffman (1999), who argue that it is time to end the Material A vs. Material B research design. Such studies perpetuate the myth that it is particular instructional programs that matter, even though 50 years of research on classroom teaching indicates it is how teachers implement and adapt particular methods and materials that sits at the core of instructional effectiveness. Duffy and Hoffman argue that researchers must focus on developing better understandings of the complexity of classroom life; teacher expertise and decision making; teacher development across the career span; and particularly, how more effective teachers manage to adjust instruction to meet the needs of individual students. We took this call seriously. We attempted to locate studies of upper elementary classroom teaching, especially studies of *effective* classroom teaching. Methodologically, these studies fell into three broad categories: observational studies, interview studies, and survey research. Some studies combined methods, but typically there was one research methodology that provided the principal data for each study.

Observational Studies

The handful of observational studies of upper elementary grade teaching support the assertion that instructional programs were relatively less important than the nature of the teacher and the teaching that children encountered. Sosniak and Stodolsky (1993), for instance, studied four fourth-grade teachers in two schools in the same urban school district. Although each teacher worked with similar curriculum materials and operated under common achievement expectations, the researchers found that these teachers did not teach "by the book" as is often suggested in the literature. Indeed, for each teacher the role of text varied from subject to subject. One teacher made heavy use of a basal reader during reading (88% of the time), but made little use of the social studies textbook (17% of the time). Another teacher relied less on the reading basal (31%) but more heavily on the social studies basal (90%). Similarly, recitation as a reading activity ranged from 8% to 58% of the time, reading workbook use from 8% to 34% of time. These teachers were in the same district, teaching at the same grade level, with the same materials.

Differences in teaching practice can, of course, translate into more and less student achievement. Over a 2-year period, Snow and her colleagues (1991) observed second- and fourth-grade teachers who differed in effectiveness. The more effective teachers were characterized as

> providing explicit instruction,
>
> using behavioral routines,
>
> challenging and involving students,
>
> creating a supportive, encouraging, and friendly classroom climate,
>
> engaging in many constructive teacher-student exchanges,
>
> offering a variety of reading materials,
>
> scheduling frequent library visits,
>
> crafting stimulating curricular activities,
>
> asking many inferential questions, and
>
> displaying student work prominently.

These effective teachers produced dramatically superior student achievement with placement in effective classrooms for consecutive years, producing high achievement levels among all students. Variety in the materials used and the instructional methods observed was noted, as was variety in classroom organizational plans (from open classrooms to traditional three-group organization).

Rather than particular programs and materials producing better achievement, then, these studies argue for a range of productive practices with common themes. In line with this, Knapp (1995) reports on a 2-year study of elementary classrooms in

three states. The classrooms differed in instructional emphasis and, ultimately, student achievement. Achievement in the "meaning-emphasis" classrooms was superior to that attained by students in "skills-emphasis" classrooms. The higher achieving classrooms were characterized by

> maximized opportunity to read,
>
> integrated reading and writing with other subject areas,
>
> a focus on meaning and the means of constructing meaning, and
>
> opportunity to discuss what was read.

In addition, Knapp notes that, "The choice of textbooks by school or district does little by itself to make up for teachers' lack of experience with the approach contained in the textbook" (p. 174).

Consistently, researchers who observed teachers nominated as effective or exemplary have reported that the use of curriculum materials and instructional methods varied widely. For instance, Pressley and his colleagues (1998) found significant differences in materials and methods for teaching reading and writing in the 10 fourth- and fifth-grade classrooms they studied. Common dimensions of instruction in these classrooms included

> use of diverse grouping patterns, including small-group lessons and one-to-one conferences;
>
> teaching of both higher order and lower level skills;
>
> focus on vocabulary development;
>
> use of diverse curriculum materials, but with an emphasis on narrative literature;
>
> frequent use of collaborative learning activities;
>
> focus on developing student independence; and
>
> integrated literacy and content area instruction.

Nine of 10 teachers in this study used tradebooks in theme-oriented curriculum units (often in a reading/writing workshop framework), while just one used a traditional basal reading series for reading instruction. Homework differed in emphasis, from exploring engaging content to exercises on surface features of written text. Writing tasks differed quite substantially, both in breadth of genres and length of pieces written. Breadth of book reading differed, but there was an emphasis on narratives in all classrooms. In short, instructional materials did not explain why these teachers were effective.

In these observational studies, variation in materials used and instructional program was characteristic of the observed effective classrooms, regardless of how teacher effectiveness was determined (such as reputational nomination or post hoc analyses of achievement). Each research team concluded that, while common themes could be identified, variation in specific materials and teaching methods was a characteristic of upper elementary teaching, even effective teaching.

Interview Studies

Some researchers have used interviews to look more broadly at the nature of effective elementary teaching, including teaching in the upper elementary grades. Ruddell (1997), for instance, summarizes his interviews, surveys, and classroom observations of "influential" teachers—teachers nominated by former students as having an enormous positive influence on their development—by reporting that these 95 teachers

use clearly formulated instructional strategies that provide opportunities for monitoring and providing feedback to students;

have in-depth knowledge of reading and writing processes and how teach them;

frequently use internal motivation; and

sparingly use external motivation.

Ruddell also documented common personal characteristics of these influential teachers, including

warm, caring, flexible;

sensitive to individual needs and motivations;

placing high demands and expectations;

enthusiastic about teaching, creating intellectual excitement, and willing to consider alternative points of view;

concerned for students as persons and attentive to students' academic and personal problems;

making instruction personally relevant; and

emphasizing logical and strategy-oriented instruction, clear writing, and critical thinking.

These teachers ranked establishing trust through personal contacts with students as a most important characteristic of their teaching. Again, no particular instructional programs characterized influential teaching.

Some of the characteristics documented by Ruddell are clearly beliefs and theories about teaching and learning. Others have also documented such features. For example, Thomas and Barksdale-Ladd (1995) interviewed and then observed nine classroom teachers (grades 1-5) who were nominated as effective or outstanding. Their analyses found nine common beliefs:

Children learn to read and write by reading and writing.

All children can learn to read and write.

Modeling is the best way to teach literacy.

Reading and writing are closely related and cannot be separated instructionally.

Children learn from other children in cooperative environments.

Print-rich environments are necessary for children to learn literacy.

Children need daily shared reading, independent reading, and guided reading.

Observing students is the only way to know who needs what teaching.

Ownership is part of learning; choice leads to ownership.

Each of these teachers planned his or her instruction based on observation of students, all had student portfolios, all engaged students in individual conferences on a regular basis, all had well-developed parent involvement programs, all integrated reading and writing with content area instruction, and all were readers themselves. As with the other studies, a lack of reliance on particular instructional materials characterized these teachers. They were more student-oriented than curriculum-oriented.

Haberman (1995) reported on a longitudinal study of effective urban teachers (Star teachers) and provided a set of 14 characteristics that distinguished the more effective teachers from those who were less effective. The first seven characteristics were documented in interviews over a 35-year period; the second seven are based on observation.

1. Persistence—The Star teachers believe that it is their responsibility to

   ...find ways of engaging all their students in learning activities.... They persist in trying to meet the individual needs of the problem student, the talented, the handicapped, the frequently neglected student...persistence is reflected in an endless search for what works best with each student...teaching can never be "good enough" since everyone should have learned more in any activity. The basic stance of these teachers is never to give up trying to find a better way of doing things. (p. 779)

2. Protecting learners and learning—Star teachers usually have a hobby or some other lifelong learning activity (such as opera, philately, Save the Wolves, computers) that they often bring to the classroom. This engagement in continually learning seems to be a prerequisite for stimulating learning in others. However, it also leads these teachers to open the curriculum to more engaging possibilities, which "frequently brings them into noncompliance with the extremely thick bureaucracies of urban schools" (p. 779). When challenged by the principal about such nontraditional activities, they negotiate because "they see protecting and enhancing students' involvement in learning activities as their highest priority" (p. 779). These teachers' focus on finding ways to engage students is a primary contrast with less effective teachers who focused on "covering the curriculum."

3. Application of generalizations—Star teachers have a sense of the big picture of their teaching—the long-term goals and their relationship with day-to-day practice. In other words, their instruction is not driven by the plethora of daily lesson activities recommended in the teacher manuals that accompany commercial curriculum materials.

4. Approach to "at-risk" students—Haberman highlights this as the most powerful factor in distinguishing Star teachers from others. While Stars may cite poverty, violence, drugs, and other factors as components in low achievement, they also cite irrelevant curricula, poor teaching, and bureaucratic schools as causes. "Star teachers believe that, regardless of life conditions their students face, they as teachers bear a primary responsibility for sparking their students' desire to learn" (p. 780).

5. Professional versus personal orientation to students—Star teachers expect to find children in their classrooms whom they cannot love and children who will not love them. But they also expect to be able to teach these kids:

   They use terms such as *caring, respect,* and *concern,* and they enjoy the love and affection of students when it occurs naturally. But they do not regard it as a prerequisite for learning.... Genuine respect is the best way to describe the feeling Star teachers have for their students. (p. 780)

6. Burnout: Its causes and cures—Star teachers learn how to protect themselves from mindless, interfering bureaucracies. They learn the minimum requirements for functioning in the system and how "to gain the widest discretion for themselves and their students without incurring the wrath of the system.... They set up networks of like-minded teachers, or they teach in teams, or they simply find kindred spirits. They use these support systems as sources of emotional sustenance" (p. 780).

7. Fallibility—Star teachers see mistakes and failure as an inevitable part of their and their students' learning.

8. Teaching style—They have a predisposition to "coach" rather than engage in "directive teaching." In other words, instructional interactions more often foster students' independent application of developing skills and strategies, as opposed to simply telling students what skill or strategy they should apply. Also, Star teachers focus on "watch

me" as they demonstrate the use of a skill or strategy.

9. Explanations of success—Haberman observed that Star teachers have a predisposition to emphasize student effort over ability. Such an emphasis reflects much of what we know from research on student academic motivation.

10. Organizational ability—Star teachers showed an important predisposition and ability to engage in planning and gathering materials to create lessons that engaged students in learning.

11. Emotional stamina—Star teachers were observed to have the ability to persist in face of violence, death, and other crises. They develop and use a support system of other like-minded teachers as "sources of emotional sustenance" (p. 780).

12. Basis of rapport—An approach to student involvement was also observed. Star teachers created a classroom that was "their" classroom or "our" classroom, not "my" classroom. They worked to develop a sense of community in the classroom.

13. Readiness—They expect a range of differences in students rather than that all students should be at the same point. And they are ready to meet these different needs.

14. Physical stamina—Teaching is hard work, and these teachers use their organizational skills to eliminate every unnecessary bit of bureaucratic paperwork, meetings, and interruptions.

Expanding to a more general model for teachers and other human service professionals, Spencer and Spencer (1993) reported a large-scale study of professional effectiveness with compatible findings. They employed the Behavioral Events Interview (BEI) to develop a "grounded theory" of job competencies by working backward from the criterion of superior teaching performance "to identify the characteristics of people who perform at these levels" (p. 135). Their "generic model" included the 14 competencies listed below in descending order of importance.

1. Impact and influence—These people tailor their presentation and language to the audience, establish credibility, and use individual influence strategies including humor, body language, and voice.

2. Developing others—They believe in students' potential and use innovative teaching methods to respond flexibly to individual needs, particularly "allowing students to use individualized ways to learn or to meet requirements" (p. 189).

3. Interpersonal understanding—These teachers take time to listen, so that they are aware of students' moods and feelings, their background, interests, and needs.

4. Self-confidence—They have confidence in their own abilities and judgments and take responsibility for problems and failings. They are prepared to question and give suggestions to superiors.

5. Self-control—Stress resistance and stamina are characteristic of these teachers. They keep their own emotions from interfering with work.

6. Other personal effectiveness competencies—These teachers accurately self-assess their techniques and learn from their mistakes. They genuinely like people and have positive expectations of others. The best teachers display "intrinsic enjoyment of their work and a strong commitment to the process of learning and to the mission of their school" (p. 191).

7. Professional expertise—These teachers expand and use their professional knowledge.

8. Customer service orientation—They probe "to discover the student's underlying needs and match available or customized services to those needs" (p. 193).

9. Teamwork and cooperation—Excellent teachers solicit input from their students, give credit to and cooperate with peers. They have a "concern to help children, and their desire to develop their own skills led teachers into mutually beneficial dialogue with other professionals" (p. 194).

10. Analytical thinking—These teachers make inferences, see causal relationships, and systematically analyze complex problems. In particular, these teachers "thought about the connections in the subject matter and how to get them across to students" (p. 195).

11. Conceptual thinking—Also important was the ability to recognize patterns and diagnose situations. They "make connections between course work and their students' lives and to make complex material clear and vivid" (p. 195).

12. Initiative—High-performing teachers go beyond the basic job requirements, "tackling problems before they become urgent or inescapable" (p. 195).

13. Flexibility—These teachers adapt their style and strategies to fit the circumstances. Indeed, the authors argue that "flexibility was critical for teachers" (p. 196).

14. Directiveness/assertiveness—These teachers set limits, confront problem behavior, and say "no" when necessary. At the same time, "the best teachers have established boundaries so well that they don't focus on directiveness" (p. 196).

Again, as with the other studies, particular programs and materials are not mentioned in this list of characteristics. Instead, effective teachers' beliefs, attitudes, and interpersonal and instructional skills dominate the interview studies.

Survey Studies

Pressley and his colleagues conducted a U.S. national survey of effective upper elementary teaching (Pressley, Yokoi, Rankin, Wharton-McDonald, & Mistretta, 1996). Their survey of a national sample of fifth-grade teachers who were nominated by their supervisors as effective found extensive reading and writing as a central theme in effective instruction. Respondents also reported that they

integrated reading and writing with content area instruction;

used diverse grouping arrangements (including cooperative groups and conferencing);

taught both higher and lower order skills (often directly);

worked to promote student motivation for reading; and

used diverse assessment tools to evaluate growth.

Again, however, no pattern of particular programs or materials was found to characterize the teaching in these upper elementary classrooms. In fact, Pressley et al. (1996) note that upper elementary classrooms seem more diverse on many curricular and instructional dimensions than primary grade classrooms.

Summary of Past Research

Taken together, these various studies of (or including) effective upper elementary grade teachers produce a dizzying array of features that might characterize good fourth-grade teachers and their teaching. Because different researchers used different research methods and because they employed different lenses to study good teaching, the breadth of characteristics identified seems unsurprising. Each list contains a mixture of constructs—beliefs, behaviors, and propensities. A summary list with some loss of detail might look something like Table 1 on the facing page. While a valuable start, such an uneven list is hard to capitalize on when designing teacher education programs. First, we cannot be sure that the various constructs we collapsed together represent, in fact, the same characteristics. Different researchers used different selection, data collection, and analytical methods and often drew from different theoretical formulations of effective teaching. The richness of variety can be seen as a potential strength of these studies, but that same richness makes synthesis ever more problematic.

Second, given current sociocultural understandings of learning, we find it odd that so little attention is given in the constructs to classroom language. As Wilkinson and Silliman (2000) point out, "the language used by teachers and students determines what is learned and how learning takes

Table 1. Summary of Features Associated With Exemplary Teachers

Personal characteristics	Studies
Emotional and physical stamina, stress resistance, persistence, and self-control	H, SS
Warm, caring, flexible, concern for individuals as persons as well as academics	R, H
Supportive, encouraging, and friendly	S, SS
Have interests and hobbies—and assume others do	H
Enthusiastic, enjoys work	H, SS
Genuinely likes people and has positive expectations of them	SS
A sense of agency (also confidence)—the feeling that what one does makes a difference	H
Accurate self-assessment	SS
Expands professional expertise	SS, R

Beliefs, attitudes, and expectations	
Expects diversity and expects to manage it	H
All children can learn to read and write—believes in children's potential	T, SS, H
Learning is social	T
Ownership is necessary for learning; students need choice	T
Error is a place to learn	H, SS
Modeling is important	T, H
Respect and trust	H, R

Instructional practice	
Organized and planful	H, R
Classroom routines; behavior, movement, lessons	S, Pb
Diverse instructional groupings	Pa,b
Arranges for student ownership	H, R,T
Believes students learn to read and write by reading and writing a lot	K, S, Pa,b
Integrates reading writing and subjects	K, T, Pa,b
Daily guided, shared, and independent reading	T
Listens and observes to adapt instruction	T, SS
High demands, but sensitive to individual needs and motivations—challenges and involves students	R, S
Flexible response to individual needs and interests	SS, H
Instruction is personally relevant, activities are stimulating	R, S
Explicit instruction, particularly of strategies	S, Pa
Displays student work along with much other print	T, S

Instructional talk	
Many constructive teacher-student exchanges	S
Discussion	K
Collaborative learning	T, Pa,b
Emphasizes strategic and critical thinking	R

Key: H=Haberman (1995); K=Knapp (1995); Pa=Pressley, Yokoi, Rankin, Wharton-McDonald, & Mistretta (1996); Pb=Pressley, Wharton-McDonald, Mistretta-Hampston, & Echevarria (1998), R=Ruddell (1997); S=Snow, Barnes, Chandler, Goodman, & Hemphill (1991); SS =Spencer & Spencer (1993); T=Thomas & Barksdale-Ladd (1995).

place…[and] exerts a profound effect on students' development of language and literacy skills" (p. 337).

Third, we are inclined to ask, as does Lampert (1985, p. 193), how exemplary teachers manage to teach—using "manage" in the sense that "a manager is one who is able to find a way to do something, and that action and invention are fused together in the management process." The crucial question then becomes, of course, what the "something" is that they are trying to do—what conception of literacy teaching and learning guides these teachers' practice—a question not adequately answered in these studies.

An additional concern, however, is that some of the constructs introduced by these studies are of little practical help. For example, it has long been reported and repeated in these studies that students in effective teachers' classrooms spend a lot of time engaged in academic work. Although intuitively consistent with other descriptors, such constructs are of little help to novice teachers or those who work with them. By contrast, it would seem more useful to know that effective teachers foster such engagement through lessons that focus on meaning and its construction, and that part of doing so involves integrating reading, writing, and subject areas (e.g., Guthrie, Wigfield, & VonSecker, 2000). Likewise, identifying how effective teachers develop "community" would seem of greater importance than finding that a "sense of community" exists in effective teachers' classrooms. Similarly, if we foreground the personality characteristics of effective teachers, then improving teaching becomes principally a matter of selecting teachers with "the right stuff"—perhaps useful at hiring time, but of limited value in developing effective teachers.

Our Study of Exemplary Fourth-Grade Teachers

Guided by the available research on effective upper elementary grade teaching, we set out to contribute to a better understanding of effective fourth-grade literacy instruction. We hoped that this work would better inform both preservice and inservice teacher development efforts. We were concerned that most previous studies of effective upper elementary teaching had gathered information on rather few teachers and their classrooms in limited geographic regions. It seemed important to broaden the sample of teachers because state educational contexts vary on many dimensions. For example, some states sponsor textbook adoptions but most do not; some states test basic skills while others test a more thoughtful literacy. Some states have limited their investments in teacher development, and others have focused their efforts in this area. We wanted to capitalize on the specificity of case studies while exploring the generality across diverse circumstances.

Consequently, our study involved classroom observations of and interviews with 30 fourth-grade teachers in 30 schools in five states (New York, New Jersey, New Hampshire, Texas, and California). The teachers were identified as exemplary through a multiple nomination process. The schools were located in a variety of communities (rural, small city, large city, suburbs). They ranged in size from small schools with enrollments of approximately 300 students to larger schools with enrollments of 800 to 1,000 students. Most schools enrolled between 400 and 600 students. In over half of the schools, minority students represented at least 25% of the student body, and in one third of the schools, minority students represented over half of the student body. The schools served substantial numbers of children from lower income families. In two thirds of the schools, more than 1 of 5 students received a free or reduced-price meal. In one fourth of the schools more than 7 of 10 children qualified for such meals.

We observed in each teacher's classroom for at least 10 full days, composing field notes that attempted to capture both the structure of classroom activity (time allocated, groupings, movement) and the essence of the language environment (who talks, nature of talk, content of talk). Audio and video recordings of classroom activities allowed closer analysis of some lessons. Additional data were gathered in (a) two semi-structured interviews with each teacher, (b) interviews with target children from each classroom, (c) samples of student writing and reading logs provided by children, and finally, (d) end-of-year achievement test performance.

We conducted a post hoc analysis of achievement test gains in the subset of classrooms where both third- and fourth-grade student achievement data were available. Not surprisingly, that analysis showed that student achievement gains outpaced expected levels of growth. These teachers nominated as effective did produce greater than expected levels of literacy growth as measured on standardized achievement tests. However, as we point out below, literacy growth is not the only indicator of quality instruction and student achievement (Battistich, Watson, Solomon, Lewis, & Schaps, 1999; Johnston, 1999; Johnston, Jiron, & Day, in press). Our analyses of the various data have been published in a variety of sources, and analyses are continuing.

Individual case studies were prepared for seven of these exemplary teachers—two from New York and California, and a single teacher case from the other three states. These teachers represented a range in years of teaching experience (5 to 25 years), gender, and ethnicity. Their classrooms represented a range of class sizes (19 to 33 students); ethnic mixes of students; student poverty levels; organization (from self-contained to departmentalized, from single grade to multigrade); and location (urban core, urban fringe, small city, rural town, and suburban community types). In short, the case study teachers worked with a variety of students in communities that varied in substantial ways.

Our contrastive case analysis (Allington & Johnston, in press) provided some common features of instruction, which we now briefly describe. Subsequently, we will connect our analysis with previous analyses.

The Nature of Classroom Talk

Perhaps the most important features of these classrooms lies in the nature of classroom talk. The observers routinely noted that students in these classrooms talked much more than has been previously reported in the research literature, particularly public talk to each other (e.g., Cazden, 1988; Dillon, 1988; Mehan, 1979; Nystrand, Gamoran, Kachur, & Prendergast, 1997). The talk was described as respectful, supportive, and productive, and it was not only modeled by the teacher in her interactions with students, but also deliberately taught and expected. Creating these conversational communities was the focus of lessons across the

year, especially at the beginning of the year, and it required building trusting relationships.

Talk between teacher and student was personalized and personal. These teachers used conversation—real conversation—to learn about students. And teachers encouraged students to engage each other's ideas—authority was more distributed than centralized. While Knapp (1995) noted that discussion was a central feature of the high-achievement classrooms he studied, we also noted that within our sample, classroom discussions included a considerable amount of "tentative" talk, which made it possible for others to complete incomplete ideas, or otherwise contribute to the group thinking. However, such conversations clearly involved an element of trust and a nonjudgmental context. It is probably no coincidence that Ruddell's (1997) teachers ranked establishing trust through personal contact with students as particularly important.

We observed that rarely were "No" or "Wrong" uttered by the teachers, except in response to gross social transgressions. Rather, they found what was productive about a response or behavior, supported the partially correct, turned attention to the process, and encouraged further thinking or reflection, even about a "correct" answer. The teachers admitted their limited knowledge of various topics, notably those raised by their students, their mistakes, and their own interests. These practices simultaneously seemed to have the effect of making the teachers "real," making personal interests acceptable and thus distributing authority, making error a source of learning about self-correction and strategy refinement, and making space for real dialogue. As with Haberman's (1995) successful teachers, those in our sample demonstrated the limits of their own knowledge and expertise—their fallibility. The routine demonstrations of how literate people think as they read and write—including errors and self-corrections—made their own and their students' thinking available as models and for discussion.

This talk also made genuine inquiry possible—indeed common—and inquiry processes a normal topic of conversation, such as "How could we find that out?" The emphasis was clearly on making meaning and the means for doing so. Normalizing conversations about the process of making meaning and accomplishing meaningful ends also meant that there was constant modeling and articulation of strategies by both teacher and students. Furthermore, when students identified the process they used for solving problems, they located themselves in a position of agency with respect to learning. Several of the teachers actively encouraged students to build identities around this agency with comments such as, "As writers, how can you solve this problem?" (Ivey, Johnston, & Cronin, 1998). Instruction was more conversational than interrogational.

The Curriculum Materials

The instruction was multisourced. Although many teachers did often dip into textbooks in science, social studies, and reading, they hardly ever followed the traditional plan for these materials. These teachers were more inclined to fill students' days with reading and writing beyond the textbooks. They used historical fiction, biography, and informational books in social studies, for instance. They drew reading materials from, or had their students locate them from, the Internet, magazines, and other nontraditional curriculum sources. This approach allowed students to work more often in materials of appropriate complexity, which seemed central to the high levels of engagement in academic work that we observed. It also made possible a sense of ownership of the topic, and it personalized instruction. Sometimes curriculum materials came from projects such as fundraising and planning for a class trip, or running a class business. In other words, relevance and meaning were important aspects of the curriculum materials teachers selected to use.

Language itself was a curriculum material—a topic of meaningful study in the materials teachers read to students, the materials students read themselves, and the texts the students composed. Even word study (a standard feature) emphasized a search for meaningful patterns, meaning acquisition, interest in words and turns of a phrase, and the strategic, purposeful selection of words.

A strong literary emphasis pervaded these classrooms. These teachers used tradebooks in content area activities to model thinking and composing strategies, as well as to promote a "just let them read" framework. The work was often situated in an awareness of state or district standards but not driven by them. Student interests were commonly the driving force accommodated by a flexible sense of the required curriculum.

The Organization of Instruction

These exemplary teachers were very planful, but at the same time, prepared to depart from and revise their plans to capitalize on the "teaching moment." Indeed, we might think of them as planful opportunists, because their plans tended to open instructional opportunities on which to capitalize. In their planning, these teachers sought learner engagement first and situated their concern for curriculum coverage somewhere lower on the agenda. Their instruction was a sort of problem setting, although that often involved problem clarification with students, and even student problem setting. In other words, their teaching focused student attention on problems to be addressed rather than simply "facts" to be learned. Although the instruction was not "individualized" in the traditional sense, it was "personalized" in that these teachers knew their students' interests and needs, strengths, and weaknesses.

We observed much use of managed choice in these classrooms. Thus, although students did not exercise full control over the instructional decisions, these teachers strategically arranged for students to have choices and make them productively, or learn from their errors. As Turner (1995) demonstrated, choice along with the use of "open" tasks—tasks that provided the opportunity for multiple "correct" answers and multiple routes for demonstrating knowledge and skill acquisition—are clearly linked to the high levels of engagement we observed.

Constant instruction took place in these classrooms, although the teachers were only occasionally in front of the class—a finding recently also reported by Taylor, Pearson, Clark, and Walpole (2000). That is, more often we observed these teachers working alongside students, individually and in small groups, than working from the front of the room. Each teacher used a range of interactional formats. A great deal of instruction was done not by the teacher, however, but by the students, who had learned to consult one another and to make their thinking available to one another. Collaborative learning was common, and students were not only learning how to learn, but how to teach and how to interact in ways that made for mutual learning. Students were expected to manage group work, and when it broke down the problem was dealt with as an important interactional problem to be solved strategically, not as misbehavior.

Tailored, collaborative, meaningful problem-solving work dominated the instructional day. The teachers focused on developing students' personal responsibility for learning with a focus on choice, goal setting, and collaborative independence. Working together was valued and viewed as developing important learning skills. Much of the work was longer term in nature—assignments that lasted for a week or more—rather than a series of small and unrelated tasks to be completed each day. Integration across subjects, time, and topics was common rather than a compartmentalized curriculum. For instance, often we found it difficult to determine whether the classroom focus was science or language arts. This integration not only worked to foster student motivation and engagement (Guthrie, Wigfield, & VonSecker, 2000; Walmsley & Walp, 1990), but also to add a coherence to the instructional day. This lesson planning orientation was likely to produce longer instructional blocks in which productive and complicated student work could be achieved.

The Nature of Evaluation

As was the case with Haberman's (1995) Star teachers, the teachers we studied evaluated student work based more on improvement, progress, and effort than on the achievement of a single a priori standard. This emphasis produced an instructional environment in which all students worked hard—unlike many classrooms where effort and improvement are not heavily weighted in evaluation. The evaluations were personalized, also, as these teachers attended to individual student development and goals. The evaluations were often holistic—rubrics designed for teachers were adapted for student use—and focused on complex achievements—thinking like a biographer, for instance. We observed many examples of performance assessment and routinely observed these teachers providing focused feedback; they often led the student to the evaluation target rather than spelling it out for students—in Cazden's (1992) terms, "revealing"

rather than "telling." Self-evaluation was also widely encouraged, shaped, and supported.

The Fit With Previous Studies

There is a substantial convergence between previous studies and our own study. Indeed, there are few items on the combined list (see Table 1 on page 157) that we did not find to be important one way or another. There are, of course, some changes in the center of gravity of the constructs, but the collective studies are clearly not at odds with one another. There are spaces for negotiation on the nature of the constructs. For example, unlike other studies, Snow and her colleagues (1991) foreground "explicit instruction." Our observations fit more with Haberman's (1995) and Taylor and her colleagues' (in press) analyses, which use the construct "coaching" as opposed to "directive teaching." It was not that these teachers were explicit all the time about everything, but rather they were explicit when they needed to be explicit, with whom they needed to be explicit, and in the context of ongoing literate engagement. Indeed, part of what we found impressive is this very ability to know when to be explicit, which entails knowing roughly what students know, what they need to know at a particular point, and what they can figure out for themselves. The difference is important, because if a teacher does all of the knowledge delivery or is overly "directive," then students do not get to be independent or in control of their knowledge construction.

Similarly, although Spencer and Spencer (1993) argue that exemplary teachers are comfortable saying no, they also point out that such teachers set boundaries so well that they do not have to spend their time telling students what not to do. We would add that in our research, "saying no" is not used much for academic matters, but might be used for serious social transgressions. However, generally these teachers turn those few observed transgressions into opportunities for learning rather than for correction.

Not only do the studies have considerable commonality, but it is also not hard to see that some of the constructs hang together quite well in clusters—given some items, one would expect other items. There are doubtless reasons for this. For example, when arriving at these constructs, personal characteristics have been inferred from teachers' behaviors. Caring is likely to be inferred from teachers' personal attention to, and flexible accommodation of, students' interests, needs, and concerns. It might also be inferred from supportive, encouraging, and friendly verbal interactions, rather than judgmental ones. Students, too, probably infer these characteristics from similar indicators.

These clusters of beliefs, attributes, instructional practices, and personal characteristics are important to consider. It is these that might ultimately give us leads on a more unified structure. For example, a teacher who genuinely likes children is likely to be interested in their experiences, is unlikely to be judgmental, and is likely to view error as an opportunity for learning rather than for correction. Similarly, Spencer and Spencer's (1993) report that effective teachers tailor presentations to their audience and have flexible responses to individual interests and needs, implies that these teachers have listened to, observed, and assessed the students; careful listening, observation, and assessment are each additional descriptors Spencer and Spencer report. Other researchers also point out that these teachers are sensitive to and accommodate individuals' interests, needs, and motivations, which is possibly why their classrooms are reported to have a wide range of difficulty of materials—and high engagement. Furthermore, it may be the careful listening and observation that makes it possible for these teachers to successfully challenge their students (often reported as "having high expectations") in ways that students can actually meet and are prepared to pick up. At the same time, the "engrossment" of these teachers in learning about each student has been emphasized by Noddings (1984) and others (Goldstein, 1999; Tappan, 1998) as a central part of both a caring relationship and the nurturing of productive relationship development.

Consider another potential cluster. In each of the studies we reviewed, there is a focus on making meaning and how to do so. Both Knapp (1995) and Cantrell (1999) also report that more meaning-centered upper elementary teachers produced students who were more successful on a range of measures of reading and writing. These teachers engage children in discussion, ask inferential questions (which can lead to discussion), and integrate subjects with one another and with children's experience, making instruction personally relevant—in other words, meaningful. In the process, these practices probably go a long way toward establishing trust and respect in the classroom. Doubtless it goes the other way, too, in that listening to students' discussion and experiences requires a measure of respect in the first place.

Such theoretically consistent clusters of descriptors are exactly what we seek in our research efforts—constructs that are coherent but at the same time practical. They provide the focusing intention, the stance, and the means for improving instruction. In our efforts to study these clusters of beliefs, attributes, and practices, we have examined teachers' epistemologies (Johnston, Woodside-Jiron, & Day, in press). We have reason to believe that the position called *constructed knowing* (Belenky, Clinchy, Goldberger, & Tarule, 1986) provides a framework that integrates a great many of the characteristics and practices of these exemplary teachers. Indeed, in Belenky and colleagues' terms, this represents an advanced intellectual position. Although in the long run this particular framework might not survive empirically, integrative frameworks like it are important to seek for two reasons. First, teachers primarily respond to students automatically from their internal frameworks. Second, if we are to make use of what we learn from exemplary teachers, coherent frameworks are more addressable than dozens of independent characteristics and behaviors.

Expanding Our Conception and Indicators of "Exemplary"

Our analyses of student achievement data show that exemplary teachers produce superior educational gains as measured on standardized achievement tests—not the most sensitive measures of complex achievement (Johnston, 1992; Linn, 2000). But when people nominated these teachers as exemplary, they were not simply interested in test scores. They were nominating people in whose classroom they would place their own children. So we also looked beyond the scores to what else these teachers contribute to children's literate development, exploring the implications of

Vygotsky's dictum that children grow into the intellectual environment around them.

Our analyses point to the sorts of achievement these teachers produced that is beyond the most sophisticated standardized tests. The "thoughtful literacy" instruction we observed produced students who independently engaged in complex literate conversations—evidence of an internalization of the thinking that was normalized as conversation in these classrooms. This kind of literate development is far from trivial, or even "icing on the cake," particularly in fourth grade. Stipek and her colleagues (Stipek, de la Sota, & Weishaupt, 1999) point out, "Even if basic skills acquisition is educators' exclusive goal…powerful developments in preadolescents can interfere with learning, [and]…cannot be ignored" (p. 433). Failing to address matters of broader intellectual and social development until adolescence, they argue, may be too late. They propose weaving into classroom activities practices that influence children's social development. Although they describe these competencies as "non-academic," others have pointed out that the desired competencies and associated relationships and propensities cannot be separated from literate development. Indeed, the discursive environment of the classroom has powerful effects on literate relationships, identities, and epistemologies (Gee, 1996; Johnston, Woodside-Jiron, & Day, 2001; Johnston, Layden, & Powers, 1998).

For us, the idea of exemplary teaching in fourth grade is fundamentally attached to questions of what we think teachers are supposed to be accomplishing. If, for example, we want them to create children who possess stacks of knowledge and skills, that is one thing; if we want them to create competent, caring, independent learners with self-extending learning systems, as well as a robust knowledge base, that is another. Teachers approach these different constructions of their practice differently, and children's voices, epistemologies, and relationships reflect their socialized experience (Allington & Johnston, in press; Johnston, Woodside-Jiron, & Day, 2001).

There are many important questions yet to ask. Why, for example, would it be significant that these teachers see fallibility as a normal and important part of teaching and learning (Haberman, 1995)? Is this merely another item on a list, or is it part of a larger conceptual frame? Why is the curriculum multisourced and multileveled? Why is so much of classroom activity characterized by the use of open tasks and student choice among assignment options? Are these separate items on a list of characteristics or a reliable cluster of instructional dimensions linked to student engagement and achievement (Guthrie et al., 1996)? We believe that the study of expert teaching has much to recommend as a strategy for better understanding the effective teaching of reading and the development of teachers who teach expertly and effectively.

Each of the various studies of effective upper elementary teachers we have discussed offer important glimpses of expert and effective teaching in these grades. There is certainly convergence among the studies, although the convergence is considerably greater when conclusions are summarized conceptually rather than item-by-item. Indeed, it is our view that future research will gain most leverage by seeking conceptual coherence in instructional analyses, invoking constructs such as those we have begun to develop in our analysis. We also believe that studies of exemplary teaching need to look particularly carefully at classroom talk, its sources, and its implications. Finally, it is essential that studies of exemplary teaching are not satisfied with narrow notions of educational achievement such as those indicated by standardized test scores. Much more is being achieved, and too much is at stake.

The authors would like to thank the following people for their assistance in the project: the classroom teachers who allowed us to study their teaching practices, and the other researchers on the project, including Kim Boothroyd, Greg Brooks, Melissa Cedeno, Cathy Collins Block, John Cronin, Jeni Pollack Day, Gay Ivey, Haley Woodside-Jiron, Susan Layden, Anne McGill-Franzen, Lesley Morrow, Steven Powers, Jean Veltema, and Ruth Wharton McDonald. The paper is based on research supported in part under Research and Development Centers Program (award number R305A6005) as administered by the Office of Educational Research and Improvement, U.S. Department of Education. However, the contents do not necessarily represent the positions or policies of the sponsor.

REFERENCES

Allington, R.L. (1991). The legacy of "slow it down and make it more concrete." In J. Zutell & S. McCormick (Eds.), *Learner factors/teacher factors: Issues in literacy research and instruction* (40th Yearbook of the National Reading Conference, pp. 19–30). Chicago: National Reading Conference.

Allington, R.L., & Johnston, P.H. (in press). *Good fourth grade teaching.* New York: Guilford.

Battistich, V., Watson, M., Solomon, D., Lewis, C., & Schaps, E. (1999). Beyond the three R's: A broader agenda for school reform. *The Elementary School Journal, 99*(5), 415–432.

Belenky, M.F., Clinchy, B.M., Goldberger, N.R., & Tarule, J.M. (1986). *Women's ways of knowing: The development of self, voice, and mind.* New York: Basic Books.

Cantrell, S.C. (1999). Effective teaching and literacy learning: A look inside primary classrooms. *The Reading Teacher, 52,* 370–378.

Cazden, C.B. (1988). *Classroom discourse: The language of teaching and learning.* Portsmouth, NH: Heinemann.

Cazden, C.B. (1992). Revealing and telling: The socialization of attention in learning to read and write. *Educational Psychology, 12,* 305–313.

Chall, J.S. (1983). *Stages of reading development.* New York: McGraw-Hill.

Dillon, J.T. (1988). The remedial status of student questioning. *Curriculum Studies, 20,* 197–210.

Duffy, G.G., & Hoffman, J.V. (1999). In pursuit of an illusion: The search for a perfect method. *The Reading Teacher, 53,* 10–16.

Gee, J.P. (1996). *Social linguistics and literacies: Ideology in discourses* (2nd ed.). London: Falmer.

Goldstein, L.S. (1999). The relational zone: The role of caring relationships in the co-construction of mind. *American Educational Research Journal, 36*(3), 647–673.

Guthrie, J.T., Van Meter, P., McCann, A., Wigfield, A., Bennett, L., Poundstone, C., Rice, M., Faibisch, F., Hunt, B., & Mitchell, A. (1996). Growth of literacy engagement: Changes in motivations and strategies during concept-oriented reading instruction. *Reading Research Quarterly, 31,* 306–322.

Guthrie, J.T., Wigfield, A., & VonSecker, C. (2000). Effects of integrated instruction on motivation and strategy use in reading. *Journal of Educational Psychology, 92*(2), 331–341.

Haberman, M. (1995). Selecting "Star" teachers for children and youth in urban poverty. *Phi Delta Kappan, 76*(10), 777–781.

Ivey, G., Johnston, P.H., & Cronin, J. (1998, April). *Process talk and children's sense of literate competence and agency.* Paper presented at the annual meeting of the American Educational Research Association, Montreal, Quebec, Canada.

Johnston, P.H. (1999). Unpacking literate "achievement." In J. Gaffney & B. Askew (Eds.), *Stirring the waters: A tribute to Marie Clay.* Portsmouth, NH: Heinemann.

Johnston, P.H., Jiron, H.W., & Day, J. (2001). Teaching and learning literate epistemologies. *Journal of Educational Psychology, 93*(1), 223–233.

Johnston, P.H., Layden, S., & Powers, S. (1998, April). *Children's literate talk and relationships.* Paper presented at the annual meeting of the American Educational Research Association, Montreal, Quebec, Canada.

Knapp, M.S. (1995). *Teaching for meaning in high-poverty classrooms.* New York: Teachers College Press.

Lampert, M. (1985). How do teachers manage to teach? *Harvard Educational Review, 55*(2), 178–194.

Linn, R.L. (2000). Assessments and accountability. *Educational Researcher, 29*(2), 4–16.

Mehan, H. (1979). *Learning lessons: Social organization in the classroom.* Cambridge, MA: Harvard University Press.

National Commission on Teaching and America's Future. (1997). *Doing what matters most: Investing in quality teaching.* New York: Author.

Noddings, N. (1984). *Caring: A feminine approach to ethics and moral education.* Berkeley, CA: University of California Press.

Nystrand, M., Gamoran, A., Kachur, R., & Prendergast, C. (1997). *Opening dialogue: Understanding the dynamics of language and learning in the English classroom.* New York: Teachers College Press.

Pressley, M., Wharton-McDonald, R., Mistretta-Hampston, J., & Echevarria, M. (1998). Literacy instruction in 10 fourth- and fifth-grade classrooms in upstate New York. *Scientific Study of Reading, 2*(2), 159–194.

Pressley, M., Yokoi, L., Rankin, J., Wharton-McDonald, R., & Mistretta, J. (1996). A survey of the instructional practices of Grade 5 teachers nominated as effective in promoting literacy. *Scientific Studies of Reading, 1*(2), 145–160.

Ruddell, R. (1997). Researching the influential literacy teacher: Characteristics, beliefs, strategies, and new research directions. In C. Kinzer, K.A. Hinchman, & D.J. Leu (Eds.), *Inquiries in literacy theory and practice* (46th yearbook of the National Reading Conference, pp. 37–53). Chicago: National Reading Conference.

Snow, C., Barnes, W., Chandler, J., Goodman, I.F., & Hemphill, L. (1991). *Unfulfilled expectations: Home and school influences on literacy.* Cambridge, MA: Harvard University Press.

Sosniak, L.A., & Stodolsky, S.S. (1993). Teachers and textbooks: Materials use in four fourth grade classrooms. *The Elementary School Journal, 93*(3), 249–275.

Spencer, L.M., & Spencer, S.M. (1993). *Competence at work: Models for superior performance.* New York: John Wiley & Sons.

Stipek, D., de la Sota, A., & Weishaupt, L. (1999). Life lessons: An embedded classroom approach to preventing high-risk behaviors among preadolescents. *The Elementary School Journal, 99*(5), 433–451.

Tappan, M.B. (1998). Sociocultural psychology and caring pedagogy: Exploring Vygotsky's "hidden curriculum." *Educational Psychologist, 33*(1), 23–33.

Taylor, B.M., Pearson, P.D., Clark, K., & Walpole, S. (2000). Effective Schools and accomplished teachers: Lessons about primary grade reading instruction in low income schools. *The Elementary School Journal, 101*, 121–165.

Thomas, K.F., & Barksdale-Ladd, M.A. (1995). Effective literacy classrooms: Teachers and students exploring literacy together. In K.A. Hinchman, D.J. Leu, & C. Kinzer (Eds.), *Perspectives on literacy research and practice* (pp. 169–179). Chicago: National Reading Conference.

Turner, J.C. (1995). The influence of classroom contexts on young children's motivation for literacy. *Reading Research Quarterly, 30*, 410–441.

Walmsley, S.A., & Walp, T.P. (1990). Integrating literature and composing into the language arts curriculum: Philosophy and practice. *The Elementary School Journal, 90*, 251–274.

Wilkinson, L.C., & Silliman, E.R. (2000). Classroom language and literacy learning. In M.L. Kamil, P.B. Mosenthal, P.D. Pearson, & R. Barr (Eds.), *Handbook of Reading Research*: Volume III, pp. 337–360). Mahwah, NJ: Erlbaum.

CHAPTER 9

Conducting a design experiment for improving early literacy: What we learned in school last year

Robert C. Calfee, Kimberly A. Norman, Guy Trainin, and Kathleen Marie Wilson
UNIVERSITY OF CALIFORNIA, RIVERSIDE

Three significant reports during the past two decades have attempted to set the research record straight about early reading (Adams, 1990; National Reading Panel, 2000; Snow, Burns, & Griffin, 1998). Each report agrees on one fundamental finding: Students in the early primary grades (chiefly first grade) perform better on primary grade reading tests if the curriculum includes explicit attention to phonics instruction delivered by direct instruction. For some reason, none of these studies highlights the First-Grade Reading Study of the 1960s (Bond & Dykstra, 1967), which found the same result—and a good deal more when the various follow-up studies and technical documents are taken into account. Adams (1990) devoted a few pages to the Study, noting that student characteristics (such as alphabet and letter-sound knowledge) were the strongest predictors of performance, and footnoting within-project variations, "a major impetus for recent research into the teacher/learning situation" (p. 43).

The three reports give less attention to several other results scattered here and there throughout the research literature. First, whatever the first-grade program, National Assessment of Educational Progress (NAEP, 2000) studies show that a substantial proportion of students are poor readers and worse writers when they leave third grade, a pattern substantially correlated with family demographics. Second, while advocates herald various experimental programs as the remedy for the "read-ing problem," none of these can produce proven effectiveness over time and situations. The "poop-out" effect observed by many observers and evident in state and national surveys may reflect several factors, including changes in assessment instruments. Most reports remain largely silent on this phenomenon. In a presentation on the National Reading Panel (NRP) report, however, Ehri (2000) showed the impact of phonemic awareness training (currently viewed as one of the strongest factors affecting early literacy acquisition) to depend greatly on what was assessed and when it was assessed. As gauged by effect size, for instance, training effects ranged from 0.9 (a "large effect") when tested immediately on phoneme awareness (testing what is taught) to 0.2 (a "small effect") when tested much later on spelling (testing for transfer).

Third, investigations consistently find that variability among teachers within programs is substantial; indeed, if researchers used "teacher/class within program" as the unit of analysis, which they properly should, then many "proven practices" would fall short of proof. The NRP report, with much to say about variations in phonemic and phonic programs, found much less about research on teachers of early reading, but offered a significant conclusion:

> [While] there is a much larger body of work on teacher education, only a very small number of studies were found to meet the initial criteria.... For teacher education to be effective, it must change

both teacher and student behavior.... Because of the small number of studies that constituted the final sample, the Panel could not answer the question of how research can be used to improve teacher education.... Based on the analysis, the NRP concludes that appropriate teacher education does produce higher achievement in students. Much more must be known about the conditions under which this conclusion holds. (NRP, 2000, pp. 5-1, 2)

Generic studies of teacher effects on student achievement, seldom covering the early grades, demonstrate that professional preparation matters— a finding all the more surprising given the coarse grain for describing preparation and the rough-cut indicators of student achievement (Darling-Hammond, Wise, & Klein, 1999; Pearson, 2000; see also Chapter 1 of this volume). Pearson's review of the generic findings advances a strong case that not only do teachers matter, but teacher preparation also matters. In fact, one of the strongest predictors of teacher effectiveness—by every criterion—is the level of preparation attained by teachers in order to become credentialed as full-fledged teachers.

What should teachers of reading in the early grades know and be able to do? The breadth of this question extends beyond the reach of this chapter (cf. Calfee & Scott-Hendrick, in press). For present purposes, what should teachers know about teaching English orthography to primary grade students? The answer must deal with a couple of complications. First is the nature of the English spelling-sound system, with its convoluted historical aggregation of languages, spoken and written (Venezky, 1970, 1999). Teaching students something about phonics is better than teaching nothing, but what critical features merit emphasis? Second is translation into the pragmatics of teacher knowledge and skill, a particularly challenging task in California, where policy initiatives force professional development activities to deal with teachers in practice, during the afternoons, on the fly, with instant results.

This chapter introduces the *design experiment* concept as a promising methodology for exploring these issues. We present selected results from two recent design experiment studies that utilized *WordWork*, a decoding-spelling program based on an analysis of English orthography, to inquire

deeply into what teachers and students need to know about phonics. This work resulted in virtually every student acquiring knowledge and skills needed to handle the reading-writing demands of the upper elementary grades. These findings are encouraging for two reasons. First, while levels of early reading achievement in the United States are far higher than implied by Cassandra alarms, our students need to do better for the nation's well-being (Carnevalle & Fry, 2000). Second, despite the policy emphasis on reading during the past few decades, including the recent emphasis on "proven practice," substantial evidence shows that students are not doing better, not even on the circumscribed indicators (such as multiple-choice tests) that dominate current practice (e.g., NAEP, 2000). The U.S. needs to aspire toward genuine success for all.

A Research Methodology: The Design Experiment

Virtually every high school graduate knows about scientific experiments: special treatment for one group, business as usual for the other, and results that should show the superiority of the special treatment. Graduates often realize the limitations of this strategy, the difficulty of doing what is supposed to be done, and the problem that sometimes the results are not as expected. R.A. Fisher (1934), who focused on agricultural studies but serves as the guru for social science and educational experiments, knew better. His writings reveal an awareness of the importance of "knowing the territory," of incorporating contextual factors in comprehensive and coherent designs and an appreciation for complexity that connects with today's qualitative methodologies.

To paraphrase the Bard, however, "The phrase is the thing." The concept of the design experiment emerged about a decade ago (Brown, 1992; Collins, 1992); it has also been referred to as "formative experiments" (Reinking & Pickle, 1993), with wellsprings in action research (Lewin, 1946), facets of the qualitative research movement of the 1970s and beyond (Lagemann & Shulman, 1999), and teacher/classroom studies (Freedman, in press; Sandholtz, 2000). The methodology for design experiments is presently sparse, but the basic concept is compelling. The challenge is to combine the rigor of systematic experimentation with the chaos of classroom realities in a way that informs practice while also contributing to theory, to collaboration between practitioners and researchers, and to thoughtful modifications in curriculum, instruction, and other factors. The idea incorporates the notion of formative evaluation, of studying the growth of student skill and knowledge over time, penetrating into the classroom processes on a monthly or even weekly schedule, as teachers (and researchers) negotiate curricular and instructional decisions.

The design experiment inverts the Fisherian invention of experimental design in several ways. Collins (1999) poses seven distinctions between traditional (1940–1970) experimental research and the design experiment approach, including (a) strict laboratory control versus messy classrooms, (b) socially isolated "subjects" versus participative informants, and (c) single versus multiple outcome indicators. These contrasts actually describe continua rather than distinctive categories, and they call for ongoing methodological decisions during the design and implementation of an investigation. We have placed these decisions into four categories: program variations, settings and situations, documentation, and systematic variability.

The first category entails the identification of program variations, whether the result of intentional or natural variations. Design experiments are presently associated with educational studies, hence the goal to discover which treatments make a difference for teachers and students. The traditional experimental approach relies on a horse-race paradigm. A predefined package is compared to a control condition (things as usual). This strategy has evoked critiques for decades (see Cronbach, 1963). In contrast, design experiments systematically tweak various program elements and explore naturally occurring quirks in routine practice.

For instance, the *WordWork* study, described briefly in the next section, explored decisions about curricular and instructional choices that appeared to be critical for the acquisition of letter-sound patterns, choices not directly informed by available empirical findings. For instance, should phonemic awareness be conducted orally before introducing the connection with letters, and if so, for how long?

Some research suggests a synergy between letters and sounds, but many programs spend considerable time with oral language games before the alphabet is taught.

The second facet centers around the range of settings and situations. Traditional approaches begin with demographic factors and random assignments. To establish the effectiveness of Program X, the researcher installs the program in a representative random collection of settings. Design experiments are more opportunistic, but then identify the contrasts among the settings—individuals, groups, and situations. Schools, classrooms, teachers, and student cohorts vary in many ways. For generalization, the researcher needs to make informed judgments about the range of variations in order to lay out a preliminary between-unit design. In our study, for instance, we began by classifying schools according to demographic factors (SES and language status), teachers by amount of experience, and students by previous achievement levels. For each program variation, we sought to assign the plan in a balanced fashion to schools and classrooms.

Third is documentation. Once the study begins, much as in qualitative methodologies, design experimenters record everything possible: treatments, participants, and outcomes. What actually happens during each variation? These data are critical if the study is to take full advantage of the potential of sequential variations. In the classical experimental paradigm, a plan is prepared and carried out, come what may. The design experiment strategy as we interpret it allows—indeed, requires—systematic redesign throughout the various phases of the study. For the strategy to work, the researcher needs to employ observations, interviews, videotapes, and student assessments to track the consequences of each phase, as a foundation for studying the outcome of variations within that phase, but also to modify subsequent phases. Suppose, for instance, that an early program variation contrasts a situation in which phonemic awareness is taught for 2 weeks with or without letters. Imagine that you discover that teachers, unless they can use letters for support, experience difficulty in communicating the concept to students. Rather than proceed with the previously planned second variation, the experimenter creates a variation of the first contrast. Employing this strategy requires that documentation be both comprehensive and transparent. All important bases have to be covered, and information has to be immediately readable so that decisions can be made quickly. A tension that appeared in our study is likely in most design experiments—developing instruments tailored to each of the planned variations, which also cut across all phases of the study.

The fourth element—adaptable variations—springs from the previous one. The design experiment should begin with a design—a conceptually reasoned plan of action. Rather than moving ahead willy-nilly, the plan adapts to contexts and circumstances, based on emerging data, as well as feedback from collaborators. For example, if teachers in one condition inform the investigator that students need more practice on a particular pattern, or if an unpredicted intrusion occurs (such as a sudden field trip), then it makes sense to reconsider the original design. Adaptations may include both treatment contrasts and instrumentation. Aside from systematic adaptability, we have discovered the importance of monitoring unplanned or natural variations. Some variations reflect departures from treatment fidelity, in which the teacher, for whatever reasons, does not carry out the planned contrasts. In other instances, practitioners may incorporate changes that reflect either sensitivity to local contexts or enhancement of the original program. In the WordWork study, unplanned variations turned out to be substantial and became essential for analyzing and interpreting the findings for student growth.

To summarize, the design-experiment concept has an intriguing ring. By capturing the tension between systematic variations and sequential adaptations, it offers promise as a methodology for formative investigations in complex settings. We take the notion of experimentation quite seriously; classroom teachers conduct millions of experiments every year, with more or less attention to design contrasts and outcomes. In order to formalize such activities in the service of generalizable research, investigators need to be serious about the design ingredients—treatments, contexts, and participants. They need to be equally careful in instrumentation, in documenting what actually happens, and the proximal consequences. The book is only begin-

ning to be written on this methodology. In the remainder of this chapter, we present our efforts to employ the technique, along with lessons that we have learned along the way.

A Design Experiment on First-Grade Decoding-Spelling

The Experimental Context

In the fall of 1998, the Riverside Unified School District in Riverside, California, USA, agreed to collaborate in a 3-year study of the WordWork concept. They were concerned about their reading scores, and WordWork offered promise. The program itself is based on the historical-morphophonemic structure of English orthography (Calfee, 1998). The curriculum (see Figure 1 on page 170) introduces students to the basic building blocks of the alphabetic system (consonants and vowels) in the consonant-vowel-consonant (CVC) pattern. Key to acquiring this pattern is learning that vowels function as "glue letters/sounds," binding consonants together into syllabic units. Students are taught individual letter-sound relations for the consonants through the articulatory principle, using the dimensions of manner, place, and voicing. Because the key to perceiving sounds is through the mouth rather than the ear, students focus their attention on the "feel" of the sounds within words. Instruction is grounded in social-cognitive theory and employs the metaphonic principle, which states that students best learn to decode and spell by comprehending letter-sound relations rather than rote practice. Therefore, explicit discussions are woven throughout lessons to scaffold young students in thinking metacognitively about decoding and spelling.

With support from the central administration, 17 teachers from four different schools volunteered to participate in the design experiment (additional detail is available from Calfee, Norman, & Trainin, in press). The schools span a range of socioeconomic status (SES) levels: (a) two low-SES schools (7 classrooms) with a preponderance of free/reduced-price lunch and minority students, and 30% limited English proficiency; (b) a middle-SES school (3 classrooms) with half the students on free/reduced-price lunch and minority status, and 10% limited English

Figure 1. Classroom Chart for WordWork Curriculum

Building a Reading/Writing Community

Working With Words

Making Sounds

Building Words: Short Vowels

Building Words: Long Vowels

Building Big Words: Compound Words

Projects

This chart shows the major components of the decoding-spelling spiral curriculum for Kindergarten through second grade.

proficiency; and (c) a high-SES school (7 classrooms) with 20% free/reduced-price lunch, 30% minority students, and less than 5% limited English proficiency. This span is typical for Riverside, California, a region of rapid growth and challenging demographics.

More than 250 first graders participated in the study, along with a handful of second graders and a special day class. This report focuses on a representative random sample of 149 students selected for detailed tracking during the project. Selection was based on teacher nominations of high, low, and average achievers, with roughly equal numbers of boys and girls.

A key element in the design experiment is the "real" environment, so we took steps to document classroom activities and treatment fidelity. Project staff conducted weekly classroom observations, teachers provided structured self-reports, and teacher reflections were an important part of bi-weekly meetings at each of the sites.

Students were assessed at the beginning of the study, at the end of each 2-week block, and 4 weeks after the conclusion of the study. Block assessments targeting specific concepts for each 2-week variation will not be reported here. Pre- and postassessments included the Tile Test (Calfee & Norman, 1996; individualized decoding-spelling) and Sentence Reading from IRAS (Interactive Reading Assessment System, Calfee & Calfee, 1981; oral reading). Phonemic awareness was tapped by asking students to explain articulation of consonant sounds in real and synthetic words. Finally, metaphonic questions assessed explicit understanding of spelling patterns. In addition to the project assessments, the school district provided several indicators for both first and second grade: reading running records, reading tests from the Scholastic series, writing samples, and second-grade standardized tests (SAT9 reading and spelling scores). These indicators provided information about transfer and long-term student progress. Parenthetically, we report this collection of measures to indicate the breadth of assessment within a design experiment; only selected results are reported in this chapter.

Planned and Natural Variations

Planned curricular variations were arranged in 2-week learning blocks. Before each block, project staff discussed the planned variations with teachers, reviewing lesson plans and literacy activities for eight daily lessons. The design provided flexibility for teacher adaptations based on day-to-day contingencies and student needs and opportunities.

The planned contrasts implemented during Year Two of the project are shown in Figure 2 as an example of the variations used in the first 2 years of the study. The design aimed to investigate both macro- and micro-level hypotheses. Four macro-level issues based on WordWork principles investigated (1) an explicit "metaphonic" strategy to help students understand orthographic structures; (2) the CVC foundation of English orthography based on phonemic analysis of consonants (through articulation) and vowels (as "glue letters"); (3) effective and efficient instruction supported by a variety of tasks and settings and with ongoing application in a broad range of reading-writing assignments; and (4) program effectiveness in promoting teacher understanding and implementation of program principles.

The design contrasts provided information about three micro-level issues: (1) curriculum combinations (for example, how to interweave phoneme awareness with letter-sound patterns); (2) time and sequence (for example, how long to spend on various components); and (3) instructional variations (for example, how to distribute direct instruction, small and large groups, and individual activities). Figure 2 on page 172 displays four 2-week block variations. As seen in Block One, the classrooms were divided into two groups. The first explored phonemic awareness with an emphasis on articulation, while the second emphasized metacognitive word building. During Blocks Two through Four, classrooms maintained an emphasis on articulatory phoneme awareness and/or metacognitive word building while varying the rate and sequence in which collections of vowels and consonants were introduced.

We quickly discovered deviations from the plan, which reflected various real-life circumstances. Some arose from structural tensions, such as differences between traditional and year-round schedules. Others reflected unexpected school or district events or staff conflicts (such as graduate exams). Finally, teachers made decisions that affected the design, ranging from "drop-outs" (some

Figure 2. Planned Variations for 2-Week Blocks

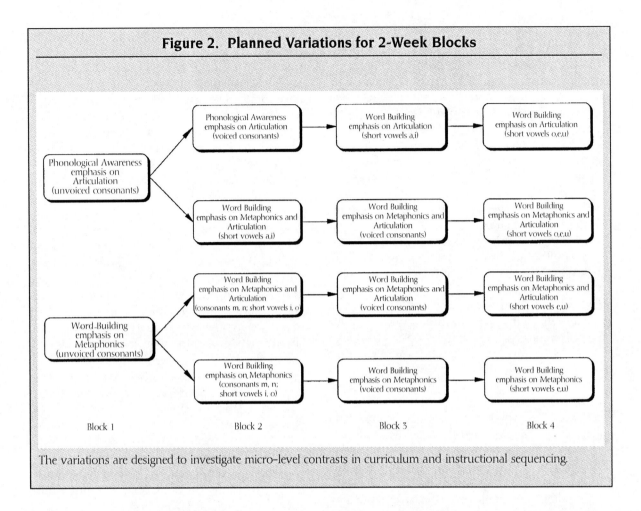

The variations are designed to investigate micro-level contrasts in curriculum and instructional sequencing.

individuals continued with previous phonics program and found themselves unable to cover WordWork as well) to "drop-ins," who varied in the emphasis they placed on the planned variations. Figure 3 on the facing page presents two examples of the divergences between planned and natural variations, predictable consequences of the design experiment concept. The figure also illustrates a finding typical in many classrooms: Although the curriculum aimed toward an accumulation of components, some elements fell by the wayside when not the focus of the block. In particular, articulatory phoneme awareness proved difficult to sustain during the later blocks.

Of final contextual note, this study took place at a time of considerable turmoil in California schools. During the preceding 2 years, the state suddenly instituted class-size reduction in the primary grades, leading to an instant shortage of qualified teachers and adequate space. Bilingual programs were eliminated throughout the state. Staff development days were cut to two per year. Finally, the Stanford Achievement Test (SAT9) was mandated for all students from second grade on, and schools were held accountable for reaching pre-established yearly growth rates, leading many to emphasize test preparation rather than curriculum standards. These events frustrated many efforts at genuine collaboration; fortunately, district and school support sustained a reasonable level of interaction.

The Findings

A detailed report of the results goes beyond the scope of this chapter, so we will present selected highlights in this section. First, natural variations

Figure 3. Examples of Differences Between Planned and Natural Variations in Two Classrooms

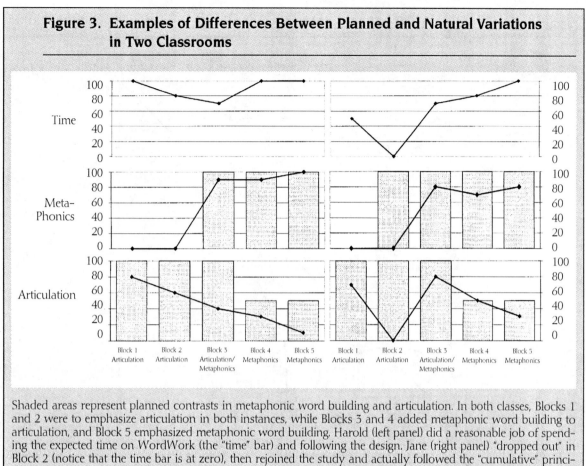

Shaded areas represent planned contrasts in metaphonic word building and articulation. In both classes, Blocks 1 and 2 were to emphasize articulation in both instances, while Blocks 3 and 4 added metaphonic word building to articulation, and Block 5 emphasized metaphonic word building. Harold (left panel) did a reasonable job of spending the expected time on WordWork (the "time" bar) and following the design. Jane (right panel) "dropped out" in Block 2 (notice that the time bar is at zero), then rejoined the study and actually followed the "cumulative" principle by keeping articulation in the mix during the last two blocks.

outweighed planned variations in many instances, and discussion of variations required greater engagement with teachers than we expected. We have just completed a second implementation year with more attention to this matter, yielding clearer results for implementation, teacher input, and student outcomes. For instance, a consistent pattern in our data supports the decision to combine letter learning and phoneme awareness training (what we have labeled metacognitive word building) within a matter of a few weeks, rather than rely on extended oral phoneme-awareness training, a finding also reported by the National Reading Panel (2000). We

are still unpacking these contrasts, and in this chapter will focus on macro-level comparisons.

Figure 4 on page 174 displays an essential finding for student achievement as assessed by Sentence Reading. By the end of first grade, the preponderance of the target students read aloud with the fluency needed in second grade. Each level on IRAS Sentence Reading corresponds to a one half of a grade-equivalent—Level 1 to a GLE of 1.5, Level 2 to a GLE of 2.0, and so on. Except for a handful of observations, all students showed growth; they were above the diagonal, and the preponderance of low-entry students met or exceeded the exit level for first grade (Level 2 or above). The high proportion of

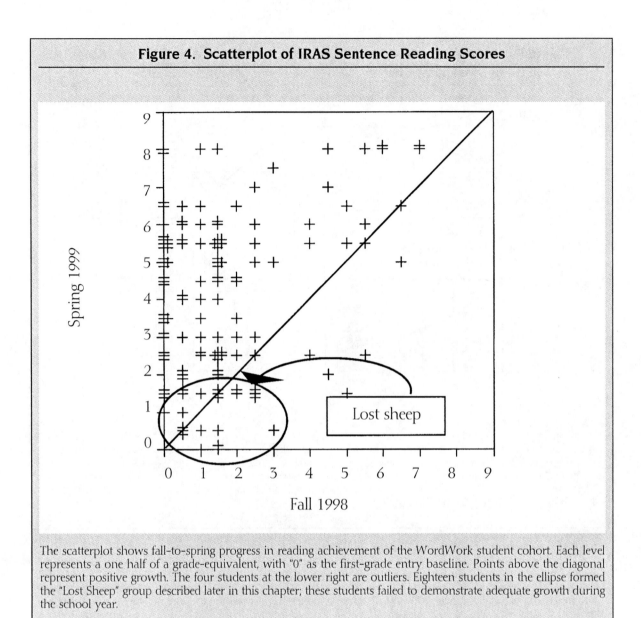

Figure 4. Scatterplot of IRAS Sentence Reading Scores

Lost sheep

Spring 1999

Fall 1998

The scatterplot shows fall-to-spring progress in reading achievement of the WordWork student cohort. Each level represents a one half of a grade-equivalent, with "0" as the first-grade entry baseline. Points above the diagonal represent positive growth. The four students at the lower right are outliers. Eighteen students in the ellipse formed the "Lost Sheep" group described later in this chapter; these students failed to demonstrate adequate growth during the school year.

low-entry students who performed well above expectations (Level 4 or above) was especially encouraging. To be sure, some low-entry students demonstrated little or no progress, a group that we consider later in the chapter.

Another set of findings centers around the impact of the design experiment on teacher understanding and practice. Three patterns warrant mention. First, the teachers in this study represented the broad range likely to appear from random selection. For a project of this intensity and given the available resources, the sample of teachers and schools was substantial, allowing us to move beyond a "boutique" investigation. The task was challenging, but if educational researchers are to be convincing about real-world research and evaluation, then models of this magnitude should become the standard.

Second, school effects appear significant in several respects. As an aside, pre-assessments showed smaller school-level differences than we expected, given the demographic spread in our sample. At the beginning of first grade, students' prereading performance was related to demographic profiles, but within-school variations were more substantial than between-school patterns. What did vary between schools was the level of support for the design experiment, reflecting a complex combination of on-site programs, experience of teachers and administrators, and the presence of other programs. As noted earlier, the current California context mitigates against school-wide efforts other than those that directly connect with standardized tests. The lesson, from our perspective, is that there is a need to incorporate school-level factors into educational design experiments.

Third, we have been impressed with the permanent effects for a significant proportion of teacher colleagues. Fully documenting this claim remains to be completed. During the past 2 school years, we have conducted end-of-year sessions for collaborating teachers, where student findings are presented and discussed. About a third of the teachers attend these sessions, which is impressive given that we can offer little more than data and cookies. The level of professional discussion has been quite remarkable, and it bodes well for case studies now underway.

The Lost Sheep: Extending the Design Experiment

Scatterplots—a foundation for exploratory data analysis (Behrens & Smith, 1996)—provide a rich portrayal of learning patterns. Figure 4 shows that most WordWork students made substantial growth on an applied performance task (reading sentences aloud) during the school year, many achieving levels expected of second and third graders. The figure also identifies a challenge: The collection of students in the lower left-hand corner of the graph, who entered first grade with little oral reading skill, did not progress during the year. Other indicators, both project- and district-based, confirmed this pattern. Detailed review of individual profiles turned up 18 students (12% of the target sample, and 40% of the low-entry students) who performed distinctively below standards, a

group we christened the Lost Sheep. The design experiment methodology provided a great deal of information about these students, including achievement profiles and instructional contexts. We worked with the district to locate these children and to initiate a targeted effort to "bring them home." The students spanned schools, classrooms, and demographics. They did share one feature—none were well prepared for literacy when they entered first grade. The data revealed two program elements that fell through the cracks: articulatory phonological awareness and metaphonic ability. Many students performed poorly on assessments of these capacities; none of the Lost Sheep could handle the tasks.

The design experiment concept, as we perceive it, provides a balance between systematicity and opportunity. The researcher has the responsibility to design an experiment, with the freedom to explore promising paths that emerge along the way. The Lost Sheep study combined data with practical tactics. First, the data—both program implementation and student profiles—centered on the two specific facets mentioned earlier. The Lost Sheep had not learned how to "make" consonants, nor were they facile in talking about word building. Second, we targeted these students, now scattered through several second-grade classrooms, for a focused treatment. With district assistance, we located 16 of the 18 students, and we arranged with principals and teachers to conduct tutorial sessions, as long as these did not interfere with regular reading, could be conducted within the classroom, and did not create disruptions. Project staff developed a program that met these conditions, which we implemented during the winter quarter. Students met in small groups (2–5 students) with tutors (project staff) in 30-minute sessions twice weekly for 10 weeks. Each session emphasized articulation and explanation, contextualized within reading-writing tasks appropriate for second graders.

Figure 5 (see page 176) shows the Sentence Reading results. Without follow-up data, these findings require a grain of salt, but offer considerable promise. Virtually none of the students could read simple sentences on entry to first grade, and with one exception, they showed little evidence of growth by the end of the year (the outlier student

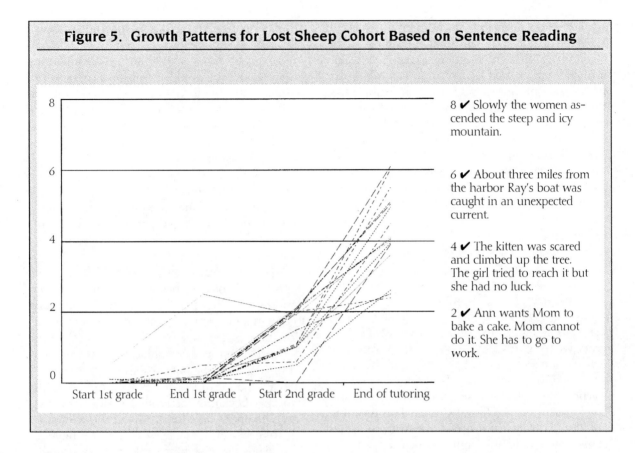

Figure 5. Growth Patterns for Lost Sheep Cohort Based on Sentence Reading

8 ✔ Slowly the women ascended the steep and icy mountain.

6 ✔ About three miles from the harbor Ray's boat was caught in an unexpected current.

4 ✔ The kitten was scared and climbed up the tree. The girl tried to reach it but she had no luck.

2 ✔ Ann wants Mom to bake a cake. Mom cannot do it. She has to go to work.

(x-axis labels: Start 1st grade   End 1st grade   Start 2nd grade   End of tutoring)

was included in the sample because of other indicators). In second grade, as they neared the winter break, all students still fell well below grade-level expectation. By the end of the tutoring sessions, student achievement on Sentence Reading increased substantially on average (roughly one GLE in 10 weeks) and individually (.5 GLE for all but one student).

As a "ministudy," this investigation has limits: small sample size, a constrained treatment, no long-term follow-up, selective outcome indicators, to name a few. But within the larger context of the design experiment concept, we would argue for both the validity and value of the findings. This is a small sample, but the achievement gains actually meet conventional criteria for statistical significance ($p < .0001$ by the sign test). To rely on this argument misses the point, however. We had observed these students for a full school year in a program in which the preponderance of their classmates showed substantial progress. While this is a constrained treatment, it is one designed around program elements identified during the preceding year as requiring additional attention. There was no long-term follow-up, although we plan to collect district data on these students; given predictive research on the prospects for students who leave first grade (or enter second grade) in the lowest quartiles, however, the short-term gains merit attention in their own right. Finally, the outcome measures can be viewed as applied performance tasks; we did not simply assess what was being taught, but asked students to read sentences of increasing complexity. Tutors also monitored students' attention to articulation and metaphonic awareness, and reported that most seemed to "get it" by about the fifth session. A substudy of self-efficacy suggests that most of the students predicted that they would do well on the final assessment because they had become more competent.

The design experiment concept invites the investigator to pursue leads that flow from a structured but flexible research strategy. The typical experimental-control paradigm permits little variation from the prescribed procedures, which typically absorb available resources. Indeed, deviations connote a loss of control, methodologically and conceptually. Exploratory strategies, in contrast, allow the investigator considerable freedom, but with little structural guidance. The 1998–1999 design experiment informed the Lost Sheep investigation in ways that depended directly on the conceptual design and variations, observations and interviews, along with ongoing and collaborative analysis of student profiles. Indeed, this follow-up seems to us a natural extension of the original design experiment, incorporating the same fundamental principles and leading to results that will shape future investigations.

Reflections on Substance and Method, Practice and Policy

A research agenda for learning to teach reading—the topic of this volume—entails questions about what to study and how to study it, about how to apply research and how to support application. This chapter has focused on teaching reading in the early grades, where we define literacy as the emerging capacity to use language to think and communicate. Although the studies in this chapter serve as illustrations about mastery of the print system, we should emphasize that a narrow focus on decoding will shortchange other important necessities, including language development, comprehension, and writing. The larger project of which these studies are a part encompasses this broad range, as do indicators of literate outcomes in the present study. On the other hand, we would argue for a central emphasis on literacy in the primary grades, and for preparation and certification of primary grade teachers who know, above all, how to teach reading. Unfortunately, today's primary grade teachers learn a little about teaching everything, with the result that they know much too little about teaching literacy (Calfee & Scott-Hendrick, in press).

A research agenda of this breadth requires a balancing act. Valid research encompasses the learning of teachers and students, indicators of thought and action, attention to both experimentation and evaluation. Learning to teach reading requires more than knowing how to follow the instructions in a prescribed teacher's manual, and it requires more than commitment to philosophical positions on literacy.

Methodology plays a significant role in shaping the research agenda. The current emphasis on randomized field trials for establishing the preeminence of "one best system" neglects a half century of evidence on the inadequacy of this methodology and the futility of this goal. The case-study alternative makes for more interesting reading, but reliance on anecdotes is risky for a host of reasons, including valid generalizability. These issues apply broadly to educational research problems, not just learning to teach early reading.

Hence there is a need to search for a different methodological paradigm, thus our exploration of the potential of design experiments. To be sure, this research strategy appears more tantalizing than tangible at present. The strengths in the available examples include the notion of flexibility and collaboration, along with some features of action research and teachers as researchers. We would add to this list the need for the structure and sequence found in traditional factorial design techniques, along with the associated analytic procedures for assessing concepts like main effects and interactions. Quantitative indicators provide the most rigorous basis for assessing such patterns, but new techniques for the examination of qualitative data also offer considerable promise (Chambliss & Calfee, in press).

The challenge is to construct a system of methodological principles that reflect more than a rejection of traditional approaches. Design is a powerful concept, indicating a plan with dimensions and structure. Experiment suggests intention. Analysis requires both strategic and tactical procedures in order to inform and convince audiences. In its current state, the design experiment concept requires a good deal of infilling if the next generation of researchers is to build on the contributions of the previous decade. Within the troubled arena of educational research (Lagemann & Shulman, 1999), the challenges that we find of greatest importance include the interplay of planned and natural variations; the development of interwoven quantitative-qualitative tools for unpacking complex data structures; and, something entirely different, establishment of professional environments that ameliorate the tensions between researchers and practitioners. It is easy to romanticize this relation, but difficult to establish effective relations with individuals and institutions.

The reality is that the practice of teaching is at best a semiprofession in the United States, creating a gap between research and practice unlike the situation in fields such as engineering or medicine. This state of affairs springs from many sources, including governmental agencies, the media, institutions of higher education, and professional organizations. The result is that practitioners are significantly distanced from research and researchers. Schaefer (1967) spoke to these issues decades ago in his concept of the "school as a center of inquiry." The design experiment offers promise as a methodological nucleus for supporting this concept, but realizing the potential will also require policy action of a character and quality seldom seen on today's radar screens. Nonetheless, the image is worth pursuing, partly for the possibilities that have emerged from such studies. Much more thought is needed to validate such investigations as "proven practice." Meanwhile, for the collaborators in such enterprise, the results clearly seem worth the effort.

Support for this chapter was provided by the Spencer Foundation.

REFERENCES

Adams, M.J. (1990). *Beginning to read: Thinking and learning about print.* Cambridge, MA: MIT Press.

Behrens, J.T., & Smith, M.L. (1996). Data and data analysis. In D.C. Berliner & R.C. Calfee (Eds.), *Handbook of educational Psychology* (pp. 945–989). New York: Macmillan.

Bond, G.L., & Dykstra, R. (1967). The cooperative research program in first-grade reading instruction. *Reading Research Quarterly, 2*(4).

Brown, A.L. (1992). Design experiments: Theoretical and methodological challenges in creating complex interventions in classroom settings. *The Journal of the Learning Sciences, 2,* 141–178.

Calfee, R.C. (1998). Phonics and phonemes: Learning to decode and spell in a literature-based program. In J.L. Metsala & L.C. Ehri (Eds.), *Word recognition in beginning literacy* (pp. 315–340). Mahwah, NJ: Erlbaum.

Calfee, R.C., & Calfee, K.H. (1981). *Interactive reading assessment system (IRAS)* (Rev.). Unpublished, Stanford University, School of Education.

Calfee, R.C., & Norman, K.A. (1998). Psychological perspectives on the early reading wars: The case of phonological awareness. *Teachers College Record, 100*(2), 242–274.

Calfee, R.C., Norman, K.A., & Trainin, G. (in press). *A design experiment exploring factors that affect early acquisition of decoding-spelling skill and knowledge.* Riverside, CA: University of California.

Calfee, R.C., & Scott-Hendrick, L. (in press). The teacher of beginning reading. In W. Slater (Ed.), *Consensus on the preparation of early literacy teachers.*

Carnevalle, A.P., & Fry, R.A. (2000). *Crossing the great divide: Can we achieve equity when Generation Y goes to college?* Princeton, NJ: Educational Testing Service.

Chambliss, M.C., & Calfee, R.C. (in press). The design of empirical research. In J. Flood, J.M. Jensen, D. Lapp, & J.R. Squire (Eds.), *Handbook of research on teaching the English language arts* (2nd ed.). Mahwah, NJ: Erlbaum.

Collins, A. (1992). Toward a design science of education. In E. Scanlon & T. O'Shea (Eds.), *New directions in educational technology* (pp. 37–53). New York: Springer-Verlag.

Collins, A. (1999). The changing infrastructure of education research. In E. Lagemann & L. Shulman (Eds.), *Issues in education research: Problems and possibilities* (pp. 289–298). San Francisco: Jossey-Bass.

Cronbach, L.J. (1963). Evaluation for course improvement. *Teachers College Record, 64,* 97–121.

Darling-Hammond, L., Wise, A.E., & Klein, S.P. (1999). *A license to teach: Raising standards for teaching.* San Francisco: Jossey-Bass.

Ehri, L.C. (2000, April). *A report from the National Reading Panel.* Paper presented at the meeting of the American Educational Research Association, Montreal, Quebec, Canada.

Fisher, R.A. (1934). *The design of experiments.* Edinburgh, Scotland: Oliver & Boyd.

Freedman, S.W. (in press). Teacher research and professional development: Purposeful planning or serendipity. In A. Lieberman & L. Miller (Eds.), *Teachers caught in the action: Professional development in practice.* New York: Teachers College Press.

Lagemann, E.C., & Shulman, L.S. (1999). *Issues in educational research: Problems and possibilities.* San Francisco: Jossey-Bass.

Lewin, K. (1946). Action research and minority problems. *The Journal of Social Issues, 2*(4), 34–47.

National Assessment of Educational Progress (NAEP). (2000). *NAEP 1999 trends in academic progress.* Washington, DC: National Center for Educational Statistics.

National Reading Panel (NRP). (2000). *Teaching children to read: An evidence-based assessment of the scientific research literature on read-*

ing and its implications for reading instruction: Summary report. Washington, DC: National Institute of Child Health and Human Development.

Pearson, P.D. (2000, April). Learning to teach reading: The status of the knowledge base. Paper presented to Reading Research 2000, International Reading Association, Indianapolis, IN.

Reinking, D., & Pickle, J.M. (1993). Using a formative experiment to study how computers affect reading and writing in classrooms. National Reading Conference Yearbook, 42, 263–270.

Sandholtz, J.H. (2000). Interdisciplinary team teaching as a form of professional development. Teacher Education Quarterly, 27(3), 39–54.

Schaefer, R.J. (1967). The school as a center of inquiry. New York: Harper & Row.

Snow, C.E., Burns, M.S., & Griffin, P. (1998). Preventing reading difficulties in young children. Washington, DC: National Academy Press.

Venezky, R.L. (1970). The structure of English orthography. The Hague: Mouton.

Venezky, R.L. (1999). The American way of spelling: The structure and origins of American English orthography. New York: Guilford Press.

CHAPTER 10

The CIERA School Change Project: Translating research on effective reading instruction and school reform into practice in high-poverty elementary schools

Barbara M. Taylor
University of Minnesota/CIERA

P. David Pearson
Michigan State University/CIERA

Concern about poor reading performance, especially for students living in poverty, is a major issue in the United States. Even though the gap in reading achievement between children living in poverty and middle-class children closed between 1970 and 1990, it remains large and has not closed at all during the last 10 years (Donoghue, Voelkl, Campbell, & Mazzeo, 1999). Many states have passed legislation that sets demanding goals, such as all children will read on grade level by the end of third grade, and states and districts have created both incentives and sanctions to encourage low-performing schools to improve their scores.

The good news is that we know a lot today about beginning reading and what it takes to teach all children to read (Adams, 1990; Kamil, Mosenthal, Pearson, & Barr, 2000; National Reading Panel, 2000; Snow, Burns, & Griffin, 1998). Recent large-scale studies point to strikingly convergent findings in terms of classroom-level and school-level variables that contribute to students' reading success (Taylor, Pressley, & Pearson, in press). Across several recent large-scale studies of effective teachers or schools (Designs for Change, 1998; Knapp, 1995;

Pressley et al., in press; Puma et al., 1997; Taylor, Pearson, Clark, & Walpole, 2000) a consistent group of features characterized effective classroom instruction, including

> balanced reading instruction,
>
> small-group instruction,
>
> higher order thinking activities, and
>
> excellent classroom management.

Our earlier work (Taylor et al., 2000) suggests several additional exemplary features of instruction, features associated with greater than expected gains in achievement—student engagement, time for independent reading, approaches to word recognition and comprehension instruction, and teacher interaction styles.

Five recent large-scale studies (see Taylor, Pressley, & Pearson, in press; also see Charles A. Dana Center, 1999; Designs for Change, 1998; Lein, Johnson, & Ragland, 1997; Puma et al., 1997; Taylor et al., 2000) also point to consistent findings in terms of building-level factors present in schools that succeed in teaching all children to read:

strong links to parents

strong teacher collaboration

ongoing professional development

strong building leadership

regular, systematic internal assessment of pupil progress

What remains to be seen is whether we can put this research-based knowledge on effective reading programs and instruction to work in our neediest schools to improve children's reading ability. There is a strong national movement in the United States to encourage low performing schools to adopt widely publicized, off-the-shelf, "research-based" school reform models (American Federation of Teachers, 1997; Herman, 1999; Herman & Stringfield, 1997; Slavin & Fashola, 1998; Wang, Haertel, & Walberg, 1998). On the other hand, recent analyses of effective high-poverty schools suggest that prepackaged programs are not the only path to success in helping all children achieve high levels of literacy. The CIERA Effective Schools/ Accomplished Teachers study (Taylor et al., 2000), the Hope for Urban Education study (Charles A. Dana Center, 1997), and the Successful Texas School-Wide Programs study (Lein et al., 1997) found that most of the effective schools in their studies were using home-grown reform models. These were models that while strongly grounded in research were also tailored to the local settings.

Purpose of the CIERA School Change Project

In the spirit of understanding how schools can create these home-grown models on their own, we have undertaken the CIERA School Change Project. The overall objective of the project is to test the efficacy of a framework designed to guide schools in developing and implementing a reading program that can improve the performance of all students. As discussed earlier, we know a great deal about effective school-level and classroom-level practices that promote reading success in the elementary grades. We also possess a great deal of knowledge about school change and the role of professional development in the change process (Fullan, 1993; Joyce &

Calhoun, 1996; Louis, Kruse, & Raywid, 1996; Lieberman, Saxl, & Miles, 1988; Richardson & Placier, in press). Despite some very compelling success stories about schools that have managed to integrate best practices on effective schools, effective instruction, and effective change efforts to achieve impressive results, we seem hard pressed to integrate and apply this knowledge in ways that will have a significant impact on the thousands of schools that are struggling to teach all children to read. To use the language of policy makers, we have yet to show that we can "scale up" these efforts.

These premises lead us to two fundamental questions:

1. Will a research-based, action-oriented, Internet-delivered framework designed to promote a grass-roots reading program—based on our best knowledge about six key program components (discussed later in this chapter)—produce robust changes in (a) schoolwide approaches to delivering reading instruction, (b) classroom teaching practices, and (c) student learning and reading achievement?

2. Across schools, what professional development activities are most effective in promoting changes in the teaching of reading and in students' reading achievement?

Perspectives of the Project

In trying to answer these questions, we have negotiated some vexing research design issues. For example, in the ideal world of experimental design, programs would be randomly assigned to schools so that we could evaluate their relative efficacy across a large and robust sample of schools. However, we do not think that we can or should randomly assign programs or even particular programmatic components to schools and teachers; to do so would violate what we have learned from the last 20 years of research on school change—that school staffs must be involved in creating the programs for which they will be held accountable. On the other hand, it is neither necessary nor desirable to invite each and every school to "reinvent the wheel." Therefore, what we have done is to offer school staffs a framework for making their own decisions about how they might create a new or significantly revised reading program. The framework consists of a set of six components, each of which must be addressed in creating or revamping a reading program. The components in the framework are classroom practice, school reading programs, reading interventions, school-home-community relations, school change processes, and professional development. For each component, the framework provides what we hope is the best available research-based knowledge to guide schools in crafting their local implementation of that component. The framework exists as an Internet-based multimedia program that provides research summaries, readings, video clips of effective practice, and teacher study group activities to guide local action. Within each component, the research permits choices in the way the component is implemented. We expect enough natural variation in the way each component is addressed to permit some experimental comparisons of the efficacy of various choices.

In this chapter, we will first describe the CIERA School Change Project. We will then present the Classroom Observation Scheme as an example of a research-based tool that can be used by teachers to help them improve their classroom reading instruction.

Method of Study

Participants

Six schools in North Carolina, Michigan, Minnesota, and California used the CIERA School Change Framework in 1999–2000; additionally, we collected data in another four comparison schools that did not use the framework. Six additional schools in Iowa, California, Michigan, and Connecticut are joining the project in 2000–2001. The schools range from 70–90% poverty, based on percent of students on subsidized lunch.

At least 75% of the teachers in a building must agree to participate in the project. Two teachers per grade are randomly selected to participate in the classroom observations. Within these classrooms, nine children are selected as target students—three each from the high, middle, and low thirds of the classroom continuum of reading achievement—

with the hope, given what we know about attrition, of yielding six students by May. As many of these same children as possible will be followed until the project ends in 2001-2002.

Student Assessments

The children randomly selected for participation are assessed in the fall and spring on a number of literacy assessments (depending on grade level), including a standardized reading test (grades 1–6) as well as assessments of the following: letter names and sounds (K–1), phonemic awareness (K–1), sentence dictation (K–1), concepts of print (K–1), instructional decoding level (from an informal reading inventory), fluency (words correct per minute), comprehension (multiple choice and short answer questions on a grade-level story, grades 1–6), and writing ability based on a prompt (grades 1–6).

Use of the School Change Framework

The staffs of each school meet for a minimum of 1 hour a month as a large group and 1 hour a week, on average, in small groups, with the School Change Framework Internet site used as a resource. Small groups, whether grade-level teams or cross-grade teams, meet as study groups to reflect on their teaching practices, their students' needs, and their reading curricula and assessments. A school leadership team made up of teachers, the principal, and an external facilitator (who spends a minimum of 8 hours a week in the building) are responsible for leading the staff through the large- and small-group activities. These activities focus on one or more of the six major areas of the framework (school change, ongoing professional development, school reading program, classroom instruction, early reading interventions, and home-school-community connections). Large-group activities include discussion and action on the schoolwide reading program as well as issues related to school change and professional development, reports from study groups, and cross-grade dialogue. Study group activities include, but are not limited to, watching and discussing video clips of effective practice, video sharing of one's own practice, discussing new instructional techniques that group members have tried, problem solving, peer coaching, and cross-grade dialogue.

Documenting Classroom Practice and Program Characteristics

On three occasions (fall, winter, spring) each participating teacher is observed for an hour during reading instruction to document her classroom practices in the teaching of reading. The observer uses the CIERA School Change Observation Scheme, described later in this chapter. Teachers receive descriptive feedback from the observers as a way of allowing them to make decisions about classroom practices they may wish to implement. Teachers also complete a log of activities covered and grouping practices for an entire week in late fall and early spring of the school year. Teachers and principals are interviewed in the fall, winter, and spring in order to document program features and participants beliefs as well as any perceived changes during the year.

Data Analysis

Data from the interviews and field notes taken by observers during school events will be used to describe the change process and complement the data from small- and large-group meeting notes and action plans. The data from classroom observations and teacher activity logs will be analyzed for relationships with students' reading and writing performance. Data also will be compared to practices identified as effective at the school and classroom level from earlier research (Taylor et al., 2000; Taylor, Pressley, & Pearson, in press). We are especially interested in how practices change over time as a function of participation in the study, and how changes in program features and instructional practices are related to changes in student performance.

Findings From the CIERA School Change Classroom Observation Scheme

As of this writing, we have only just begun to analyze data from the first year of the study, and we are not able to share our most precise and elab-

orate analyses of student performance or the relationship between student performance and teacher practices. We can, however, share some preliminary correlational data on the relationship between teacher practices and student performance, and we do so with all the requisite cautions about not jumping from correlational observations to causal interpretations.

We hope—indeed, we believe—the Observation Scheme is one example of a tool, based on research, that can be useful for teachers and administrators in their efforts to improve classroom reading practices. The purpose of this observation system is to give teachers in grades K–6 data related to their grouping practices, literacy events or activities, materials, interaction styles, expected student responses to the literacy events, and students' engagement rate. Teachers will also receive data on the mean scores on teacher practices for all teachers at their grade level across the study as well as the relationship of teacher practices with achievement. Teachers are encouraged to interpret these data individually or with help from colleagues (such as a peer coach, the external facilitator, members of their study group) to understand, reflect on, broaden, and enhance the quality of their classroom reading instruction.

The observation system combines qualitative notetaking with a more quantitatively oriented checklist process. It works this way: The observer takes field notes for a 5-minute period, recording a narrative account of what is happening in the classroom, including where possible and appropriate, what the teacher and children are saying. At the end of the 5-minute notetaking episode, the observer first records the proportion of children in the classroom who appear to be on task, or doing what they are supposed to be doing. Then the observer codes the three or four most salient literacy events (category 4 codes) that occur during that 5-minute episode. For every category 4 event, the observer also codes who was providing the instruction (category 1), the grouping pattern in use for that event (category 2), the major literacy activity (category 3), the materials being used (category 5), the teacher interaction styles observed (category 6), and the expected responses of the students (category 7). An example of a 5-minute observational segment is provided in Figure 1. Note that at the end of the narrative notes, the observer notes the proportion of on-task students (11/12 in this segment). On the lines below the notes, the observer has recorded the codes for the various phenomena (behaviors, groupings, artifacts) observed during the 5-minute segment (see Figure 2 on the facing page for a list of the codes for all the categories).

The observer tabulates and enters the data from the hour-long observation onto a coding summary sheet, which is a numerical summary of the relative frequency with which the different codes were observed during the observation period. Finally, at the end of the observation, observers answer eight general questions pertaining to overall approach and emphasis, instruction, grouping practices, materials, student participation and engagement, classroom management, classroom environment, and other comments.

Each teacher receives feedback after the observation. The feedback consists of the actual notes taken during the hour-long observation and the numerical summary sheet completed by the observer (the relative incidence of occurrence of the various codes for each category). To help interpret the summary, each teacher also receives an explanation of the observation codes, a summary of the Effective Schools/Accomplished Teachers study (Taylor et al., 2000) as well as a summary of findings from the 1999-2000 School Change Study. These two reports provide some data that teachers can use as benchmarks to help them interpret the observational data. For example, the most accomplished teachers in the Effective Schools/Accomplished Teachers study had 95% of their students on task on average based on the count taken every 5 minutes;

in contrast, the least accomplished teachers had 64% of their students on task on average.

Field Testing of the Observation Scheme

During the 1997-1998 school year, the CIERA School Change Classroom Observation Scheme was used in the classrooms of 92 teachers in grades K–3 in 14 schools ranging from 28-92% poverty in Los Angeles, California; Longmont, Colorado; Minneapolis/St. Paul, Minnesota, and rural Virginia. Four schools, ranging from 38-92% poverty (mean 59% poverty) surfaced as particularly effective in teaching all students to read. The classroom practices of the teachers in these four schools, as well as the practices of the six moderately effective schools and the four least effective schools, are presented in Taylor et al. (2000). Briefly, we found that the students in the most effective schools spent twice as much time in small-group as opposed to whole-group instruction, whereas the reverse was true for the students in the least effective schools. More teachers in the most effective schools were frequently observed coaching in word recognition during reading as a way to help students apply phonics to actual text than were teachers in the other schools. More teachers in the most effective schools were frequently observed asking higher level questions than were teachers in the other schools. Additionally in this study, the practices of the most accomplished teachers (those who exhibited the most characteristics of a profile of effective teaching) across all schools (41% of the sample) were compared with those of the moderately accomplished teachers (32% of the sample) and the least accomplished teachers (27% of the sample).

Figure 2. Codes for Classroom Observations

Level 1 Who	Code
Classroom teacher	c
Reading specialist	r
Special education	se
Other specialist	sp
Student teacher	st
Aide	a
Volunteer	v
No one	n
Other	o
Not applicable	9

Level 2 Grouping	Code
Whole class	w
Small Group	s
Pairs	p
Individual	i
Other	o
Not applicable	9

Level 3 General Focus	Code
Reading	r
Composition/writing	w
Spelling	s
Handwriting	h
Language	l
Other	o
Not applicable	9

Level 4 Specific Focus	Code
Reading connected text	r
Listening to text	l
Vocabulary	v
Meaning of text, lower m1 for talk m2 for writing	m1 m2
Meaning of text, higher m3 for talk m4 for writing	m3 m4
Comprehension skill	c
Comprehension strategy	cs
Writing	w
Exchanging ideas/Oral production	e/o
Word ID	wi
Sight words	sw
Phonics p1 = letter sound p2 = letter by letter p3 = onset/rime p4 = multisyllabic	p1 p2 p3 p4
Word recognition strategies	wr
Phonemic awareness	pa
Letter ID	li
Spelling	s
Other	o
Not applicable	9

Level 5 Material	Code
Textbook, narrative	tn
Textbook, informational	ti
Narrative trade book	n
Informational tradebook	i
Student writing	w
Board/chart	b
Worksheet	s
Oral presentation	OP
Pictures	p
Video/film	v
Computer	c
Other	o
Not applicable	9

Level 6 Teacher Interaction	Code
Tell/give information	t
Modeling	m
Recitation	r
Discussion	d
Coaching/scaffolding	c
Listening/watching	l
Reading aloud	ra
Check work	cw
Assessment	s
Other	o
Not applicable	9

Level 7 Expected Pupil Response	Code
Reading	r
Reading turn-taking	r-tt
Orally responding	or
Oral turn-taking	or-tt
Listening	l
Writing	w
Manipulating	m
Other	o
Not applicable	9
# students on task/ # students in room	

Significant differences in classroom practices across the levels of teacher accomplishment (Taylor et al., 2000) revealed that the most accomplished teachers were able to keep 96% of their students on task on average, as compared to 84% on task for the moderately accomplished teachers and 61% for the least accomplished teachers. The most accomplished teachers provided about twice as much small-group time as compared to whole-group instruction. More of the most accomplished teachers were frequently observed providing coaching in word recognition during reading to help students apply phonics to the reading of actual text. More of the most accomplished teachers asked higher level questions and had students write in response to what they had read. Also, 48% of the most accomplished teachers had a preferred interaction style of coaching, whereas 75% of the least accomplished teachers had a preferred interaction style of telling students information. We believe these types of data, which can be gleaned from the CIERA Classroom Observation Scheme, can be useful in helping teachers reflect on various aspects of their reading instruction repertoire.

Use of the Observation Scheme in the CIERA School Change Project

During the 1999–2000 school year, the CIERA School Change Classroom Observation Scheme was used in the classrooms of 120 teachers in grades K–6 in nine schools across the United States. These schools ranged from 70–95% poverty. In the pages that follow we highlight results from the classroom observations. We report for grades K–1, 2–3, and 4–6.

Across all grades, whole-group instruction was coded more than small group instruction; specifically, for about 55-70% of the time (segments coded) compared to 20-35% of the time for small groups. This is similar to what was found in the moderately effective and least effective schools in our earlier Effective School/Accomplished Teachers study (Taylor et al., 2000). It should be noted, however, that in our earlier work, a performance advantage for small-group instruction was found. Similarly, in this data set, in kindergarten, students' spring literacy scores (using fall scores as a covariate) were negatively related to the amount of whole-group instruction provided ($r = -.38$) and positively related to the amount of small-group instruction ($r = .38$). In grades 4–6, small-group instruction was found to be positively related to growth in students' standardized reading comprehension ($r = .16$).

Across all grades a relatively (some would say alarmingly) small amount of higher level questioning or writing related to stories read was observed. This was coded for 4% of the segments in grades K–1, 13% of the segments in grades 2-3, and 12% in grades 4-6. In contrast, lower level questioning was coded 30% of the time in grades K–1, 41% in grades 2-3, and 46% in grades 4-6. Even with a relatively small occurrence, higher level questioning, along with writing about text, was found to be positively related to growth in reading in kindergarten and grades 4-6. These findings echo those of our earlier work (Taylor et al., 2000), in which we found that higher level questions distinguished both the most effective schools and the most accomplished teachers. Furthermore, other research (Knapp, 1995; Pressley et al., in press) has found that a hallmark of effective teachers is their emphasis on higher level thinking.

In kindergarten and grades 4-6, the incidence of the activity code of "other" was negatively related to students' growth in reading during the year at kindergarten ($r = -.32$ with residual letter name) and at grades 4-6 ($r = -.15$ with Gates comprehension). "Other" was coded when it was not clear what literacy activity was occurring during a particular segment, and it was often indicative of not being particularly focused on literacy learning at that moment in time. Not surprisingly, we have known for some time that "content covered" or academic learning time is important for students' learning (Fisher et al., 1980; Stallings & Kaskowitz, 1974).

Across all grades, informational text was seldom a part of the lessons we observed; it was coded only 2% of the time in grades K–1, 10% of the time in grade 2-3, and 10% of the time in grades 4-6. Similar findings have been recently reported by Duke (2000) in a study of first-grade classrooms. In contrast, narrative text was coded 34% of the time in kindergarten and Grade 1, and 40% of the time in grades 2-6.

Telling and recitation were major interaction styles of teachers in all grades, with telling coded from 46–58% of the time and recitation coded from 56–64% of the time across grades K–1, 2–3, and 4–6. However, telling was found to be negatively related to students' growth in emergent literacy in kindergarten ($r = -.29$ with residual phonemic awareness) and grade 1 ($r = -.38$ with residual instructional reading level), as well as spring scores in literacy in kindergarten, grade 1, grades 2–3, and grades 4–6. In our earlier study (Taylor et al., 2000), we found that the least accomplished teachers had a preferred interaction style of telling. It may be the case that telling children information is not the best way for children to learn or to be engaged in their learning.

In contrast, coaching was only observed from 14–21% of the time across grade K–1, 2–3, or 4–6. However, coaching was found to be positively related to students' reading growth in grades 2–3 ($r = .18$). Again, this echoes findings from our earlier work (Taylor et al., 2000) where we found that coaching was the preferred interaction style of the most accomplished teachers. Pressley et al. (in press) also found that coaching, or scaffolding, was a hallmark of highly effective first-grade teachers, as did Roehler and Duffy (1984).

Across all grades, students were coded more often as engaged in passive responding than in active responding. Passive responding, which included turn-taking during oral reading (for example, round robin), oral turn-taking when answering questions, or listening to the teacher was coded 45% of the time in grades K–1 and 58–60% of the time in grades 2–6. In contrast, active responding (reading, writing, and manipulating) was coded from 28–30% of the time across grades K–6. Passive responding was negatively related to students' achievement in kindergarten ($r = -.28$ with concepts of print). Passive responding was also found to be negatively related to student time on task across all classrooms ($r = -.19$). In contrast, active responding (reading, writing, and manipulating) was positively related to kindergarten students' growth in concepts of print ($r = .23$) and in rhyme ($r = .29$), as well as first-grade students' growth in reading fluency ($r = .26$). Active responding was also found to be related to spring reading scores in grades 4–6 ($r = .23$ with Gates reading comprehension, and $r = .26$ with Houghton Mifflin reading comprehension).

Similarly, research by Pressley et al. (in press) found that children in the classrooms of the most effective elementary teachers were engaged in reading and writing much of the time.

Discussion

Again, we caution readers that these data are preliminary. We have a long way to go in sorting out the specific and detailed influences of instruction on student achievement. Even so, we hope that they provide useful hypotheses about instructional practices, and we hope that our findings will encourage others to look at instruction in a careful and detailed manner, as we have done with our Observational Scheme. Preliminary results from the analysis of the classroom observations suggest that small-group instruction may have an edge over whole-group instruction in terms of enhancing students' growth in reading, a finding supported by other recent research. Higher level questioning and writing about text are beneficial to students' reading growth, but they appear to be woefully under-used as instructional activities.

The teacher's chosen interaction style, or instructional delivery style, and students' expected response to instruction are related to each other and tied to students' growth and performance in reading. Telling appears to be an over-used, and not particularly beneficial, instructional technique. On the other hand, coaching children as they attempt to perform a transferable action or strategy appears to be a beneficial, but under-used instructional technique. In terms of pupil response, if a teacher frequently is engaged in telling students information or if students are listening to others take turns reading or orally responding, they are not very actively engaged in their own learning. However, active responding by students, whether this be reading, writing, or manipulating, shows positive relationships to students' growth in reading in grades K–1 as well as related to students' reading achievement in grades K–6.

Most of the findings reported in this chapter are not surprising. Observers of teaching will tell you that good teachers elicit more active responding and greater engagement on the part of students. But it is important, we think, that we have been able to document the efficacy of these teacher actions in the sorts of schools in which students are most in need of our very best instructional practice. The good news is that teachers can use the classroom observation system to get data on their instructional repertoire (including grouping practices, types of literacy activities, interaction styles, and student response activities) with an eye toward reflecting on what they find and then making instructional changes to improve students' reading performance. It is to this end that we hope the research and tools reported on in this chapter are found to be useful.

Importance of the CIERA School Change Project

Currently, the improvement of our children's reading achievement is a major U.S. goal. Schools know that a wealth of information exists to help them move toward this goal, but access to all the most relevant information in a format that helps schools take action remains elusive. We believe a strategy that includes the best research available on reading pedagogy and school change within the framework of teacher involvement and ownership over the change process stands the very best chance of creating the knowledge that will help us achieve this goal. The Internet-based delivery system in the CIERA School Change Project will make the framework widely and readily available to educators across the United States who want to improve their local schools. Finally, we invite all readers to learn about the CIERA School Change Observation Scheme and the CIERA School Change Framework by visiting us at http://www.school change.ciera.org.

This research was conducted as part of CIERA, the Center for the Improvement of Early Reading Achievement and supported under the Educational Research and Development Centers program, PR/Award Number R305R70004, as administered by the Office of Educational Research and Improvement, U.S. Department of Education. However, the contents of the described report do not necessarily represent the positions or policies of the National Institute on Student Achievement, Curriculum, and Assessment; the National Institute on Early Childhood Development; or the U.S. Department of Education, and you should not assume endorsement by the federal government.

Portions of this chapter have appeared in Taylor, B.M., & Pearson, P.D. (2000). The CIERA school change classroom observation scheme. Minneapolis, MN: University of Minnesota. Reprinted with permission.

REFERENCES

Adams, M.J. (1990). *Beginning to read: Thinking and learning about print.* Cambridge, MA: MIT Press.

American Federation of Teachers (AFT). (1997). *Raising student achievement: A resource guide for redesigning low-performing schools.* (AFT Item Number 3780). Washington DC: Author.

Charles A. Dana Center, University of Texas at Austin. (1999). *Hope for urban education: A study of nine high-performing, high-poverty urban elementary schools.* Washington, DC: U.S. Department of Education, Planning and Evaluation Service.

Designs for Change. (1998). *Practices of schools with substantially improved reading achievement* (Chicago Public Schools) [Online]. Available: www.dfc1.org/summary/report.htm

Donoghue, P.L, Voelkl, K.C., Campbell, J.R., & Mazzeo, J. (1999). *NAEP 1998 reading report card for the nation.* Washington, DC: U.S. Department of Education, Office of Educational Research and Improvement.

Duke, N. (2000). 3.6 minutes per day: The scarcity of informational texts in first grade. *Reading Research Quarterly, 35,* 202–224.

Fisher, C., Berliner, D., Filby, N., Marliave, R., Cahen, L., & Dishaw, M. (1980). Teaching behaviors, academic learning time and student achievement: An overview. In C. Denham & A. Lieberman (Eds.), *Time to learn.* Washington, DC: National Institute of Education.

Fullan, M.G. (1993). *Change forces: Probing the depths of educational reform.* Bristol, PA: Falmer.

Herman, R. (1999). *An educator's guide to school-wide reform.* Washington, DC: American Institutes for Research.

Herman, R., & Stringfield, S. (1997). *Ten promising programs for educating all children: Evidence of impact.* Arlington, VA: Educational Research Service

Joyce, B., & Calhoun, E. (1996). School renewal: An inquiry, not a prescription. In B. Joyce & E. Calhoun (Eds.), *Learning experiences in school renewal: An exploration of 5 successful programs.* Eugene, OR: ERIC.

Kamil, M.L., Mosenthal, P.B., Pearson, P.D., & Barr, R. (Eds.). (2000). *Handbook of reading research: Volume III.* Mahwah, NJ: Erlbaum.

Knapp., M.S. (1995). *Teaching for meaning in high-poverty classrooms.* New York: Teachers College Press.

Lieberman, A., Saxl, E.R., & Miles, M.P. (1988). Teacher leadership: Ideology and practice. In A. Leiberman (Ed.), *Building a professional culture in schools.* New York: Teachers College Press.

Lein, L., Johnson, J.F., & Ragland, M. (1997). *Successful Texas school-wide programs: Research study results*. Austin, TX: Charles A. Dana Center, University of Texas at Austin.

Louis, K.S., Kruse, S., & Raywid, M. (1996). Putting teachers at the center of reform: Learning schools and professional communities. *NASSP Bulletin, 80*(580), 9–21.

National Reading Panel (NRP). (2000). *Teaching children to read: An evidence-based assessment of the scientific research literature on reading and its implications for reading instruction*. Washington, DC: National Institute of Child Health and Human Development.

Pressley, M., Wharton-McDonald, R., Allington, R., Block, C.C., Morrow, L., Tracey, D., Baker, K., Brooks, G., Cronin, J., Nelson, E., & Woo, D. (in press). A study of effective first-grade literacy instruction. *Scientific Studies of Reading*.

Puma, M.J., Karweit, N., Price, C., Ricciuti, A., Thompson, W., & Vaden-Kiernan, M. (1997). *Prospects: Final report on student outcomes*. Washington, DC: U.S. Department of Education, Planning and Evaluation Services.

Richardson, V., & Placier, P. (in press). Teacher change. In V. Richardson (Ed.), *Handbook of research on teaching* (4th ed.). Washington, DC: American Educational Research Association.

Roehler, L.R., & Duffy, G.G. (1984). Direct explanation of comprehension processes. In G.G. Duffy, L.R. Roehler, & J. Mason (Eds.), *Comprehension instruction: Perspectives and suggestions* (pp. 265–280). New York: Longman.

Slavin, R.E., & Fashola, O.S. (1998). *Show me the evidence! Proven and promising programs for America's schools*. Thousand Oaks, CA: Corwin Press.

Snow, C.E., Burns, M.S., & Griffin, P. (1998). *Preventing reading difficulties in young children*. Washington, DC: National Academy Press.

Stallings, J., & Kaskowitz, D. (1974). *Follow through classroom observation evaluation 1972–1973* (SRI Project URU-7370). Stanford, CA: Stanford Research Institute.

Taylor, B.M., & Pearson, P.D. (2000). *The CIERA school change classroom observation scheme*. Minneapolis, MN: University of Minnesota.

Taylor, B.M., Pearson, P.D., Clark, K., & Walpole, S. (2000). Effective schools and accomplished teachers: Lessons about primary grade reading instruction in low-income schools. *The Elementary School Journal, 101*, 121–166.

Taylor, B.M., Pressley, M., & Pearson, P.D. (in press) *Effective teachers and schools: Trends across recent studies*. Washington, DC: National Education Association.

Wang, M.C., Haertel, G.D., & Walberg, H.J. (1998). *What do we know: Widely implemented school improvement programs*. Philadelphia, PA: Center for Research in Human Development and Education.

CHAPTER 11

Teachers talk back to standards

Jennifer I. Berne

MICHIGAN STATE UNIVERSITY AND OAKLAND COMMUNITY COLLEGE

In *Tinkering Toward Utopia*, Tyack and Cuban (1995) present their belief that policy documents and policies should be repositioned as hypotheses rather than edicts. This idea has great appeal because it suggests that ideas are not complete unless they are put into practice and examined from a classroom context. In other words, when ideas come down from the state, district, or building level, if we consider them as drafts of ideas, as hypotheses that may or may not produce the consequences desired, then we do two things. First, we empower the practioners to use these ideas flexibly, and to borrow what they see as helpful and omit that which is not consistent with what they as professionals consider productive. Second, we spend time noticing and thinking about the results of the policy. Rather than simply assuming that the policy will fail or succeed in total, considering it as a hypothesis allows us to think about *pieces* of policy that can remain, or changes in the new policy that might improve the outcome.

Though this sounds like a simple idea, it has come to influence my thinking about my work as I examine standards documents for English language arts teachers and as I observe teachers of English language arts. It is odd that I even have to make that distinction because standards documents and the teaching of subjects should go hand in hand. However, it often seems that teaching continues oblivious to standards and that standards get written, discussed, and sometimes put into "policy" without the input of teachers, and parents, and/or students. In this, those of us who study policy and practice often do it in two separate realms. Because the enactment and consideration of standards documents are often divorced from the work of teacher educators and those who work with inser-

vice teachers on professional development, they become two separate issues. Standards documents can be miles from the world of chalkboards and students and standardized tests that have become the work of teachers and teaching in so many U.S. schools. This is true, in large part, because those who write and consult on standards often do not see them as hypotheses, but rather as the last word in teachers' responsibilities.

Standards documents are big and bold, and we often find very good ideas in them. However, what we often do not find is any clue how to take these ideas into teacher education classrooms, what these ideas look like in the real world of the classroom, how a teacher might know if he or she is achieving them, and where to turn for help. All of these gaps might be filled if we shrink away from the idea of standards as policy and embrace the idea of standards as hypotheses.

As part of an inquiry into the ways standards are framed rhetorically, I did a survey of five major standards documents:

the American Federation of Teachers' (AFT) *Reading IS Rocket Science: What Expert Teachers of Reading Should Know and Be Able to Do* (1999) (see Appendix C of this volume for the executive summary of this document);

the International Reading Association/National Council of Teachers of English's (IRA/NCTE) joint publication *Standards for the English Language Arts* (1996);

the Council of Chief State School Officers/ Interstate New Teacher Assessment and Support Consortium's (CCSSO/INTASC) document drafted by the English Language Arts Sub-

Committee *Model Standards for English Language Arts Teachers* (draft of March 1, 1998);

the International Reading Association's (IRA) map of knowledge bases useful for reading professionals, titled *Standards for Reading Professionals* (1998); and

a standards document jointly authored by the National Evaluation System and the California Commission on Teacher Credentialing Reading Instruction Competence Assessment (RICA) Content Specifications (published by National Evaluation System Inc. and California Commission on Teacher Credentialing).

What I found in this comparative survey is beyond the scope of this chapter; however, it occurred to me that across the board, I was unable to see how a teacher might use these very impressive documents to the benefit of students. I could see their value in framing teacher education curriculums, especially in their relationship to liberal arts coursework, yet this could not have been their only intended audience. It was obvious that a great deal of work went into these texts, so it seemed implicit that all sorts of people interact with them.

In the way that student standards are meant to clarify the work of teachers and students, standards documents for teachers need to speak both to teacher educators and to the teachers themselves. This moves teachers away from roles as passive recipients of a teacher certification curriculum to enactors of their own principles and policies. Indeed, virtually all standards documents state explicitly or implicitly that teachers need to become their own decision makers. NCTE notes that elementary teachers develop as professionals by learning from their own practice and the knowledge and practice of others. The CCSSO/INTASC document frames it this way: "Teachers are reflective practitioners. They continually assess and adapt their practices in light of their experiences with students and based on scholarship related to their profession. Teachers are actively involved in their own development as professionals" (1998, p. 7). It is only logical, then, that this activity should start with a way to take control of the very standards that suggest that teachers need control of their professional lives. Despite the fact that there is something odd about empow-

ering teachers by telling them that they should be empowered, this is not enough to believe they should not be.

If we circle back to policy as a hypothesis, we see that if we take standards documents for teachers out of the realm of done deals and into the realm of discussion starters, we have positioned both teachers and standards in an entirely new way. If standards are to be texts that we can talk back to in the significant ways that we want children to become active readers of texts, they become hypotheses to be tested rather than mandates to be followed. However, it is not enough for teachers to use standards and view them flexibly. Standards writers must also see the value in a document that will constantly be in draft form, that fluctuates naturally and necessarily, and that is deadened if it is not put to use.

Because I had an idea that standards, like policy, might be a hypotheses, colleagues and I decided to see what might really happen if we asked practicing teachers to work with, not against, nor as puppets, for standards. In this spirit, we worked on a piece of inquiry that might help us understand what it would mean to let the voices of practicing teachers interact with the voices of standards writers (who, to be fair, sometimes are practicing teachers, and often also are influenced by teachers). These teachers had no particular investment in standards, nor did they actively oppose the influence of standards on the dialogue around literacy education.

Background of the Project

My colleagues and I wondered what a professional development opportunity that asked teachers to become critical readers of standards might do both for the teacher's consideration of his or her work and for the profession that is still struggling with the assessment and evaluation of teachers against some objective list. When we began working with standards and wondering how they might read to various groups of teachers, we were daunted. The range of skill sets, the depth of required understandings, the breadth of disciplinary knowledge, and the range of intellectual activities seemed untenable, yet nobody seemed to want to get up and say that any given child should have a teacher who could not demonstrate competence on all these measures. So we were faced with another dilemma: If we decide to expect all these things, how can we know if a teacher has achieved them, and how can that teacher know if he or she had done them? Furthermore, what assistance can policy makers or teacher educators offer on behalf of teachers?

With those questions in mind, we set to construct an activity for teachers to look at standards and speak back to them or in support of them in a safe environment, away from the pulls and pressures of a building, an administrator, or a particular set of standards.

The teachers with whom we worked were part of a group that had been heavily involved in the creation of "I can" statements for students. These were statements that took the competencies required of students in the state of Michigan and placed them in language that children (as well as their parents) could understand. Instead of an abstraction riddled with language that was constructed by policy makers, these statements were direct and tangible. (For a further discussion of this project, please see Raphael et al., 2001). From the experience of taking large intimidating statements and changing them into simple actions by which a student might express competency, we understood how powerful it could be for learners to go from abstract policy to statements that were resonant with their own experiences from their own work. We decided to use this idea to flesh out standards documents for teachers.

Teacher Standards Survey

From my participant observation of this group, I knew that these teachers were reflective about their own practice, reliant on current research to inform their instructional practices, and thoughtful about literacy and learning. Because I knew them well, I felt comfortable asking them to look at a cross-section of standards documents for K–12 teachers of English language arts and to rank them according to the importance they played in the teachers' own classroom work. I then asked the teachers to omit those standards that they felt were not important enough to be included on a short list of standards

and add those that were not included in our original list. I also asked that they give us any additional comments in written, verbal, or electronic form. I told them that this was part of the work for my dissertation and that they should consider it seriously if briefly (this was only weeks before winter vacation). The original list I distributed is shown in Figure 1 on the facing page. I was careful to list these standards in an arbitrary order, taken from the range of the five documents that I had studied. To be fair to each document I reviewed, I selected one or two of the first three standards they offered. I tried to offer the standards that seemed to be most important to the standards writers in each particular case. I did not attempt to load the list in any way, to have special favorites, or to plant duds. It actually was not the content of the standards in which I was interested, but rather I was interested in the form of the teacher's responses.

I asked the teachers to return the documents to me after the winter break, and when they did, I was surprised at what I received. These far-from-ordinary teachers—teachers who were used to critical reflection and arguing for the importance of their own work—sent me back documents that were merely renumbered. They had no comments, no additions, and with the exception of one, no deletions. This led me to think harder about the ways that standards documents do and do not speak to teachers. I had intended on using teachers' responses to study how less-accomplished teachers might use standards as tools rather than feel that standards were thrust upon them; what I found instead was that even these relatively accomplished and experienced teachers were turned off by this task. Instead of an insight into standards documents, this became a question of how teachers were reading documents and in what ways these documents may have been disallowing a dialogue that some standards writers argued they were designed to promote.

Group Discussions of Standards

Step two involved gathering these teachers together to see if I could determine what might be preventing them from working on the survey in a way that would let me see their interaction with the

Figure 1. List of Standards Distributed to Teachers

1. *I understand subject matter.* Knowledge of a subject includes both familiarity with basic facts and information as well as an understanding of the ways of thinking and doing within the discipline.

2. *I know students.* Knowledge of students includes understanding how different people may develop and learn. This also includes the way students act individually and the effects of groups on individual learning and behavior.

3. *I am skilled in curriculum planning and design.* Teachers can identify large curricular goals and design units to support those goals in coherent fashion.

4. *I am comfortable with the psychology of reading and reading development.* Teachers know the characteristics of good and poor readers, as well as how reading, writing, and spelling develop.

5. *I have studied the language structure of English.* This includes phonology, phonetics, morphology, semantics, orthography, and syntax.

6. *I can work with others to support students.* I am comfortable asking colleagues and administrators for support and letting parents know when their insights or expertise are needed.

7. *I am reflective about my practice.* When I attempt innovations or use tried and true methods, I have a decision-making system for analyzing what actually happens.

8. *I know how to use and interpret various assessment measures.* These might include performance and other authentic assessments, as well as standardized instruments.

texts. This time we met in person, and many of the teachers were apologetic about the job they had done on the initial task. My colleagues and I asked them again to look at the same list, this time in small working groups comprised of four or five teachers from different schools, districts, or communities. This time we asked them not to rank the various standards because we thought that this may have been too binary a task. Instead, we asked them to come to a group consensus on one or two standards that they felt they would like to describe. They were then asked to devise a story starter based on the literacy work they had been doing with struggling readers that explicated the particular standard they had chosen. Story starters, it was explained, are merely pieces of a fuller picture that serve to represent and suggest an anecdotal moment. The university researchers and teacher educators also decided to be participant/observers in the groups in order to better understand the ways teachers were interacting through discussion and the ways the standards were directing those discussions.

These groups were lively and quite critical of the standards. They had amazingly detailed and rich conversations about what particular standards said about teachers' work and about the way they might approach literacy teaching and learning. One of the groups, for instance, discussed instructional strategies that would cross over many of the standards. By isolating an instructional activity—they used "closing community share," an instructional frame with which they all were familiar and used regularly—and pulling the components of their own planning, instructional activity, and assessment, they could see which standards were put to use in the service of instruction. For instance, they saw that part of this activity involved assessment, part understanding students as learners, part sense making and theory building. They wondered where in the standards these components were represented and how the field was going about preparing teachers to accomplish them. Several admitted that they were still trying to understand, for instance, what "understanding students as learners" (CCSSO/INTASC, 1998, p. 7) really meant. All helped the discussion resolve in the idea that standards should be culled from best practice instruction rather than from instruction defining itself as an exercise in the display of standards.

Another depiction came about because of a discussion of the activity of "retelling." One instructor asked how others knew they were teaching adequately this important lower elementary skill. They wondered which standards might help them perform a real instructional activity and which were more theoretical. From this discussion of retelling and standards came the resonant idea that "reasoned improvisation" made up the most important work of teachers in their daily activities. This group decided that when planning fails and when theory is not accessible, great teachers can use reasoned improvisation to positive ends.

How did a discussion of teacher standards lead teachers to these conclusions? The act of pulling different pieces out of different standards and imagining how those pieces played out instructionally, led them there. This group combined and coordinated standards. The arrowing back and forth on their lists is evidence of the way that they thought about standards in particular interactions with one another.

It was incredible to look at the way these teachers wrote all over the same documents I had offered to them individually. In the small groups, there were comments and foldings and pictures doodled all over my text—in contrast to the pristine ways that they had returned the documents to me when I had asked them to respond individually. We also saw that instead of using one standard or one story starter, these teachers were more comfortable traversing standards and stories to come up with explications that arose out of real-world experiences. In this, they resisted the original task and made a task that was far more challenging and theoretical. In a way, they refused to act and discuss in a way that was neat and categorizable as standards are, but instead took to a task as messy and indeterminate as the world of a classroom.

Another group came up with a visual picture of teaching that encompassed many of the standards that they felt were important. They placed assessment in the center of their picture and allowed all the other components of their work to fall around it. They did not believe, in the end, that it was helpful to list standards without metaphorically and analytically linking them to one another to make meaning. They spoke eloquently of the ways in which standards could support their work and could support their students, yet they had to remove the standards from their empty position on a list. They believed very much in the standards, yet they felt them abstract and indeterminate.

Like the first group concluded, the standards did not give us a clear picture of what a teacher would look like in practice as he or she showed competence in a particular standard. Instead, they theory-built about the most important pieces of their work and related these pieces visually (through a nature-based metaphor) to one another. Also like the first group, they resisted categorizing or isolating standards in their work. They built a relationship through a visual scheme in the way that the first group built a relationship through particular teaching frames.

How much of the outputs of these groups were attempts to build consensus is unclear. Research has suggested that teachers, particulary, often avoid conflict as part of their core behavior (Florio-Ruane, 2001). There certainly seemed a uniformity to the end result that needs further inquiry. Nonetheless, the output from this activity was at least meaty enough to produce reflection in the teachers if their own self-reports are to be believed—and I do believe them.

Also important, the teachers were truly stimulated by this activity. One told me later (and helpfully, while the video was running) that something about working in this way made her stomach flutter and ache with excitement. She felt this activity had been truly important for her and the way she thought about documents that attempted to define her work.

Another remarked that going through these standards with teachers from other buildings, communities, and cultural contexts was the enriching part for her. Before this activity, she believed that her work was similar to the work of all teachers. After, she decided that the cultural context in which she worked was even more powerful than she had once believed. She commented that the standards made her believe that her teaching, in general, resembled teaching everywhere else. After working through standards and conversing with teachers from all around, she felt the chasm was wider than she had once thought.

The results of the presentations the small groups offered were multidimensional, visual, linked to actual practice, and theoretical. They are wonderful models of the definition of teachers' work by teachers, and they look nothing like a list of standards. They look much more like an attempt to understand and talk about complex problems of practice through stories, through visual imagery, through collaboration. It is important to remember that these presentations arose out of the desire to understand and explicate standards, and this is a value for standards documents that must not be lost.

Teacher professional development might benefit on many fronts from this kind of activity. It does at least two important things: It requires reflection about practice, and it reminds us that the indeterminate world of the classroom cannot always be assessed against a list of unproblematized standards. A teacher's work is art and science because it can be rooted in principles and enacted through improvisation. This is not to demean the work and good of standards lists. It is only, to return to an idea that we began with, a way to begin a conversation about teaching—not a way to end one.

In another context, I was able to find another dimension to the standards usability question. This time I saw that it was not the "magical-ness" of groups that allowed teachers to speak with and interact around standards. I tried this activity in a group of cooperating teachers who were attending a conference on how to best work with interns. I asked them to take that same list of standards and determine how their interns might respond to it and how interns might work in interaction with other interns around them. The response was about the same as the response I had gotten the first time I sent around the standards to the group in the mail and asked them to respond individually: They talked around the issue a lot. They seemed to want to say that the standards were fine and that they only needed to be put in easier language for their interns to be able to use and understand. I was not sure they understood how one might interact with a standards document—though nobody asked me to clarify the task—and nobody stated that they found the activity problematic or difficult. Yet the results were the verbal equivalent of the renumbering I had seen from the original group of teachers.

Conclusions

Though it would have been nice to figure out that standards documents are useful for groups to work with but too daunting for individuals, that is not what I found. Instead, I found that the initial group used characteristics of the teacher network that they were to come together and use the standards in productive ways. These teachers had built trust and context with one another over a long period of time. Perhaps because of this history, their work together was jump-started from the beginning. They had trust; they had respect; they were used to sitting together and working on difficult issues around teaching and learning. In the following ways, Lieberman and Grolnick (1996) define the ways in which teacher networks bring people together and organize their work:

> agendas that are more often challenging than prescriptive; learning that is more indirect than direct; formats for work more collaborative than individualistic; attempts at change more integrated than fragmented; approaches to leadership more facilitative than directive; thinking that is more multiperspective than uniperspective; valuing both context-specific knowledge and generalized knowledge; and structurally and organizationally more movement-like than organization-like. (p. 44)

As you can see, then, the particular characteristics of groups of teachers in a network can move toward meanings that arbitrary groups of teachers cannot or will not.

These experiences lead me to some tentative conclusions:

1. Texts will speak louder than teachers unless we give teachers specific ways to speak back to them. This may be in the form of formal professional development activities specifically geared to critical analysis of texts like district competencies, standards, or curricula. However, this will work only if we decide as a community that we really want teachers

to have the tools that will cause more decentralized decision making when the current political climate seems to suggest we want more.

2. In practice, when documents like these are given to teachers in mandated settings, they are read as authoritative and general. When they are placed in a context that is safe, collective, and nonthreatening, standards become something more dialogic. and useable.

3. Teachers can find ways to speak back to documents like this when the exercise is positioned as an activity that places teachers and their work at the center of the conversation within diverse groups that foreground differences but also have worked together over time and in trusting, active ways. These kinds of settings produce ideas that are generative, contextualized, and adaptable to different contexts—in these ways nonstandard. The image from standards documents is often that of the teacher as lone ranger who only asks for help if he or she cannot solve a problem alone. We found, to the contrary, that standards are often activated in meaningful ways within a discourse community.

4. Finally, we were interested to see that teachers did not develop rubrics or even examples of standards in the ways we expected they might. Instead, they took one or two key examples of rich classroom practice and used them as ways to criss-cross landscapes (Spiro, Feltovich, Jacobson, & Coulson, 1995), revealing kinds of teacher knowledge in action.

In his keynote address to the Reading Research 2000 audience, P. David Pearson (2000) noted that standards documents for teachers are often more alike than they are different. (See Pearson, Chapter 1 in this volume, for further discussion of standards documents.) He argued that standards documents can be put to very good use if they are considered within a large context of teacher learning and development. He also noted that they often represent the latest in the base of teacher knowledge. None of these ideas are called into dispute by my study of standards. One of the reasons projects like this can be helpful to the field is because scholars like Pearson are coming to embrace standards as important components in the dialogue around teacher preparation. It is thus an exciting time to imagine all their uses and to play with them in the service of professional development. Standards can become an important part of the professional development of teachers if we think of them as tools for teacher learning, rather than as skills that teachers should have already learned. It is up to those of us who care about the field to pursue this ideal.

REFERENCES

American Federation of Teachers (AFT). (1999). *Teaching reading IS rocket science: What expert teachers of reading should know and be able to do.* Washington, DC: Author.

Council of Chief State School Officers/Interstate New Teacher Assessment and Support Consortium (CCSSO/INTASC). (1998). *Model standards in English language arts for beginning teacher licensing and development: A resource for state dialogue.* Washington, DC: Author.

Florio-Ruane, S. (with deTar, J.) (2001). *Teacher education and the cultural imagination: Autobiography, conversation, and narrative.* Mahwah, NJ: Erlbaum.

International Reading Association (IRA). (1998). *Standards for reading professionals, revised.* Newark, DE: Author.

International Reading Association & National Council of Teachers of English (IRA/NCTE). (1996). *Standards for the English language arts.* Newark, DE, & Urbana, IL: Authors.

Lieberman, N., & Grolnick, M. (1996). Network and reform in American education. *Teachers College Record, 98*(1), 7–45.

National Evaluation System/California Commission on Teacher Credentialing. (1999). *Reading instruction competence assessment content specifications.* Sacramento, CA: Author.

Pearson, P.D. (2000, April). *Learning to teach reading: The status of the knowledge base.* Presentation at the Reading Research 2000 Conference, Indianapolis, IN.

Raphael, T.E., Florio-Ruane, S., Kehus, M.J., George, M., Hasty, N.L., & Highfield, K. (2001). Thinking for ourselves: Literacy learning in a diverse teacher inquiry Network. *The Reading Teacher, 54,* 596–607.

Spiro, R.J., Feltovich, P.J., Jacobson, M.I., & Coulson, R.L. (1995). Cognitive flexibility, constructivism, and hypertext: Random access instruction for advanced knowledge acquisition in ill-structured domains. *Army Research Institute.* Paper MDA903-86-K-0443.

Tyack, D., & Cuban, L. (1995). *Tinkering toward utopia: Reflections on a century of public school reform.* Cambridge, MA: Harvard University Press.

SECTION FOUR

CONCLUSION

CHAPTER 12

A proposed research agenda for teacher preparation in reading

Cathy M. Roller

International Reading Association

I write this final chapter after watching President Bush declare, "Bipartisan education reform will be the cornerstone of my administration." He has pledged to work with the Congress to make sure that "no child is left behind" (Bush, 2000). I am both hopeful and apprehensive—hopeful because I share the president's top priority, apprehensive because he and I may have different ways of realizing that priority. I am convinced that improving U.S. schools, and particularly the reading instruction in those schools, requires an ambitious research agenda for teacher education—a research agenda whose themes are woven throughout this volume.

Teacher Development

One important message of this volume is that teacher education, both preservice and inservice, can be effective. In the opening chapter, P. David Pearson summarized a body of work that converges on this finding. While most of this evidence is correlational and qualitative, the finding rests on a substantial empirical base. The effectiveness of teacher education was also an important finding of *the Report of the National Reading Panel* (2000). However, I do not want to make too much of this finding. While in general teacher education is effective—that is, teacher learning is reflected in student learning—there is much that we do not know about teacher development and the relationship between teacher learning and student learning. Teacher development is the first item on my proposed research agenda.

As Pearson (see Chapter 1 in this volume) and Dorothy Strickland (see Chapter 2 in this volume) point out, our understanding of teacher development is limited. This volume presents characterizations of beginning teachers (see Grossman et al., Chapter 4; Flint et al., Chapter 5), and characterizations of teachers from particular programs (see Grossman et. al.; Flint et. al; Lalik & Potts, Chapter 6). It also presents characterizations of exemplary and effective teachers (see Allington & Johnston, Chapter 8; Taylor & Pearson, Chapter 10). However, none of the chapters focus on the development of reading teachers *across their careers*. In this, the present volume reflects the field. There are a few descriptions of beginning teachers as they move into, through, and out of their teacher preparation programs and into the first years of teaching, and there are a growing number of converging descriptions of exemplary teachers at various grade levels. We are studying the larvae and butterfly, but what occurs in the chrysalis is a mystery.

The descriptions of exemplary teachers are encouraging, however. Our studies of exemplary teachers show again and again that it is what teachers actually do in the classroom with curriculum materials and not the curriculum materials themselves that produce high reading achievement. Since the First-Grade Studies (Bond & Dykstra, 1967), we have known that the differences in student achievement are often greater for teachers using the same materials and methods than are the differences for teachers using different methods and materials.

Chapter 8 in this volume, authored by Allington and Johnston, which focuses on upper elementary (grades 3, 4, and 5) teachers and teaching, provides a summary table of features associated with exemplary teachers. It is a valuable start, even with the authors' caution about its utility given the different data selection, data collection, analytical methods, and theoretical frames of the various studies. Their study is substantially convergent with earlier studies, and they suggest there are clusters of beliefs, attributes, instructional practices, and personal characteristics that might ultimately lead to a more unified construct of exemplary teachers. They propose "constructed knowing" (Belenky et. al, 1986) as a framework that integrates many of the characteristics and practices of exemplary teachers. A unified construct would be a useful step in theory development.

The CIERA study (see Taylor & Pearson, Chapter 10 in this volume) identifies characteristics of exemplary primary teachers in high-poverty schools and takes another important step toward theory development. The observation instrument developed in earlier studies (Taylor & Pearson, 1999) captures some of the characteristics of effective teachers and provides a way for practicing teachers to compare their own teaching to that of effective teachers from effective schools. This work is headed in the right direction. Although it is crucial to describe and define both end goal and initial states, ultimately we must go far beyond these descriptions to understand how beginning teachers become exemplary teachers. Hence I echo Pearson's call for long-term longitudinal studies of teacher development. And I would note, as Allington and Johnston (this volume) do, that the longitudinal studies will have to involve studying teachers and students in classrooms as they use the language of instruction to become readers and writers.

The Relationship Between Teacher Learning and Student Learning

The second item on my agenda is studying the relationship between teacher learning and student learning. As Pearson (this volume) points out, this is a difficult relationship to pin down. Many of the studies supporting teacher education effectiveness are either very narrow (focusing on a very specific top-ic, such as teaching summarization over a short period of time) or very general (focusing on relationships between students' higher pass rates on state exams and teachers' scores on national exams, or focusing on achievement of students whose teachers were traditionally versus alternatively certified).

The logistics of following teacher learning and relating it to student learning are daunting. When teachers and students learn in a variety of settings over a long period of time, and both of them learn in complex environments where a host of variables other than teacher learning may contribute to student learning, it is difficult to track specific student performances to any particular cause. Our approaches to date, either focusing on very specific information or relying on very general correlational data, are insufficient to make a strong case for teacher education. To adequately study the relationship between teacher and student learning, long-term longitudinal studies of teachers and students *as they interact in classrooms* must focus on student learning as well as teacher development.

A major part of this agenda must explore the effects of socioeconomic status, race, ethnicity, and cultural differences on reading achievement. As Au and Maaka (see Chapter 7 in this volume) point out, poverty, race, culture, gender, and ethnicity are persistently and tenaciously related to reading achievement and are also are related to the demographics of the teaching force. In addition, an overwhelming majority of teachers are female and white. We need to recruit minority teachers (see Au & Maaka, this volume; Strickland, this volume), but we also must help white female teachers learn to teach children unlike themselves to read and write, and our research agenda must include systematic study of these effects. Our longitudinal studies must carefully examine these factors and be of significant size and scope to allow follow-up work with the particular groups of children.

However, longitudinal studies require substantial investment. Longitudinal studies—particularly those that follow students and their teachers into their classrooms and carefully analyze how the words and actions of teachers influence the words and actions of students—are prohibitively expensive given the total dollars that are currently spent on research in reading instruction. As educators we have been too ready to accept the adjective "prohibitive," and too ready to do our best under rigid constraints.

Gaining the necessary understandings to ensure that all children learn to read requires a significant increase in the spending on classroom instructional research. A simple comparison of spending on education and health research supports this point. The primary source of funding for reading education researchers has been the Office of Education Research and Improvement (OERI). Over the last 25 years, OERI has funded centers for studying reading, and several other centers and grant programs have focused on reading. Over the lifetime of these centers, the government funding has totaled $50 million (Sweet, 2000). Meanwhile, OERI's annual budget is 1/360th of that of the National Institutes of Health (NIH). If everyone at NIH stayed home for just one day, the savings would allow OERI to double its budget (Sweet, 2000).

But even if the funding were sufficient, the task would remain daunting. Classroom environments are complex , and it is difficult to control appropriate variables. Many of the characteristics of children and teachers are innate and cannot be assigned randomly. Often the conditions of true experiments cannot be achieved, and we must rely on quasi-experimental and correlational designs in which causal attribution is more difficult. Often qualitative approaches are necessary to get full answers to our questions.

Calfee and his colleagues' (see Chapter 9 in this volume) use of the design experiment is a promising conceptualization for the conduct of research in complex educational settings. The design experiment allows us to begin studies within reasoned parameters, but does not lock us into parameters that soon prove inappropriate. It includes the detailed observation and rich description of qualitative methodologies. The design experiment is appropriate for the kind of longitudinal studies we need to conduct. For example, Calfee et al. did not start out to study the teaching and learning experiences of their "Lost Sheep." However, the data clearly indicated there were a small number of children who did not benefit from the instruction. It was sensible, and indeed ethical, to locate those children and intervene. If longitudinal studies were

conducted on a large enough scale, they would allow a series of smaller follow-up experiments that would serve the needs of the children and the teachers involved, and help us to understand the causal relationships. It will take very large-scale research efforts to get the information we need to help all children learn to read and write.

A Reading Teacher Education Database

A third item on my research agenda is developing a database that allows us to provide descriptions of teacher education and professional development. As noted in Chapter 3 of this volume (Hoffman, Roller, & the National Commission on Excellence in Elementary Teacher Preparation for Reading Instruction),

> Today, again as in the 1960s, we find ourselves under attack for our shortcomings in teaching reading—only this time the attack is not on teachers or schools, but it is leveled directly at the teacher education community. We are charged with failure in preparing teachers with the knowledge and skills they need to be effective. We are charged with failure to infuse our programs of preparation with understandings from research on teaching and learning to read.
>
> Whether we are guilty of these charges or not is a matter for extended discussion. What is true and what we are clearly guilty of is having no data to respond to these attacks. We know little more today that we did 25 years ago about what is going on in reading teacher education. In this regard, and without question, we have been professionally irresponsible and negligent—not just because we have not collected the data that would allow us to confront the absurd attacks being made, but because we have not been continuously collecting data from which we can learn how to make ongoing improvements in reading teacher education. We are a community of reading researchers active in teacher education who have not been systematic about studying our own practices.

Although we may find these words harsh, we cannot argue that we have studied our own practice systematically. In fact, we do not collect the basic data necessary to provide simple descriptive statistics. For example, recently a researcher contacted me to find out about the number of certified reading specialists in schools and whether that number has been declining or increasing. I found that the National Center for Education Statistics' School and Staffing Survey collects data about the numbers of teachers who report "reading" as their assignment, but that they do not collect information about certification. When I checked in several states, I found the states could provide the number of reading specialist certificates issued, but they could not tell me if or where those teachers were teaching. Although I may yet find an answer, I am not optimistic about finding data that connects reading specialist certification with practicing teachers. We, as a profession, should be systematically collecting such data, and one of my recommendations is the International Reading Association take the lead in developing and maintaining such a database.

Improved Assessment Plans

A fourth item on my research agenda is developing better assessment systems that can provide all the appropriate audiences (students, parents, teachers, schools and school districts, states, the public, and policy makers) with the information they need. Many of the assessment systems currently in place are not adequate to meet these demands, and as educators, we are appropriately critical of them. However, policy makers are repelled by educators' rejection of standardized tests; they read our criticisms as wanton and irresponsible attempts to avoid accountability.

Policy makers have a right to demand information that indicates whether our schools and teachers are succeeding in teaching all children to read and write. If we as educators feel that standardized tests are not appropriate indicators of this, then we must provide a measure or measures that *are* good indicators. In the opening chapter of this volume, Pearson notes that Connecticut has developed a low-stakes, high-information, performance-based assessment system that provides students, parents, teachers, schools and school districts, and policy makers with good information for improving instruction. The system involves administering two reading tests at grades 4, 6, and 8: The Degrees of Reading Power (Touchstone Applied Science Associates) and the Reading Comprehension Test

(Harcourt Brace Educational Measurement). One test focuses on identifying students' reading levels and the other focuses on measuring comprehension by having students read a variety of 400- to 800-word texts with a combination of both multiple-choice and open-ended items (Baron, 1999). The comprehension test was modeled on the National Assessment of Educational Progress (NAEP) tests. Although scores are widely reported in a variety of formats, no specific promotion, graduation, or teacher salary decisions are based on the test scores. Furthermore, Connecticut put several reforms in place at the same time, and in the end, has produced dramatic achievement gain on the NAEP—a test that in no way can be represented as measuring only basic recall and regurgitation of facts.

The Connecticut example shows that it is possible to improve reading achievement without attaching high stakes to assessment information. What is necessary is good assessment—assessment plans that provide good information about students' progress, strengths, and weaknesses at classroom, school, district, and state levels. There are a number of state assessment programs that show promise.

Assessment of teachers and teaching is an essential aspect of my proposed research agenda in reading. As Pearson indicates (see Chapter 1), National Board for Professional Teaching Standards (NBPTS) and Interstate New Teacher Assessment and Support Consortium (INTASC) are developing reliable methods for assessing teachers using a combination of paper-and-pencil tests, portfolios, interviews, and observations. In Appendix A of this volume, you will find the executive summary of one the first attempts to determine whether NBPTS-certified teachers produce greater student achievement than similar teachers who did not earn certification. They did. This suggests that the evaluation system is capturing valid and reliable measures of teaching expertise. We need to pursue these efforts and put them to broad use to improve the teaching of reading.

Policy Research Specific to Reading Instruction

The fifth item on my agenda is policy research. We are beginning a third decade of education reform, and in the area of reading, there is very little research on the tools that have been employed—standards, assessments, and incentives (or consequences). Although there has been some attempt to analyze standards in reading and writing (Wixson & Dutro, 1999), there seem to be no major attempts at measuring the effects of standards reforms on reading achievement from within the field. The existing studies are funded by government and farmed out to think tanks such as Rand (Grissmer, Flanagan, Kawata, & Williamson, 2000) and the National Education Goals Panel (Baron, 1999).

We have a small cadre of policy researchers in reading education: Richard Allington, Kathryn Au, Anne McGill-Franzen, Sheila Valencia, and Karen Wixson have published policy analyses in our major reading and education journals, and in the *Handbook of Reading Research: Volume III*. John Guthrie and his colleagues from the former National Reading Research Center have produced technical reports. And the National Reading Conference Yearbook has published some state-level analyses of policy issues. However, a review the references from Valencia and Wixson (2000) and McGill-Franzen (2000) shows that there are remarkably few studies examining the impacts of the major policy initiatives of the 1990s. We must begin to make use of the large databases from NAEP and other NCES data banks to examine large policy issues in the area of reading.

Improved Researcher–Policy Maker Communication

My sixth agenda item comes both from considering seriously the findings of the research collected in this volume and my own recent experiences with policy makers. One of the major problems researchers face is that our conceptions of effective teaching are not shared by policy makers and the public. This is nowhere more evident than in chapters on teacher preparation in this volume. In the Grossman et al. chapter (Chapter 4), and to some extent in each of the other three programs examined in this volume (Flint et al., Chapter 5; Au & Maaka, Chapter 7; Lalik & Potts, Chapter 6)

the tension between constructivism and ownership and skill orientation and structure surfaced.

Ownership is a complex construct based on a constructivist view of learning. Many reading educators view ownership as a critical element for creating intrinsic motivation for literacy activities (see Au & Maaka, Chapter 7 in this volume). Intrinsic motivation, they believe, is necessary to creating lifelong readers who use reading in complex ways. Reading educators' vision of good instruction is that it is student centered and that the mark of truly skilled teaching is the ability to adjust instruction to meet the individual needs of each child. Effective teachers are "responsively adaptive" as well as "technically competent" (Duffy, 2001). Our studies of exemplary teachers support this view.

Structure, on the other hand, is more focused on what the teacher should do and technical competence. It represents the desire to have things spelled out, to have a series of discrete steps that if followed will result in student learning—a recipe if you like, or a script. In the Grossman et al. (Chapter 4) study and the Lalik and Potts (Chapter 6) descriptions of beginning teachers and reading teacher education programs, as well as in the Flint et al. study (Chapter 5) of beginning teachers, we hear the comments of students who want to be told "how to do it."

I was fascinated by the ways the tensions between ownership and a constructivist view of teaching and structure and a more skills-oriented view of teaching resolved themselves in the various programs. Charles, the secondary student from the Grossman et al. study, struggled against his teacher preparation program because he felt he was not getting enough structure, was not learning "how to do it." When he began his practice and encountered a very structured approach to teaching writing, he was ecstatic with a program that his preparation program would not have embraced. The program promised technical competence. However, as he used that program, he became disenchanted with the structure because he noticed that student ownership—something he believed was very important to student achievement—was destroyed by the rigidity and the teacher control and made responsive adaptation difficult. His struggle made me wonder if some teachers might best develop into responsively adaptive teachers if they experienced first a very structured teaching environment. These are questions we have not answered, which may be at the root of differing views of effective urban teaching. It may be that different kinds of teaching are effective in different environments and at different points in teachers' careers.

The teachers from the Lalik and Potts study (see Chapter 6 in this volume) also reported this tension:

> It was an extremely useful program. You didn't give me a lot of real specific strategies, and at first when I got out of the program, I was…thrown into a classroom. I was really a little upset about that. As I've taught more, I've realized how smart that is. While it's difficult the first year, you have such a strong foundation coming out of the program of beliefs and convictions. That's what carries you through the difficult times. It's not the strategy you pull out of your back pocket…. You search out strategies, strategies you feel will work for you, [strategies that] will best support your philosophy.

However, the elementary teachers from the Grossman et al. study (see Chapter 4), as well as the program beginning teachers from the Flint et al. study (see Chapter 5), seemed less aware of this tension. The commonality in the three elementary programs seemed to be that the students had learned to do constructivist teaching by seeing their professors model it and by having many opportunities in their preparation programs to implement constructivist teaching with guidance and support. Au and Maaka's description of the Ka Lama preservice program also emphasizes professor modeling and opportunities for preservice teachers to practice constructivist methods (see Chapter 7 in this volume). In the Flint et al. study, the program beginning teachers, even when they were required to adopt materials and practices that were not congruent with constructivist practices, were able to modify required practices and "teach against the grain." In these cases, teaching practices that were constructivist seemed also to provide enough structure for the beginning teachers.

Now step back a moment and imagine a policy maker reading this. Policy makers are decision makers. They want to take specific actions to achieve specific goals. We have told them that be-ginning teachers experience a tension between constructivist approaches to teaching and ownership, and more skill-oriented approaches and structure. As researchers, we draw the conclusion from a study of beginning teachers that "Teacher education provided these teachers with a set of tools with which to continue their learning and refine their practice. In the relatively brief amount of time allotted for the professional preparation of teachers, providing tools that enable teachers to continue their development may be the most important legacy of all."

As I read this conclusion, I think back to the conceptualization of teaching as constructivist and the strong vision of teaching that the programs were able to communicate to the beginning teachers. Although beginning teachers often do not enact this vision in their beginning year, it is clear that the vision guides their reflection and helps them adjust their practice. This is an important finding and contributes to our understanding of teacher development. In fact, I believe this is a very important finding. It is also a finding that is being reported in a variety of teacher education program studies. For example, Linda Darling-Hammond (1996) reports that "a clear shared vision of effective teaching" characterizes successful teacher preparation programs.

But a policy maker? Constructivist? Ownership? Mr. Policy Maker's question is, "What can I do to improve reading achievement?" Or more cynically, "What can I do that will convince my constituents that I am helping to improve reading achievement?" I wonder how he will respond to Lalik and Potts's conclusion that

> Given our conversations with teacher educators and practicing teachers, it seems that at least in one program we studied the social reconstruction framework remains viable. That is, the particular version of social reconstructionism in practice seems to help literacy teachers and teacher educators raise issues of social justice and transformation and find practices consistent with their understandings of those issues. (see Chapter 6 in this volume, p. 134)

Mr. Policy Maker is likely to ask, "But could they teach children to read and write? If they could, what did they do?" Remember, Mr. Policy Maker keeps his eye on the ball. His focus is on specific goals such as, "What can I do to make sure that all children learn to read and write in school?" His perspective is much more consistent with the skills-oriented perspectives that focus on structure. Social justice and transformation may not be high on his priority list. Although he may be sympathetic to Kathy Au's and Margaret Maaka's determination to teach native Hawaiian children to read, he may become impatient when told a major focus of their program is producing social change, or that their program will achieve a level of success when at least half the cohort are residents from the Wai'anae Coast. When Flint et al. cite as an indicator of their success as teacher educators that beginning teachers "teach against the grain," Mr. Policy Maker will begin to sputter. And Jennifer Berne's notion that "teachers view standards as hypotheses so that teachers will talk back standards" will send him out the door (see Berne, Chapter 11 in this volume).

Vast distances lie between the perspectives of professional researchers and policy makers. And while I myself believe that each of the quotations above says something very valuable about teacher education programs, and that having teachers talk back to standards, social justice, and social change are appropriate goals for teacher education programs, I cringe at my imagined conversations with policy makers. We *need* them to help us fund research efforts that will help us teach all children to read and write.

That was a long introduction to my sixth and final research agenda item: We need to have research on the best ways to communicate our complex notions of effective teaching to policy makers. Most of our attempts at this are counter-productive. A colleague reported an incident in which a policy maker had asked a question. The colleague said he did not know the answer, but he knew a researcher who would, and so the policy maker called the researcher and posed his question. The answer was long, and very soon the policy maker held the phone away from his head and mouthed, "yada, yada, yada." We must learn to sound like something more than "yada" to policy makers.

I believe we have the knowledge and technology to do this. I recall a powerful example that Purcell-Gates & Dahl (1991) report: The class had been working on beginning consonant sounds, and they had worksheets with pictures and letters. The

pictures and letters had been cut into chunks, and the children were to paste the letter that represented the beginning sound next to the picture that began with that sound. An observer overheard Mary Anne asking another child where he was going to put his *b*. She said she was going to put hers next to the fox because she liked it. She was unfazed by his response that the fox was a wolf and so the *w* went with it. She returned to her task and continued to focus on cutting and pasting instead of on the relationships between letters and sounds. Although there had been extensive instruction in beginning sounds and letters, and most of the children understood the task, Mary Anne did not get it. If she is going to learn to read, someone is going to need to do something extra with her. Her teacher needs to be responsively adaptive.

This example of a child who was not benefiting from explicit phonics instruction has remained with me for more than a decade. Examples are powerful. When Elliott (1996) commented in the *Journal of Literacy Research* on several researchers' contributions to a dialogue, Literacy and Educational Policy (Green, Dixon, Pearson, Quint, & Alvermann, 1996), he noted that "every policy-sensitive person will admire the powerful images she [Quint] creates though her direct quotations; a policy maker would die for a speech writer who could produce such compelling statements." However, he also noted that Quint failed to connect these images to practical, *implementable* actions. We must learn to connect powerful images to specific actions that both reflect our understandings about good reading instruction and that policy makers can implement.

Final Thoughts

To summarize, I propose six important topics for a research agenda in reading teacher education:

teacher development;

the relationship between teacher learning and student learning with particular attention to socioeconomic, racial, ethnic, and cultural factors related to reading achievement;

a reading teacher education database;

improved assessment plans;

policy research specific to reading instruction; and

researcher–policy maker communication.

However, a research agenda, while necessary, is not sufficient to improve reading achievement. We must simultaneously attend to some of the practical challenges that Dorothy Strickland raises in her chapter (see Chapter 2 in this volume). If we know that children are struggling to read and we provide them with inexperienced beginning teachers, paraprofessionals, or special educators with no specific training in reading, we cannot expect our research agenda to have impact. If we continue school financing practices that ensure that children who are most needy have more children per classroom, fewer and older reading materials, and crumbling school buildings, we cannot expect research to result in a system that teaches every child to read and write.

In conclusion, I return to President Bush's proposal, "Leave No Child Behind." The goal is one I and all reading educators passionately share. I am encouraged by the focus on providing resources to failing schools before invoking sanctions. Hopefully, the resources will be ample and sufficient. President Bush's proposal recognizes that resources are not equitably distributed and that many teachers and children work in untenable conditions. We do know how to teach children to read. Perhaps now we have the political will to do what has been given short shrift until now—teach *all* of America's children to read and write.

REFERENCES

Baron, J.B. (1999). *Exploring high and improving reading achievement in Connecticut*. Washington, DC: National Goals Panel.

Belenky, M.F., Clinchy, B.M., Goldberger, N.R., & Tarule, J.M. (1986). *Women's ways of knowing: The development of self, voice, and mind*. New York: Basic Books.

Bond, G.L., & Dykstra, R. (1997). The cooperative research program in first-grade reading instruction. *Reading Research Quarterly, 32*, 348–427.

Bush, G.W. (2000). *No child left behind* [Online]. Available: edworkforce.house.gov/press/press107/NoChildLeftBehind.pdf

Darling-Hammond, L. (1996). *What matters most: Teaching for America's future*. New York: National Commission on Teaching and America's Future.

Duffy, G. (2001, January 26). Personal communication.

Elliott, E.J. (1996). Critical issues: Literacy and educational policy, part three. *Journal of Literacy Research, 28*, 590–595.

Green, J., Dixon, C., Pearson, P.D., Quint, S., & Alvermann, D.E. (1996). Critical issues: Literacy and educational policy, part one. *Journal of Literacy Research, 28*, 289–324.

Grissmer, D.W., Flanagan, A.E., Kawata, J.H., & Williamson, S. (2000). *Improving student achievement: What state NAEP test scores tell us*. Santa Monica, CA: Rand Education.

McGill-Franzen, A. (2000). Policy and instruction: What is the relationship? In M. Kamil, P.B. Mosenthal, P.D. Pearson, & R. Barr (Eds.), *Handbook of reading research: Volume III* (pp. 889–908). Mahwah, NJ: Erlbaum.

National Reading Panel. (2000). *Report of the National Reading Panel: Teaching children to read*. Washington, DC: National Institute of Child Health & Human Development.

Purcell-Gates, V., & Dahl, K.L. (1991). Low-SES children's success and failure at early literacy literacy learning in skills-based classrooms. *Journal of Reading Behavior, 1*, 1–34.

Slaven, R. (2001). Personal communication.

Sweet, A. (2000). *OERI reading research: A brief history*. Briefing paper prepared for Rand.

Sweet, A. (2001, February 1). Personal communication.

Taylor, B.M., & Pearson, P.D. (1999, May). *A national study of effective schools and accomplished teachers of reading in the primary grades*. Paper presented at the Reading Research 1999 Conference, International Reading Association, San Diego, CA.

Valencia, S.W., & Wixson, K.K. (2000). Policy-oriented research on literacy standards and assessment. In M. Kamil, P.B. Mosenthal, P.D. Pearson, & R. Barr (Eds.), *Handbook of reading research: Volume III* (pp. 889–908). Mahwah, NJ: Erlbaum.

Wixson, K.K., & Dutro, E. (1999). Standards for primary-grade reading: An analysis of state frameworks. *The Elementary School Journal, 100*, 89–110.

National Board certification and the reform agenda: Executive summary

Gary R. Galluzzo

NATIONAL BOARD FOR PROFESSIONAL TEACHING STANDARDS

Purpose

The purpose of the study was to investigate three important questions about the validity of the National Board for Professional Teaching Standards' (NBPTS) system for assessing and certifying accomplished teachers. These questions included

Do teachers certified by NBPTS differ significantly from teacher candidates who did not earn certification, in terms of the quality of their classroom teaching practices?

Do teachers certified by NBPTS differ significantly from teacher candidates who did not earn certification in terms of the quality of work produced by their students on classroom assignments and on external modes of student assessment?

Do teachers certified by NBPTS differ significantly from teacher candidates who did not earn certification in terms of their post-assessment professional activities?

Participants

The study focused on a sample of 65 teachers from three geographic locations: North Carolina, Ohio, and the Washington, D.C., area. In addition, all the teachers in the study had gone through the National Board's certification process in one of two NBPTS certificate areas: Early Adolescence/English Language Arts and Middle Childhood/Generalist. Thirty-four teachers were Early Adolescence/English Language Art teachers, of whom 13 earned National Board Certification and 21 did not. The remaining 31 teachers were Middle Childhood/Generalists, of whom 18 earned National Board Certification and 13 did not. This sample was recruited from all eligible candidates from all years the Early Adolescence/ English Language Arts and Middle Childhood/ Generalist assessments were available. Of the 1,556 teachers who sought National Board Certification in these two certificate areas between 1993–1994 and 1998–1999, eligible study participants included only those candidates whose final scores on the NBPTS assessments met the following guidelines: (1) candidates for National Board Certification whose total scores on an assessment were at least one-and-one-fourth standard deviations below the certification score; (2) candidates for National Board Certification whose total scores on an assessment were between one fourth and three fourths of a standard deviation below the certification score; (3) candidates for National Board Certification whose total scores on an assessment were between one fourth and three fourths of a standard deviation above the certification score; and (4) candidates for National Board Certification whose total scores on an assessment were at least one-and-one-fourth standard deviations above the certification score. These groups were defined to ensure that dependable differences between National Board Certified Teachers and non–Board Certified teachers could be detected.

Design and Methodology

The study was designed and carried out by a team of researchers at the University of North

Carolina at Greensboro (North Carolina, USA). Members of the research team included university educational researchers, teacher educators, assistant principals, curriculum specialists, and highly experienced practicing and retired English Language Arts and elementary and middle school generalist teachers.

The study was based on a comprehensive review of the vast research and scholarly literature on expert/novice comparisons, comparative teaching practices, and studies of schooling effects and outcomes. From the analysis of this literature emerged the 15 dimensions on which the two groups of teachers were compared. Thirteen of these dimensions were related to the skills and abilities of excellent teachers; two of the dimensions were related to student learning, and a final attribute was a complex combination of both student outcomes and teacher characteristics.

The evidence analyzed in the study was obtained from a variety of sources: teachers' instructional objectives and lesson plans for a particular instructional unit; classroom observations of all 65 teachers' classrooms; and scripted interviews of the teachers and their students. All of this information was obtained and evaluated by observers and assessors who had no knowledge of the teachers' certification status. The information gathered for each teacher was compiled into a "casebook," which served as the basis for evaluating teachers along the 13 teaching dimensions related to the skills and abilities of excellent teachers. In addition, evidence about student learning was obtained from two sources: (1) products and artifacts of the observed unit of instruction created by a randomly selected sample of students, and (2) student writing samples created in response to prompts developed by the research team. Measures of student motivation and self-efficacy were also obtained. Finally, evidence about the extent to which National Board Certified Teachers and their non–Board Certified counterparts engage in a variety of professional activities outside of the classroom was obtained via a series of structured telephone interviews.

To assess the degree to which the teachers in the sample possessed the attributes characteristic of expert teachers that emerged from the literature review, a rigorous, highly articulated assessment protocol was developed and applied to each casebook. The protocol was developed, tested, and refined by senior members of the research team and experienced teachers with over 50 years of combined experience in teacher assessment and evaluation. Trained assessors, all recently retired or practicing teachers in the relevant discipline, scored each casebook. All assessors were unaware of the certification status of the teachers in the study.

Findings and Conclusions

In every comparison between NBCTs and non–NBCTs on the dimensions of teaching excellence, NBCTs obtained higher mean scores. In 11 of the 13 comparisons, the differences were highly statistically significant. In eight of the comparisons, differences between the two groups held up against what is generally regarded as the most stringent statistical test available. The conclusion seems clear: The National Board Certified Teachers in this sample possess, to a considerably greater degree than noncertified teachers, those characteristics of expert teaching that have emerged from the body of research on teaching and learning. Specifically, they possess pedagogical content knowledge that is more flexibly and innovatively employed in instruction; they are more able to improvise and to alter instruction in response to contextual features of the classroom situation; they understand at a deeper level the reasons for individual student success and failure on any given academic task; their understanding of students is such that they are more able to provide developmentally appropriate learning tasks that engage, challenge, and even intrigue students, but neither bore nor overwhelm them; they are more able to anticipate and plan for difficulties students are likely to encounter with new concepts; they can more easily improvise when things do not run smoothly; they are more able to generate accurate hypotheses about the causes of student success and failure; and they bring a distinct passion (i.e., deep commitment to their students' academic success) to their work.

On 2 of the 13 dimensions (Monitoring Students and Providing Feedback and Responding to the Multidimensional Complexity of Classrooms), NBCTs obtained higher mean scores than non–

NBCTs, but the differences did not reach conventional levels of statistical significance. Because of design and scorer training improvements made during the course of this research, the authors of this report are reasonably convinced that these two differences also will be found to be statistically significant in future studies.

To investigate the differential effects, if any, that NBCTs have on student learning, the research team selected two different student outcome measures: a student product in response to an instructional assignment by the teacher tied to the instructional unit we observed, and an "external" measure of writing in response to an age-appropriate prompt devised by lead teachers on the scoring and observational teams. Trained assessors evaluated the responses of students to the instructional assignment using an elaborated scoring classification scheme designed to assess a student's depth of understanding. As before, assessors were unaware of the certification status of the teachers in the study.

The evaluation of the student responses to teacher assignments provided evidence that is both compelling and consistent: The National Board for Professional Teaching Standards, through its series of comprehensive performance assessments of teaching proficiency, is identifying and certifying teachers who are producing students who differ in profound and important ways from those taught by less proficient teachers. These students appear to exhibit an understanding of the concepts targeted in instruction that is more integrated, more coherent, and at a higher level of abstraction than understandings achieved by other students.

The evaluation of the responses to writing prompts designed by the teachers on the research team as "external" indicants of achievement not directly tied to the teacher's specific instructional objectives at the time of observation provided evidence that was less compelling. The decision to use writing as one of the measures of student outcomes was motivated by a desire to gauge the effects teachers have on a universally valued student outcome that is common to virtually all school curricula. In comparisons of the student writing scores, only students of National Board Certified Middle Childhood/Generalist teachers obtained writing scores with statistical significance above that of non–Board Certified teachers. Differences between the writing scores of the full complement of students, as well as students of English Language Arts teachers, while in the expected direction, were not statistically significant.

Evidence of the effects that National Board Certified Teachers have on measures of student motivation and self-efficacy were inconclusive, in part, we speculate, because such effects are inherently more elusive and measures of these effects are less sophisticated.

Consistent and reliable differences in the number and variety of professional activities the teachers in the sample engaged in were not discernible. In addition, the separate sample of 40 National Board Certified Teachers interviewed to determine how schools, school districts, and other entities were using their talents indicated that, with rare exception, they have not noticed an increase in the use of their expertise since obtaining National Board Certification. It is hoped that with the increasing numbers and visibility of National Board Certified Teachers in all certificate areas, this pattern will change.

Finally, it should be noted that a limitation of the present investigation is the absence of adequate and appropriate measures of entering student ability. Attempts to match students with standardized test scores from state records were largely unsuccessful. Although we have no compelling reason to believe that students differed systematically at the beginning of the observational year, future research in this area should consider the collection of such information as part of the study design.

Report of the NEA Task Force on Reading 2000: Summary

Reading From the Perspective of Expert Teachers

The field of reading instruction is rich in conflicting theories and approaches, although the current controversies are not new. Indeed, much relevant research is not particularly new either. Now, as in the past, research results are often conflicting and lead to diverse instructional programs based on those results.

The debates about the best ways to teach reading have been taking place for almost a century. In spite of current reports, based on reviews of research, that both whole language activities and phonics activities contribute to reading success, experts and policy makers continue to argue about the proportion of instructional time to be given to specific types of reading activities and the sequence of instructional activities. But amid all the discussion by special panels of experts and statements by policy makers, the voices of teachers—the people whose expertise is based on real teaching experiences in real classrooms—are not usually heard.

While reading debates are not new, the intense politicization of reading instruction is a relatively recent development. The implementation of specific approaches to reading has been claimed by some political groups as part of their agenda. Constituents of other groups view that agenda as an effort to disenfranchise teachers and students. In the midst of the rhetoric and intense feeling generated by both sides, it is difficult to set an unbiased, apolitical course. Some have tried to stake out a middle ground by calling for a "balanced" approach to reading. Unfortunately, this stance promotes the notion of only two competing aspects to reading instruction. It leaves open the possibility of criticism

for placing the fulcrum for the "balance" too much to one side or the other.

It would be beneficial to take a different stance that moves beyond the debate. A focus on *complete* reading programs could offer such a stance. The promotion of complete reading programs would include recognition of several critical aspects of reading achievement.

1. A complete reading program includes the development of language and thinking skills as well as phonemic awareness; phonics; decoding; word recognition; comprehension; positive reading habits and attitudes; vocabulary; and a sense of the organization of texts such as stories, articles, and reports. All are essential to addressing all the components in the early stages of literacy learning.

2. A complete reading program addresses reading as one of several aspects of literacy. Others include listening, speaking, writing, using information from text, and responding thoughtfully and critically to text.

3. A complete reading program builds on the cultural and linguistic diversity that students bring to the classroom and enables all students to understand and appreciate cultural diversity.

4. A complete reading program provides for the reading success of all students, including those with special needs. Materials and instruction are adapted to accommodate those students.

5. A complete reading program involves *all* of the child's teachers, including parents and resources in the community providing

language development and models of the importance of reading.

6. A complete reading program provides teachers with the instructional and assessment tools to plan and deliver to each student the instructional activities that best support that individual's achieving a high level of reading proficiency.

7. A complete reading program aims to raise the achievement of all students. Therefore, it must be flexible in meeting the needs of all students. This might entail more instructional time for some students and more access to books for others. It might emphasize more opportunities to develop thinking skills related to reading for some students while providing more opportunities to develop fluency for others.

8. A complete reading program acknowledges that reading, like all cognitive skills, is linked to the physical well-being of children. That well-being starts before birth with sound prenatal care and continues with healthcare for preschoolers as well as school-age children. It involves parents having adequate knowledge about providing for their children's health and development.

9. A complete reading program is built on a wide range of significant research and thinking related to both the theory and practice of reading instruction. Significant research and thinking includes experimental studies; descriptive studies; case studies (a realistic way to conduct research on whole school programs); meta-analyses of research; and reasonable, reflective writings on theory and best practice. While some advocate using only experimental research in planning reading programs, doing so eliminates important contributions to the understanding of how children develop language and reading skills. For example, Piaget and

Vygotsky, two influential contributors to the understanding of learning in young children, did no experimental studies.

10. A complete reading program incorporates findings of research related to several factors in reading, not just a limited set of skills. Beginning readers, for example, need to learn about the structure of stories and sentences as well as word structure of words, which means that research in those areas is important. Another area of relevant research involves the variety of characteristics of materials used with beginning readers. Recent research, such as that on the importance of young students having access to classroom libraries of rich, multilevel reading materials, should also be considered.

As suggested here, a complete reading program has several components that contribute in varying ratios to the achievement of literacy. It is analogous in several ways to a balanced diet. Completeness in both diet and reading is achieved by providing diverse components in ratios that are not necessarily equal. In addition, the ratios might vary with individual needs and with development. For example, infants do not eat five servings of fruits and vegetables as recommended for children and adults. In a similar fashion, beginning readers might require different amounts of certain types of reading activities than more proficient readers. Just as some infants do not do well on milk products and need special formulae, so beginning readers may have special instructional needs.

Advocating a complete reading program addresses all the factors involved in literacy achievement and supports the understanding that there is no one-size-fits-all answer to the successful teaching of reading.

Teaching reading IS rocket science: What expert teachers of reading should know and be able to do: Executive summary

The most fundamental responsibility of schools is teaching students to read. Indeed, the future success of all students hinges upon their ability to become proficient readers. Recent scientific studies have allowed us to understand more than ever before how literacy develops, why some children have difficulty, and what constitutes best instructional practice. Scientists now estimate that fully 95% of all children can be taught to read. Yet, in spite of all our knowledge, statistics reveal an alarming prevalence of struggling and poor readers that is not limited to any one segment of society:

About 20% of elementary students nationwide have significant problems learning to read.

At least 20% of elementary students do not read fluently enough to enjoy or engage in independent reading.

The rate of reading failure for African American, Hispanic, limited-English speakers, and poor children ranges from 60% to 70%.

One third of poor readers nationwide are from college-educated families.

Twenty-five percent of adults in this country lack the basic literacy skills required in a typical job.

Research indicates that, although some children will learn to read in spite of incidental teaching, others never learn unless they are taught in an organized, systematic, efficient way by a knowledgeable teacher using a well-designed instructional approach. And, while many students from high-risk environments come to school less prepared for literacy than their more advantaged peers, their risk of reading difficulties could be prevented and ameliorated by literacy instruction that includes a range of research-based components and practices. But, as the statistics testify, this type of instruction clearly has not made its way into every classroom.

Indeed, a chasm exists between classroom instructional practices and the research knowledge base on literacy development. Part of the responsibility for this divide lies with teacher preparation programs, many of which, for a variety of reasons, have failed to adequately prepare their teacher candidates to teach reading. Fortunately, this situation is being corrected, thanks in large part to recent basic research on reading that has allowed the community of reading scientists and educators to agree on what needs to be done. This new information about language, reading, and writing is just beginning to shape teacher preparation and instructional programs. This knowledge must also form the basis of high-quality professional development for practicing teachers.

What Does the Research Say About Effective Reading Instruction?

Well-designed, controlled comparisons of instructional approaches have consistently supported these components and practices in reading instruction:

Direct teaching of decoding, comprehension, and literature appreciation;

Phoneme awareness instruction;

Systematic and explicit instruction in the code system of written English;

Daily exposure to a variety of texts as well as incentives for children to read independently and with others;

Vocabulary instruction that includes a variety of complementary methods designed to explore the relationships among words and the relationships among word structure, origin, and meaning;

Comprehension strategies that include prediction of outcomes, summarizing, clarification, questioning, and visualization; and

Frequent writing of prose to enable deeper understanding of what is read.

Toward a Curriculum for Teacher Preparation and Inservice Professional Development

Because classroom instruction, more than any other factor, is crucial in preventing reading problems, it is a primary focus for effecting change. A comprehensive redesign of teacher preparation in reading instruction, founded on a core curriculum that defines the knowledge and skills necessary for effective practice, is vital to improved classroom instruction.

Such a research-based core curriculum would provide much more extensive, demanding, and content-driven training to inform classroom practice. Specifically, a core curriculum for teacher preparation must include components for

understanding reading psychology and development;

understanding the structure of the English language;

applying best practices in all aspects of reading instruction; and

using validated, reliable, efficient assessments to inform classroom teaching.

This core curriculum can also serve as the basis for inservice professional development for the vast number of current teachers who have not been exposed to the research-based knowledge.

Changing Teacher Preparation and Professional Development in Reading

If higher standards and substantive courses of preparation are adopted now, the two million new teachers projected over the next decade may be equipped to minimize reading failure in all but a small percentage of students. To achieve that goal, a range of initiatives needs to be considered:

Research should guide the profession.

Core requirements and standards for new teachers should be established.

Teacher education programs should be aligned with standards for students and licensing requirements for teachers.

Professional development institutes should be created for professors of education and master teachers.

Developers of textbooks and instructional materials should be encouraged to improve their products.

High-quality professional development must be available for teachers.

An investment in teaching should be made to attract and retain high-caliber teacher candidates.

The fact that teachers need better training to carry out deliberate instruction in reading, spelling, and writing should prompt action rather than criticism. It should highlight the existing gap between what teachers need and what they have been given. It should underscore the obligation of teacher preparation programs to provide candidates with a rigorous, research-based curriculum and opportunities to practice a range of predefined skills and knowledge, as well as the need for licensing authorities to assess that knowledge.

The knowledge and skills inherent in effective reading programs must be part of every teacher's reading instruction repertoire. Good, research-based teacher preparation programs, coupled with high-quality professional development for classroom teachers, can assure that this is so.

Author Index

Page references followed by *f* and *t* indicate figures and tables, respectively.

Subject Index

Page references followed by *f* and *t* indicate figures and tables, respectively.

form and, 20; and teacher quality, 20–29; for writing, 80–99. *See also* reading teacher education

TEACHER EDUCATION RESEARCH: directions for, 26–28, 163, 181; need for, 18; scaling up findings in, 11–12; status of, 4–19; and teacher quality, 20–29; on transitions, 80–99. *See also* reading teacher education research

TEACHER EXPERTISE: level of, 17; maldistribution of, 8–10, 9*f*; and reading instruction, 207–209

TEACHER LEARNING: and student learning, 15–17, 199–200; views of, 11–13, 154–155

TEACHER QUALITY: factors affecting, 20–29

TEACHER ROLES: by student diversity, 56*t*

TEACHER TURNOVER: in Hawaii, 137; preparation and, 7, 8*f*

TEACHING: observational studies of, 151–153, 183–187, 184*f*–185*f*; as profession, 10–11, 178; transitions into, 80–99

TEACHING STRATEGIES: in Ka Lama program, 142; teachers on, 128

TEACHING STYLES, 154–155

TELLING: incidence of, 186–187

TERMINAL VIEW OF TEACHER LEARNING, 11–13

TEXAS: teacher preparation in, 24

TEXT, 16–17

TEXTBOOKS FOR READING TEACHER EDUCATION, 45, 45*t*

TITLE I PROGRAMS, 22

TOOLS FOR BEGINNING TEACHERS, 92–94

U

UNIVERSITY OF HAWAII, 136–148

UNIVERSITY OF TEXAS AT AUSTIN, 104–111; destinations of graduates of, 103*t*; program description, 101–102

V

VERMONT: teacher preparation in, 22–23

VIABLE: definition of, 121

VISION: in Hawaiian education, 141; and teacher education, 96–97. *See also* philosophy

W

WORDWORK PROGRAM, 167–175, 170*f*

WRITERS' WORKSHOP, 80, 85, 87–89, 91–92, 94; for preservice teachers, 142

WRITING TEACHER EDUCATION, 80–99; strategies for, 84; tools in, 92–94